739

THE MAN YOU LOVED TO HATE

THE MAN
YOU LOVED
TO HATE

ERICH VON STROHEIM AND HOLLYWOOD

RICHARD KOSZARSKI

OXFORD UNIVERSITY PRESS
Oxford   New York   Toronto   Melbourne
1983

Oxford University Press

Oxford London Glasgow
New York Toronto Melbourne Auckland
Delhi Bombay Calcutta Madras Karachi
Kuala Lumpur Singapore Hong Kong Tokyo
Nairobi Dar es Salaam Cape Town

and associate companies in
Beirut Berlin Ibadan Mexico City Nicosia

Library of Congress Cataloging in Publication Data
Koszarski, Richard.
   The man you loved to hate.
   Bibliogaphy: p. Includes index.
   1. Von Stroheim, Erich, 1885–1957.
2. Moving-picture producers and directors—
United States—Biography. I. Title.
PN1998.A3V647 1983 791.43'0233'0924 [B] 82-14519
ISBN 0-19-503239-X
ISBN 0-19-503379-5 (pbk.)
Printing (last digit): 9 8 7 6 5 4 3 2 1

Printed in the United States of America

For Diane

Preface

Hollywood. In the beginning there were more characters on the street than on the screen.

Directors in puttees, fake aristocrats with wavering accents, manufactured love goddesses straight from the dime store counters, you could find such people on every corner.

The place was part Coney Island and part Gold Rush boomtown, and any spot with qualities like these was bound to attract its fair share of charlatans and eccentrics. It was the right time and place for outrageous behavior and oversized personalities, especially that mad decade between the war's end and the coming of the talkies.

This situation couldn't last forever, though. It didn't take long for things to settle down in the movie factories, for sober businessmen to rationalize the haphazard production policies of their predecessors, and for the comet that was silent Hollywood to disappear over the horizon.

Soon people were looking back on those few years and wondering whatever happened to those characters. Some had died young. Some simply lost their public. Others drank themselves into oblivion. A few even toned down their acts and joined the new order in better shape than before.

The world they lived in is now a vast feeding ground for nostalgia addicts and popular culture vultures. John Gilbert, Rudolph Valentino, Fatty Arbuckle, and a host of others, many long since forgotten, once held tremendous power over the imaginations of audiences around the world. They reflected their times even as they took a major role in shaping them.

Lumped together with this group for many who remembered was the one they called "the man you love to hate." Erich von Stroheim.

Like Valentino or Arbuckle, von Stroheim's name still means something even to those who have never seen one of his films. True, the image is vague, but the general outlines are there, and for those with an interest there is quite a substantial bibliography to help flesh it out.

Lately much of this writing has centered on the duplicity of von Stroheim's Hollywood persona, the fact that the self-image he and his films created was at such wide variance with the truth. It is known now that the man was not the émigré heir of a noble line, but the eldest son of a Jewish hatter. So his films of imperial decay are no longer read as the gossipy re-creations of a renegade Hapsburg, but the fantasy construction of someone on the outside looking in.

These revisionist analyses share with the classic line a preoccupation with von Stroheim's injection of his off-screen personality into his films, and his subsequent use of the films to feed that off-screen personality. With unparalleled self-assurance von Stroheim used the big budget Hollywood film as an autobiographical tool. It would be too simple to say that he rebuilt Vienna on the Paramount lot just so he could play the handsome prince. If this were all that von Stroheim and his cinema were about then he really would belong with that roster of silent screen characters, and there would be no reason at all for a book like this.

Von Stroheim was certainly one of the most extravagant personalities of his time, but he was no mere eccentric. The strangest thing about him was not his monocle or his adopted ancestry, but the fact that he acted as if the movies were an art form and not an entertainment medium or an investment opportunity.

Unlike von Sternberg, Mizoguchi, Hitchcock, or John Ford, he was not in the strict sense a professional film director. He could not be handed a script and told to direct. He was certainly able to create great films, films of elegant structure and startling insight, but he was not able to do this to order.

And unlike Eisenstein, Balasz, Freeburg, or the other film theorists of the 1920s, he had no formula for film technique. He claimed he hated technique and he certainly hated formulas. He knew that he was an artist, and that chance had made the cinema his canvas. His problem was how to get his ideas up onto the screen, and his only conscious solution was to be direct, avoid fancy stylistic tricks, and maintain complete honesty in the face of his material. In practice he would drive his actors through dozens of takes, make impossible demands on his designers, and spend months fiddling with the editing. It was as if he were trying to shape the films through sheer force of will. This was interpreted at the time as a "mania for realism," but it was really so much more.

Von Stroheim never felt that the rules of Hollywood applied to him.

He operated as if he were a poet shaping sonnets, and an especially private poet at that; his work was always rooted in his own experience, real or imagined. This was true whether or not he was playing a part in the film, or even if the film were adapted from some outside source. The only important point was that the project, in theme and subject matter, be able to serve as a variant on his own "story," that ongoing narrative of which the movies were only one part. Because of this he had no interest in demonstrating his style on some amorphous material. Lubitsch, Lang, or Welles were all willing and able to do this, but not von Stroheim. Von Stroheim was simply not playing this game, and this is why it is improper to compare his body of work with that of a professional film director. One doesn't expect to find Hart Crane or Edgar Allan Poe exercising the same muscles as Longfellow or Tennyson.

Von Stroheim did have one near relative in Hollywood, however, for there was one other who saw film as a medium of personal expression through which he could project essentially intimate feelings and observations before a mass audience. This of course was Chaplin, and like von Stroheim, Chaplin's art incorporates many of the same autobiographical strategies. Chaplin was never a tramp, but the Tramp character does help him reflect the workhouse world of his youth. His films return over and over to the same situations and locales, reaffirming the same basic concerns with food, shelter, and companionship. With the central presence of the Tramp character to carry these films, Chaplin's films never strayed very far from his essentially private world.

Like von Stroheim, Chaplin's statements on the "art" of film invariably avoided coming to terms with problems of technique, and both directors were known to labor over their productions for years before finally releasing them to the public. Compare this almost handcrafted relation to the medium with the efficient professionalism of Ford, Hitchcock, or Lubitsch.

But while Chaplin and von Stroheim shared many of the same working principles, there were crucial differences between them. Most obviously, the financial success of Chaplin's films allowed him to continue his work long after von Stroheim was forcibly retired. And with this success came the full artistic control that was always denied von Stroheim. Then too, von Stroheim's business judgment was consistently faulty, and while Chaplin's shrewdness was able to help guarantee his continued freedom, von Stroheim's contracts were frequently disastrous. Finally, von Stroheim encouraged his audience to confuse the man on screen with the man behind the camera, something that never happened with Chaplin.

Ultimately, he was alone in Hollywood.

Von Stroheim's place in the American cinema has long been obscured behind a screen of bizarre rumors and anecdotes. *Photoplay* magazine once called him "Hollywood's one real genius," and they were not making the claim lightly. They sensed the difference between art and artistry, between inspired technique and true creativity.

Von Stroheim was a personal film artist who operated, for a time, at the highest levels of Hollywood studio production. This paradox is at the core of his great contribution to cinema: his ability to marshal the resources of mass production in the service of a single artistic vision.

How was this possible? How was this wandering soldier of fortune able to accomplish so much with such limited training and education, and why was he forced to stop? To know this we must examine the creation of each of his films in as much detail as surviving documents permit. If we can re-create the process by which von Stroheim's ideas took shape on film, not only will the works come to mean more to us, but the man himself may finally emerge from behind that self-imposed cloak of mystery.

March 1983   R.K.

Acknowledgments

I must express my sincere appreciation to all those who have contributed to this study over the years. The information, access, and support of every kind which so many generous people have provided can never be adequately acknowledged.

First let me thank those who knew and worked with Erich von Stroheim for sharing their memories with me: J. J. Cohn, Thomas Quinn Curtiss, Melvyn Douglas, Fritz Feld, Harold Henderson, H. R. Hough, James Wong Howe, Paul Ivano, Ted Kent, Paul Kohner, I. B. Kornblum, Carl Laemmle, Jr., Anita Loos, William Margulies, Samuel Marx, Lewis Milestone, Hal Mohr, Ray Rennahan, Leonard Spigelgass, Alfred Werker, Grant Whytock, and Fay Wray.

Special thanks to Mrs. Valerie von Stroheim and to Josef von Stroheim for sharing their memories of Erich as husband and father.

For her graciousness to my wife and me during a frightfully cold and snowy evening at Maurepas, my warmest thanks to Mme. Denise Vernac.

At the studios, Carl Bennett of M-G-M, Bernice Mosk, John Boswell and William Kenly of Paramount, Alex Gordon of Twentieth Century-Fox, and Vera Culwell, David Riback, Andrew Lee, Serafina Burgos, and Jerry Evans of Universal, all helped provide crucial access to previously unavailable material.

At libraries and museums around the country, Paul Myers and his staff in the Theater Collection of the New York Public Library, Eileen Bowser, Mary Corliss, and Charles Silver of the Museum of Modern Art, Paul Spehr, Pat Sheehan, David Parker, and John Kuiper of the Library of Congress, and George Pratt and James Card of the George Eastman House/International Museum of Photography, all put up with my insistent queries for too many years. John Huntley of the British Film Institute, Henri Langlois of the Cinémathèque Française, and Gero Gandert of the Stiftung Deutsche Kinemathek helped from overseas.

The American Film Institute's Louis B. Mayer Oral History Program came through with a crucial Research Associateship in 1971. My thanks to Bruce Henstell, David Shepherd, and Anne Schlosser from those far-off days, and to Larry Karr and Audrey Kupferberg ever since.

Additional support was provided through a 1978 stipend from the American Council of Learned Societies for travel and photographic research.

Thanks to Patrick Montgomery, with whom I spent many long hours, for permission to use material gathered by Film Profiles, Inc., for our documentary portrait of "The Man You Loved To Hate," and to Gregg Burton and William Loeffler for initiating the project.

To Arthur Lennig, whose infectious accolades may have driven me to von Stroheim in the first place, and to William Sloan, whose classes spawned my first von Stroheim research.

To Annette Michelson and Jay Leyda, for helping to shape this material during its early NYU days, and to Anthony Pipolo and Jonathan Rosenbaum, for similar help at a more recent date.

To William K. Everson, whose encouragement and support turned enthusiasm into reality, and to Kevin Brownlow, whose exhaustive fault-finding was a real compliment.

To Sheldon Meyer, an editor who can really wait out a manuscript, and Leona Capeless, who had the last word on everything.

And finally to Marc Wanamaker and Mark del Costello, Tony Slide and Bob Gitt, David Bradley and John Hampton, Eddie Brandt and all the gang, Carol Pipolo and Rita Sirignano, Robert Regan and John Hagen, Jon Gartenberg and Monty Arnold, Dale Henderson and Werner Sudendorf, Joel Finler and Miles Kreuger and Andrew Sarris, who will all be able to see themselves in here somewhere.

R.K.

Contents

THE MAN YOU LOVED TO HATE

Prologue

When American immigration authorities closed the books on the 1909-10 fiscal year, they found that for the first time they had registered over one million new arrivals. But while they assembled a mountain of statistics to differentiate according to age, sex, race and nationality, in the popular imagination this influx was wholly faceless. The tide had long since become a torrent. Historians had declared the frontier closed years earlier, and the pressure added by the new arrivals was no longer so easily channelled westward. Agitation to restrict this flow was rising, and would soon lead to a series of notorious exclusionary acts, effectively closing the open door and institutionalizing a growing fear of alien infiltration.

Sailing from Bremen on November 15, 1909 was the German steamer *Prince Friedrich Wilhelm,* to the examiners at Ellis Island just one more delivery van adding its manifest to the season's total. The processing of these arrivals was orderly and efficient, each immigrant being numbered and tagged, and registered by hand in gigantic logbooks. Rejects were segregated, the balance put on ferries to lower Manhattan where they disappeared into the city.

To one 24-year-old émigré the fate to avoid was the fate of anonymity. Like most of the others he was arriving with little more than the clothes on his back. He had some money and some prospective connections, but neither could be expected to open many doors. There had to be a way to differentiate himself from this mob, and he found one that was cheap and easy. Erich Oswald Stroheim, as he had once been called, disappeared during the course of a difficult ten-day Atlantic crossing. In his place appeared a man who presented himself to American immigration officials on November 25 as Erich Oswald Hans Carl Maria von Stroheim.[1]

Thus ennobled, "von" Stroheim gained at least a psychological edge over most of the *Friedrich Wilhelm*'s other cargo. It might not help immediately, but Americans were notoriously title crazy, and who could tell what opportunities might present themselves. He had come to America to start with a clean slate, and if the old life was to be left behind, why not make the most of it?

From the day Erich von Stroheim landed in America he treated his early life as a fiction, and to the day he died he stuck to the outline of his story with only minor embellishments. As an artist von Stroheim chose to make his own life his prime artwork. The films would come later, and would only project this effort before a wider public. They would draw on the facts of his life, as well as the myth he had already begun to spin around it. While other filmmakers sought to filter their sensibilities through a variety of plots and characters, von Stroheim felt that a director should confine himself to "pictures portraying life and customs with which he is familiar."[2]

What was that life? A press release issued by Universal around 1920 offers a typical version, designed for public consumption.

> Born September 22, 1885, in Vienna, the son of a German Baroness and Austrian Count, he received his early education in the war colleges of Austria Hungary, graduating on August 18th 1902 from the Imperial Military Academy at Wienerneustadt, a second lieutenant. Between 1902 and 1909 he saw regular service with the 4th Dragoons, 14th Huzaars, and 3rd Regular Uhlans. In 1907 he was detailed to the war college at Vienna where he passed rigorous examinations sub auspices Imperatores, which carried with it the award by the Emperor of a diamond ring with the royal initials engraved upon it. This ring he pawned in Los Angeles during the days of no food and no work, after having clung desperately to it, until he was in actual danger of starving to death. In 1908 he served in the war of the Bosnia Herzegovina annexation and was wounded at Benjaluka, where he went into the fray upon horseback and came out in an ambulance with 16 inches of lead in his body. For this he received the Franz Josef Cross and the Annexation medal. . . .[3]

Much of this information can be checked, and little of it is true. Kevin Brownlow, who has investigated the military side of von Stroheim's Austrian career, writes that "History does not record any military action during the annexation in which Stroheim could have been wounded."[4] He also finds no mention of the name von Stroheim in 1908 military rank lists of the Austro-Hungarian army. Denis Marion, who was the first to investigate the actual circumstances of von Stroheim's early years, was able to confirm only one fact in this account: the date of birth. After interviewing surviving relatives and uncovering what documentary evidence remained in Vienna, he announced that Erich Oswald Stroheim's origins were distinctly bourgeois. His parents were Benno Stroheim and Johanna Bondy, practicing Jews who registered the births of their sons Erich and Bruno (born February 18, 1889) in the archives of Vienna's Jewish community. Benno Stroheim, born in Gleiwitz, Prussian Silesia, was originally a dealer in felt, straw, and feathers. He later became a hat manufacturer. Johanna was born in Prague. Marion was told by Emil Feldmar, a von Stroheim cousin, that Erich's military service was limited to a few months spent as a private soldier, that he deserted before the end of his regulation year, and that he emigrated to America as the result of some mysterious indiscretion.[5]

Such is the revisionist account. On the other hand, von Stroheim's line is defended by Thomas Quinn Curtiss, who in 1970 published what might be called the authorized biography.[6] A longtime friend who also had access to von Stroheim's personal papers, Curtiss tells the story as von Stroheim himself would have told it, dismissing Marion's documents as Nazi forgeries and ignoring the presence of Feldmar entirely. The Curtiss book is quite valuable in offering the von Stroheim version as a touchstone against which all other accounts may be measured, and there are many gaps in these early years which can only be filled by turning to Curtiss.

Why, for example, did von Stroheim leave his own country and sail for America? Feldmar's hints of "youthful misdemeanor" are fleshed out by Curtiss with a melodramatic tale straight off the gaslight stage. As a young lieutenant von Stroheim is hobbled with debts, the result of expensive tastes in women and the costly requirements of life in the officer class. He is talked into a shady deal by an unscrupulous Jewish moneylender, and rescued by his well-connected uncle, Emil Bondy, who pays off the debt on the condition that Erich leave Austria once and for all.

This story is as good as any, especially since von Stroheim, not long after he arrived in America, used it as the basis for the first of many semi-autobiographical works, a short play which he called "In the Morning." With a little bending and twisting it can be made to fit Marion's facts as well, but the specifics of von Stroheim's life in those days are not our concern at the moment.

What is important is to sense the air of mystery and contradiction which von Stroheim brought to America with him, and in which he wrapped himself for the next half-century. Whether he was or wasn't an officer in the Emperor's Life Guard Mounted is of little concern to history. What happened when von Stroheim processed that claim through Hollywood's dream factory is something else entirely.

Records of the Immigration and Naturalization Service, only now available through the Freedom of Information Act, tell us something of von Stroheim's intentions on his arrival. There is the usual physical description: the applicant has fair skin and brown eyes, is 5'5'' tall, and is distinguished by a cut on the forehead. He lists his race as "Hungarian" and his occupation as "clerk." His destination is East 21st Street in Manhattan, the address of a friend named Max whose last name is illegible. Could this have been Max Grab, whose Max Grab Fashion Company, an import house, was then located at 38 East 21st Street?

Curtiss mentions Max Grab, but claims that von Stroheim only began there after a brief period of odd job work and a two-year hitch in the New York State National Guard. Grab is said to be an ex-Austrian officer, and a letter from Uncle Emil arranges the introduction.[7] Perhaps von Stroheim did start out looking for work as a clerk, but his English may not have been up to Max Grab's standards. By his own account his first job was wrapping packages at Simpson-Crawford's, a Sixth Avenue department store, during the 1909 Christmas season. He then began to move around the fringes of New York's German community, working in various menial occupations. He was a singing waiter in a Yorkville rathskeller, and once even claimed to have worked in a brothel—Sigmund Romberg played the piano and he turned the pages, or so he said.[8]

The annual muster roll of Troop 8, Squadron C, of the New York National Guard shows that von Stroheim's two-year hitch was in fact closer to two months. He enlisted as a private in that unit on January 30, 1911, and is shown as "removed from rolls" on March 27. Squadron C was quartered in the 23rd Regiment Armory at 1579 Bedford Avenue in Brooklyn, out near Eastern Parkway. It was across the road from the Bedford Riding Academy, the only public riding academy in Brooklyn. Curtiss says that von Stroheim caught the attention of Squadron C's Captain Edward McLeer[9] by getting a fallen horse to rise. It's entirely possible that von Stroheim was handling horses for the Riding Academy at that time, a type of job we know he held in California a few years later. In any case, we can only guess at von Stroheim's activities during the 14 months between his arrival at Ellis Island and his brief National Guard enlistment.[10]

Apparently von Stroheim simply stopped showing up at the Armory, and perhaps Max Grab was ready for him now. The 1911 Trow Directory shows that Grab had moved his place of business to 15 East 32nd street that year, and possibly there were job openings. Grab was in the garment business, as was Erich's father Benno, and von Stroheim could be expected to have a general familiarity with the operation. But he does not seem to have been too happy with Grab, who sent him on the road as a traveling salesman.[11] After only a few months with the company there was trouble back at the home office and he found himself out of work, stranded in San Francisco.

All things considered, it was not a bad spot for someone of von Stroheim's tastes and abilities. San Francisco was a gold rush boom town masquerading as a graceful European capital, and von Stroheim was still in the business of passing himself off as a European count. The whole area was awash in redevelopment, and while business opportunities were many, the tempo of life was still more congenial than what he had found in the tenement neighborhoods of New York.

By 1912 San Francisco had nearly completed the tremendous task of rebuilding the lost downtown business district, flattened and burned out by the 1906 earthquake and fire. Readying the city for the Panama-Pacific Exposition, which was to open in 1915, was a goal which absorbed enormous public and private energies. Across the Bay, Oakland prospered as well. It was the terminus of the transcontinental railway and a major shipping port for the Orient. Thousands had settled here after fleeing the devastation in San Francisco, and in 1909 the city annexed enough of the neighboring countryside to triple its surface area. There was a German community here as well (which von Stroheim would parody mercilessly in *Greed* a decade later), and the new arrival soon found a place for himself.

Overlooking the Bay in Marin County was Mount Tamalpais, a rustic hideaway whose fabulous views were much favored by hikers and sightseers. The Tavern on the summit was an elaborate retreat served by the famous "crooked railroad," and noted for its sumptuous suppers. But a more modest dining spot, the West Point Inn, stood about two miles from the summit at a juncture of the railroad line. The innkeeper, Capt. Henry Masyon, was remembered by one local historian for "his suave manner, his military bearing, and his Franz Joseph beard." Rumor had it that he was "an Austrian nobleman formerly attached to the court of the Emperor."[12] Von Stroheim soon found his way to the West Point Inn.

According to Curtiss, Capt. Masyon (or Masjon) was an "old Austrian acquaintance" of von Stroheim, and soon put the new arrival to work. At the tiny chalet Erich had to do a little of everything, from general maintenance to waiting on table, and it was while trying his hand at the latter that he first met Margaret Knox. In the summer of 1912 Margaret Knox was 33 years old—six years older than von Stroheim—in fragile health, and if not yet a spinster, then at least well past prime marrying age. Von Stroheim promptly spilled a bowl of soup on her,[13] the beginning of a chaotic two-year relationship which would lead to his first marriage, his first literary effort, and his first trip to Hollywood.

Margaret's mother, Dr. Myra Knox, was a pillar of the Oakland community and lived in an elaborate Victorian mansion at 958 14th Street. The 1912 Oakland City Directory shows that Margaret lived there with her mother, but apparently she also had a bungalow of her own in Mill Valley. The spilled soup proved a powerful token, for von Stroheim soon moved from the Inn to Margaret's cabin. Capt. Masyon had characterized her as an "emancipated" type (the suffrage amendment had passed in California the year before) but even so such an act must have been especially bold in 1912. Von Stroheim captivated her with tales of his military adventures and his life at court. She in turn began to educate him in language and literature, and encouraged him to try his hand at writing. Years later von Stroheim remembered *The Red Badge of Courage* and *Spoon River Anthology* as two of the works Margaret introduced him to,[14] and painted an idyllic picture of their life in Mill Valley. He told Tom Curtiss that he wrote a story for *Smart Set* at this time, but no story with his byline appeared in that magazine. Another strange claim was that Erich and Margaret had collaborated on a *Grand Guignol* playlet called "The Black Mask" which was performed by San Francisco actor Holbrook Blinn on the vaudeville circuit. Why he should have made this claim is unclear, since "The Black Mask" was the work of the well-known British dramatists F. Tennyson Jesse and H. M. Harwood. "The Black Mask" is the story of a disfigured maniac who hides his face behind a mask, and wins himself a bride by dangling her over a mine shaft, letting her choose between death at the bottom of the pit and life with him. For some reason von Stroheim appropriated this play as part of his own work.[15]

But one piece at least does survive, an early sketch for von Stroheim's cycle of Imperial films called "In the Morning." Alluded to by Curtiss and Peter Noble under a different title,[16] this first literary effort has never been examined by critics or historians, a pity since it displays the preoccupations of future von Stroheim films in surprisingly well-developed fashion. It was deposited with the copyright office on November 16, 1912, and although von Stroheim claims to have written it at Margaret's Mill Valley cabin, the return address on the original manuscript is Dr. Knox's home in Oakland.

The play is set in the Paris apartments of Nicholaus Maria Erwin Count von Berchtholdsburg, called Nicki. The period is contemporary (prewar), and as such is the only von Stroheim work to deal with this era right at the moment, and not as a period re-creation.

Nicki is an attaché in the French capital and wears the uniform of an Austrian lieutenant of hussars. A gambler and a womanizer who consistently lives above his means, he finds at the beginning of the play that his aunt has cut him from her will. He is deeply in debt to a moneylender named Eppsteiner, whom Nicki refers to as "The Jew—damn the shark." Eppsteiner, having heard of Nicki's tremendous losses at cards the night before, arrives to offer more credit (at an increasing rate). He suggests that Nicki could solve his problems if he would "marry rich," but Nicki finds the idea unpalatable, since all of Eppsteiner's eligibles have "more or less bent noses."

Without even the prospect of funds for repayment, Nicki sends Eppsteiner away and orders his valet Franz off to the pawn shop with the last of Nicki's personal jewelry. While Franz is out, Nicki's mistress Mizzi Dorfler stops by with the usual run of bills from Paquin and Mirabelle. Nickie tells her of the collapse of his financial prospects, how his aunt had learned that it was he who murdered her beloved parrot after the bird had called Nicki a "good for nothing parasite."

Mizzi is a music hall artiste whose small salary must necessarily be supplemented by the favors of a patron like Nicki, and the Count sees a parallel with his own situation, that of an army officer expected to supplement his regulation pay with outside sources of income. She is no gold digger, however, and offers to return all of his expensive jewelry, though Nicki finds it dishonorable to accept such a favor.

In fact, Nicki's secret plan is to blow out his brains after one last night with Mizzi, since he could not face the only alternative, exile to "the less sensitive American continent." Mizzi sits down at the piano and plays the duet from *Waltz Dream* for him, then leaves for the theater. Franz returns with 2000 francs from the pawnship and Nicki writes a few notes, intended to settle his key debts, which Franz will deliver in the morning.

Just then a mysterious stranger appears at Nicki's doorway, Fipe la Main Rouge he calls himself, a notorious highwayman. Foiled in an attempted hold up he has run into the nearest doorway for protection.

Nicki is amused and offers him some refreshments. It soon becomes apparent that the stranger is also of a noble line, for he teaches Nicki a thing or two about the proper preparation of a champagne cup.

The stranger quickly sizes up the situation by rummaging through Nicki's correspondence when the Count leaves the room for more supplies. He explains to Nicki how he came to this criminal state, and how with "every tie broken, the veneer goes quickly and the primitive—the predatory comes through." Out of gratitude for Nicki's hospitality he saves the Count from himself by binding him to a chair and emptying his revolver.

In a lengthy philosophical monologue the stranger opines that they are brothers, that they both take from society. He confesses that he, too, once considered suicide while in Nicki's position, but found it "cowardly." In any case, dying for this ideal of honor is absurd, the very concept is "a figure of straw, an invention of our corrupt, degenerate, demoralized upper four hundred called society." Real courage is not expressed by one who throws away his life for a hollow ideal, but "to fight every tomorrow, in a world which does not understand—which does not want to understand. To fight alone—always alone. *That* takes courage."

On his way out the stranger takes with him a copy of Max Nordau's *Paradoxes,* "a philosophy of every day, for every one." He is, he finally admits, Prince Otto de Casco, brother of the man to whom Nicki has lost a fortune at cards, and for whom he is now prepared to give his life. That honorable gentleman, the Prince says, earns most of his income from a brothel on the Rue L'Humbert.

In the morning Nicki is discovered by Franz, who brings a telegram saying the Aunt has died (without changing her will) and left her estate to Nicki after all. "I shall change," Nicki says as the morning sun begins to fill the room, "bring me a plain civilian coat."

The work looks backward to von Stroheim's avowed reasons for leaving Vienna, and forward to a whole string of filmic variations on the same story. We will meet Nicki and Mizzi again, although the moneylender disappears from von Stroheim's work, which in the future would scarcely *refer* to a Jewish character, much less use one in so sinister a role. For example, when Prince Nikki in *The Wedding March* is forced to "marry money," the unpleasant choice is no longer a Jewess, but a lame cornplaster heiress.

The interplay between Nicki and his valet is pure von Stroheim, as is the luxurious attention to the trappings of ceremonial uniforms which the Count puts on and off several times. Mizzi is a worthy lover, and the Count can look forward to a real happy ending with her after the curtain. In future works von Stroheim would usually break apart his female characters into two distinct personalities: a soubrette would be expected to be a gold digger, while unselfish love would be the province of an uncorrupted innocent.

The ambiguous presentation of the central character is perhaps the most interesting part of "In the Morning." This is not a stock caricature, but a man with good and bad sides, the first of many von Stroheim characters whose sensitive soul lies trapped behind a monstrously inflated *persona*. He behaves the way he does since he is a creature of society, operating according to its "degenerate" dictates. We can hate him for being a parasite, and admire him for his honesty, elegance, and true sense of honor. As the play reveals, despite his position in a corrupt society, he himself is not beyond salvation.

One wonders just what audiences might have made of the stranger's choice of reading material, Nordau's *Paradoxes*. Von Stroheim said that it was Margaret who revealed the world of literature to him, but was she the one who had so absorbed the philosophy of this German physician, author, and Zionist? Nordau was the author of many critical and satirical works. *Paradoxes* was published in 1885, but perhaps more relevant to von Stroheim was his two-volume study *Degeneration,* which related genius and degeneracy. This doesn't seem to have been something he picked up in Mill Valley.

Curtiss reports that von Stroheim submitted the manuscript to the Essanay Film Company for consideration as a film script.[17] This was a popular practice at the time, encouraged by the rapidly growing studios which were always starved for potential story ideas. But there was no film sale, and von Stroheim was forced to turn his attention elsewhere.

He had been living with Margaret for over half a year when they were married on February 19, 1913. The marriage certificate is a typical von Stroheim document, in which he swears that his mother is the Baroness Bondy, that his father is Benno "von" Stroheim, and that his occupation is that of importer. Margaret lists her age as 18, approximately half the correct figure. After the brief Unitarian service at Dr. Knox's home the von Stroheims returned to Mill Valley, where their situation quickly deteriorated.

Money problems began to destroy the relationship. Von Stroheim could find no work worthy of his talents and fell into depression and fits of violence. Within two months he began to drink heavily, turning his rages on Margaret, whom he would curse and threaten, sometimes locking her in the bungalow. By August he was coming home drunk at least once a week; finally, after he blackened her eye and punched her on the side of the head until her ears began to bleed, Margaret escaped back to her mother in Oakland. Von Stroheim followed, and managed to arrange a reconciliation (throughout his career he was able to talk people into almost anything). The couple took rooms down the street from Mrs. Knox at 616 14th Street, but the situation failed to improve. Dr. Knox had no regard for von Stroheim by this point, and Erich saw her attempts to keep Margaret away from him as being motivated simply by his failure to earn a "respectable" living—which they probably were. At times when Margaret would try to leave the apartment to visit her mother von Stroheim would forcibly restrain her, cursing the two women and threatening more violence. By their first anniversary Margaret had separated from him and was living in her mother's home again. Von Stroheim would make violent scenes in the street. He had a tremendous and inflexible sense of responsibility, and his failure to support his wife, combined with the frustrating inability to find fulfilling work, soon drove him to this unforgivable behavior. In a sense the story is an eerie parallel to that of Mac and Trina in *Greed,* a couple drawn together by "ungovernable instincts" slowly reduced to the level of bickering dogs, with poverty and drink behind it all.

In May of 1914 von Stroheim was screaming to Margaret over the phone. "You God damn dirty beast. I have you and your mother in my fist and I am going to squeeze you. I am coming right down to the house to raise hell. If I could get hold of you I would smash your face!"[18] Margaret filed for divorce the following week. Von Stroheim was served on May 29, but failed to appear at the hearing to contest any of the evidence against him. Margaret received her final decree on grounds of extreme cruelty, but did not win the award of $100 per month she sought in alimony. Although her health made it difficult for her to support herself she did have considerable family resources, and von Stroheim, who was practically reduced to the life of a tramp at this point, would have little chance of delivering such an amount. Whether those six illicit months at the cabin figured in the decision is unknown.

Von Stroheim often told the story of how, during the summer of 1914, he worked at Lake Tahoe for Traite and Mann, rowing tourists around the lake, catching and frying their fish, handling their horses, and occasionally even filling in as lifeguard. But while he was good with horses and may have been adequate as a fisherman, he apparently could not swim a stroke. Jim Tully, in a famous profile of the director published in *Vanity Fair* made much of the elements of fraud and bluff in von Stroheim's personality, seeing these as the key to his success in Hollywood. "In a game that is mostly bluff," Tully wrote, "the lifeguard who could not swim was bound to come into his own."[19]

Lake Tahoe is located up above the California gold country, about 150 miles from San Francisco. Von Stroheim retreated here after the disaster with Margaret, seeking to lose himself in the anonymity of the wilderness. Years later his script of *Greed* would re-create this journey in the story of McTeague's flight from San Francisco to Placer County after his murder of Trina. Von Stroheim never seems to have remarked on this parallel, but like so much else in his work it is hardly a coincidence.

While working at Tahoe von Stroheim did more than play mountain guide. He turned on the charm when the need arose, and in the case of Emma Bissinger, at least, won himself a much needed supporter. Mrs. Bissinger, wife of a wealthy San Francisco hide merchant, was fascinated by von Stroheim's stories and impressed by his ambition. When the season ended and von Stroheim shipped down to Los Angeles with a trainload of horses he decided to stage a production of his play, with himself in the lead. He needed five hundred dollars to put on the show, and cabled Emma Bissinger for the money. It arrived the next day, no questions asked.[20]

Curtiss reports that the play went on one night at the Alhambra, where the audience reacted by throwing vegetables. This delicious story may have some truth in it, although the Alhambra was showing first-run features at the time and did not use live acts. In fact, *Variety*'s detailed reports on the Los Angeles legitimate scene fail to mention any such performance during the summer or fall of 1914, although it is possible the event passed unnoticed.

What *Variety* did not overlook was the growing war in Europe, a catastrophe which had an immediate and lasting effect on, among other things, the future of the American film industry. Until that moment it was the European cinema, and especially such French producers as the Pathé Frères, which was firmly in control of international markets. But by 1914 many changes were in the wind: feature length pictures had supplanted shorts as the main item on cinema bills; picture palaces were replacing the old nickelodeons; improved technology made the filming process itself far more reliable; stars had come to dominate the marketplace; the old Motion Picture Patents Company, a conservative trust led by Thomas Edison and the other original cinema patentees, was crumbling under an attack by vigorous new independent producers; and in America the entire film industry was on the point of transplanting itself from East Coast cities to the expansive reaches of southern California. Had the European producers been able to compete on equal terms over the next few years perhaps the outcome would have been different. But the economic and aesthetic momentum suddenly passed to America, and to Hollywood, and for once von Stroheim found himself in the right place at the right time.

Kevin Brownlow reminds us that von Stroheim was "technically" a deserter from the Austrian army who failed to respond to the call to arms in 1914, although Curtiss claims that he did, in fact, offer his services to the consulate.[21] Be that as it may, the only war von Stroheim fought that year was the Civil War, for with hundreds of others he was pressed into service on D. W. Griffith's epic *The Birth of a Nation.*

A trained rider and expert horse handler, von Stroheim had little trouble finding work on this lavish production, which seems to have employed half the drifters in Hollywood. Griffith's film told the story of the Civil War and Reconstruction through the eyes of one southern family. The great director juggled costly spectacle sequences and intimate family episodes, tender love scenes and attempted rapes, fantastic melodrama and realistic depiction of historical incident. Expense was not an issue. Griffith demanded that settings and performances reach an ideal standard, and spent whatever was required. Rebuilding the Old South with the resources available in this sleepy community was no mean feat in 1914; props and costumes which might have been rented from a supply house back East needed to be hand crafted in southern California. Achieving the degree of quality he demanded cost Griffith $110,000 and 108 reels of negative—fantastic amounts for the period and easily enough for ten or twelve normal features.[22]

And on top of this financial gamble Griffith made aesthetic and even political demands on his audience. New techniques in editing and photography offered viewers a type of spectacle they had never before experienced, while Griffith's rabid social theories stirred up an unprecedented storm of reaction. Griffith dared everything, challenged all the rules, and ultimately achieved a brilliant critical and commercial success. The demands he made on his audiences and his backers paid off handsomely, and fully justified his eccentric, even monomaniac production methods. This was the film which introduced Erich von Stroheim to the movies.

He claims to have appeared in half a dozen extra roles, usually in blackface, but only one is vaguely identifiable today: the man who falls off the roof during the guerilla raid on Piedmont. This was one of von Stroheim's favorite stories, and he told it different ways at different times, but always included the fact that the fall needed to be filmed three times in order to please Griffith's exacting eye. Today the actor in this long shot is not identifiable, and at least one authority doubts that von Stroheim appears in the film at all.[23]

Did von Stroheim work as an actor in *The Birth of a Nation,* or did he simply appropriate this landmark film as a suitable vehicle for his entry into pictures? It may never be possible to prove this one way or the other, but I once saw an extraordinary reel of outtakes from *The Birth of a Nation* which tended to back up von Stroheim's story. Included were three separate takes of the man falling off the roof, clearly the work of an inept, though eager, stuntman. How would von Stroheim have known that this simple fall required as many as three takes unless he was there on the spot himself—if not taking the fall, then at least taking notes.

When shooting ended on *The Birth,* Griffith busied himself with its exploitation, and work at his studio on Sunset Boulevard proceeded without him. In addition to the films which he personally directed, Griffith supervised the work of other directors whose day-to-day activities supported the studio overhead. Von Stroheim kept returning here each day, hoping for work as an extra. Apparently he was uninterested in the other studios in town, perhaps because he felt he had an "in" with the Griffith people.

He reports a series of episodes, alternately hazardous and boring, in the life of a Hollywood extra of 1915. Most of these seem to involve horses—riding a horse off a pier in one unnamed picture, or being knocked off his horse due to a faulty stirrup in Jack Conway's *Captain Macklin.* But usually there were long, fruitless waits in the "cattle yard" with the other hopefuls. He walked the eight miles from downtown Los Angeles each morning, subsisted on a handout meal of crackers and milk, and generally walked home each night with no prospect of dinner.[24] Von Stroheim had taken many odd jobs in the six years since he arrived in America, but work as a movie extra must have been one of the least remunerative: the pay was three dollars a day, when you worked. Of course there were other things he could have done, but the movies exerted a special appeal. The other extras wanted to be the next Henry B. Walthall or Lillian Gish. Von Stroheim wanted to be the next D. W. Griffith.

There are conflicting accounts of what happened next, but all sources agree that while hanging around the Mutual lot in the early spring of

1915 von Stroheim ran into the Broadway director John Emerson. Emerson had been working for the Shuberts and for Charles Frohman, and had just arrived on the Coast as part of a large Broadway contingent signed up by Mutual president Harry Aitken.[25] According to Curtiss he was set to act in and direct an adaptation of Ibsen's *Ghosts,* and when von Stroheim saw him Emerson was costumed for the leading role. Seizing the opportunity for what it was worth, von Stroheim stepped forward and criticized a decoration on Emerson's lapel. Claiming to be an expert on European civil and military decoration he volunteered to provide a proper ribbon, a service for which Emerson was properly grateful. But when von Stroheim returned the next day he learned that Emerson had quarreled with scenario editor Frank Woods and was off the picture. According to this account he did not see Emerson again until the filming of *Old Heidelberg* later that summer.[26]

This was the story as von Stroheim told it, dramatically satisfying, but somewhat careless of the facts. There is no record of Emerson ever having been assigned to *Ghosts,* although of course that could have been possible.[27] Instead he was acting in a film called *The Failure,* shot simultaneously and released only three days after the Ibsen picture. Von Stroheim appears in bit parts in both *Ghosts* and *The Failure,* and may have confused the two films. *The Failure* was directed by Christy Cabanne and John Emerson co-starred with Wahneta Hanson. *Reel Life,* the Mutual house paper, ran a photo of Emerson and von Stroheim in their issue of May 22, 1915.[28] This was probably von Stroheim's first appearance in any form of motion picture publicity, although he received no credit for what was probably just a few days' work.[29]

Unfortunately, all trace of *The Failure* seems to have vanished, although there is always the possibility a stray print will turn up somewhere. But von Stroheim's bit in *Ghosts* does survive, a few teasing moments in which he appears in chin whiskers and moustache as a registrar working in the office of a school in which young Oswald is placed. Despite being pushed all the way over to the edge of the frame he is largely successful in his efforts to upstage the star performers down front. Emerson may in fact have left this picture because of the gross liberties taken with the text. The man did have a reputation to maintain. There is no mention of syphilis, although much is made of Oswald's "inherited taint," now apparently alcoholism. An odd pain in Oswald's neck now seems the only sign of something outside the ordinary. Henry B. Walthall plays both Oswald and his father, Captain Alving. *Ghosts* was directed by George Nichols, one of Griffith's

Von Stroheim's first real part, a monocled villain in *Farewell to Thee.*

favorite character actors and later a key member of von Stroheim's own stock company.[30]

Von Stroheim's success in these small roles soon separated him from the rest of the hopefuls, and that summer he appeared in his first real part, receiving screen credit as the villain in a one-reel melodrama called *Farewell to Thee.* He and Lucille Young played a pair of adventurers trying to cheat one of her old sweethearts out of a recently inherited fortune. They track their victim to Hawaii, where the first order of business is to remove an inconvenient native wife from the scene, then lure the unsuspecting heir back to the mainland. But when the erstwhile victim discovers Lucille entertaining von Stroheim by playing "Aloha Oe" on her guitar he realizes the truth of the situation and forces a confession from her. He returns to the islands for a reunion with the wife and a happy ending.[31]

This was a period when actresses often played active and adventurous leads—Ruth Roland and Pearl White made careers of this sort of thing in the serials. But a dominant villainess was not quite so common, at least not until the misogynistic *film noir* era some thirty years later. For the record, von Stroheim's character was called Jackson, although how that explains his monocle is uncertain. No prints of *Farewell to Thee* appear to survive, and the film is not mentioned by von Stroheim or any of his major biographers.[32]

John Emerson now came back into von Stroheim's life, hiring him as actor, assistant, and technical adviser for a production of Wilhelm Meyer-Förster's *Old Heidelberg*. The relationship with Emerson was to last two years, and would be the single most important influence on von Stroheim's early career. As Emerson's assistant von Stroheim had direct access to the studio hierarchy, and even to Griffith himself. He gained valuable experience in all aspects of production, and when Emerson's unit struck gold with a series of Douglas Fairbanks films, von Stroheim found he was tied up with a winner.

There are two versions of how all this came about, and the difference in tone is instructive. Apparently, Emerson asked von Stroheim if he had even been in Heidelberg. According to Curtiss "It would have been very easy for von Stroheim to lie, but he had only been in Germany once, when he traveled from Vienna to Bremen. 'No,' he answered. 'But I do know the students' customs and costumes, as we have a student corps in Austria, too'."[33] That was von Stroheim's version, but Anita Loos, wife of John Emerson, remembered it differently. In her autobiography, *A Girl Like I,* when Emerson pops the question von Stroheim answers, "I am a graduate of the university, sir."[34] Whatever the case, Emerson did hire von Stroheim to tell him all about Heidelberg, and the extra was now behind the camera, giving orders instead of taking them. It was one year since he had entered films.

Von Stroheim was now earning fifteen dollars per week, not a big advance over three dollars a day, but at least the work was steady.

> My duties were to engage the fitting types for officers and students and other supernumeraries, to provide their costumes and uniforms, to have them fitted, to see that they were dressed properly and "made up" correctly, to provide for transportation for all people and the working crew, to find fitting locations, to get permits from Police to work in public parks and streets, to order and call for "box lunches," to distribute them, to burn up the boxes and papers after lunch, to be made up myself, to act one of the main parts, to write out the pay checks, to handle petti [sic] cash, to have all necessary props and to call half the night the needed people for the next day, over the phone.[35]

"Emerson started him off as technical adviser on life in the university town," remembered Anita Loos, "but before long Von was playing an important part in the picture. By the time the film was completed, Von's wide general culture had made him so indispensable that Emerson engaged him permanently as his assistant, in which capacity Von remained until his genius would no longer be held down."[36]

Von Stroheim's friend Sigmund Romberg would not present *The Student Prince* until 1924, so this 1915 adaptation was based directly on the novel, an impressionistic work of *fin-de-siècle* fiction, and its highly successful stage adaptation. Von Stroheim was heavily influenced by the narrative structure of *Old Heidelberg,* and made use of its conflict between duty and romance in most of his Imperial films. But if he took from this story then he also added something to it of his own, and in Emerson's film his hand is visible quite clearly, not only in the arrangement of background action which might be expected of an assistant director, but in that characteristic obsession with fate that strikes any viewer familiar with von Stroheim's own films.

In the original, young Prince Karl meets the charming Katie during his student days at Heidelberg. But this imagistic whirl of romance, drinking parties, and Student Corps festivities is doomed to fade, and Karl must give up Katie and the world of his youth when duty calls him to the throne. Changes in the film version turned this schmaltzy tale into a much more somber and realistic drama. War is always in the background. Katie's father returns with one arm and one medal. A title announces "the reigning prince has ordered that each crippled soldier be given a hand organ," a suspiciously Stroheimesque notion. Later in the film a large-scale war breaks out across the middle of Meyer-Förster's narrative. The Prince is against the war and so are the people, who turn to rioting in the streets. When Karl assumes the throne he calls the whole thing off, but he still cannot have Katie. The adaptation has added a level of grim reality which shifts the story from simple *noblesse oblige* to something much more fatalistic.

The question remains, who was responsible for this change in tone? Emerson was a major Broadway director and would have been expected to provide his own adaptation. Would he have paid attention to the eager dramatic suggestions of his new technical assistant, or was it the assistant who found Emerson's adaptation so compelling that he later incorporated much of it into his own work? Unfortunately, there are few surviving Emerson films which might help us identify his own hand here, and those which exist are mainly Douglas Fairbanks comedies written by Anita Loos. Inserting the war was obviously a topical consideration, and allowed the introduction of strong pacifistic sentiments then popular on the Griffith lot, where *Intolerance* was about to go into production. Von Stroheim might have suggested playing the romance against the war, or the idea might have come from "supervisor" Griffith, whose own films frequently made use of this device. In any case, von Stroheim was close enough to the decision so that his own scripts for *Merry-Go-Round* and *The Wedding March* must be read accordingly. But certainly von Stroheim is visible here in the background details, in the "customs and costumes" of the students, and in the one armed organ grinders providing ironic counterpoint to Meyer-Förster's lovely romantic militarism.

Wallace Reid played Prince Karl, and Dorothy Gish was Katie. Neither has much Viennese authority, but there is little that von Stroheim could have done about that. He does have the Prince appear with an unexplained black armband later in the picture, an expression of *Weltschmerz* (so he claimed) that would soon become a trademark.[37] Von Stroheim played the part of Lutz, Prince Karl's valet, a small part but one which allowed him to display his entire catalogue of obnoxious Teutonic mannerisms. He leers, hides behind his monocle, primps, struts, and generally holds himself like a ramrod. Already audiences were being taught to hate the man.

Emerson now took advantage of the opportunity to return East where he was to direct two more films, vehicles for Triangle stars Norma Talmadge and Douglas Fairbanks. This was the end of 1915, and while film companies generally left New York for California in the winter, it was a chance to catch up on the Broadway scene for Emerson and the rest of his unit, many of whom were homesick New Yorkers. Von Stroheim busied himself with his usual preparatory duties, and took time off for some personal business as well.

Little is known about von Stroheim's second marriage, to New York seamstress and dressmaker Mae Jones. Curtiss is the only biographer to discuss it at length, and his information is clearly at variance with the few facts available. According to this account, von Stroheim had known Mae Jones during his first years in New York, then picked up the relationship when he returned with Emerson to work on the Fairbanks film. They didn't see each other again until the close of shooting on *Hearts of the World* in 1918, and "when his first wife's divorce decree was granted," he proposed marriage. Their brief, unhappy union produced one son, Erich von Stroheim, Jr.[38]

There is an inexplicable loss of several years here. Margaret Knox's final decree came down on November 10, 1915. Erich von Stroheim, Jr., was born nine months later, August 25, 1916.[39] All efforts to pin-point the date of the Jones–von Stroheim marriage have been unsuccessful, although it appears to have taken place in New York, not Los Angeles. References to von Stroheim in this period by friends and co-workers always omit Mae Jones, and the relationship may in fact have foundered very early on. Mae does seem to have accompanied him to the Coast when he returned with Emerson after the New York shooting was over.

The two films Emerson directed on this New York trip were solid "Hollywood" entertainments, enlivened by fashionable Anita Loos scripts and first-class star performances. Von Stroheim had small parts in both, playing the member of a criminal gang in Fairbanks's *His Picture in the Papers* (he wore an eyepatch to make his bit more noticeable), and a snooping society reporter in Norma Talmadge's *The Social Secretary.* He was uncredited in the Fairbanks film, but was billed as "The Buzzard" in *The Social Secretary,* a fascinating location picture with much footage of Riverside Drive and the area around the Soldiers and Sailors' Monument.

When Emerson and von Stroheim returned to the Coast they made *The Flying Torpedo,* a preparedness film which predicted the invasion of America by foreign hordes. The attackers are eventually driven off with the aid of "flying torpedoes," remote controlled missiles devised by an eccentric inventor later murdered by a gang of international crooks. Von Stroheim, again teamed with Lucille Young, was one of the crooks.

More significant was Emerson's version of *Macbeth,* produced to highlight Aitken's latest theatrical acquisition, Sir Herbert Beerbohm-Tree. Tree's services were acquired for $100,000, and various Shakespearean titles were suggested for his first appearance, *Macbeth* finally being chosen for the pictorial richness of its narrative. The production was elaborate and expensive, with considerable location work and costly interior settings. Reviews speak of lavish pictorial effects, the most noteworthy being the vision of the three weird sisters, cited by the *New York Times* as "a triumph."[40] According to Anita Loos (who served, uncredited, as title writer on this picture) von Stroheim was responsible for this. He hired three young female impersonators to play the sisters and wired them up so that sparks would fly from their fingertips. But after $10,000 had been spent on this electrical effect, "the current proved too strong, and before it could be turned off three gaunt young female impersonators were screeching curses that

Shakespeare would have gratefully plagiarized could he have heard them."[41]

But the public would have none of this. Despite the film's pictorial richness Emerson's direction was unable to overcome Tree's theatrical acting style. In fact, Tree insisted on reciting all of the dialogue for each of his scenes, forcing Emerson to turn an empty camera on him most of the time, and saving his film for those moments which would actually be retained in the silent film. Praised by critics for the artistic quality of its production, the film failed to interest audiences. Robert Hamilton Ball reports that during the first screening even Tree fell asleep![42]

Von Stroheim always liked to be associated with films on which all thought of cost was sacrificed to artistic effect, but even he must have been appalled at the results of Tree's "artistic" performance. In his own films he would stay away from actors trained in the theater, and even avoid professional "movie stars" whenever possible. Griffith's use of untrained talent, moulded by the force of the director's will, would remain his great example.[43]

Among von Stroheim's duties on *Macbeth* was the creation of a large parquet floor for the banquet hall of Macbeth's castle, but when Emerson arrived to film this one day he found it had disappeared—spirited away by Griffith for use in his own film *Intolerance*.[44] This massive production was soaking up all the resources of the Triangle-Fine Arts lot, and soon von Stroheim again found himself pressed into service by Griffith, this time as assistant director as well as bit actor. While he was first assistant to Emerson and responsible for all the physical aspects of production, with Griffith he was only one of many. Joseph Henabery, Elmer Clifton, George Seigmann, and W. S. Van Dyke were all ahead of him, and his work on the set seemed limited to supervising segments of the crowd during mass action scenes (although he did tell Curtiss that he was asked to go to the Jewish section of Los Angeles to recruit realistically bearded Biblical types).[45]

But just as his suggestions filtered through in the background of films like *Old Heidelberg,* he seems to have had a hand in certain corners of *Intolerance* as well, notably in the modern episode. Set in a contemporary American city against a background of street crime and labor violence, this episode would have appealed to von Stroheim's sense of realism, and its ambience does carry over to such later films as *Greed* and *Walking Down Broadway*. Most clearly influenced by von Stroheim is the decoration of Walter Long's apartment, the decadent lair of a "musketeer of the slums." We learn about Long through a series of close-ups of the things in his room, a technique which von Stroheim would use over and over in his own films, but which is rarely seen in Griffith. And what things! A copy of "Loves of Lucille" on the night table, a statue of a nude along which the camera lovingly tilts—elements that would be more at home in *Queen Kelly* than in this overdecorated tenement. Long's apartment is contrasted with that of Mae Marsh, "the little dear one," where the only ornamentation is an icon of the virgin and a "hopeful geranium." Von Stroheim's obsession with religious imagery is well documented, but his use of the solitary geranium as symbol is not so well recognized. In films like *Queen Kelly, Walking Down Broadway,* and *La Grande Illusion,* the "hopeful geranium" echoes certain ideals of the main characters which are in danger of being overwhelmed by the force of circumstance. Griffith does use flowers as symbols, but not in as vigorous or consistent a way as von Stroheim.

The contrasting worlds of these two characters predict the study in contrasting milieus which would mark nearly all the films of von Stroheim and become one of his most familiar devices.

"Count Von Stroheim" received billing (along with Baron Von Ritzau) as one of two pharisees in the Judean episode of *Intolerance.* Surviving prints of the film imply that this is the pair we see during the marriage feast at Cana, demanding that all activity stop while they pray. But the figures are unrecognizably bearded, and recent photographic analysis by Arthur Lennig suggests that neither of the pair is von Stroheim. It must be remembered that today's prints of *Intolerance* are considerably shorter than those of 1916, and that the Judean episodes suffered the most. Pressure from organized Jewish groups forced Griffith to trim much of this episode, notably scenes involving the crucifixion. Russell Merritt, who has closely investigated this controversy, suggests that von Stroheim actually appears only in the cut sequences—nailing Christ to the cross! Von Stroheim's only recorded comment on his appearance in the film was simply "I'm one of those guys yelling 'Crucify Him!'."[46]

Von Stroheim was never one of Griffith's closest aides, but he realized the true significance of Griffith's contributions much better than Henabery, Seigmann, Clifton and the others. "He was the man who had put beauty and poetry into a cheap and tawdry form of amusement," von Stroheim remembered. Not only did he invent or develop a score of technical devices, but he was the first to devote these to a serious end, the first to realize "the potentialities of the medium." In a lengthy tribute to Griffith given at his mentor's death in 1948, von Stroheim singled out Griffith's understanding of "the psychological effect of a proper and correct costume on an actor," and his "sacred duty to show everything, may it be sets, costumes, uniforms, customs or rituals, as correctly as humanly possible."[47]

This emphasis on the "correct" relationship between character and setting made a tremendous impact on von Stroheim. Griffith's other assistants never quite grasped the reason for D.W.'s fussy perfectionism. And they never came near equaling it in their own films. Von Stroheim saw and learned. Unlike the others he never chided Griffith as a romantic dreamer, because he, too, shared the same dream.

But von Stroheim was Emerson's man, and returned with him to New York in the summer of 1916 while Griffith was putting the final touches on *Intolerance*. Their first film was a Mary Pickford for Artcraft, *Less Than the Dust,* a grim production which failed to find an audience. Then while Emerson was between pictures von Stroheim found he was able to get work elsewhere, and assisted Allan Dwan on a Norma Talmadge picture for Selznick, *Panthea*. Dwan had been a director on the Fine Arts lot while *Intolerance* was in production, and knew von Stroheim from the old days.

> I made him a Russian officer with a Prussian attitude and a whip. We had some tough looking White Russians we'd picked up—he played their officer and he was very commanding, cracking his whip at them. He made the mistake of socking them with it a couple of times and finally they started to beat the hell out of him. I had to pull him out from under a lot of Cossacks.[48]

Von Stroheim continued the film strictly behind the camera.

Douglas Fairbanks had organized his own production company for Artcraft and signed Emerson and Loos to create his films for him. Von Stroheim continued as assistant director on several of these, but by 1917 America found itself in the war and Fairbanks grew nervous about his Teutonic a.d. After *In Again, Out Again* von Stroheim's name disappeared from the credits, and on *Wild and Woolly* only a single trade paper mentioned his contribution. He claims to have appeared in *Reaching for the Moon,* heavily disguised as a vegetable in a dream sequence.[49] Finally he was dropped altogether. "I was discharged on account of Doug's apprehensions about having a man with a German name in his employ when even German-fried potatoes had to be rebaptized 'Liberty' potatoes," von Stroheim remembered years later.[50]

Yet this was a cloud with a silver lining. While Fairbanks the all-American had no use for von Stroheim in those days of national hysteria, whole new avenues were opening before him instead. He took advantage of his looks, name, and reputation, and carved out a new career as a professional Hun. At the Pathé studio in Jersey City Heights he worked for director George Fitzmaurice in *Sylvia of the Secret Service,* an espionage thriller starring Irene Castle and Antonio Moreno. Arthur Miller was cameraman, and remembered von Stroheim's work on the film.

> [He] was a sort of technical director for this picture. Von had considerable knowledge of German militarism, or at least everyone thought he had. The plot of *Sylvia of the Secret Service* had something to do with the Germans blowing up an ammunition dump, and Von went to New York to research the names of the different explosives to be painted on the cases stored at such a place. . . . These were the war years, and between his appearance and the sort of questions he was asking, it was no time at all before he was in the clink. The studio, of course, immediately went to his rescue and he was released. I am convinced, though, that the clever Von Stroheim pulled the whole thing off for its publicity value.[51]

During wartime was such behavior thoughtless, foolish, or carefully calculated? Miller's conclusions are shared by many of those who worked with von Stroheim during the war. Anita Loos remembers that between takes on one film,

> Von, dressed in the Prussian uniform of the movie's villain, would stalk over to the Plaza Hotel, engage one of the fiacres stationed there, and ride arrogantly through Central Park, accepting the jeers of American patriots along his way with an imperious twist of his monocle.[52]

This was a risky way of getting attention, but von Stroheim always took advantage of the opportunity to live dangerously. When the war was over and he could no longer arouse this sort of reaction simply by parading through the streets, he found other ways.

At the Vitagraph studio he played the Hun in *For France,* and again at Metro in *Draft 258,* directed by his old Fine Arts colleague Christie Cabanne. Unfortunately, the only one of his early Hun roles to survive is *The Unbeliever,* an Edison picture made with considerable Marine Corps cooperation late in 1917. Von Stroheim's behavior here would seem to have been typical of similar roles elsewhere. As Lt. Kurt Von Schnieditz he suspects a Belgian family of signaling the Allies with windmill vanes, so he shoots a mother and child as spies. "You foul fiend!" gasps Marguerite Courtot, their daughter and the real enemy agent. Such films generally blamed atrocities like this on isolated fanatics who pushed the "good Germans" into the background. After shooting another old lady, von Stroheim is himself shot by one of these good Germans, while his troops rise in revolt with cries of "Long Live Democracy!"

Von Stroheim spent quite a few months in New York during 1916 and 1917, but after breaking with Fairbanks he became so identified with Hun performances that this was the only work available to him. Curtiss describes him in those days as "lonely and depressed."[53] What was his relationship with Mae Jones, and their infant son, Erich, Jr.? "What his social life was I don't know," remembered Anita Loos. "I think he was very unhappily married and sort of under a cloud. He was not a happy man. He was always in trouble then. And I think most of the time he was having his domestic troubles."[54]

Von Stroheim had taken cheap lodgings at 152 West 49th Street when D. W. Griffith passed through town. Griffith had accepted a commission from the allied governments to create a film on the great war, but was having troubles of his own. "Viewed as drama," Griffith said, "the war is disappointing."[55] Von Stroheim saw him in New York and convinced Griffith that what was needed was an experienced technical adviser. Something would have to be done in Hollywood to juice up the "disappointing" footage shot in Europe, and von Stroheim was just the person to help. In the D. W. Griffith collection of the Museum of Modern Art is the following telegram, sent by von Stroheim to Griffith on November 2, 1917:

> As per your request beg to remind you that you engaged me for your company anticipating possible demand. I have ascertained exact number of uniforms on hand of costumer here anxiously awaiting your order to leave respectfully Von Stroheim.

Griffith sent for him at once.[56]

The new film would be called *Hearts of the World,* and von Stroheim apparently assumed the villain's role was his for the asking. But once again he misjudged his real closeness to Griffith, and Lillian Gish reports that he "broke into tears" when the part went to George Seigmann instead.[57] In retrospect this decision was not surprising. Despite his admitted success in the earlier Hun roles von Stroheim was still more important as an adviser than as an actor. And Seigmann, who was much better established in the Griffith camp, was also closer to the physical type Griffith needed. In order to better menace Lillian Gish the director required someone of substantial size for the climactic rape scenes. Seigmann simply repeated his role of the power-crazed mulatto governor in *The Birth of a Nation,* which had been Griffith's intention all along.

So von Stroheim was limited to only a few incidental villainies. He is a prominent participant in the "dungeons of lust" sequence, but his best scene, where he reads out a list of civilians to be deported, was missing from most prints until very recently. *Hearts of the World* was a great success, but von Stroheim had so small a part that he could not have attracted much attention in it. Those who claim to remember him are invariably confusing him with Seigmann (who plays a character named Von Strohm) or are thinking of a later film, Universal's *The Heart of Humanity*. That film would prove a major stepping stone in von Stroheim's career, but appears to have come his way due to his work *behind* the cameras for Griffith, not in front of them.

Before moving to Universal von Stroheim made one last appearance on the Griffith lot, playing opposite Dorothy Gish in *The Hun Within,* another Christy Cabanne film. In later years von Stroheim tried to make much of his Griffith connection, not out of any sense of self-aggrandizement, but because he honestly felt himself to be Griffith's true heir. This is something that never seems to have occurred to Griffith himself, who much preferred the company of men like Seigmann, Henabery, and Elmer Clifton. Von Stroheim was too alien a presence for this tight little group, and while Griffith was clever enough to use von Stroheim for specific tasks he never allowed him to be one of the inner circle. It was only with Emerson that von Stroheim managed that sort of relationship, and through Emerson that he was able to spend as much time with Griffith as he did.

But the *appearance* that he was a Griffith protégé did count for something in Hollywood. "Allen Holubar needed a man of Griffith experience in his forthcoming production," Universal admitted, and so von Stroheim began work on *The Heart of Humanity*.[58] Supposedly he was again just an actor here, but in retrospect the von Stroheim touch is more clearly in evidence than in any of the other pre-directorial works. As the title indicates this film attempted to copy the success of the Griffith picture as closely as possible. In addition to von Stroheim repeating in a similar role another supporting actor, Robert Anderson, was also brought over from the *Hearts of the World* cast. Much of the narrative structure was lifted intact, and significant chunks of dialogue also turned up, this time spoken by von Stroheim, who finally achieved the role Seigmann had played in the earlier picture.[59]

One "major" difference was that in Griffith's film the engaged lovers are separated by the war before their marriage, while here they have been married for a brief time before the hero leaves for the front. Griffith's characters were Belgian, and the action naturally flowed back and forth around their little village. In the Universal version director Allen Holubar used Canadians instead, so his heroine must join the Red Cross in order to take part in the action at the front. Even in the smallest details *The Heart of Humanity* echoes its predecessor, and

Allen Holubar's
Super-production

"THE HEART
OF HUMANITY"

The Picture that
will Live Forever

Starring DOROTHY PHILLIPS

"Altogether beautifully done"—MOTION PICTURE WORLD

JEWEL
Productions Inc.
1600 Broadway, New York City

By 1918 the von Stroheim image was already being used to sell his films. Just visible here are the black arm band and slave bracelet (a gift from Valerie) which will recur throughout his career.

von Stroheim had to call upon all his "Griffith experience" to lend a few touches of characterization or symbolic shading. Early on in the film Dorothy Phillips is metaphorically compared to a squirrel, a pastoral symbol already considered a Griffith cliché. But as she prays at a roadside shrine the photography transforms *her* into a madonna, and von Stroheim's own sensibility becomes more apparent. When the Hun himself appears as a threatening premonition the comparison is to a spider, and a particularly nasty one crawls across the face of the woodland madonna.

Griffith was a master of rape scenes, but even he never created one as unnerving as that in *The Heart of Humanity*. Only in this one scene does the picture really come alive, and only here do we get the feeling that von Stroheim's contribution went far beyond mere "technical advice." Von Stroheim has finally trapped Dorothy Phillips, tantalizing in her rumpled Red Cross uniform. With the smoke and flames of the burning city rising outside the window he slowly strips off his field jacket and unbuckles his gleaming leather shoulder harness. But Dorothy has been caring for the town's orphans, and an especially noisy one is locked in the room with them. As the child cries helplessly von Stroheim begins to rip off the nurse's uniform with his teeth. Screams from Dorothy mingle with those from the infant until finally von Stroheim has had enough. He walks over to the cradle, picks the child up, and throws it out the second floor window.

Few in the audience ever forgot this scene. They forgot the last-minute rescue by United States Marines, they forgot the name of the film's insipid hero, but they never forgot "the scene where von Stroheim throws the baby out the window."

Despite the fact that the film did not open until a month *after* the Armistice, it did tremendous business all through 1919. Kevin Brownlow points out that, contrary to popular belief, films about the war did not disappear after November but continued to be released for several more months as "vengeance" pictures, and *The Heart of Humanity* proved to be the greatest success of all.[60] D. W. Griffith had bet Los Angeles exhibitor Sol Lesser that *The Heart of Humanity* would fail to gross $7000 its first week at the Kinema Theatre. It took $10,000.[61]

In addition to a sudden flush of public notoriety von Stroheim gained three things from *The Heart of Humanity*. First, he met an English actor named Gibson Gowland, here playing a German soldier in scenes of trench warfare.[62] Von Stroheim would use him as an actor later on: he would be the ideal McTeague. Second, von Stroheim was able to demonstrate his eagerness and proficiency all over the Universal lot during the shooting of this lavish production. It was experience that would stand him in good stead a few months later when he returned with a script of his own. And finally, he met his third wife, an extra and "hand model" from Detroit named Valerie Germonprez.

In a sense, Valerie Germonprez was another mysterious Hollywood character. She always dressed in high style and drove to work in a big new Buick, far above the means of the average extra. One rumor had it that she was a Belgian spy, observing German activity in the movie colony. In reality she was lucky enough to have a sister who was a dressmaker and a brother in the car rental business. He gave her the Buick so she wouldn't have to accept rides from movie people.[63]

Von Stroheim met her while she was playing the part of an ambulance driver. "Where is this ambulance coming from?" he demanded. "The front," she said. "As clean as this?" He stooped down and picked up fistfuls of mud with his kid-gloved hands, and spattered the pure white van until it was dripping. "Now it looks like it came from the front!" he announced, and continued his rounds of inspection. "There's a fellow with something wrong with him," she thought, but even then Valerie knew that all he wanted was to attract her attention.[64]

A few days later von Stroheim appeared again, asking for a date and beginning an insistent courtship that went on for over a year. Valerie would come home and find him waiting on her doorstep. He had quite a reputation to overcome, and didn't always go about this in the most effective way. He took her to a downtown theater where *The Unbeliever* was still playing. "When I got in there and saw he was an officer shooting this old lady I thought, 'We'd better get out of here before they turn on the lights'!"[65] Then they would go to French restaurants where the other diners would throw rolls, most of which would hit Valerie.

But for a good Catholic worst of all were von Stroheim's two previous marriages. It is unclear if Valerie knew at the time about Margaret Knox, but his marriage to Mae Jones was still in effect, and that divorce was not final until July of 1919.[66] Somehow von Stroheim was able to explain all this to Mrs. Germonprez, who gave him one year to "make good" and allowed him to continue calling on Valerie. The religious question itself was no problem. Von Stroheim was always a practicing Catholic when Valerie knew him; it was decades later before she learned any different.

Von Stroheim never learned to drive a car. Even in *Sunset Boulevard,* where he appears to "drive" onto the Paramount lot, the car is simply being towed along as he sits behind the wheel making the proper gestures. So when *The Heart of Humanity* was finished it was Valerie who drove him around to the various studios, now in search of work as a writer or director. Von Stroheim had a script called "The Furnace" which he had written in 1918 with Roberta Lawson, but no one was interested in it once the Armistice was signed. And there were other reasons for disliking it as well. A reader's report dug out of the M-G-M story files by Arthur Lennig tells the story:

> A synopsis is not made because this is a war story with all its unhappy and regrettable details, even going so far as to have one of twin daughters of an American father and a Belgian mother, executed on the evidence of a German surgeon, and the other daughter afterwards marries the German. In spite of the fact that he is supposed to be a good German and not in sympathy with the war, this is rather too much to ask an American public to accept. If the author of this story thinks that in its present form it would be tolerated by the American public, he has the same colossal and, to them, very regrettable misunderstanding that the Germans had of the American people before the war. The idea . . . is too appalling for words.[67]

It was not the last time that von Stroheim would ask too much of the American public.

There may have been other early von Stroheim screenplays, now lost to history. All we can say for sure is that his imagination was prolific, and that whenever he did come up with an idea he liked he would keep reshaping it until it sold. Even "The Furnace" would come back again, as a 1925 treatment called "The Crucible."

One of the studios von Stroheim would travel to was Universal, across the Cahuenga Pass from Hollywood proper. The pass was a dangerous glen and he carried a pistol under the seat as protection against highwaymen. One day he and Valerie saw a gypsy camp in a grove of eucalyptus trees just off the main road. Von Stroheim, irrepressibly superstitious, stopped to have his fortune told. He crossed the gypsy's palm with silver and she made one prediction. "You will become very famous," she said, "over that hill." And pointed in the direction of Universal City.[68]

Blind Husbands

Until the coming of Orson Welles, *Blind Husbands* was the most impressive and significant debut film in Hollywood history. It remains the most surprising even today, since Welles's record in theater and radio was well known, while von Stroheim emerged directly from the ranks of melodramatic villainy. We know how Welles came to work for RKO, but what enabled von Stroheim to move from near-anonymity to an unprecedented writing, directing, and acting triumph, literally overnight?

Von Stroheim had not worked since completing *The Heart of Humanity* for Carl Laemmle late in 1918. The market for Prussian villains had dried up with the November armistice, and his writing projects had come to nothing.[1] He was living alone at the Hollywood Hotel, a picturesque landmark on Hollywood Boulevard already past its prime. To add to his troubles he fell victim to the great influenza epidemic as it swept through Los Angeles. Hundreds died, and the film industry was at a standstill, casts and crews decimated. At the last minute he was taken in by the Germonprez family—very lucky for him since he had certainly run out of money again. Cared for by Valerie, he passed the time concocting motion picture plots and developed an idea of his into a scenario called *The Pinnacle,* a romantic triangle set against snow-capped European peaks. Each night he would act it out in detail for the family, then scribble away long afternoons on a school-room pad supplied by one of the younger Germonprez brothers. He had no money, and given the still prevalent anti-German hysteria, no prospects. He would borrow cigarettes from Valerie's brother Louis, carefully rationing them to stretch the supply. More than anything he would ever write this script carried so much of his hope for future success. To promote it he devised an elaborate personal sales campaign, and Universal's Carl Laemmle was the prime target.

Laemmle was the obvious mark for several reasons. True, von Stroheim had done well for him in *The Heart of Humanity,* stealing the acting honors and providing the needed "Griffith experience," but he had done that for other studios as well. Von Stroheim's campaign here was based not on simple business ties, but on a canny assessment of the man and his studio. In marketing terms, Universal was the Woolworth's of the motion picture business. The Paramount program offered high-priced stars like Pickford, Fairbanks, and William S. Hart in a series of increasingly costly productions, but Laemmle had long since dropped out of this prestige competition. Instead he produced his films cheaply and in quantity, effecting economies by keeping salaries low and employing mass-production techniques at his huge studio at Universal City. Unwilling to pay the now-obligatory six-figure salaries to important stars, he managed without them, investing heavily in westerns, serials, and short comedies, for which top dramatic stars were unnecessary. While Universal continued to produce occasional "Jewels" to head their season's output, available personnel for these more elaborate productions were few, and hardly impressive by the standards of other studios. As soon as a star or director achieved wide success Laemmle inevitably failed to meet their increased salary demands and they moved elsewhere. John Ford, Lon Chaney, and Mae Murray were all in the process of outgrowing Universal when von Stroheim made his approach there. Rudolph Valentino had already left. Because of this there was always a tremendous staff turnover, particularly among the more talented or popular figures. Newcomers were always being hired to fill the gaps, at suitably meager salaries, and von Stroheim was counting on just such an opportunity.

He was also counting on taking advantage of Laemmle's idiosyncratic business methods. It was a standing joke in Hollywood that Laemmle's studio was staffed with personal relatives and other *lansmen,* German Jews from the area around Laupheim, Laemmle's birthplace.[2] Rival studios were controlled by men like Goldwyn, Zukor, Mayer, and Fox, with very different ethnic roots in eastern Europe. The holdovers from the early days of cinema, WASP-run studios like Blackton and Smith's Vitagraph, were few in number and dwindling in power. Neither of these groups could be expected to warm to von Stroheim's Teutonic demeanor, but Universal was a different matter entirely. Only here could von Stroheim be sure of escaping the still-rampant anti-German prejudices of the immediate postwar years. Even better, as a German speaking émigré himself, von Stroheim was able to play directly to Carl Laemmle's sentimental attachments.

Finally, von Stroheim hoped to take advantage of Laemmle's well-known gambler's streak. For years he had run his studio on hunches, and his capricious disposition made the effective functioning of studio operations nearly impossible. Studio managers came and went, their authority unclear, their tenure uncertain. At regular intervals Uncle Carl would come out from New York and institute all sorts of wild changes, and von Stroheim was determined to be there when he did. He would make the gambler an irresistible offer. He would show him that *The Pinnacle* could be produced for a song, with inexpensive actors of small reputation. He would *give* him the script, and direct it for nothing. He would take $200 a week for acting.[3] What could he lose?

But first von Stroheim had to break through the wall around Laemmle. The studio head was surrounded by a retinue of hangers-on whose best interests were served by isolating Uncle Carl from people like von Stroheim, whose pleas could easily cause yet another capricious policy swing. Von Stroheim fortified himself by making a novena to St. Rita, then set on a daily ritual of waiting outside the president's office. He did not drive, and had no money for carfare. He would walk from the Germonprez house to Universal City, a distance of some miles across the Cahuenga Pass.[4] The executive offices at Universal City were in a whitewashed hacienda just off Lankershim Boulevard, warmed by the heat of the San Fernando Valley. Von Stroheim would hike out here each day, but was never able to get close enough for a hearing. There were too many others with the same idea, actors, writers and all sorts of Hollywood promoters, who would hang around the oversized pepper tree that stood in front of the main office. Eventually he changed his tactics and decided to show up on Laemmle's doorstep instead. Carl Laemmle, Jr., the studio head's eleven-year-old son, ran to answer the bell and immediately recognized von Stroheim, but the household staff refused to allow him in without an appointment.[5] Von Stroheim tried to talk his way past them, but their orders were clear. Finally Uncle Carl himself heard the commotion. "Who is this who only wants to see me for five minutes?" That was all it took. Von Stroheim and Laemmle disappeared into the library and closed the doors behind them. Von Stroheim knew that once he began his story his five minutes could stretch indefinitely. He was a fabulous storyteller, acting out all the parts, describing the *mise en scène* in exhaustive detail, painting a word picture so detailed that the film seemed finished already. A long time passed. When they left the roon von Stroheim had convinced Laemmle to allow him to star in and direct *The Pinnacle*. The price was right. But while Laemmle often acted on hunches, he was no fool: von Stroheim must audition again for the studio manager, Joe Stern.

This time Valerie drove him, but she did not go into Stern's home with Erich. She waited in the car and watched the men's shadows on the drawn shades of a bay window. As Erich paced the room acting out all the parts again she could follow the plot perfectly. The climax of *The Pinnacle* occurs on a rocky peak, as the villain spots a dark bird of prey hovering symbolically nearby. On the window shade she saw Erich raise his arms over his head, miming the bird in flight. She knew how von Stroheim's story came out, but the climax of the other drama taking place in Stern's house that night was another matter entirely. She had to wait a long time for him to walk out the door.[6]

But Stern was a Laemmle yes-man, and his reaction should have been predictable. The project was in the bag, and only details of production remained to be settled. According to one source, the budget von Stroheim prepared was $25,000, slim, but not unreasonable.[7] The studio continued to make program pictures for less than that well into the 1920s. Von Stroheim went home to prepare the details of casting and budgeting; in the days before the producer system this was still the province of the director. He himself would play the villain, while the rest of the cast would be old friends and associates, the beginnings of a stock company system, learned from Griffith, which he would continue through all his later films. Francellia Billington and Sam de Grasse would be an American couple on holiday in Croce Bianca, a mountain resort near the Austro-Italian border. They were familiar faces from his days at Mutual, where they had appeared together in films like *Tangled Paths* (1915). Von Stroheim may never have worked directly with Billington at that time, but the lot was small and he would have certainly run across her during the long stretches between scenes. Sam de Grasse, of course, had worked with him in *Intolerance,* and later in Fairbanks's *Wild and Woolly,* on which von Stroheim was technical adviser. Gibson Gowland, a burly British actor he had met during *Heart of Humanity* would be Sepp, the mountain guide, and there was even a small part for Valerie. Behind the cameras Universal had obviously decided to support the production, and assigned one of their top cameramen, Ben Reynolds, along with his young assistant, William Daniels. These two would spend the next five years working for von Stroheim.

Production began on April 3, 1919, and despite the director's detailed preparations both budget and shooting schedule soon began to grow. While von Stroheim had worked out every detail on paper well

Detailed setting and familiar actors: Francellia Billington and Sam deGrasse.

ahead of time, he continued to refine the picture as he went along, changing the script by adding or subtracting action and characters— mostly adding. Soon after the film was released Carl Laemmle claimed that it had cost ten times what von Stroheim had projected.[8]

Not surprisingly, the more cash the studio sank into the production, the more eager they were to ensure its success by any means possible. They convinced fan magazines like *Photoplay* and *Picture Play* to carry special features on von Stroheim intended to desensitize potentially troublesome audience reaction. "In real life," wrote *Picture Play*'s Celia Brynn, "there is not a better-liked man on the Universal lot than this same 'Horrible Hun' who goes by the nickname of 'Von,' and they will tell you that his heart is as big as all outdoors, that he is as square as they make 'em, and is a prince of good fellows."[9] The article goes on to carefully explain how the film satirized the German *"Kultur"* mentality, neatly diverting its readers from a less jingoistic interpretation. American troops were only just returning from the war, and Universal was taking no chances on a misinterpretation of the sentiments of *The Pinnacle* or its director. All domestic advertising dropped the "von" from his name, and press releases announced that he had given up his royal title, anyway. The studio conspicuously promoted the lie that he had been an American citizen for ten years—he would not in fact be naturalized until February 19, 1926. As it happened, the need for such behavior was short-lived, and the "von" reappeared for his next picture only a few months later.

By the end of shooting on June 12 the film had grown into one of Universal's most important productions. Many elaborate costumes had been hand sewn, a compact but finely detailed Alpine set had been constructed on the back lot, and a location trip to Idlewild, the mountain range just beyond Palm Springs, was thrown in for added realism. The negative cost had reached $112,144.83, and a further $140,173.34 would soon be charged against it for advertising and selling expenses.[10] If von Stroheim was counting desperately on the film's success, so was Universal.

Von Stroheim spent the rest of the summer cutting the picture, struggling to select the best takes from the mass of footage he had accumulated. Unlike John Emerson he lacked a firm background in the theatre and experience in directing actors. He had observed Griffith at work, but the master's handling of actors was impossible to duplicate. In order to achieve his effects von Stroheim would create an "atmosphere" on the set, then run the actors through the scene over and over until he felt they had achieved an ideal. This technique was often maddening to actors and crew, but invariably resulted in performances of tremendous power and conviction. It also resulted in huge amounts of footage which von Stroheim was agonizingly slow in reducing to manageable length. Griffith edited *Intolerance* in a matter of weeks, but von Stroheim would spend months in his cutting rooms, and was usually forced to surrender a partially edited print to anxious studio executives. Universal eventually sent in Grant Whytock, a young editor whose career would cross von Stroheim's more than once. He brought the film down to 7711 feet by eliminating what von Stroheim remembered as an entire reel, although Whytock claims that "practically nothing" was cut.[11]

The studio had been promoting the film for months, anxious to recoup its investment, but also well aware of the extraordinary quality of the picture. Press screenings for Hollywood representatives of the fan magazines went very well, and *Photoplay*'s Julian Johnson broke the release date with an unqualified rave.

> It seems to me that the master has produced a pupil—we are doing in pictures what the first masters of the Barbison school did in painting—von Stroheim is the direct descendant of Griffith, and in its perfection of detail, its semblance to all the small realities of life, its omission of no touch or trifle which lends to illusion and the gratification of intelligent observors, *The Pinnacle* is a Griffith picture.[12]

Along with *Broken Blossoms* and *The Miracle Man,* Johnson put it at the top of the year's releases. With such plaudits already behind it the film was shipped to New York on August 28, 1919, where the sales office demanded an immediate title change. Since the picture had been advertised and even reviewed as *The Pinnacle* this change was no small decision, and came from R. H. Cochrane himself, Universal's vice-president and publicity director, and Laemmle's most trusted associate. It seems unlikely that the demand came from Laemmle, whom legend claims was surprised to find that the film was not about card playing ("There ain't no pinochle in it!").

The New York office considered film titles as the proper responsibility of the sales department and often ran inter-departmental competitions to retitle films which arrived from the coast. In this case some 500 prospective titles were received, including "Thy Neighbor's Wife," "The Perfect Rotter," "The Love Snake," and (interestingly enough) "Foolish Wives." Advertising manager Edward S. Moffat submitted the winning title, *Blind Husbands*. Von Stroheim was livid, and reacted immediately with a full page ad in the *Motion Picture News* under the heading "A Protest to the Trade."

> When I went to Mr. Laemmle and sold him this story I sold him more
> than a mere story—I sold this gentleman part of *myself*. "The Pinnacle"
> was the child of my brain—and heart. I had created it—I loved it. . . .
> And the *title* was just as much a part of the picture as any scene in it. I
> had thought of it always as "The Pinnacle"—the name exactly and pre-
> cisely fitted the picture. It was the *only* title for it—of that I am sure.
>
> But now Mr. Laemmle—without consulting me—is about to change the
> title.
>
> He is going to change it to "Blind Husbands." *"Blind Husbands!"* Can
> you imagine it to yourself? A beautiful title, a meaningful title, a title
> that meant everything to the man who created it, a title that represented
> months and years of creative effort in producing this picture—all tossed
> away in a moment for a name which is the *absolute essence of commer-
> cialism*. A name in which there is no beauty—no sense of the artistic. A
> name which I would have rejected in disgust had it been submitted to
> me. I would, in fact, have been ashamed of myself had I even thought
> of it. . . .[13]

Von Stroheim even claimed to have been made physically ill (*"Blind
Husbands,* Ugh!"), but his arguments probably carried little weight with
the exhibitors who subscribed to *Motion Picture News*. The following
week "Carl Laemmle" provided a much more clearly targeted response,
boasting of the very commercialism von Stroheim scorned. "Art is a
glorious thing in pictures, but when it comes to the *title, commercialism
must come first,"* he wrote. "Otherwise there would not be enough
money in it to pay for the art!"[14]

As *Blind Husbands* the film premiered at Washington's Rialto Theatre on October 19, 1919, and was immediately booked for the first
available date at New York's palatial Capitol, largest and finest of
Broadway's new picture palaces. Universal's product was seldom seen
in the best Broadway houses, and the studio jumped at the booking,
even though it meant a two-month delay before getting into New York.
Until then the studio took what bookings it could (New York dates even
then seemed "official" premieres) and began playing off the picture
around the country. "Maybe you don't know who this Stroheim person
is," wrote one Chicago critic. "Maybe you don't care. But if you happen
into the Ziegfeld Theatre this week you're going to find out and you're
going to remember."[15]

As was the fashion, feature pictures were presented with an elaborate atmospheric prologue designed to add color, sound, and three-
dimensional spectacle to the silent photoplay. At the larger theaters
these could be quite impressive, and often received as much notice from

reviewers as the picture presentation. For the film's December 7 New
York opening Major Edward Bowes, manager of the Capitol, and John
Wenger, his art director, created a special setting with original vocal
music as a "frame" for *Blind Husbands,* but critics hardly had space to
mention it.[16] Wrote the *New York Telegraph:*

> If we are not very much mistaken, *Blind Husbands* will introduce to the
> industry a new "super director"—Eric von Stroheim. Unlike many other
> directors who aspire to the ranks of the fortunate, he is not a near-
> Griffith a near-De Mille, or a near-Tourneur. His work is quite in a class
> by itself. It has individuality and originality. . . . The atmosphere is
> deeper than mere realism. The details are truly remarkable. The interiors
> of the Alpine Inns, the wayside shrines, and the peasant types were all
> the work of a man who knew very much what he was doing.[17]

Variety stated bluntly:

> This picture is exceptional . . . this former Griffith heavy has written,
> directed, and acted in a feature that makes others shown on Broadway
> seem like a novel by Chambers beside a masterpiece by Sudermann or
> Schnitzler . . . every exhibitor should show it or consider himself at
> once the manager of a second grade house.[18]

This was a time of hyperbole and cliché in film reviewing, but *Blind
Husbands* seems to have brought out the best in a host of otherwise un-
imaginative reviewers. Not only did the trade almost without exception
recognize the status of this new work, but they were quick to see that
von Stroheim's strength lay in a new realism of character and setting,
and that his themes had more than a bit of Griffith—and Schnitzler—
about them. "There is no play for heroics, no bid for big climaxes,"
wrote Laurence Reid. "These come spontaneously, without effort. And
so the picture does not assume the aspect of a photoplay, but resembles
a slice from life."[19] Even the *New York Times,* never home to the most
sophisticated film criticism, had an explanation for von Stroheim's
success.

> Mr. Stroheim, unlike many directors, grasps the fact that the screen is
> the place for moving pictures, and that whatever is to be done on it with
> artistic finish must be done pictorially.[20]

A recent flood of over-titled features had made a number of reviewers
sensitive on this point, and the *Times* was not alone in praising von
Stroheim's ability to replace words with images. "If the promise that is
borne of his first performance as a director is fulfilled, the screen will
be greatly enriched."[21]

The studio publicity department did not rest with a simple title change. Under the heading *"Blind Husbands* the Wonder Picture" von Stroheim's face glared down from the façade of Universal's offices at 1600 Broadway. Manhattan and Brooklyn were plastered with 191 billboard-sized 24-sheet posters announcing the film's imminent arrival. In fact, over 158,000 posters of various sizes were distributed across the country during the film's first year of release, by which point receipts of $327,084.06 had been registered (average receipts for a typical Universal five-reel feature in this period were $55,000).[22] The studio certainly maximized its selling effort on the picture, but von Stroheim had given them something highly salable to work with.

Von Stroheim's plot was simple, but laced with elements designed to appeal to an audience's taste for exotic adventure. Dr. Robert Armstrong and his wife Margaret are American tourists visiting the Hotel Croce Bianca in Cortina, a mountain resort in the Austrian Dolomites, Lt. Eric von Steuben arrives with them on the post-coach, a serpent introduced into an Alpine Eden ("In the Alps there is no sin," a rustic placard declares). The period is unclear. As the film was going into release studio publicity material announced the period as "three years after the close of the present war," somewhat unusual since this places the action at least two years in the future! Various critics noted this, but none seemed to care. Obviously a decision was made early on during production not to present this as a pre-war story, and post-dating the action appeared the only solution. None of this affects the charming, prewar ambience of the film in the slightest.

The lieutenant's part was an extension of "the man you love to hate," the Prussian villain created by von Stroheim in films like *The Heart of Humanity*. That character was a simple rapist, however, having his way with women through the use of terror and physical violence. Lt. von Steuben occupies himself with most of the women in the cast, but operates as a "lounge lizard," a smooth and unscrupulous seducer. Although a stock villain who undergoes no psychological development in the course of the film, von Steuben is at least an interesting symbol, man's libido unrestrained by the bonds of conventional society. The film concerns itself with how the overly civilized marriage of Robert and Margaret reacts to the intrusion of this destabilizing element. The symbolic nature of this triangle was brought out in one of the script's more exotic scenes, in which the figures of von Steuben and Margaret dissolve into those of Pan and a shepherdess, with Pan playing his pipes into the lady's ear (no such scene survives in existing prints).

The lieutenant busies himself with women of all classes, including a local peasant girl, the hotel waitress, and the aristocratic American visitor. While the husband is obviously a good sort, he fails to exhibit any outward signs of romantic affection, something which von Steuben notices and decides to take advantage of. As the doctor busies himself with his mountain climbing plans, von Steuben works on a conquest of his own, gradually winning the attention of the neglected Margaret.

The sexual symbolism of mastering mountain peaks is clearly brought out, and von Stroheim's placement of this sexual duel against such a background strongly recalls the work of Ibsen or Strindberg (remember that Hedda and Tesman honeymoon in the Dolomites). Along with this very conscious Freudian allegory exists a religious symbol system as well, incorporating the rituals of von Stroheim's adopted Roman Catholicism. For example, the feast being celebrated in the village during the course of the film, the "Gala Peter," commemorates Christ's ascension of Mt. Tabor and His Transfiguration, an extension of the film's central metaphor.[23] The combination of religious and sexual imagery would be continued in each subsequent von Stroheim film.

Margaret resists von Steuben's advances, but various clues have begun to make Robert suspicious. At the film's conclusion he and the lieutenant are climbing to The Pinnacle alone, and it is apparent that the Austrian's tales of rock-climbing prowess are nothing but machismo fantasies. He cannot move another step without the doctor's expert advice. At this point a note from Margaret to the lieutenant refusing his advances is glimpsed by the doctor, but blows away in a fateful gust of wind before he can read it. The doctor demands to know if Margaret has been unfaithful, threatening to drop von Steuben over the edge if he lies. The lieutenant, reasoning that the doctor will not believe the truth, "confesses" that she has. Armstrong keeps his word and hauls him back over the edge, but cuts the rope between them and descends alone. This sort of no-win situation involving suspicion and guilt will occur again in von Stroheim's films, notably in *The Devil's Pass Key*. But here it is inelegantly handled, and even became a topic of humor at the time, as the cartoon by Segar indicates.[24] On his way down the doctor finds the note and learns its true contents, clearing Margaret's name. The lieutenant, with a symbolic vulture hovering overhead, falls to his death while attempting the descent. The film closes as it began, with a tracking shot of Robert and Margaret in the post-coach, now leaving Croce Bianca a little wiser for their holiday adventure.

That Margaret stops even to consider the attentions of von Steuben was a daring break with tradition, and has long been noted as the film's most innovative plot element. In fact, there were a few earlier American films which tried to deal with passion and guilt in terms of some psy-

chological complexity (especially those of the demagogical woman director Lois Weber) and certainly the early Swedish and Italian cinemas often handled this theme. But never had such ideas been presented with the dramatic force which von Stroheim was able to marshal. The realism of setting he called for was a necessary stylistic adjunct to his theme, and was further emphasized by an exceptionally intelligent use of camera and editing. The very first sequence of the picture, as the three principals travel in the coach to Croce Bianca, announces the arrival of a new master of psychological realism. On the one hand, the scene prefigures Murnau's famous streetcar ride in *Sunrise,* but von Stroheim never hesitates to use Griffith's analytic editing techniques to telegraph certain points directly. A series of close-ups establishes an immediate tension among the travelers, and the attraction of a shifting glance for a well-turned ankle is demonstrated with considerable wit. Although only a first work, the level of professionalism seen here puts most films of the period to shame, a fact quickly recognized in the first reviews.

Von Stroheim had the experience of several years with Griffith and Emerson to his credit, but the power of his first film hardly comes from this alone. Rather, like so many of his later works, it draws its strength from deeply personal roots. In the work of no other great director are autobiographical elements so crucial, and such elements are stronger than usual in *Blind Husbands*. This is von Stroheim's version of his days in the Austrian army, his experiences in the resort hotels of northern California, and his whirlwind seduction and courtship of Margaret Knox. That the officer is a direct projection of von Stroheim himself is beyond question. The sound-alike name is only a clue, but there are other similarities as well. According to the preparation sheets, von Steuben wears the 1908 Jubilee Cross, the Annexation Medal, and the Marianer Cross—all decorations von Stroheim claimed to have won himself. Both have been assigned to the same front, taken part in the Bosnia-Herzegovina campaign, and are lieutenants attached to the fourth regiment of dragoons. It is possible that the detailed reconstruction of the Hotel Croce Bianca at Cortina was created out of guide books, but the style of the man seems to indicate a personal knowledge of this actual place.

To this background von Stroheim added incidents from his experiences in America, especially his time spent in resort hotels at Lake Tahoe and Mt. Tamalpais. In places like these he observed at first hand the behavior of well-to-do Americans on holiday, and seems to have had particular success with the ladies. He had no trouble talking Emma Bissinger into a gift of $500 to produce his play in 1914, for example. Most interesting of all is the connection between Margaret Armstrong and Margaret Knox. Margaret Armstrong and her husband are the only well-bred Americans in von Stroheim's entire body of work. Others are pictured as uncouth and money-grubbing, sometimes kind-hearted and well-intentioned, but hopelessly lacking in grace of any sort. Yet notes in the script here constantly remind us of the "good taste" of Margaret's wardrobe and jewelry, and a trio of embarrassing American vulgarians are supplied mainly to make this crystal clear. Margaret Knox was such a woman, a certified member of Oakland's high society (you can look her up for yourself in the Oakland *Blue Book*) and, like the character in the film, had a doctor in the family as well.[25]

All of which draws us to the conclusion that von Steuben's pursuit of Margaret is patterned on von Stroheim's pursuit of Margaret. But here is where real life and the filmmaker's vision differ dramatically. Von Stroheim won his Margaret, and began a relationship which ended in the divorce courts not long after. That he suffered considerable guilt over these events is certain. That the spectacular death of his alter ego, von Steuben, extirpates much of this guilt, is also more than likely. When he came to rewrite this script for a proposed talkie remake in 1930 he made only one major change: the lieutenant no longer had to die.

Although prints of *Blind Husbands* are generally available today, they are all significantly shorter than the film which caused such a sensation in 1919. On July 14, 1924, Universal reissued the film in a streamlined version from which 1365 feet had been eliminated, over 19 minutes of running time.[26] Titles were altered, snippets of action removed, and at least one major scene taken out entirely, where von Steuben and Margaret visit a small local chapel. Between 1927 and 1936 Universal operated the Show-At-Home Movie Library, a film rental service through which selected Universal features and shorts were made available on 16mm for home use. Most silent Universals which exist today can trace their genealogy to prints made up for the Show-At-Home library. Unfortunately, by the time *Blind Husbands* was made available the negative had already been cut for the 1924 reissue, and so the original release version seems lost to us. In 1941 the Museum of Modern Art Film Library requested a print and also was sent the 1924 version, 6346 feet of 35mm film. All surviving prints appear to descend from one of these cut-down versions. The Museum, not being aware of the cuts made for the reissue, has always assumed they hold and distribute the substantially different 1919 version. What was left of the original negative, suffering from the initial stages of nitrate decomposition, was destroyed in Universal's Woodbridge and Kearney, New Jersey, vaults between 1956 and 1961.

The Devil's Pass Key

For decades the most shadowy of all von Stroheim's completed projects has been *The Devil's Pass Key*. Although rumors of its existence are heard from time to time,[1] it has been officially "lost" for so long that even our sharpest historians tend to pass right over it in recounting their histories of von Stroheim's films. For example, Kevin Brownlow, in *The Parade's Gone By . . .* writes, *"Blind Husbands,* directed by Erich von Stroheim, brought Universal wide prestige and von Stroheim was given carte blanche for his next production, *Foolish Wives."*[2] *The Devil's Pass Key* is not mentioned in this book. Many minor histories repeat this same oversight, and even von Stroheim himself on occasion overlooked the film, as in a 1941 article in which he moves from *Blind Husbands* to "my next film, *Foolish Wives."*[3] *The Devil's Pass Key* never seems to have been particularly close to von Stroheim at any time, and this may go far in explaining his own lack of concern with it in later years. The story was not an original of his, and von Stroheim's own personal commitment of time to the project was very brief, a mere seven months between first encountering the material in September of 1919 and shipping the completed print east in April of the following year (with half of *this* period devoted to editing problems). Indeed, none of von Stroheim's other completed projects was dispatched so quickly and efficiently. On arrival in New York to promote the film in June of 1920, von Stroheim managed to give an interview to the *New York Times*[4] without once mentioning the film, instead complaining loudly about "the tyranny of the happy ending"—a rather spectacular example of which he wrote into *The Devil's Pass Key*.

Coming as it does between his first film (*Blind Husbands*) and his first great film (*Foolish Wives*), perhaps it was bound to be forgotten by von Stroheim as well as his critics, but even investigative historians are faced with special problems here. Not only has *The Devil's Pass Key* been out of circulation for over half a century, but even in comparison with the earlier *Blind Husbands* there is a scarcity of available research material on the picture. The same handful of stills appears in each book or magazine article, and there is a surprising dearth of contemporary references to the film, this despite the fact that what references do exist are among von Stroheim's best. So historians are faced with an unusually difficult problem here, even for a von Stroheim film: there is no print, supporting materials are scarce, and memories of eyewitnesses are dim. In a lengthy series of letters to his biographer Peter Noble in 1947, von Stroheim had not a single comment to make on the film. Perhaps Denise Vernac was right when she told Bob Bergut, "C'est en rétrospective qu'il apparait indigne de l'ensemble de l'œuvre de Stroheim."[5]

Studio records indicate that Mahra de Meyer, address New York, was paid $750 for the rights to her unpublished story "Clothes and Treachery" in August of 1919. The story has not survived, but an investigation into the background of the author reveals some information of value. Mahra was in fact the Baroness de Meyer, née Olga Caracciolo, only child of the Duke of Caracciolo and god-daughter of Edward VII. She married the wealthy Jewish photographer Adolf Meyer-Watson in 1899, and in 1902 helped him gain the title of Baron of the kingdom of Saxony. The pair traveled in the highest Edwardian social circles (Edward was whispered to be her true father) and at the start of the war established themselves in New York. Here Baron de Meyer gained considerable fame as a portrait photographer, and in the pages of Condé Nast publications created a new school of fashion photography patterned after the style of the photo-secession. A recent biography of de Meyer by Robert Brandau and Philippe Jullian pictures Olga (familiarly known as Mahra) as a prime force behind the Baron's photographic success, largely due to her contacts with major artists in England and France, as well as such patrons as Edward and Serge Diaghilev.[6]

At first it did not seem that there could have been any contact between von Stroheim and the de Meyers as early as 1919, although Jullian feels that it was "not at all impossible that she wrote for von Stroheim" in this period.[7] The Baroness had a circle of German friends, and had also done some journalistic writing in her youth. But in the novelization of von Stroheim's film *Merry-Go-Round,* we find an acknowledgment to Count Mario Caracciolo, implying direct contact between von Stroheim and at least one member of this noble Neapolitan house by 1922.[8]

If exact information on von Stroheim's relationship with the Caracciolo family could be established it would help explain whether the original story for this film was suggested for purchase by the director himself, or simply acquired by the studio and turned over to him.

Von Stroheim began work on the screenplay on September 8, 1919, finishing on October 29, at which point he was paid $250 for his efforts. Early press reports list that he will be the "star" of the production,[9] and eventually he did write himself in for the part of the Count De Trouvere, but he later decided against this and the part was eventually played by Jack Matheis. During the course of production "Clothes and Treachery" was also known as "His Great Success," "The Charge Account," and "The Woman in the Plot," before finally emerging as *The Devil's Pass Key*.

A unique description of von Stroheim's early working methods was given by a reporter who visited the set during production:

> After calling the company together and discussing a few points the work began. "His Great Success" is a big story containing an after-the-war problem and laid in Paris at the present time. With the orchestra playing the dreamy "Je t'aime Waltz" over and over, while an intense scene between Clyde Fillmore and Una Trevelyn was being directed, I grew deeply interested in watching Mr. Von (as he is affectionately addressed by his company), for he acted out the entire scene in detail for each one, rehearsing several times until it was satisfactory. He knew exactly what he wanted portrayed—subtle touches—mere suggestions which carry such weight in the psychology of a picture.
>
> "Here is a play," said Mr. von Stroheim when the scene was over, "with all the allure, the vivacity and the lightness of Parisian life, with a tragedy, and it must be handled very carefully to express the meaning desired. I try to have the scenes taken consecutively, whenever possible, and the big, crashing final scene will be made last of all, for by that time the actors will fully grasp the undercurrents and depths of the preceding situations. Taken now, they would not feel the true values."
>
> "Yesterday we had some highly emotional scenes and—" "You should have seen him," interrupted Una Trevelyn. "While he was making me cry as if my heart would break, I looked up and he was crying, too—he feels everything he is directing. He knows all about period furniture and decorations, and all the great paintings," went on Una, as we watched him arrange the yellow satin drape on the table in the foreground of the set.
>
> "And music," said Sam de Grasse; "he has a thoro (*sic*) acquaintance with the musical classics and knows what should be played during each scene to bring out the best efforts. He plays the violin himself."
>
> "He knows all literature, too," chimed Clyde Fillmore, "I can't see how he has managed to learn so much in his few years, it must be the result of his continental education."[10]

Here we see von Stroheim the Griffith disciple, acting out each part for each player, stirring up his performers until *both* actor and director are really crying, not merely acting the part. But unlike Griffith, von Stroheim here espouses the ideal of shooting in sequence, a tactic much discussed at the time, and employed mainly by those directors who felt the need of eliciting particularly "realistic" performances from their players.

Like Griffith, von Stroheim tended to avoid "movie stars" and pretentiously dramatic actors whose technique was blatantly non-naturalistic. The cast of *The Devil's Pass Key* was recruited largely from the world of vaudeville and musical comedy. Clyde Fillmore was hired on the strength of his performance as a "demobilized lieutenant" in a Thompson Buchanan comedy caught by von Stroheim in Los Angeles; this was his first film.[11] Maude George was an Australian musical comedy actress who had played with Nat C. Goodwin in stage and screen comedies, as well as having appeared in Lois Weber's *Idle Wives* and William S. Hart's *Blue Blazes Rawden*. Mae Busch obtained her part in the most idiosyncratic fashion of all. Arriving in the casting office:

> Miss Busch glanced around the outer office, saw that already there was a crowd waiting, and started to leave. She remarked non-chalantly that it wasn't worth her while to wait. And behind that reckless demeanor— that willingness to walk out of a big engagement rather than be subjected to the humiliation of being judged with several other candidates, Von Stroheim saw that she was just the girl with the mettle to carry off the role he had in mind. She was engaged and all the patient others dismissed.[12]

But Curtiss states that von Stroheim had seen her as a dancer in a musical comedy five years earlier.[13] Sam de Grasse was by now a von Stroheim regular. He was repeating a role similar to the one he played in *Blind Husbands,* and prior to that von Stroheim had worked with him on Griffith's *Intolerance* and Emerson's *Wild and Woolly*.

As von Stroheim shot his footage a rough-cut was being assembled by one of Universal's editors, Grant Whytock, and with the end of shooting on December 4, 1919, von Stroheim settled down to the arduous task of completing the editing of the picture, a job which was to take nearly five more months. Making sure the editing room was well stocked with easy chairs and plush carpeting, von Stroheim moved in for a long siege. According to Whytock:

> He'd come in the projection room and we would discuss what to do and then we would do it, and then we would run it again, and we would function along pretty well. He was methodical; he had to have forms.

One of his problems was that he had to have everything detailed out so
that the German mind—all the numbers had to fit or it wouldn't work.
Any transpositions or changes used to confuse him. He would run up
and have a discussion with the head scenario writer to see if it would
work.[14]

Apparently von Stroheim had already begun the habit of shooting
dozens of takes in the hope of somehow making a magical selection in
the cutting room, a practice he shared with Rex Ingram. Again according to Whytock:

> We had I think twenty-one or twenty-two scenes of one scene—Clyde
> Fillmore, who played the lead, came in in a foreground shot, sat down
> at a table in a cafe and we selected takes down to—oh, three or four, and
> he'd say, "Well now, I don't think I got the right ones." So we'd have to
> put them all back together again.[15]

This went on for months, with von Stroheim taking footage out and
then replacing it, not only to find that one magical take, but trying as
well to trim a reel or so from the film's running time. All during their
work that winter von Stroheim told Whytock the story of his life, and
of his plans for a film of *McTeague* which he was formulating in screen
terms as they both tried to complete *The Devil's Pass Key*. Meanwhile,
the *New York Times* reported on January 25, 1920, of von Stroheim's
plans for *McTeague*.[16] After tiring of von Stroheim's indecisiveness,
Whytock pleaded to be replaced by a neophyte cutter and left to join
Rex Ingram's company.

The exact running time of *The Devil's Pass Key* has long been debated, for what documentary evidence exists is contradictory. Two continuities of the film were preserved by Universal. The first is dated
March 16-18, 1920 (the date the continuity was composed) and lists
1,223 shots with a total length of 8,819 feet packed onto eight very
full reels. A second continuity, listed as "revised" in seven reels and
dated April 9-10, 1920, does not include a footage count, but totals
1,163 shots, or 60 shots fewer than the earlier version. A calculation
for the average length of shots in the original tells us that 60 shots
should take up some 433 feet of film, and we would have to add to that
the accumulated trims from the beginning and end of nearly every shot
in order to obtain a total excision of one reel.[17] In fact, Universal's
house paper, the *Moving Picture Weekly,* reports in its official press
sheet that the length of the film in general release is "approximately
7,500 feet,"[18] a length of film that could conceivably have been issued
on seven reels, and which agrees with the copyright length of seven
reels (September 3, 1920). References to the film by certain historians

as 12,000 feet—as long as *Orphans of the Storm*—have no basis in fact. This is important, since it shows that von Stroheim's penchant for lengthy narratives did not develop until *Foolish Wives,* and that *The Devil's Pass Key* was well within the accepted limits for an important feature of that period—even in its original cut.

It should be remembered that there were significant industrial pressures which forced the release of the film at a predetermined length. As its name implies, the Universal Film Manufacturing Company was a factory which contracted to supply theaters with a given program of film releases. These would be pre-sold in advance from season to season. It was most important that every release fulfill expectations exactly, not only as to genre and star, but in regard to running time as well. Theater managers wished to maintain regular showtimes from week to week in order to encourage the filmgoing habit. A familiar complement of short subjects—also of predetermined length—was likewise part of the standard theater program. So the week's feature necessarily had to add up to the number of reels agreed upon well in advance. A nine-reel film submitted in place of a seven-reeler was no bonus, but a monstrosity which would inevitably off-balance the theater manager's neatly scheduled program (and perhaps adversely affect grosses as well as filmgoing habits). If von Stroheim would not cut *The Devil's Pass Key* to standard length, the studio would—and did. Universal knew that if they did not deliver a picture of program length, theaters would complain and take action themselves: it was not unknown for individual managers to edit prints to their own satisfaction, and abuses involving projection speeds were widely commented on. These restrictions did not impinge on von Stroheim as noticeably in later films—particularly with "specials" like *Foolish Wives*—but they continued to affect the industry's less prestigious releases down to the advent of television (at which point that medium picked up the tradition, and developed it to the extreme).

Universal has preserved a variety of written materials on this property, ranging from an early two-page outline to the detailed continuities mentioned earlier. These provide us with an excellent insight into how von Stroheim's early projects would grow as he developed them for the screen. While the original de Meyer story is unavailable, the brief synopsis entitled "The Charge Account" is probably the closest to it in terms of plot and characterization, and we reprint it here. Although the names of the characters would later change, the actors indicated as playing these parts were in fact those who ultimately appeared in the film. Six reels is the projected length.

François Bagrange is an author of talent, but he is a dreamer and has never had any success with his work. He has a small income on which he has lived comfortably, but it is not enough to supply his beautiful young wife with the luxuries which have always been hers. Yvonne loves her husband but believes that she keeps his love by reason of her beauty. Yvonne is of a noble family and François is madly in love with her. She buys the most expensive costumes and François believes that she pays for them out of the money which he gives her. Yvonne has no idea of the value of money and easily falls a victim to Madame Malot, an unscrouplous (*sic*) modiste, who has persuaded the girl that she has unlimited credit. At the proper time, Madame Malot springs her trap. Yvonne is in debt to her for the sum of fifty thousand francs and Madame Malot expects the girl to get a rich lover to pay her bills.

Madame Malot tells Yvonne that she knows a rich American who will pay her bills. That he will loan her money which François can repay. Hugh is living a gay life in Paris but he is kind at heart and when he sees that Yvonne is innocent and unsophisticated, he tells her that he cannot let her have the money, in fact he has spent more than his income. He advises her to tell her husband and gives her his card, telling her that if Madame Malot gets nasty, he will help her. Hugh drops his card case in the room. Madame Malot finds it later and sees that it contains some letters from a woman of high position. She gets the help of Flora, former mistress of Hugh, and together they plan to blackmail the woman, Mme. De Mereuil. Mme. De Mereuil is clever and not lacking in courage. She goes to Hugh and with the help of a detective they catch Madame Malot. Hugh forces the dressmaker to give Yvonne a receipted bill and to return the letters to Mme. De Mereuil.

A scandalous society paper publishes an account of the affair and Yvonne is suspected of being the woman in the case. François reads the article and insists on taking it for the plot for a play. Yvonne protests, but François is not suspicious. The play is a great success, but François and Yvonne are cut by their friends who believe than François knows of the indiscretions of his wife. An old friend finally tells François the truth. He will not allow Yvonne to explain but begins suit for divorce. Yvonne goes to Hugh who has returned from America. Hugh explains to François. Yvonne is taken back by a penitent husband.

A later, though less detailed, synopsis makes Americans of the playwright and his wife, and changes their names to Warren and Yvonne Cartright. Hugh Randolph becomes "an American Army officer stationed in Paris." He is apparently quite wealthy and never leaves for America. The climax is now a dramatic confrontation in which Warren holds a pistol on Yvonne and Hugh and is only at the last minute convinced by Hugh's explanation.

The only extant shooting script, titled "His Great Success," fleshes out these ideas and further refines the characters. The playwright and his wife are now called Warren and Grace Goodwright, and the other man is Capt. Rex Strong, American military attaché. Mme. De Mereuil has become the Countess De Trouvere and Flora is now called La Belle Odera. "With an agility unbelievable in a roué as senile as Paris" the post-war social whirl has picked right up, valse and fox trot replacing military airs. The script opens at the Grand Prix, where the main characters are seen promenading, and gossips inform us of their individual stories. We see the Count and Countess De Trouvere, "she young charming and beautifully dressed—he a decrepit old roué" (von Stroheim has indicated himself to play this part). The exposition in this opening leaves much to be desired. One title actually reads:

> "Well, I'll be darned! There's Goodwright, who came over with the YMCA. Got stuck on one of them dames that drove an ambulance and married her the same day the armistice was signed. I s'pose he thought that she had money, but her uncle died and left a lot of debts, so they've got to live on $3000 a year he's got coming from some stock he owns."

But while stated here in a clumsy fashion, we do see clues to later glories, such as the marriage on the day of the armistice, and the immediate linking of marriage and money (which doesn't materialize). And remember that von Stroheim met Valerie Germonprez (whom he would marry soon after *The Devil's Pass Key* opened) while they were both acting in the World War I film, *The Heart of Humanity*—he as an officer, she as the driver of a Red Cross ambulance.[19]

A war profiteer remarks that Warren has wasted his life and never sold anything. "Give me my ammunition any time. Too bad the war is over." Rex Strong and La Belle Odera are a third couple, and as they all meet we sense that Rex, now with Odera, has also been involved with the Countess. He seems interested in Grace as well, much to Odera's irritation. After the race von Stroheim intercuts two scenes, Grace and Warren at home, and Odera and Rex at Mme. Malot's dress shop. Odera has a rotten temper and we learn that she is with Rex only for his "American dollars." Grace arrives at Mme. Malot's. She feels that she must keep herself beautiful in order to hold her husband's love, and so has spent heavily on what she thinks is credit.

Rex notices her again as he leaves with Odera, contrives to return, and arranges to meet Grace for tea. Meanwhile Warren's new play has been rejected because of its weak plot. Odera has followed Rex and Grace as they ride through the Bois de Boulogne and is furious. Back at the shop we see Mme. Malot arranging a back-room assignation between an old roué and a woman dressed in mourning. After some time the woman emerges and tearfully pays Mme. a clothing bill. Rex and

Grace arrive at her flat after a harmless afternoon tea and Warren greets them. Rex declines his invitation to come up. Later, Mme. Malot hands Grace a bill for 19,000 francs, a scene that is intercut with Warren having another of his plays rejected as having "no plot."

Mme. Malot suggests she may have a solution if Grace lacks the money. At Odera's apartment the dancer becomes furious with Rex and vows vengeance when he walks out on her. Mme. arranges to set Grace up with Rex, who says he will loan Grace the money. But in Madame's back room Grace cries when he steals a kiss. Rex understands, promises her his help if needed, and offers his card; however, he leaves his wallet behind. Mme. Malot is furious that Grace has not obtained the money from Rex, and demands she produce it "damn quick." Grace goes home and looks at the dresses which she feels hold her husband's love for her; she thinks that these will be the last.

Odera dances the Tarantella at the Pre-Catalan Café. In the audience Rex notices that he has lost his wallet and borrows some money from Warren, who happens to be seated at the next table. Later Mme. Malot visits Odera in her lavish bathroom. She is smoking and enjoying a pedicure as Mme. proposes a little scheme. At the Goodwrights' Grace tells Warren, "You wouldn't love me if I didn't look pretty."

The next day the Countess De Trouvere receives a blackmail letter and consults with Rex, as her husband the Count visits Odera in her bath ("That old wreck again!"). To pay the blackmail money the Countess has been told to deliver it to a woman in a cab. This turns out to be Grace, working under Malot's orders to deliver a package she will receive to Odera's apartment. Rex and two detectives follow, and soon Odera, Grace, Malot, and Rex are together at the apartment. Trapped in her scheme, Madame is forced to write a receipt for 19,000 francs to Grace.

The story is leaked by a detective to one "Alphonse Marier, social scavenger on the staff of 'The Whip'" (reminiscent of the character played by von Stroheim in John Emerson's *The Social Secretary*). All who read the story recognize the unnamed husband as Warren, except for Warren himself, who finds it a good idea for a new play. Under the title "His Great Success" the play is produced immediately. During intermission the talk is all about how Warren has used his own wife's indiscretion as the basis for his story, and while the audience roars at his new comedy, Warren misses the irony. While Warren goes down on stage to answer the audience's calls of "author!" Rex goes to the Goodwrights' box to silently comfort the embarrassed Grace.

Warren goes off to a party at Odera's, but when Grace pleads a

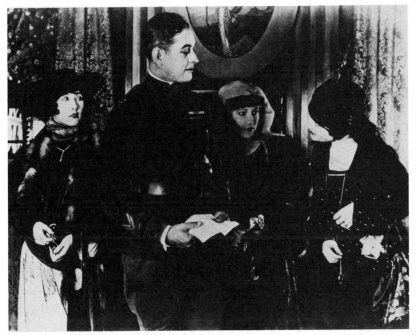

The American officer turns the tables on the designing madame: Mae Busch, Clyde Fillmore, Una Trevelyn, and Maude George.

headache he sends her home with Rex. At the party the drunken Marier lets the cat out of the bag. Warren punches him and walks slowly home, where he knows he will find Rex and Grace. After taking a gun from his bureau he asks Grace if any of her debts were paid by another man. He refuses to listen to any explanation. As they sit a black cat runs across the room and catches a mouse, causing Grace to scream and jump on a chair. Rex takes advantage of the confusion to wrestle the gun from Warren and explain to him the real situation. In a flashback we see how the Count had nearly found Rex in the Countess's boudoir. The Countess later wrote him a compromising letter which was found by Mme. Malot in Rex's wallet. The money was paid to save the Countess's reputation, Rex says, but Warren doesn't believe it. Rex and Grace are disgusted with Warren's lack of faith and start to leave. Warren says he will forgive her, but they insist he must *believe* their story, and this he cannot do. After he thinks they have gone Warren smiles sadly at "the tragic jest of fate" and prepares to blow his brains out, but Grace has stayed behind, goes to him, and all ends happily.

By the time the story appeared as a film von Stroheim had made further changes in it. An overall improvement was the reworking of the titles, which were no longer awkward and overlong, but written in the form of sentence fragments connected by multiple hyphens—the style of title-writing used in *Foolish Wives*. Otherwise few substantial differences existed between the final shooting script and the first known cut of the film.

Von Stroheim directly stated his theme by opening the film with an introductory title quoting Elbert Hubbard (a popular philosopher of the prewar period who was lost on the *Lusitania*): "To be deceived is less shameful than to be suspicious." He greatly streamlined the Grand Prix sequence. Much wordy exposition was dropped here and visual interest was increased by such photographic touches as the use of binocular masking to suggest point of view shots. Considerable use was made of interpolated stock footage of the King and Queen of England. The war profiteer became a sugar merchant. And in one extra bit of action a spectator is shown as so involved in the race that he doesn't notice his wallet being lifted. At the finish he turns excitedly and shakes hands with the pickpocket. This metaphoric action prefigures the later course of the film.

At the performance of the play an optical trick showed the performers on stage dissolve into Rex and Grace—the real-life people who have inspired them. This heavily emphasized the irony of the play-within-the-film. Warren reacts to the crowd's reception by remarking, "It seems to strike home with many."

Finally, the confrontation scene was considerably reworked. The cat-and-mouse metaphor disappeared (to return in *Greed*), and Warren merely gave up the idea of using the gun instead of having it wrestled from him. "Sounds good, but where's your proof?" he asks when he hears Rex's story. "I see you miss the scrap of paper that turns up at the end of every play—but this is no play—and all the proof we have is—our word," answers Rex. This served to underline again the film's theater metaphors, as well as commenting on the sort of plays that Warren Goodwright was trying to write. Von Stroheim either hit on the idea of life-as-theater, or decided to emphasize it so heavily, only after shooting had begun, since nearly all the changes that have been wrought in the shooting script seem designed to emphasize it. Warren's lack of faith was also strongly underlined, as Rex's plea to BELIEVE grew in large letters on the screen. Grace, before going to reconcile with Warren, was seen behind a curtain weeping next to a statue of Jesus Christ, a use of religious iconography that would later become even more prevalent.

In the "revised" seven reel version few changes of such significance were made. In the first scene showing the activity at Mme. Malot's approximately 20 shots (one-third of the total) were removed to speed up the action. These consisted mainly of milieu details and CU reaction shots that were probably unnecessary. The entire sequence of fourteen shots showing Grace and Rex at tea in the Inter-Allied Gardens was removed; there was now no way of knowing how the two spent their afternoon. A brief sequence of a dozen shots where Warren tells Grace his play has been rejected was cut in half. The first three shots of the scene in which the Countess receives the blackmail letter were removed (she was having breakfast in bed). Several shots of the audience at the play performance were cut, including all those showing "the president's box." And a pair of shots in the final sequence showing candles flickering was removed (a difficult hand-coloring job; see below). Along with a few other odd shots here and there this was the extent of the trimming of von Stroheim's original cut as seen in the final print. There is no reason to feel that these cuts were made against his will.

The initial advertising for *The Devil's Pass Key* centered on a series of back-page teasers in the *Moving Picture Weekly,* beginning on March 20, 1920, and running for several months. This was exceptional, in that the back page was usually devoted to a different Universal release each week. The finished print, probably at 7,500 feet, was shipped to New York on April 5, 1920 (just before the typing of the final continuity), and the initial press screenings were held that month. Thomas Quinn Curtiss reports that von Stroheim suffered a "physical collapse"[20] after the April previews, but in June he was in New York talking with reporters, and giving interviews like any visiting screen celebrity.[21] Laemmle decided to delay release of the film in order to take advantage of the considerable personal publicity that was being won by von Stroheim, maximize publicity on the new film, and avoid a scheduling clash with the still current *Blind Husbands* release. No further cutting or censorship seems to have been involved. Indeed, the delay irked at least one of the New York critics, who on reviewing the film in August noted that it had been previewed in April, and asked, "Why it was not booked when the enthusiasm was in the ascendant."[22] Perhaps Laemmle prolonged his teaser campaign just a bit too long.

Universal provided the following "Advertising Punches" to exhibitors as keys in exploiting the film, and they bear repeating here:

1. The fact that it was produced by Eric von Stroheim, the man responsible for the success of *Blind Husbands.*

2. The fact that the public has been anxiously awaiting the second von Stroheim production since he scored his first sensational hit.

3. The true Parisian atmosphere of the story, written by Baroness De Meyer.

4. The many interesting and unusual situations superbly handled by director and cast.

5. The scenic detail showing Paris in its various phases.

6. The importance of the cast, headed by Sam de Grasse, Clyde Fillmore, Una Trevelyn, Maude George and Mae Busch.

7. The fact that Sam de Grasse, who played the husband in *Blind Husbands,* has a similar role in this feature.

8. The exact reproduction of the Grand Prix, the turf classic of Paris, with its thrilling races and brilliant crowd.

9. The sumptuous scenes showing the interior of the Theatre Français on the night of a premiere.

10. Elaborate views of Mme. Malot's fashionable costume establishment with its scores of beautiful manequins.[23]

Note particularly that parts one and two are geared to von Stroheim's personal popularity and the hoped for expectations of the public for his next film, and that five, eight, nine, and ten emphasize the spectacle and verisimilitude which were to gain so much greater notoriety in his later films. Universal learned early to link von Stroheim to the phenomenal attention to detail which he lavished on his films. Elsewhere in the pressbook Universal told exhibitors that "One of the remarkable features of *The Devil's Pass Key* . . . is the seemingly endless series of tremendure (*sic*) scenes which figure in the story. One of these, a reproduction of the Grand Prix in Paris, the European racing classic, is declared to mark the limit of screen realism."[24] And later, "The exact reproduction of the Theatre Français in Paris, with its lobby, auditorium, orchestra, boxes, stage and dressing rooms,"[25] is similarly touted. Such phrases would be heard again later.

Perhaps the most amusing aspect of Universal's ad campaign reflected the current success of C. B. De Mille's first "bathtub" epics (*Don't Change Your Husband, Why Change Your Wife?,* etc.). According to one blurb entitled "Voluptuous Luxury in *Devil's Pass Key* Scenery," the bathroom scene of the picture features an expensive and carefully tiled reconstruction copied from the photograph of the "natatorium of a Parisian stage favorite before the war."[26] The reference is to the Spanish gypsy Caroline Otero, popularly known as La Belle Otero (1868-1965). Otero, perhaps the most famous courtesan of *la belle epôque,* has been described by her biographer, Arthur H. Lewis, as "a woman so lacking in morals, so grossly materialistic in outlook, and, though she was often billed as an artist, so totally lacking, save one, in any genuine talent."[27] Strangely enough, Otero's first success was won in America, where during the 1890-91 season she was exploited at New York's Eden Musee as the "mysterious Spanish beauty, international Queen of the Dance." One critic remarked of her performance, "We have seen Otero sing, we have heard her dance,"[28] but public acclaim for her near pornographic exhibitions was enormous; she returned to Paris with an international reputation. The high point of her career was perhaps her thirtieth birthday party, at which she was accompanied by King Leopold II of Belgium, Prince Nicholas I of Montenegro, Prince Albert of Monaco, the Grand Duke Nikolai Nikolaevich of Russia, and Albert Edward, Prince of Wales[29]—an entourage out of a von Stroheim film, at least. The Baroness de Meyer was certainly familiar with Otero in prewar Paris, at least by reputation, and possibly on a more personal level: Albert Edward later became Edward VII, who as we have seen was rumored to be Olga's true father. Certainly Otero is the basis of the gypsy dancer in "Clothes and Treachery," but it was von Stroheim who changed her name from Flora to La Belle Odera (one of the less fortunate examples of the director's early penchant for symbolic naming). This adds a *roman à clef* quality to the role which is unique in von Stroheim's cinema, and which is particularly clear since American audiences could be expected to recognize Otero/Odera due to the dancer's prewar popularity here. The Lewis biography is stocked with stories of sex, money, free-spending degenerate nobility and high-stake gambling (most of her gains were squandered across the gaming tables at Monte Carlo). That these elements appealed to von Stroheim is evident in the catalogue of obsessions that runs through his films. Characters similar to Otero, often played by Mae Busch, would appear in later von Stroheim films as well. His fascination with the character must have been highly developed even at this point, for the role won the acclaim of even the film's detractors. "Just one character of *The Devil's Pass Key* really lives," wrote the *Motion Picture Classic*. "It is the *cocotte* Odera, realized with fine Parisian verve and piquancy by Mae Bush (*sic*)."[30]

The Devil's Pass Key was finally shown to the public on August 8, 1920, at New York's Capitol Theatre, and was given a proper send-off by Major Edward Bowes and his resident factotum, S. L. "Roxy" Roth-afel. The usual elaborate stage show featured Liszt's 13th Hungarian Rhapsody, arranged and conducted by Erno Rapee, a "Scarf Dance" ballet devised by Alexander Oumansky, and a final number "in a per-

son of a score or more pretty young woman singers, headed by Bertram
Peacock and in charge of William Axt, in a musical act called 'Carna-
val,' and a typical French cabaret scene. As the singing ended the leader
of the singers, garbed as Satan, sang a line or two and quietly left the
stage as the picture began to unfold on the screen."[31] Even the organ
background to one of the Prizmacolor scenic shorts was designed to
impress, and as the huge pipe organ broke into "Praise God from
Whom All Blessings Flow," history records "men and women turning
from one to another, eyebrows lifted, uttering little gasps and exclama-
tions under their breath."[32] Church music had not been heard in a
Broadway movie house before, according to the *New York Tribune*
critic, who not only remarked on the incident but chose to headline her
review of *The Devil's Pass Key,* "Church Hymn on Capitol Organ
Marks New Departure."[33] In addition to all this, Will Rogers's *Illiterate
Digest* and the popular Capitol Newsreel (compiled and edited by the
theater management) were also on the bill, no doubt leaving the audience exhausted by the time von Stroheim's film came on. While these
prologues were to be expected in the large Broadway picture palaces of
the period, von Stroheim's other films generally avoided being so totally overwhelmed, usually because their own length precluded any extended festivities.

The Devil's Pass Key was well received by the New York critics,
and cemented von Stroheim's reputation as among the finest American
directors. "Despite sweltering heat an SRO audience was held rapt with
the enthralling interest, realism and charm so admirably pictured," remarked *Billboard*[34] on the film's premiere, and it was another eight
months before Universal finally answered the demands of small exhibitors for a chance at the film.[35] As we saw earlier the film was sold on
realism, and critics and audiences alike were quick to pick up on this.
Von Stroheim's clever mixture of stock footage and elaborate Hollywood settings convinced many that they were actually looking at a Eu-
ropean-made film. "The scene is Paris, and the film was obviously
taken there," wrote the *New York Globe,*[36] but the *Morning Telegraph*
was only amused that "the audience applauds the screen counterparts
of King George and Queen Mary in *The Devil's Pass Key* under the
impression that they are actually the rulers of Britain."[37] In fact they
most likely *were* the rulers of Britain, although the critic of the *Morning Telegraph* was unaware that stock footage could be so interpolated.
Billboard, more familiar with such trickery, was even themselves un-
sure of where reality ended and von Stroheim's film began: "That
many of the animated scenes were pieced in—especially the racetrack

at Longchamps and the arrival of the King and Queen (this, too, may
have been camoflaged (*sic*)), an immense crowd of people at the opera
and other scenes of Parisian life—has not interfered with the success of
the picture."[38] But while Americans were more than satisfied with
von Stroheim's Paris, Parisians were simply outraged. According to one
French review quoted by Denis Marion:

> I can only shrug my shoulders with amazement viewing the grotesque ver-
> sion of Paris constructed by Stroheim at Universal City. The Café de la
> Paix displays a charming notice, which, far from listing the price of re-
> freshments, declares: "FORBIDDEN TO URINATE." The Bon Marché
> Department Store is shown as an insignificant little haberdashery on Rue
> de la Paix of the most destitute appearance. Antique Second Empire
> buses, vintage 1880, have reappeared on our streets (while the story
> takes place after the Armistice!), our good police have a commanding
> officer whose helmet resembles a jockey cap, etc.[39]

Nonetheless, it was with this film that Erich von Stroheim won the
support of both critics and audiences that enabled him to produce
Foolish Wives, a film whose notoriety eventually obliterated the memory of its less auspicious predecessor. The *New York Times* put its im-
primatur on von Stroheim's talents in a review that was not only unusually thoughtful, but for the *Times* remarkably astute as well:

> . . . he has realized that the substance of the photoplay is the dra-
> matic motion picture, not the subtitle, nor the spectacular scene, nor the
> beauty or the tricks of any star, nor the sentiment or surprises of any
> story, but moving pictures that have meaning, that are where they are
> in a photoplay because they are an integral part of it, telling in them-
> selves some essential incident of the story, exposing suddenly some un-
> expected, but consistent, or anticipated, but not obvious, side of the
> character of one of the people in the plot. It is by his accomplishments
> in moving pictures, therefore, that his story is unfolded forcefully and
> his characters are definite and comprehensible individuals.
>   When Mr. von Stroheim uses a close-up, for example, it is because at
> that particular moment spectators are naturally straining to see some
> character or detail of action more closely, and when he suspends the
> story's action to introduce what is known as "atmosphere," it is because
> at the particular moment there is dramatic significance between the re-
> lation of the action and its environment.[40]

Perhaps what interested von Stroheim in the Baroness de Meyer's
story was the chance it gave him to combine two of his chief preoccupations: autobiographical art and sexual humiliation emphasized to the
point of extreme irony. *The Devil's Pass Key* is the only von Stroheim
film to deal with artistic creation (here playwrighting) and in it Warren
Goodwright achieves success through a dramatization of the affair

which has caused all Paris secretly to laugh at him. "You must write
of life as it is—real drama is all around you—being played on the streets
of Paris now—That is what we want—!" charges Warren's publisher,
summarizing what we may take as von Stroheim's own artistic credo.
Warren takes his story from the newspapers, to von Stroheim a true
twentieth-century oracle (remember of course that the words of the
oracle require correct interpretation). Newspapermen like Harry Carr
and Thomas Quinn Curtiss were among von Stroheim's closest friends,
and it seems that the journalistic approach of ex-reporters like Frank
Norris and Stephen Crane (whose *Maggie* von Stroheim once wanted
to film) was what first attracted him to their works. For von Stroheim,
newspaper truth is (or should be!) the holy writ of realism. Yet if presented in half-truths, or manipulated unscrupulously—as the gossip
Marier does—it can become the most powerful of lies. Warren does not
realize how potent a dose of realism is contained in the little story he
chooses to dramatize, how it is in fact his own story. From the stage
he tells the applauding first-nighters, "Whatever excellence my play
has, it owes to its subject—drawn from real life—." The world has
laughed at him once, and now, through his art, it has the chance to
laugh even more gleefully. The film indicated that Warren's humiliation as a suspected cuckold is somehow more severe because of his own
ignorance, which makes him unable even to confront the situation which
all Paris is laughing at. The play-within-the-film takes this idea one further step, adding irony to insult, as the audience recognizes first Rex
and Grace as the characters in the play (accomplished for us through
special effects which identify the audience of *The Devil's Pass Key* with
the audience of "His Great Success"), and finally gets to view the spectacle of Warren himself on stage, seemingly oblivious to the real joke.
Warren is the victim of a double irony: (1) he is unaware of the true
source of his play and (2) although derided as a cuckold, he is in
fact the husband of a faithful, though foolish, wife. It is the news-
paperman, drunk, who tells him the real truth about the first of these,
but he must resolve for himself the truth of the second. Here is where
the invocation of Elbert Hubbard comes in, "To be deceived is less
shameful than to be suspicious." It should be kept in mind, however,
that the deception here is not an adulterous one, but merely the result
of Grace's withholding the true facts in the case from her husband.
Would von Stroheim have taken the same attitude here if adultery were
really involved? Would Warren's suspicions be so "shameful" in that
case? The parallel story of the Count and Countess De Trouvere is

important here. The Count has *really* been cuckolded by Rex, and the guilty pair have evidently been able to keep him in complete ignorance of the affair. Yet he is derided throughout by von Stroheim as an old fool, seemingly because of the undiscovered liaison going on right in his own house. Is it better that he is not suspicious? That he patronizes Odera, Rex's current inamorata, lends an amusing twist to the proceedings, reminiscent of the works of Schnitzler which were on von Stroheim's mind at the time.

But by far the most interesting character in this film is Rex Strong, one of the most complex and fascinating of all von Stroheim's early creations. As an adulterer and general rake, Strong, the "other man," would generally be the villain of the piece. Yet von Stroheim imbues him with so many fine qualities that to modern eyes at least he emerges as the obvious hero. Rex is dashing and elegant, well versed in Continental manners and modes, unwilling to take advantage of Grace, and even generous enough to offer to pay her bill at Mme. Malot's with no ulterior motive. In contrast, Warren is a dull writer who can only achieve fame in the most ironic way possible, suspicious to the point of instantly believing the worst of his wife, and at the end a would-be suicide. Even when Grace comes back to him at the finale, he *still* has not indicated that he has faith in her—von Stroheim leaves that whole issue unresolved. Judging from his performance in *Blind Husbands,* Sam de Grasse probably played him as self-righteous and inflexible, a cold fish WASP of the worst variety. Today Rex might seem the obvious hero of *The Devil's Pass Key,* but given the societal values of 1920 not one reviewer has a good word for him. Instead most agreed with the *New York Tribune* that, "It is difficult for us to imagine that any American army officer would conduct himself as dishonorably as Captain Rex Strong is shown to conduct himself in Paris."[41] We can see here the seeds of chauvinist outrage which would later be directed against the picture of the American ambassador in *Foolish Wives,* and against the picture of America itself in *Greed.*

Rex is the center of a Continental *reigen* thrown just slightly askew by the intrusion of the American innocents abroad, Grace and Warren. A chart of the liaisons, successful and unsuccessful, licit and illicit, looks like this:

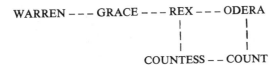

This shows Rex surrounded by the film's females, each representing a different type of relationship for him. He is clearly the focal point of the action, while Warren must inevitably be seen as a fifth wheel. Odera and Grace are opposites, and the Count becomes the inverse of Rex, an "old wreck" scorned for the very alliances which von Stroheim finds so vital in the young officer. In a later film the Count would no doubt have been played by Tully Marshall, and it is significant that von Stroheim thought of himself for the role here. In the enclosed world of von Stroheim's films the "Tully Marshall character" (whose importance grows as the director grows older) must be seen as the inevitable degenerate end of the young roué. What charm the young rakes possess drains away with their youth, and Rex must some day become the Count, just as in *The Merry Widow* Danilo will one day become another Baron Sadoja (at least if "true love" never intervenes). There are no charming *old* rakes in von Stroheim's cinema, only an embarrassing senility spiked with occasional bouts of *locomotor ataxia,* the fruits of youthful indiscretions.

But for all his admirable virtues Rex is at least in one way the most serious transgressor in von Stroheim's moral universe. While von Stroheim's films often deal with the libidinous exploits of a wide range of characters, Rex is the only major character in any von Stroheim film we actually catch in the act of adultery. In his films at least, von Stroheim seems to share with Griffith the ideal that the marriage bond is "life's cleanest and sweetest," and that transgressions here are beyond the pale. Remember that such rakes as Von Steuben and *Foolish Wives*'s Count Karamzin try and fail to seduce the married heroines of their films, and that the dalliances which do occur are invariably with serving maids, whores, or unattached ladies of dubious ancestry. When we see Rex in the boudoir of the Countess, barely avoiding detection by the Count, we are witnessing a unique episode in von Stroheim's cinema. It is significant that (1) this is shown in flashback, itself a very rare occurrence in a von Stroheim film; and (2) the cuckolded Count is, as has been mentioned, a cameo role that von Stroheim had once intended for himself.

Many critics have identified a so-called "von Stroheim character" standing in for the director in most of his films, but in *The Devil's Pass Key* (a film very much concerned with autobiographical narrative), von Stroheim can be seen in *all* the male roles. Rex Strong is not merely a man you love to hate (as the *New York Tribune* did), but a man we can both love *and* hate. Although an American on the outside, he is underneath a true Continental, a successful womanizer, *bon vivant,* and man of the world, and clearly first cousin to the later Karamzin, Danilo, and Prince Nicki. Warren, the troubled and insecure playwright who follows the trail of realism all the way into autobiography, can also be seen as a projection of the film's young *auteur.* The Count De Trouvere, a young roué grown ridiculously old, was as we have seen literally to have been played by Erich von Stroheim. And even Marier, hard-drinking scandal-monger for "The Whip," is a re-creation of an early von Stroheim screen role, as seen in John Emerson's *The Social Secretary.*

An early work, *The Devil's Pass Key* doesn't present women in much more than two-dimensional roles, with perhaps a hint here and there of more interesting things to come. Grace Goodwright is the interchangeable heroine of von Stroheim's first three films—indeed, one critic[42] instantly recognized her as an "incredibly foolish wife" and even a "stupid wife" (a title von Stroheim never used). Maude George as the procuress (the pun on "madame" must have delighted von Stroheim) is already the cynical promoter of sex for money, already the woman who will warn Karamzin, "It's the money, not the woman, we want," and advise Prince Nicki that the answer to all his problems is "Marry money!" Her performance here must have been the same one that enlivens *Foolish Wives* and *The Wedding March.* Lending an air of *roman à clef* to the proceedings (as discussed earlier), Mae Busch plays a famous courtesan of the day, a woman of no morals and only one talent, which she, too, would again play for von Stroheim.

I have saved for this moment a discussion of what to me seems the most valuable element of *The Devil's Pass Key,* von Stroheim's experiments in photographic stylization and color effects. D. W. Griffith's *Broken Blossoms* had opened in New York on May 13, 1919, and was widely acclaimed for its photographic effects, which included soft-focus gauze shots clearly patterned after photo-secessionist portraiture, and a complex tinting and toning pattern which even incorporated the use of projected color beams thrown from the balconies. Von Stroheim tried to duplicate, perhaps even surpass, Griffith's achievements in his manipulation of the visuals in *The Devil's Pass Key.* Fortunately, careful notes on the visual effects were included by those who compiled the studio continuities.

With Ben Reynolds, von Stroheim devised a process called pastelography in an apparent attempt to copy the gauze effects developed for Griffith by Henrik Sartov. According to the *Moving Picture Weekly:*

The effect of pastelography is to give moving pictures the appearance of paintings, and while the effect of soft diffusion is obtained, there is none of the murkiness which appears in some of the ultra-futurist photo dramas, so difficult for the eye to follow.[43]

With no print of *The Devil's Pass Key* to refer to we can only assume that the process was the same as used for such shots as that of the monk in *Foolish Wives,* or Mother McTeague in *Greed,* frozen tableaus which give the impression of being printed on a burlap-grained fabric; Reynolds also worked on those films. How this was received at the time is unclear. The *New York Times* complained that "the lighting of some of the scenes . . . seems somewhat crude to the writer. There are bright spots on shiny walls that suggest the rays of powerful studio lamps rather than the illumination of a normally lighted room."[44] Of course, this may not refer to the "pastelography," and later on the *Times* saw fit to praise other photographic touches. If we agree that the shots mentioned above from *Foolish Wives* and *Greed* give us an indication of the look of this process, then we can certainly see it as an influence on Cavalcanti's *La P'tite Lili* (1927) a one-reel short featuring Catherine Hessling and Jean Renoir. That film was shot entirely in this fashion, and one wonders if perhaps Renoir, an admitted von Stroheim disciple, was responsible for the idea. According to Andre Bazin, "the idea of shooting [*La P'tite Lili*] through a sort of burlap cloth provided the artistic justification for the dull gray photography [due to bad weather]."[45]

The *New York Times* did, however, find something to like about the film's visual style, and commented at length upon a contrast between the "soft focus" photography of one scene and the "sharp as reality" appearance of another:

> In one instance, however, modulated lighting, or perhaps, soft focus, is used to good effect. Warren Goodwright and his wife meet in the husband's study in circumstances foreshadowing tragedy, he with the knowledge that his play has been rejected, she with the pain of her experience with Capt. Strong fresh in her mind and the realization that the payment of Mme. Malot's bill is dependent upon the sale of the play. The scene is dim; details are subdued; there seems to be a shadow over everything. The effect is that aimed at, and usually missed, by the playing of low, slow music. The crisis is intensified, and the tension is held in the following scene, when Grace Goodwright faces the unyielding Mme. Malot and the harsh facts of her situation in the pitiless glare of the next day. Something has to be done, overpowering discouragement has to be shaken off, and there is no softening by lights or lens. The scene is as sharp as reality.[46]

It is clear, then, that as early as his second film von Stroheim was aware of the dramatic effect which could be produced through boldly contrasting visual styles, an extremely precocious insight for a film shot in 1919. But judging only from contemporary reviews it is hard to establish the complete success of these experiments. Such contrasting visuals were of course developed to their fullest in *The Wedding March* several years later.

One of the few substantial references to *The Devil's Pass Key* by a later critic-historian is made by Eric Elliott in his seminal *Anatomy of Motion Picture Art:*

> The credit for introducing colour as a psychological influence on the film scene has been given to *The Devil's Pass Key*. In the story, after a repentent woman's vigil with her disillusioned husband, the last hours of night show dark and blue; but as dawn breaks the room becomes perceptibly brighter, until the sunglow brings promise of life and dreams anew.[47]

Elliott's memory can be supplemented by this unusual account from the *Moving Picture Weekly* headlined "Color Plays Important Role in *The Devil's Pass Key*":

> Color as one of the *dramatis personae* of a film play is utilized for the first time in history in the final scenes of Eric Von Stroheim's *The Devil's Pass Key*. Universal chemists interpreted in the metaphor of color a phase of dramatic action unwieldy of exposition by action or sub-titles. Experts say there is more drama in manipulated color than in natural color photography. Universal is making plans for a tremendous business on this masterpiece when it is released early in the fall.
>
> Technically known as a "color lap dissolve," the effect is a laboratory process of dyeing developed under the guidance of S. M. Tompkins, superintendent of the Universal film laboratories, and his assistant, Jack Guerin. No camera attachments are necessary in photographing scenes to be treated by this method, and the effect may therefore be used at any time with any scene. Tompkins and Guerin are now rounding up all available film dyes and coloring chemicals preparatory to an extensive series of experiments in this branch of color work. This research was ordered by Producing Manager Bernstein.
>
> The initial experiment in *The Devil's Pass Key* follows the night-long vigil of a repentent woman in the room with her disillusioned and despairing husband. During the cold morning everything is dark blue. Through the French windows the dawn is seen to break. A glow grows against the sky, and gradually the sun rises, flooding the room with the hopeful pink of a new day. It is symbolic of what has passed in the minds of the two in that room. And so the picture is ended.
>
> Here is a case where the manipulation of color was the dramatic punch itself; where the subtle hint of the prism told its own story better

than it could have been told in a sequence of scenes, at the same time giving the audience the satisfaction of being able to use its own imagination.[48]

I have quoted this at some length not only to demonstrate how much early film history was dependent on such sources as press agents hand-outs, but to give a feeling of the "high class" tone that Universal attached to the newly prestigious von Stroheim pictures in so much of their advertising. The sentiments indicated here are admirable, and the comments on the use of non-naturalistic color imply a familiarity with the projected-color experiments of the *avant-garde* theater of the day.

The continuity refers to this sequence as being given a blue tone and pink tint, and if the effect described in the previous article was achieved, then the pink gradually increased in relative intensity until it completely dominated the blue, a chromatic sunrise effect producing the glorious "happy ending" which von Stroheim disclaimed. In this period it was standard procedure to tint (dye the clear portion of the film) or to tone (chemically alter the silver in the emulsion and therefore turn the blacks into some colored silver salt) but a combination of tinting and toning was used more rarely. "These methods give an image whose clear portions or highlights show the color of the tinting dye, whereas the shadows and half-tones project a tint intermediate between that of the tinting dye and the toned deposit,"[49] says an Eastman Kodak technical manual. But if tinting or toning individually was common, and combined tinting-toning more scarce, then a tinting-toning process which changes in relative intensity was rare indeed, and if produced *en masse,* a considerable laboratory feat.

But while the color effects of the conclusion were remarked on by both critics and press agents, a potentially more revolutionary color effect was overlooked by all. The continuity of reel four (o.v.) shows the following in its description of Odera's dance at the Pre-Catalan Café. Rex, Warren and Grace are in the audience, and a standard amber tint has been employed up to this point:

91. Int. Cafe   Amber
People seated at the tables—dancer comes on in b.g.—dances—lights are turned down leaving Odera in the spot-light—[in pencil] *color changes.*

92. Int. Cafe   Rose
Odera dancing—people at tables

93. Close Up In Cafe   Red
Odera dancing

94. Close Up in Cafe   Green
    Odera dancing

95. Close Up of Rex   Green
    Seated smoking—the shadows pass across his face

96. Close Up of Rex   Violet
    Smoking—shadows on his face—he looks off

97. Int. Cafe   Violet
    Odera dancing

98. Int. Cafe   Green
    Odera dancing

99. Close Up of Odera   Green
    Dancing

100. Close Up of Rex   Green
     Smoking

101. Close Up of Rex   Rose
     Smoking

102. Close Up of Odera   Rose
     Dancing

103. Close Up of Rex   Rose
     Watching O looks off

103a. Close Up of Rex   Violet
      Watching—looks off

104. Int. Cafe   Violet
     Odera dancing

105. Int. Cafe   Red
     Odera whirls about—dancing—kneels

106. Int. Cafe   Green
     Odera in b.g. dancing—people at tables

107. Int. Cafe   Amber
     Odera finishing her dance—people at tables—they applaud—
     Odera rises—runs across

Although the continuity does not list the length of the individual shots, we inevitably get the feeling of rapid cutting in this sequence, in effect a rhythmic montage of the colors amber, rose, red, green, and violet. Note particularly the use of red and green, to von Stroheim colors inevitably bound up with passion and lust (the train which passes McTeague and Trina when they first kiss has one lamp hand-colored green, another red).[50] Odera's dance sequence is chromatically enhanced by "manipulated color" in a sequence perhaps unique in the silent cinema, and more to be expected in a Soviet classroom experiment than an Erich von Stroheim picture.

As well as these more complex tinting and toning elements, the film has its share of sequences tinted in the standard fashion—Rex's fight with Odera in red, certain "portrait" shots of Grace in lavender, etc. Inevitably the use of hand-coloring of firelights also came into play, but just as the tinting-toning of the climax had more than a decorative end, so does the hand-coloring of candlelights in the final sequence. As Rex and Grace return to her home after the performance they sit down next to a candelabra blazing brightly with many small points of light (hand-colored red). By the time Warren arrives home these have all flickered out, victims not so much of passing time as passing hope. Hand coloring was infinitely more troublesome than tinting or toning, and limited to relatively few moments in selected release prints. Von Stroheim remembered that only six copies of this particular film included the hand-colored footage.[51] An obviously stylized and non-realistic effect, it nonetheless fascinated von Stroheim, who incorporated it in as many of his films as possible. Still, his efforts were seldom appreciated. "Von Stroheim, who produced the picture, strived for color effects, but succeeded only in painting candle lights red,"[52] carped the *New York Evening Mail*. Whether the fault was in the execution of the sequences or the eye of the beholder is something we are today unable to judge.

The Devil's Pass Key has no tombstone, but there is a death certificate. Official notice may be found in the Universal print department "Junk File." On July 5, 1940, inspectors at the company's Woodbridge, New Jersey, negative storage facility noticed that part of reel five was suffering from terminal nitrate decomposition. Less than a year later, on May 8, 1941, the entire negative was destroyed. The film was barely twenty years old. Perhaps a fugitive print does still survive today, its existence jealously guarded or maybe just ignored. But as far as the official record goes, von Stroheim's film died at an especially young age.

Foolish Wives

When Erich and Valerie went east to attend the press screenings of *The Devil's Pass Key* they planned to stop at several major cities along the way for publicity purposes. It would also be the first real vacation for either of them since the day Carl Laemmle had agreed to go ahead with *The Pinnacle*. These first two films had been made back-to-back, and now they could bask for awhile in von Stroheim's sensational success as writer, director and star. A new contract was clearly called for as well, and New York was where it would have to be negotiated. Carl Laemmle would outline the general terms, but the final haggling would be done by a group of lawyers and corporate executives headed by R. H. Cochrane.

As Laemmle saw it, he had given von Stroheim his start when all others were indifferent, and for this the director owed him everything. Apparently he hoped to keep von Stroheim on long-term contract for little more than the $200 per week he had earned for acting in *Blind Husbands*. But von Stroheim had other ideas and was able to talk Cochrane into considerably better terms. Valerie remembers that as soon as *Blind Husbands* appeared von Stroheim was deluged with offers from the larger studios, including one appeal to work for William Randolph Hearst at Cosmopolitan.[1] Cochrane was always the most realistic of the men around Laemmle, and knew full well the extraordinary value of Universal's new discovery. On May 19, 1920, he signed with von Stroheim a contract calling for $800 per week for directing, with an additional $400 for working as an actor as well. And this was only for the first six months; escalator clauses would raise this to $1750 and $1000 after three years. Laemmle "hit the ceiling" when he heard this, but von Stroheim had already taken off across the country.[2] Four days later in Chicago he announced his engagement to Valerie. He had made good.

According to Valerie it was Laemmle himself who had come up with the idea for the next von Stroheim film, a picture using the now familiar von Stroheim ingredients, but placed against the background of Monte Carlo, famed as Europe's capital of gambling and romantic intrigue. The film was first announced under the title *Monto Carlo*,[3] but von Stroheim wanted something with more bite. Sitting with Valerie in a New York restaurant just before their return to the coast they looked for a solution. "My first film was called *Blind Husbands*," said Erich, "and the new one should be about wives. What are wives?" "Foolish," she said.[4]

Laemmle had given the go-ahead for this project even before they had left for New York, and set construction had started on April 6, 1920. So hardly were they off the train when the new picture was ready to go into production. Von Stroheim would play Count Sergius Karamzin, a Russian adventurer living on the Riviera with two "cousins" (Mae Busch and Maude George). They would become involved with the American attaché and his wife, allowing a splendid display of spectacle, melodrama, and sex. It would be von Stroheim's most lavish and ambitious project. A new turn in the postwar film industry had seen spectacle dominate the theaters: Metro was filming *The Four Horsemen of the Apocalypse* and D. W. Griffith had paid a quarter of a million dollars for the rights to *Way Down East*. *Foolish Wives* would be Universal's answer. The studio had never handled so elaborate a production, but they would learn. Who better than von Stroheim to show them the way? But somehow, things never worked out as planned.

The cameras began turning on July 12, 1920, and continued, with time off for death and disaster, until June 15 of the following year. Almost from the beginning everything went wrong. The production history of *Foolish Wives* was a nightmare without precedent, a bad dream from which von Stroheim never fully recovered. He had devised a script which called for the reconstruction of large parts of Monte Carlo, a palatial resort on the Mediterranean coast. To achieve this, the main façades of the Casino, Hotel de France, and Café de Paris began to rise on the backlot at Universal (an earlier plan to construct them on Catalina Island was soon abandoned). "Monte Carlo—in California," claimed the ads, which for over a year featured the growing construction in any paper that would provide the space. But since Universal City was landlocked, the opposite sides of these build-

Monte Carlo reconstructed at Universal City. Von Stroheim behind the cameras.

ings—supposedly overlooking the Mediterranean—had to be constructed
on suitable locations along the California coast. Location scouts selected
a spot called Point Lopus, near Del Monte on the Monterey Peninsula,
three hundred miles from the studio, and not far south of San Francisco.
Although Elmer Sheeley was the head of the art department at Universal, actual design work for *Foolish Wives* was handled by Richard
Day, the first assignment in one of the most significant careers in
motion picture art direction.

Day had been a captain in the Canadian army during the war, and
since then had been working as a newspaper and magazine illustrator.
In 1920 he had come to Hollywood in an attempt to find work in the
movies, but was unsuccessful and on the point of returning to British
Columbia. By purest accident von Stroheim saw him sitting in a Los
Angeles hotel lobby and struck up a conversation. One thing led to
another, and Day found himself designing the massive *Foolish Wives*
production, one of the most elaborate scenic projects in Hollywood
history.[5] Day soon became a key member of von Stroheim's floating
production unit, designing films as diverse as *Foolish Wives, Greed,*
and *The Wedding March.* Von Stroheim's own design ideas were unwieldy amalgams of minute detail and sweeping panorama; Day was
able to translate these into practical terms, constructing plaster and
lathe cities across studio backlots, and transforming real locations into
dramatically satisfying environments. After leaving von Stroheim he
spent a long and distinguished career at M-G-M, Goldwyn, and Twentieth Century-Fox.

For months a crew of 50 to 75 men hauled mountains of lumber up
the Pacific coast and out to the relatively inaccessible Point Lopus.
Not only was the location difficult, but the weather was unpredictably
fierce. After many weeks of backbreaking effort violent storms destroyed
much of the set, forcing construction to begin all over again.[6] At Universal City things weren't going much better. Construction of von
Stroheim's sets monopolized the resources of the studio and other directors claimed they were unable to acquire needed workers and building
materials. Working on those portions of the sets already completed, von
Stroheim began to film take after take of each scene, running up as
much as 326,000 feet of negative. While not completely without precedent, the figure was high enough that one trade paper quipped, "Page
George Eastman. Tell him there's a regular customer outside."[7]

Von Stroheim's unit was growing more and more self-contained, and
the group began to feel itself as somehow apart from the rest of the
studio operations. Ben Reynolds and William Daniels were again behind

the camera, and von Stroheim had collected a hard core of technical assistants, including his brother-in-law Louis Germonprez and Albert Conti, a fellow authority on costumes and military ritual. This group maintained its loyalty to von Stroheim, not to the studio. They worked to isolate themselves from executive pressure and considered orders from studio management as unwarranted interference.

In the middle of production Laemmle had another hunch and appointed his twenty-year-old secretary, Irving Thalberg, as head of the studio. Unlike most of the sycophants on the Laemmle payroll, Thalberg was not only an able administrator but a shrewd judge of public tastes and filmmakers' abilities. While previous studio heads were content to let sleeping dogs lie, Thalberg was unable to stand by and watch von Stroheim take over the studio. Costs were mounting far over budget projections, and no end of shooting was in sight. Finally he sent a message to the set ordering von Stroheim to his office. In full imperial regalia, von Stroheim, accompanied by his squad of assistants, stormed over to Thalberg's office. Thalberg had a set of plans all drawn up, intending to bring the production to an efficient halt before it swallowed all of Universal's working capital. To back him up he found a clause in von Stroheim's contract in which the director "agrees that he will direct as ordered by the Producer." Von Stroheim laughed it all off with a bluff, claiming that Thalberg would have to fire him if he wanted to begin giving orders. "Remove me as the director and you remove me as the star," he said, "and you won't have a picture."[8] Von Stroheim had already appeared in too many key scenes to be replaced. He strutted back to the set. Thalberg had lost the first round.

Since the studio couldn't do very much to stem the rising costs they decided to play them up for as much publicity value as possible. As early as October 23, 1920, the studio house paper, *Moving Picture Weekly,* was claiming, "He's going to make you *hate him!* even if it takes a million dollars of our money to do it!" And the following month it threatened that "Those theatres that paid $4000 for *The Devil's Pass Key* will pay $10,000 for *Foolish Wives.*" In New York the head of foreign publicity, Paul Kohner, hit on a new way to plug the "million dollar" angle. He had the studio erect a gigantic electric sign across three floors of the Astor Hotel at Broadway and 45th street. Throughout the summer of 1921 it boasted "The cost of FOOLISH WIVES up to this week," with a figure changed weekly by the studio publicity department. Contrary to popular belief, von Stroheim's name was not spelled with a "$" on this sign—only Carl Laemmle's name appeared in the five-foot-high letters.[9]

The publicity departments on both coasts were working overtime on such stunts, and it is hard to know the truth behind many of the *Foolish Wives* stories. Did he really shoot dozens of takes of pigeons being loosed at a trap shoot, hoping that they would fly out to sea when the birds insisted on traveling inland? Every week the papers uncovered a new sensation, one more extravagant than the rest. One of the wildest stories, and definitely no publicity stunt, involved von Stroheim's arrest by federal agents on charges of counterfeiting French currency to use in the gambling episodes. Soon after his return from the East von Stroheim told his property master, Chester Rodgers, to obtain imitations of French fifty and thousand franc notes. Rodgers instructed one of the staff scenic artists, Gleb De Vos, to draw samples of these bills in the form of stage money—plainly marked as such and not likely to be confused for the real thing on the street. When De Vos said he could not possibly hand draw 500 examples of each before they were needed for shooting, someone suggested they photoengrave the bills and have them printed up. At this point De Vos began to worry about the operation and spoke to Secret Service agents, who promptly arrested him, Rodgers, von Stroheim, and the operators of the engraving and printing plant. The Treasury Department was looking for a test case involving the printing of such stage money and decided to make an example of von Stroheim. It was years before the nuisance charges were completely dropped.[10]

When the crews had finished rebuilding the sets at Point Lopus von Stroheim and his company traveled up the coast to shoot the seaside footage, which would be matched in with the scenes shot at Universal City. It was von Stroheim's first extended location trip and he enjoyed himself immensely. Away from all studio supervision he elaborated more scenes onto his script and ran up costly overtime delays, keeping a large company in residence at the fashionable Del Monte Hotel. He hosted the high society of San Francisco and Oakland, and even pressed them into service as dress extras during scenes on "Monte Carlo's" ocean promenade.

While von Stroheim's personal assistants were intensely loyal, hired "outsiders" often grew impatient with his all-night shooting schedules and unpredictable temper tantrums. After cursing out the electricians and carpenters at the Del Monte location once too often the group threatened to quit *en masse* unless von Stroheim apologized. Von Stroheim, always terribly contrite after such outbursts, graciously obliged.[11]

In an effort to force von Stroheim back to the studio Thalberg cut off all funds to the location, but this tactic backfired as well.[12] Von Stroheim simply continued shooting, running up hotel bills all over northern California and charging the expenses to the studio. Thalberg paid off the irate innkeepers and waited for von Stroheim to return.

As costs on Paul Kohner's sign approached the $750,000 mark the worst disaster of all hit the production. Rudolph Christians, who had been playing the American attaché, husband of the film's "foolish wife" and the nominal hero of the picture, suddenly died. The studio sent out word that "he had completed all his scenes necessary to the picture,"[13] but this was far from the truth. Production stopped while the country was scoured for a Christians look-alike. All national casting agencies were contacted, and even detectives hired to find a suitable stand-in.[14] Finally the studio signed Robert Edeson, a familiar Hollywood actor. But Edeson only had a general resemblance to Christians and von Stroheim had to shoot over his back, place him in shadow, and generally work around him for several key scenes. A moonlight water carnival where the cousins were to romance the attaché while Karamzin went to work on the wife was the most troublesome. Unable to shoot the scene properly von Stroheim had to forget about the attaché's romantic temptations, thus eliminating a major subplot. At the climax of the picture the American realizes the Count's duplicity, knocks him down, and challenges him to a duel. To paste this scene together von Stroheim used footage of Christians originally shot for other scenes, clips from an earlier Christians picture, and even (he claimed) traveling matte technique to match the old Christians footage with the needed location. None of this worked out very well. Despite von Stroheim's reputation for fastidiousness of detail he and his staff completely broke down on the Christians matter. They didn't even bother to color Edeson's hair properly, simply throwing in the towel when even nature seemed to conspire against them.

Von Stroheim now began to suggest reshooting many of Christians's scenes with Edeson, and going out on location to Del Monte again. Thalberg would have none of this. Von Stroheim was shooting the water carnival scenes at West Lake Park in Los Angeles. Costly arrangements had been made to film everything in one night, but von Stroheim came back once more the next evening. He planned to work again the following night, but when he arrived the cameras were gone. Thalberg had sent out a crew to return the equipment to the studio. Shooting was over.

It was June 15, 1921. *Foolish Wives* had been in production for eleven months, and von Stroheim had shot 326,000 feet of negative.[15]

Editing *Foolish Wives* in the summer of 1921, ice bucket within arm's reach. On the table, 19,000 feet of film.

From an initial budget of $250,000 costs had escalated rapidly: to $750,000 according to von Stroheim, to $1,124,498 according to the studio.[16] Now the film would have to be edited to a reasonable length, and for von Stroheim, the hard part was only beginning. The length of 326,000 feet was substantial, but not unprecedented. Universal itself had claimed that 300,000 feet were shot for *The Heart of Humanity*, although that must have included a lot of footage taken by multiple cameras recording battle scenes, something not the case here. After removing retakes, duplicate scenes, and spoiled footage, there still remained 150,000 feet of "actual constructive action,"[17] which by August of 1921 von Stroheim had edited down to 30 or 32 reels.

As luck would have it, *Foolish Wives* had been in production just before the Fatty Arbuckle, Wallace Reid, and William Desmond Taylor scandals erupted. The tabloids were filled with outrage at the sex-and-drug orgies seemingly sweeping Hollywood, and across the country agencies for the suppression of vice turned their sights on the movies. Von Stroheim himself was never implicated in any such scandal, but his films were known to be strongly "Continental," and those who had seen some of the footage as it piled up felt *Foolish Wives* was certain to come under direct attack. To outflank such a move, Universal hosted a junket of censors from across the country, putting them up at fancy hotels and generally providing the royal treatment. On the night of August 18, 1921, a screening of the *Foolish Wives* rough-cut was held at the Beverly Hills Hotel. It began at 9:00 p.m. and lasted until 3:30 the next morning. Universal said the print they saw was 17,000 feet long, assembled on 24 reels, but the running time seems to indicate the 30-reel print usually credited to von Stroheim.[18] The studio submitted the film to the censors as a work in progress, and solicited their advice on its future cutting. As might be expected, von Stroheim was furious at the studio for allowing his film to be used for target practice. He felt the picture was complete as it was, and wanted it shown in just that length, on two separate evenings. Films like Fritz Lang's *Dr. Mabuse, der Spieler* and Joe May's *Das Indische Grabmal* were in fact being shown that way in Europe. But Universal had had enough of von Stroheim's demands. They took the cutting of the film away from him and assigned it to Arthur Ripley, one of the studio editorial staff. Ripley was ordered to reduce the film to 14 reels in time for a long delayed New York premiere. Universal had earned as much publicity as possible out of the film's production costs, so now they turned their energies to its excessive length. Ripley had the picture down to 18 reels by November 29, then boarded a specially equipped train to continue work on the trip east. Title writer Marian Ainslee, cutters Bob Roberts and Daniel Mandell, and von Stroheim's assistant Eddie Sowders all accompanied Ripley, working shifts to reduce the film on schedule. The train roared through Salt Lake City, Omaha, and Chicago, trailing thousands of feet of cut von Stroheim footage in its wake.[19] On arriving in New York Ripley collected a bonus for his labors, and collapsed in his hotel room, not to emerge for several weeks. Daniel Mandell was so distressed by the experience that for a time he left the motion picture business entirely, although eventually he did return to continue one of the most distinguished careers in film editing.[20]

Von Stroheim, who had been out of the picture for some time, traveled to New York on a separate train to make one last effort to intercede for his creation. As the print was being readied for its January 11 premiere at the Central Theatre Sigmund Romberg arranged a musical score to accompany it (in those days more an arrangement of stock melodies, with perhaps one or two original themes, than an entirely original musical composition). The weather was bad the night of the opening, but the theatre was packed with dignitaries and motion picture celebrities. Visiting German director Ernst Lubitsch was in the audience, as were Sam Goldwyn, Nicholas Schenck, Pat Powers, William Fox, and Roxy Rothafel.[21]

The print shown that evening ran some three and a half hours, and was listed in the trades as 14,120 feet long.[22] But clearly the studio had no intention of issuing the film at this length for general release, since shortly before the premiere they had sent Julius Stern to New York to take over further editing from Ripley, who was still confined to his hotel room.[23] Stern had worked his way up the Universal ladder and was now serving as "second vice president." Putting *Foolish Wives* into shape would be his big chance, and judging from the opening night reaction that would be no easy task.

Although von Stroheim was giving interviews all over town accusing Universal of showing "only the skeleton of my dead child,"[24] even the skeleton had too much fat on its bones for most of the first nighters—at least the way Ripley and Stern had patched it together. The daily reviewers, fan magazines, and trade papers argued vehemently about the picture's merits, but all agreed on one thing: it was much too long. The *Moving Picture World* even accused the studio of irresponsible behavior in presenting it at such a length.[25] Most of the last-minute editing had affected the film's final hour, and this is where it was suffering most at the premiere.[26] Clues planted in the early reels, intended to support last-minute climaxes, had been eliminated, leaving the end of the picture in a state of dramatic collapse. In the most acute example, the editors had turned the climax of the picture into "the most absurd incident that has ever been portrayed on local screens."[27] "A great audience burst suddenly into howling gusts of laughter," wrote one witness. "Without warning, as a hen might lay an egg, the heroine had given birth to a baby. It was outrageous; it was uproarious. Von Stroheim had been seen to rise, white as death, and leave the theatre, to disappear God knows where. Broadway hummed with rumors of suicide."[28] Stern worked away at the film every day, presenting his new changes at each performance. The New York State Censorship Board, which had already passed the film on the basis of one list of cuts, felt compelled to submit another, an unprecedented action; Stern dutifully incorporated these as well. Within ten days he had eliminated another 3500 feet.[29] "The baby was extracted, but the story, as von Stroheim intended it, never came out of the ether."[30]

The film went into general release in ten reels, although no exact footage count seems to have survived. At this length it played out its run throughout the country, and in at least one 1927 revival.[31] Then in 1928 Universal decided to recut the film for a general reissue, perhaps with music and sound effects added. Editorial department head Maurice Pivar assigned cutter Ted Kent and title writer Walter Anthony to the project. They reduced the film to 7655 feet, completely restructuring the narrative and changing the names and descriptions of the characters. The American attaché became a traveling businessman, and all the scenes of pageantry that accompanied his reception were discarded. But for some reason this version was not publicly shown at that time. According to Kent, von Stroheim was called in to look at the film and prohibited its release, although he had no such right in his contract.[32] In later years *Foolish Wives* gained some circulation in the 16mm market through the Show-At-Home Movie Library, and since Kent and Anthony had cut up the original negative it was their version, with their names on the main title, that was distributed non-theatrically after 1928. It was still their version that was sent to the Museum of Modern Art in 1936 when the new Film Library requested a print. But no one at the Museum was aware that the film had been substantially altered in 1928, and they began showing it as the 1922 general release version, a significant misrepresentation. When von Stroheim saw this print he accused Iris Barry, curator of the Film Library, of ordering further cuts in the film herself![33] For almost 35 years American critics writing about this print felt that they were discussing the same picture widely shown in 1922, despite obvious differences in plot, length, and the names of characters.[34] As it happened, European archives also held prints of *Foolish Wives,* of about the same length, but not until the early 1970s did anyone bother to compare the various versions. Although the lengths were similar, it turned out that the material involved was substantially different. The European prints, badly tattered and with titles translated from one language into another, were authentic descendants of the 1922 version as prepared for export, containing at least bits and pieces of nearly all the scenes Kent and Anthony had removed. Under the aegis of the American Film Institute, von Stroheim scholar Arthur Lennig cannibalized the two prints to produce a restoration of 9682 feet, not von Stroheim's version, but considerably closer to it than anything seen in the past half-century.[35]

With such a history it becomes difficult to offer even a summary of the plot of *Foolish Wives,* much less any detailed criticism. Although the newly restored version is a considerable improvement over anything seen lately, it is still nearly an hour shorter than the "skeleton" disowned by its director at the premiere. To experience the film which von Stroheim created we would have to go back to the version last seen at the Beverly Hills Hotel censor convention. Barring that, his shooting script gives the best clues to his intentions, and fortunately it has been preserved by the von Stroheim family.

For the third time von Stroheim presented his "innocents abroad" plot, now increasing the symbolic weight of the text by making the "blind husband" an American attaché, official representative of his country in foreign lands. Andrew J. Hughes is a good man, but again lacking in all refinements or social graces. His wife Helen exhibits the worst excesses of the *nouveau riche,* toadying to titled foreigners and patronizing the less prosperous acquaintances from the States who cross her path. Under the influence of a book she frequently refers to called "Foolish Wives," by Erich von Stroheim, she fails to see her husband's worthy qualities and falls under the spell of a Continental adventurer, Count Sergius Karamzin, played by von Stroheim.[36] The film makes use of Griffith's technique of parallel development by juxtaposing Hughes's actions with the Count's throughout the picture. We see Hughes in the morning, shaving in his underwear, as his wife goes about her toilette in another room. Then we see the Count, rousted out of bed by his two "cousins," one of whom retrieves from his bed the wig she left the previous evening. Hughes is presented to the Prince of Monaco and has difficulties with so simple a task as removing his gloves. The Count turns the same gesture into an erotic exercise as he stalks Mrs. Hughes on the veranda of the Café de Paris. The Count and his cousins live in the Villa Amorosa, an exotic retreat reminiscent of a deconsecrated abbey. He fleeces American wives and passes counterfeit money in the Casino. His cousin Vera specializes in American husbands, while Olga, with the aid of a scandalous photo album, runs a service which provides "charming companions" for wealthy clients. They are played by Mae Busch and Maude George, echoing similar roles from *The Devil's Pass Key.* There is a palpable sexual tension here, heightened by the fact that the Count seems to prefer Olga's affections, driving Vera to fits of jealous rage. Maroushka, their servant maid, is pregnant by the Count and pleads with him to keep his promise to marry her.

Cesare Ventucci supplies the group with counterfeit bills. His wife committed suicide when he lost everything at the gambling tables, leaving him to raise their half-witted daughter (the wife's picture, which Ventucci reveres as an icon, is a photo of Valerie). Now he seeks revenge against the system by helping the Count pass the worthless currency in the Casino. The Count is also developing an interest in the daughter.

The group learns of the arrival of Mr. and Mrs. Hughes, and plots to involve them in their schemes. The Count makes the acquaintance of Mrs. Hughes and offers to show her Monte Carlo, warning her against the actions of unscrupulous sharks. For several days they visit the Casino and other points of interest, the Count captivating Mrs. Hughes with his Continental attentions while the husband remains skeptical. Von Stroheim wants us to know that Hughes and the Count are two sides of the same coin, his standard dramatic ploy, and various scenes are introduced to make this clear. The glove scene mentioned above serves this function, as does the pigeon shooting episode. On the ocean promenade the Count displays his skill as a marksman by slaughtering an entire flight of six birds. Hughes is disdainful, and objects that shooting tame birds is not sporting. Under the influence of her new companions, Helen feels "embarassed over her husband's provincialism," and fails to see the true nobility of his position. Jean Renoir, who was moved by *Foolish Wives* to make a new career as film director,[37] pays tribute to this scene in the rabbit hunting episode of *La Règle de Jeu,* another example of sophisticated savagery.

At a water carnival the Count maneuvers Helen into one of the small boats while his cousins sail off with Hughes in another. Helen's resistance is further tested the following evening when on a walk through the countryside with the Count they are caught in a violent thunderstorm and must spend the night in the hut of an old witch. The witch predicts "Blood! . . . Death! . . . and New Life!" Helen is saved for the moment by the fortunate arrival of an old monk who also seeks shelter from the tempest. This episode is von Stroheim's first significant use of natural forces as metaphor, a device which occurs again in the storm scenes of *Greed. The Wedding March,* and *Walking Down Broadway.*

The Count has been using Helen to help him pass Ventucci's money across the gaming tables at the Casino, but the next day the management catches her at it. Now the target of suspicion, he must act quickly. Luring her to his villa that evening he confesses the need of 30,000 francs to pay a debt of honor. Helen forces the money on him. Unfortunately, the distraught Maroushka, feeling betrayed by the Count, sets fire to the tower room where this assignation takes place. The fire department must be called out to fight the blaze, and the Count, a coward, jumps first. During all this Hughes has been playing a little poker with the cousins in their private casino elsewhere in the villa. He catches both cheating and learns of Olga's work as a procuress as well. To get back at Hughes, Olga slips a photo of Helen into the album, accusing her of infidelity with the Count. Hughes rushes back to the hotel to find his wife gone, then notices the fire engines racing up to the villa. He returns in time to send Helen home in an ambulance and confronts the Count. Hughes knocks him down with one punch, and the Count challenges him to a duel with pistols. Hughes accepts, wishing to demonstrate to Helen that he, too, can live up to Continental codes of honor. Returning to the hotel, he writes her a note explaining his decision, knowing that since the Count is a crack shot he is certainly going to his death at dawn. The Count decides to spend the evening with Ventucci's daughter, but accidentally wakes up her father as he creeps into her window. Ventucci murders the intruder and stuffs his body down a sewer, along with that of a black cat which the Count had killed on his way over. Olga and Vera, trying to flee with their gains before the police arrive, are caught and exposed as fugitive criminals. The Count's body, along with the dead cat and an empty case of champagne bottles, drifts out to sea, where it is eaten by an octopus. Hughes returns to the hotel when his opponent fails to show for the duel. To his surprise, Helen has given birth to a child—she hid the knowledge from him for fear that he would leave her behind when he left for Europe. Wiser for her experiences, Mrs. Hughes is reconciled to the fact that "the mate for the American woman is the American man."

This was the last of von Stroheim's films dealing with the clash of American and European ideals in postwar Europe. He exhausted this idea in three highly sophisticated films before Hemingway or Fitzgerald even came to the subject. But in von Stroheim's case the device was largely a transposition to exotic locales of a confrontation he himself had experienced only on this side of the Atlantic. *Foolish Wives* is an especially satisfying end to the trilogy since we now get to see the most interesting character, the villain, dominate the action on all levels. Von Stroheim's Karamzin is a bravura performance, balanced with just the right amount of sly wit and self-deprecating humor. Helen falls under the charm of this rogue with hardly a struggle, but so does the audience. Despite the fact that director von Stroheim lets us see the character from the beginning as a cheat, coward, fraud, and pimp, we fall irresistibly before his elegance and quick wit. The old "man you love to hate" magic is examined directly and shown to be powerful stuff indeed. Such ambiguous qualities in a villain were novel and obviously puzzling to some reviewers, who preferred their morals more clearly defined. Von Stroheim still has not advanced to the point where this character can be said to grow emotionally—that would not come until his next film. Nevertheless the character is sketched with a vitality rare in films of the period, and the entire conception seems to look forward to the racier pre-code films of the 1930s.

Again, part of the strength would seem to come from autobiographical roots. Like his creator, Karamzin is a bogus Count who has learned to use his wits in exerting a profitable influence over title-conscious Americans. Von Stroheim's marriage to Margaret Knox again comes to mind. And the sequence in which Karamzin wheedles 30,000 francs from Mrs. Hughes inevitably suggests von Stroheim's ability to extract $500 from Emma Bissinger, a story we have from his own hand. Karamzin, in another sense, is the "director" of this story, setting in motion little scenarios involving the cousins, Maroushka, and Mrs. Hughes, always with himself at the center. He moves the action of the picture by outrageous play-acting, as when he feigns tears in order to inveigle a few francs from his servant girl, or pretends that a "debt of honor" forces him to ask Mrs. Hughes for 30,000.

Although von Stroheim and Karamzin both share a fetish for uniforms and a rapacious appetite for the opposite sex, the two are not identical. *Foolish Wives* is a much more finely developed work than *In the Morning* or *The Pinnacle,* and von Stroheim is able to step back here and have a bit of humor at the expense of his own outrageous persona. It would be a necessary step on the road to such fully developed characters as Prince Nikki in *The Wedding March.* As in all the early films, however, a horrible death is meted out to the von Stroheim character. The director would later claim that such endings were forced on him, or at best accommodations with prevailing censorship standards, but the delicious self-annihilation we see in films like this belies the statement. Despite his claims to the contrary, censors and audiences of the time simply did not demand such fatal punishments. In Griffith's *Way Down East,* filmed just before *Foolish Wives,* the villain tricks Lillian Gish into a false marriage, impregnates and abandons her. When their paths next meet he causes her still more problems, and she is exiled out into the great storm. For all this he is knocked down by Richard Barthelmess and allowed to go on his way, with hardly a show of repentance, much less punishment. No one forced so brutal an ending on *Foolish Wives* but von Stroheim himself. Had he directed *Way Down East,* it would have been the villain going over those falls, not Lillian Gish.

As we said earlier, Andrew Hughes is a projection of the "opposite" type of character: sincere, trustworthy, open, naïve, uncomplicated. When the film was released many felt that von Stroheim had pictured our emissary as "a perfect ass,"[38] and it is clear that as Julius Stern

excised more footage many of Hughes's scenes were at the top of the list. The studio was so sensitive about this issue that when Kent and Anthony recut the film in 1928 they removed his diplomatic status altogether, making his position in the film nearly pointless. But he does still survive as counterpoint. Through most of the film he is not openly hostile to Karamzin, and perhaps senses the link between them. At times in their conversation we feel that we are eavesdropping on von Stroheim talking to himself. "You're a Devil with the women, aren't you?" "Not less and not more than other men. Of course I have acquired some experiences and I have found that they are all alike." "In other words, you mean that they are all for sale?" "Some like the money, some are in love with love." "I know one that's different." "Who could that be?" "My wife." For von Stroheim these were real conflicts, and the battle between the cynic and the romantic haunted his private life even more than his films.

As a heroine, Mrs. Hughes remains two-dimensional, a pawn over which the men will battle. Worse than this, she shares many of the negative qualities of Grace Goodwright and lacks the refinement of Margaret Armstrong. Von Stroheim found a model named Patsie Hannon to play the role, and promptly rechristened her—Margaret Armstrong! After a few months of shooting the studio gave her the name Miss Dupont, but von Stroheim's position is clear from the name he picked. She was one of his least imposing discoveries and enjoyed a strikingly brief career.

Otherwise, the structure of the plot is perhaps overly familiar, with only different incidents plugged in to maintain interest. Gambling as a subtext may have been Laemmle's suggestion, but von Stroheim develops it with an authority all his own. Gambling itself held little fascination for von Stroheim but his belief in fate was overpowering, and he was convinced that life itself was a wheel of chance, programmed by fate to its inevitable conclusion. The fixed roulette wheel, an image central to *Foolish Wives,* is important not just for its aura of forbidden glamour, but for its key position in the film's metaphoric structure.

Universal's publicity campaign for *Foolish Wives* was a model of its kind, and served to keep the name of the film on every filmgoer's lips during nearly two years of production. But such campaigns inevitably produce a backlash, and many were lying in wait for the picture, hoping for a flop and eager to emphasize any point of weakness. In addition to the length, many critics found the picture of Americans clearly objectionable, and resented von Stroheim's "making fools of the only decent people in the story."[39] One influential fan magazine went so far as to headline its review "an insult to every American."[40] Jingoistic passions were still high so soon after the war, and it was no good for von Stroheim to admit at the end that his Americans did have compensating virtues after all. A large part of the audience, even the professional audience, was simply not ready for this. "They refused to see me as a Russian, they could not forget the war films," von Stroheim wrote years later. "To them I remained the German who mocked the inviolability of American womanhood and the sacredness of matrimony."[41]

A few critics, like von Stroheim's chief early supporter, the *New York Tribune*'s Harriette Underhill, sensed the novelty and greatness which even the "skeleton" revealed. In a sensitive interview with the director shortly after the premiere, she told him it was "the best picture I ever saw."[42] But in the end the insistent cutting of the film took its toll. Critics and audiences alike sensed the gaps in plot and characterization, and reacted with impatience and boredom. It might be true that the picture "teems with scenes that mean something,"[43] but if the film "collapses in its last hour"[44] what would be the point? In Europe things were different, with films like Renoir's *Nana* a clear homage to everything von Stroheim was trying to do in *Foolish Wives,* but that didn't help him in his dealings with Hollywood studio heads.

Most crucial here was the bottom line, and when the film grossed only $869,285, it was not even enough to cover the negative costs, much less prints and advertising.[45] The first to complain were the exhibitors, since Universal had charged an increased rental for the picture. "I'm going to get every dollar I can for that production because I've got to," said Carl Laemmle. "You need no diagram to show you why."[46] With business below expectations theater owners were left holding the bag, and were quick to make their anger known. "The most absolute insult to intelligence, in my opinion, ever put on the screen, rotten and sickening," wrote one theater manager.[47] But instead of blaming Laemmle and Universal, they turned their attacks directly on von Stroheim. The editorial writer of a leading trade paper called him "the silly villain who shot the bank roll in an egotistic endeavor to glorify himself," and suggested that Carl Laemmle "either shoot von Stroheim at sunrise, or step on him and squash him."[48]

More than any other branch of the industry the exhibitors are concerned with the balance sheet alone: they earn no credit for a *succès d'estime.* Unfortunately for von Stroheim, they would prove to have long memories.

Merry-Go-Round

The controversy surrounding the picture turned *Foolish Wives* into an unprecedented media event which firmly established von Stroheim as a major figure in the industry. Where before there had only been Griffith, occasionally challenged by men like Rex Ingram, C. B. De Mille, or Maurice Tourneur, now there was von Stroheim: the student had equalled the master. This extravagant reception was not simply the work of Universal's publicity mill, but a genuine outpouring of interest in a man the public recognized as an extraordinary talent. For a time the Central Theatre was packed with the curious, and though censors and critics continued to rage, it seemed that the film might still go on to sweep the country. Griffith's *Orphans of the Storm,* which had opened earlier that month at the Apollo, was nearly ignored in the public prints as *Foolish Wives* monopolized New York's attentions. True, much of this concern was wildly critical, and often tinged with wartime xenophobia, but each new attack only seemed to fuel von Stroheim's fires. He moved into the Waldorf-Astoria and poured out his heart to sympathetic journalists like Harriette Underhill, damning the studio and savaging his critics.[1] Von Stroheim was emotionally exhausted by life at the center of this hurricane, and with no particular project in mind he enjoyed himself by revisiting old haunts like the Blue Ribbon, a Hungarian-Viennese restaurant he knew from his early days in New York. Universal had bought "McTeague" for him, but once again he put the Norris novel aside. He saw that another old project, *The Affairs of Anatole,* had been botched by Cecil B. De Mille, whose uncomfortably wholesome adaptation managed to flatten Schnitzler's wry *soufflé.* The book seemed not to have been touched.[2]

At any rate, von Stroheim sensed that he had exhausted the "innocents abroad" plot which had carried his first three films, and given the volatile state of his relations with Universal he was open for suggestions. The foreign publicity department in the company's New York office was manned by a young Bavarian émigré named Paul Kohner, one of Uncle Carl's more successful imports. He had created a job for himself translating Universal's standard press releases and placing the results in European publications eager for any news from Hollywood. The giant *Foolish Wives* electrical sign had been another of his ideas, one for which he had pocketed a fifty-dollar bonus. But Kohner had grander ambitions than film publicity, and just before the *Foolish Wives* premiere he arrived at von Stroheim's suite determined to make an impression.³ Initially, of course, it was von Stroheim who made the impression, greeting Kohner in the nude, ceremonially bowing and clicking his heels (a feat even for him), and completely ignoring the mysterious young lady who walked across the room and left with a cheerful wave of the hand. Kohner and von Stroheim immediately found plenty to talk about, although the young publicist was at first surprised to hear "Von" speak in a distinctly working-class Viennese accent.⁴ They talked for hours, sharing a nostalgia for the old country and an admiration for the films of Erich von Stroheim. It had been a long time since von Stroheim had met so sympathetic a *Landsman*. Kohner had plenty of story suggestions to offer as well, and his wide reading of European literature—especially the German classics—was tremendously impressive. "All that von Stroheim seemed to have read were military manuals," Kohner remembered.⁵ He had an officer's knowledge of the Viennese theater, of Schnitzler and Lehar, but Schiller and Goethe seemed new to him. Kohner proposed films of Feuchtwanger and Hoffmanthal, Thomas Mann, Stefan Zweig, and Franz Werfel. Von Stroheim had been away from Vienna since 1909, and for most of the war must have felt utterly abandoned and culturally isolated. In the days before the arrival of the UFA émigrés there were few Germans or Austrians in Hollywood, and those that were there—like the Laemmles—spent their time making films like *The Kaiser—Beast of Berlin*. His new friend had struck an obvious chord: von Stroheim's next film must be about Vienna.

Kohner remembers two suggestions which seemed especially appealing. The first was Leo Perutz's "From Nine to Nine," the fatalistic tale of a student falsely accused of theft, who spends 24 hours as a manacled fugitive. The other, *The Story of Hannerl and Her Lovers,* was a novel by Rudolf Hans Bartsch which featured a poor lieutenant, his young *susse madel,* and a fatal wedding averted at the last moment by the coming of war. Von Stroheim ordered an option on this one immediately. He invited Kohner to a closed screening of *Foolish Wives* at the Universal offices, after which Kohner was more than happy to spell out his own ideas on the film's cutting and advertising. He even sat down at the piano in von Stroheim's suite and ran through a selection of Viennese favorites he felt were suitable for the score. For the next two weeks Kohner kept feeding von Stroheim story ideas, outlining the plots of Heinrich Mann novels while joining the director and his friend Sigmund Romberg in a tour of New York's restaurants, night clubs, and whore-houses. By the time he left New York von Stroheim knew exactly what he wanted to do next: rebuild the Vienna which had disappeared forever.

As it happened, Universal did not option Bartsch's novel at this time, and announced instead that Ludwig Ganghofer's *Castle Hubertus* would be the next von Stroheim production.[6] But he had ideas of his own about Vienna, and needed only a central image on which to hang them. He found it in the Prater, the great amusement center of Franz Josef's capital, and its famed midway attraction, the Merry-Go-Round. Just as the wheel of chance had been a central image of *Foolish Wives,* so this spinning carousel would tie together his story of prewar Vienna.

Von Stroheim went to San Francisco to attend the opening there of *Foolish Wives,* then stayed on to work on his new script. Returning home on the evening of March 14 he dictated the first draft of *Merry-Go-Round* to Louis Germonprez, now officially his business manager.[7] They showed it to Thalberg the next day and he encouraged them to develop it. On March 30 von Stroheim returned with a more detailed synopsis, and for the next three or four days was in constant consultation with Thalberg. The negotiations were tense. Von Stroheim still owed another film under his contract, and Universal was loath to let him go, especially in light of his sudden, sensational notoriety. Yet the cloud of *Foolish Wives* hung heavily over both parties. Ultimately, von Stroheim promised to behave, and Thalberg agreed to accept the promise. He reasoned that he could control the film if he put his foot down right at the start (*Foolish Wives* had already gotten out of hand before he had arrived as production head). But there were also special conditions, lessons he had learned on the last picture, and the most important of these was prohibiting von Stroheim's appearance in the picture as an actor. By preventing von Stroheim's appearance in the picture Thalberg was implicitly threatening him with removal from the production if things began to get out of hand. He would not allow von Stroheim the advantage he had wielded so effectively during the filming of *Foolish Wives*. Von Stroheim accepted this, but the knowledge that Universal had taken this first step must have been a chilling blow to the confidence he had built up since his first film for Laemmle three years earlier. He would no longer have the run of the lot, and there would always be a Thalberg agent looking over his shoulder. Still, he believed that Universal really wanted him to make this film, and that no matter what happened, the notion that Thalberg might somehow take the film away from him was too bizarre to contemplate.

Von Stroheim and Germonprez left the studio and traveled up the coast to Ventura County, where they took rooms at the Pierpont Inn and began work on the final script. Three times a week Germonprez would carry the new pages back to the studio and return with Thalberg's notations. Once Thalberg himself showed up, passing through with director Hobart Henley on a location trip. On May 1 the new script was completed, but Thalberg demanded revisions and had his own version prepared five days later. When von Stroheim rejected it Thalberg handed the material to an "impartial" third party, Universal story editor Lucien Hubbard. Hubbard produced a script of his own which no one liked.[8] Finally, von Stroheim and Thalberg thrashed out their differences, and on May 17 the studio officially accepted the story by paying von Stroheim $5000 for his scenario. Von Stroheim did agree to prepare an "abridged continuity," and with Lucien Hubbard retreated to a small bungalow in a corner of the Universal lot. It was not uncommon for silent filmmakers to estimate the running time of each scene in a script, especially when an elaborate story was involved, and von Stroheim had to demonstrate that *Merry-Go-Round* would emerge in an acceptable length. Lucien Hubbard helped him with this:

> Mr. von Stroheim enacted each scene; for instance, simulating the trotting of horses in the arrival of a carriage, the opening of the carriage door and the exit therefrom of the characters, while I held a split-second watch and we agreed on the probable length of time it would take to enact the scene during the actual filming of the picture.[9]

The final script was delivered on June 20, 1922. In an atmosphere of uneasy truce, preparations went ahead for a film which needed to surpass *Foolish Wives* in imagination, sumptuousness, and notoriety.

Today at least three scripts exist claiming to be the final version of the original (von Stroheim) screenplay. In addition, the 26-page treatment first shown to Thalberg also survives, as do "revised" continuities prepared by other writers. All four von Stroheim drafts are remarkably

similar, featuring the same cast of characters and the same general plot
structure. They differ in incident and in the refinement of various motifs, and although none are dated, a 976-scene version preserved by
Universal seems to embody his concerns most fully.

A montage introduces us to "Vienna, with a code of morals all its
own . . . bravely idling away the hours . . . to the strains of Strauss
and Lehar . . . not knowing of tomorrow." To illustrate this, a trick
shot is indicated to show a composite Viennese orchestra in which Mo-
zart, Beethoven, Shubert, Mahler, Kreisler, Lehar, and a host of others
all keep time in waltz tempo. We see a "choice product of that Viennese
atmosphere," Count Franz Maximilian von Hohenegg, still sleeping off
the previous night's revels. In an elaborate *toilette* sequence, von Stroheim starts the Count on his day in a welter of corsets, moustache
pressers, and discarded stockings.[10] His fiancée, Komtesse Gisella von
Steinbruch, is secretly involved with one of her stablehands. She tele-
phones the Count to make sure he will attend her dinner party that evening, but he claims pressing regimental business. "What are her colors?" she asks. That morning is Holy Thursday, and the Count must
attend the ceremonial footwashing, where in imitation of Christ's hu-
mility the Emperor will wash the feet of twelve poor and aged subjects.[11]
The elaborate ritual is interrupted by "The yearly demonstration of
Vienna's working men," who storm through the streets in front of the
cathedral waving red banners and shouting "Down with the parasites."
Just as the mob begins to grow violent a fresh detachment of the Emperor's palace guard scatters them. "It is positively a sin not to turn
our machine guns on this poisonous vermin," mutters the Minister of
War, the Count's prospective father-in-law. "Sooner or later we will,
though," answers one of the Count's friends. "I'd love to do the aiming," responds another. The Count is more thoughtful: "After all they
play their little game as we play ours . . . It just depends on which
side you are!" The friends blame his mood on last night's lobster
dinner.[12]

That evening the Count and his friends take some girls to The Ice
Bird, the Prater's garden restaurant. Meanwhile Gisella leaves her party
for an interlude in the stables.[13] At the Prater the Count and his friends
amuse themselves at a shooting gallery where the Count wins a pair of
dolls—an officer and a young girl. Next stop is the Merry-Go-Round,
where the Count first sees Agnes, the young ticket-taker and organ-
grinding accompanist.[14] To better his chances—all such girls have been
warned about the attentions of officers—the Count passes himself off as
Franz Meier, a necktie salesman. Agnes is fascinated, and the Count is

more than usually interested. He leaves her the girl doll as a souvenir, then moves on to the next booth, a Punch and Judy show manned by Agnes's father, Sylvester. Both concessions belong to a brute named Huber who has designs of his own on Agnes and is seething with jealousy. He grabs the doll and smashes it to bits.

Later that night we learn that Agnes already has an admirer, Bartholomew, the hunchbacked barker at Mrs. Rossreiter's Wundershow, where a human torso and an orangutan named Boniface are the chief attractions. Bartholomew is addicted to lotteries in the hope of winning enough money to win Agnes's affections. While Agnes and her family at the Prater break bread for a humble meal, the Count and his friends are having a binge of their own. The scene is introduced with a close-up of a champagne bottle from which the camera "tracks back" to reveal the party, one of many references to camera movement in this 1922 script. Von Stroheim cuts between Agnes repairing her doll with wheat paste and the tipsy Count slicing up his doll with a fruit knife so that all the sawdust can run out.

The next day Agnes's invalid mother undergoes a traumatic death scene, calling her family to her side. But Huber refuses to let the girl leave her post at the grind organ, and crushes her foot as she weeps, snarling, "Smile, damn you, smile." The script indicates Agnes and her tears to be shot through a veil, recalling similar textured effects in *The Devil's Pass Key* and *Foolish Wives*. Huber forces her father to leave the death bed and return to the Punch and Judy show, which he carries on, Pagliacci-style, until a sudden shower scatters the crowd. Von Stroheim intercuts the scene of the mother's death with another of the Count's parties, where a naked girl emerges from an oversized punchbowl.

A few days later, while the Count is lounging around his apartments reading Arthur Schnitzler's "Reigen," the sight of the little doll reminds him of Agnes and he returns to the Merry-Go-Round to find her. Huber tells him she has been fired for being a tramp, but in fact she and her friends are away at her mother's funeral. When Agnes returns to the deserted Merry-Go-Round, Huber, furious over the Count's visit, attempts to rape her. Agnes's father hears her cries and breaks into the locked concession, slashing through the canvas flap with his pocket knife. After a terrible fight Sylvester is hauled away in a police wagon. Next day Agnes and Bartholomew go to St. Stephen's to pray for her father's release, and on leaving they see the Count emerging from Mandelbaum and Rosenstein's haberdashery. She assumes this is where he works and he plays along. On hearing her story he instantly hatches a plan, and claims that he knows someone who can help free her father. Leaving Bartholomew stranded on the sidewalk, the Count takes her to Mme. Elvira's house of assignation, mounting an elaborate charade to impress Agnes with his concern. Elvira disappears, ostensibly to make arrangements for the release, but actually to sit in the next room, occasionally looking up from her copy of "Dr. Freud's Psycho Analysis" to peek through the keyhole.

As soon as they are alone the Count begins to romance Agnes with sweet talk and violins, when suddenly, "the bare male animal in all its ugliness" emerges and he drags the struggling girl off to a couch. "You are just like Huber and the rest of them . . ." she screams. But the Count's higher nature stops the assault and he apologizes, making up to her later as he drops her near her home. As the Count drives away Agnes buys a sausage from a street peddler and is shocked to discover pictures of the Count and his fiancée in the newspaper used to wrap the wieners. The resemblance must be a coincidence, she thinks.

At Gisella's birthday party the Komtesse breaks off their engagement as they waltz across the dance floor. She has no interest in an arranged marriage, and anyway, didn't she see the Count outside the cathedral the other day, "flirting with democracy?" In a lengthy dance medley which ends to the strains of the "Merry Widow Waltz," she announces herself a truly modern woman and offers a toast "to love." The Count is surprised, but also a little relieved. That night Gisella runs off with her groom.

The following morning the Count arrives at the Prater with Sylvester, whom he has had released from jail. The Count is still claiming to be a necktie salesman, and laughs when shown the grease-stained newspaper clipping. That night he and Agnes play a romantic love scene in the gardens of the Prater as the abandoned Bartholomew cries himself to sleep.

In the morning Agnes visits the cathedral again, to confess her seduction. As the priest grants her absolution an old sacristan is busy blotting up melted candle wax with a flat iron. At the end both soul and carpet are again immaculate.

Sylvester is now doing a clown act for Mrs. Rossreiter's Wundershow, and Huber takes his revenge by sabotaging a heavy sign which falls and smashes the old man to the ground. An ambulance rushes him to the hospital, which is just that day being inspected by the Emperor—and the Count. Von Stroheim intercuts here a scene of the assassination at

Sarajevo. At the hospital Agnes is shocked to see the Count, who is unable to acknowledge her. The Emperor and his party leave a small gold coin. Sylvester dies.

The next day the Count visits Agnes but she refuses to see him. She feels that she has been lied to by a slick officer. She loves a necktie salesman. That night Huber is killed by the orangutan, avenging a thousand insults. Huber's wife is arrested for the murder. As a comet streaks through the heavens the old Emperor signs the declaration of war. The Count goes to the front. An elaborate montage conveys the war mainly in symbolic terms—shots of marching feet rather than massed batallions. The war drags on, the army is decimated, and Vienna starves. Agnes and Mrs. Huber work in an artificial limb factory. Bartholomew is a grave digger. The orangutan has been sold to a clinic.

At the war's end the Count's valet returns, with a mechanical arm. He has come to see Mrs. Huber, whom he had grown fond of while working as the Count's intermediary. He tells of the Count's painfully prolonged death in battle. Von Stroheim surveys Vienna at the close of the war. We see the Count's old friends, their fortunes gone, shoveling horse manure, or polishing the boots of Polish Jews. Gisella is a streetwalker. The Count's home is now owned by Gisella's onetime lover, the groom, who has grown wealthy as a profiteer. The Count arrives there—he had not been killed, it turns out, but only had one leg blown off. He collects a few of his things from the old janitor who had stored them while he was away. We see Vienna through his eyes, with everything changed. The Emperor's palace is now a storehouse. The old world is gone. He applies for a job with Mandelbaum and Rosenstein . . .

Back at the Prater fortune has been kind for a change. Bartholomew has finally won the lottery, and is sharing his winnings with everyone. The women have just been let go at the artificial limb factory—"everybody's got arms and legs by now." Bartholomew admits his love for Agnes when they hear that the Count is dead, and she agrees to marry him. That spring the Prater is being newly decorated. The Count's valet has married Mrs. Huber and the wedding party returns to the Merry-Go-Round. A senile old man in a wheelchair appears. He is Gisella's father, once the Secretary of War. His wife is the brothel madame, Elvira. He insists on riding the Merry-Go-Round, and the celebrating party starts it up for him. Elvira and Agnes recognize each other, bringing back memories of the Count. The midway has begun to show signs of life. Agnes grows nostalgic and hears the strains of a violin, as she had once heard it at Elvira's. She follows it and sees the Count, white-haired, nickel-plated steel braces shining beneath his trouser leg. She still loves him, but cannot marry him—she has promised herself to Bartholomew. But the hunchback has followed and sees them. "Camera on truck tracks up to Bartholomew, until his face fills the entire screen (like I did with Dale Fuller in *Foolish Wives*)." Agnes and the Count walk a little ways, then part. The smoke of a gun shot rises from behind a lilac bush; Bartholomew has killed himself. "Upon such sacrifice . . . the gods themselves throw incense." In the last shot the Merry-Go-Round is turning once more.

As in many of von Stroheim's original scenarios, one central theme or image is often fleshed out by plot structures borrowed from earlier dramas. That Schnitzler was on his mind is clear not only from the sight of the Count reading "Reigen," but from the circuit of liaisons among the classes with which the plot is filled. The notion of planting a fictional narrative within a larger historical framework was an old Griffith trick, and one that had served particularly well on *Orphans of the Storm*. Von Stroheim must have been aware of the attention drawn to Griffith's successful rejuvenation of the old theatrical warhorse "The Two Orphans," by throwing in the French Revolution. For his story von Stroheim took large elements of the "Old Heidelberg" plot and updated them the same way. The impossibility of marriage between no-bleman and commoner is solved by the great war which erupts across the center of this film. Fate was becoming increasingly important to him, and this war is pictured in no uncertain terms as a caprice of the gods: a symbolic insert shows just such a figure toying outrageously with life's carousel. It should be remembered that the John Emerson film of *Old Heidelberg,* on which von Stroheim worked as an actor and assistant director, also incorporates a great war to resolve its romantic dilemma. *Merry-Go-Round* would take that simple idea and develop it with special resonance.

If the script has one major problem it is von Stroheim's uneasy handling of the large new assortment of subsidiary plots and characters. We expect, for example, some sort of confrontation between Huber and the Count, but none occurs. Gisella seems a major character early on, but her fascinating story soon drops out of the script. Censorship considerations do not seem to have come into play there: the situation is dropped as abruptly in all the treatments. One reason for the great strength of von Stroheim's later film, *The Wedding March,* is that similar situations occurring there have been resolved, instead of being left awkwardly hanging. Another structural problem lies in the shift of focus away from the "von Stroheim character." The dynamic Karamzin held together an equally sprawling narrative in *Foolish Wives,* and there was never any question of where the center of that film lay. Here our interest keeps shifting from the Count back to Agnes, and neither is especially compelling. This problem, too, would be solved in *The Wedding March,* where additional motivation for the characters provides dramatic depth lacking here. But it is important to see that the tentative shift of interest from seducer to victim does mark a new phase in von Stroheim's career. In the earlier films this "von Stroheim character," officer or pseudo-aristocrat, was the most sharply defined, if only on the level of melodrama. Von Stroheim was then still interested in talking about himself through the figure of his movie-made persona, but now things begin to change. The Count is a real human being, whose experiences trigger a dramatic maturation. There is also more time to talk about Agnes, and we learn enough about her life away from the Count to empathize with her sorrows and joys. This had not been the case in earlier films, and in Agnes, von Stroheim creates his first dramatically successful female, an indication of a general shift in his interest. Later projects would accord more and more attention to the women, who gradually supplant the "von Stroheim character" in interest and importance (see *Queen Kelly,* for example).

As usual, it is clear that we are intended to see the good and bad characteristics of a single individual displayed in two related characters. Both Huber and the Count attempt to rape Agnes, and she recognizes that they are "all alike" as far as their carnal appetites are concerned. But Huber is simply a *bête humaine* (done in by another beast) while the Count has incorporated a veneer of civilization which enables him to reconsider his actions at the last moment. Bartholomew is a sexual outcast as far as von Stroheim is concerned, but the deformity is only emblematic of his shyness in sexual relations.[15] In a world where aggressive lady-killing is all, to be sexually disadvantaged is the lowest and most pathetic state. So in one way Bartholomew is the obverse of both Huber and the Count, sexual men of action. Von Stroheim associates him with the orangutan Boniface in order to express those emotions he keeps deep inside. While he thinks of consoling Agnes, it is Boniface who strokes her hair. While he seethes at Huber's outrageous behavior, it is the beast that murders him. Von Stroheim's fascination with the naturalism of *Greed* is well known, but that preoccupation was never so transparent as in the character of Bartholomew/Boniface.

One shouldn't get the impression, though, that *Merry-Go-Round* is nothing but a pastiche of von Stroheim's stock formulas overlaid on an early sketch for *The Wedding March.* For even in that great film von Stroheim shies away from dealing with the ultimate horror: postwar Vienna. To him this is a dead city, with gaiety and life drained out of it. No matter how strongly he underlines the decadence of the Hapsburgs, we are forced to sympathize with their world of "alt Wien" in the powerfully nostalgic homecoming episode. This sequence strongly recalls the Little Colonel's return to Piedmont in Griffith's *The Birth of a Nation,* and with similar intent. No matter what his true origins, von Stroheim completely identified himself with the *ancien régime,* and its fall was traumatic. He dwells on the injustice of prewar society, but in the end finds it preferable to what replaced it, "socialists and reds (who) have forgotten their dreams of social equality and are aping the aristocracy."[16] Von Stroheim could not go home again, but he could bring this dead world to life by recreating it on screen. This is the real reason for the attention to minute details and rituals which could never be picked up by human eyes alone. He had the Emperor Franz Josef's carriage sent to Hollywood for use in the film,[17] but not simply because he wanted to integrate a realistic prop. He wanted it because it was part of the true cross.

In rebuilding Vienna von Stroheim was not just outdoing De Mille or Griffith in details of realistic splendor. He was exorcising some of his deepest feelings, dredging up conflicts so intense that no longer could he keep them fully bottled up. Earlier von Stroheim films were sophisticated tracts, sharply cynical and devoid of compassion or sentiment. But in this script we feel the pain of great personal loss, an emotional shudder new to his work, and not very common anywhere on the screen prior to 1922. Whatever the truth of his days in Vienna, the ambiguities of *Merry-Go-Round* reveal a continuing internal struggle. He faced the fall of this dynasty with all the emotion of a true convert.

Von Stroheim would have liked to play the Count, the first of several Stroheimesque noblemen who defraud the public by claiming common birth.[18] The part was custom made, but Thalberg wouldn't allow it. Instead, von Stroheim had to find a substitute, and the best available was a small-time actor named Norman Kerry. Born Arnold Kaiser in Rochester, New York (von Stroheim must have appreciated this), Kerry had made films for the Fairbanks unit as far back as 1916 (*Manhattan Madness*), and it is possible von Stroheim knew him from those days.[19] After a stint in the army he had no difficulty finding work in relatively minor films, but *Merry-Go-Round* proved to be his big break. He signed a long-term contract with Universal and appeared as romantic lead in many of their silent classics, including *The Hunchback of Notre Dame* and *The Phantom of the Opera*. His career faded with the coming of sound. For Agnes, von Stroheim used a discovery of his

Von Stroheim with his alter ego, Norman Kerry, in the lobby of the Los
Angeles *Examiner* building.

own, Mary Philbin, second prize winner of a Chicago beauty contest he had judged in 1920 while returning from his contract-negotiating trip.[20] Philbin appeared in a walk-on in *Foolish Wives* as a crippled girl trying to cross a street on crutches,[21] but before von Stroheim could find a real part for her she had already appeared in a string of program pictures. The studio's most important star until the end of the silent period, she was often teamed with Norman Kerry, though her most remarkable performance was opposite Conrad Veidt in Paul Leni's *The Man Who Laughs*.[22]

The original synopsis shown to Thalberg in March indicated a few of the performers von Stroheim had in mind, notably Mary Philbin and stock company members Maude George (Elvira), Cesare Gravina (Sylvester), and Dale Fuller (Mrs. Huber). Von Stroheim's original choice for Gisella was Gertrude Astor, a tall blonde noted for her vamp routines, and today remembered best from such films as *The Cat and the Canary* and Harry Langdon's *The Strong Man*. But just before shooting von Stroheim replaced her with Dorothy Wallace, a James Montgomery Flagg model with only one previous film to her credit.[23] Although her brief appearance in the film as released is entirely credible, this was her last screen role.

The von Stroheim production unit was carried over directly from *Foolish Wives:* Eddie Sowders and Louis Germonprez served as his personal assistants, and art director Richard Day translated von Stroheim's ideas into practical terms. The Prater would be the main attraction here, but there were still palace interiors to design and outside locations to pin down. Standing sets at the Goldwyn studio would be used for palace exteriors and some street scenes, while the lobby of the *Los Angeles Examiner* building doubled as the foyer of the Count's apartments.[24] Ben Reynolds was replaced behind the camera by Charles Kaufman, but William Daniels remained on second camera. Von Stroheim's technical advisers, Albert Conti and Ned Lambert, would be of even greater importance here, the former also being assigned a role as one of the Count's fellow officers.

There was another member of the team not selected by Stroheim, but still very much a part of the proceedings. Thalberg sent down a "unit production manager" named James Winnard Hum, and gave him full authority over all expenses and details of physical production. From the moment Hum appeared on the set von Stroheim identified him as the enemy. Von Stroheim's style of directing called for a free use of the script and considerable improvisation in terms of "added scenes."[25] Occasionally he would decide at the last minute that certain props were crucial, and would hold up all work until they could be located. It was the production manager's job to lean on von Stroheim in these moments, and von Stroheim seems to have agreed to this state of affairs when Thalberg approved the production. But von Stroheim either never took this seriously, or ignored the reasons for the manager's presence. As soon as Hum began complaining about von Stroheim's "stalling," the director flew into a rage. Not only did he refuse to cooperate, but he counter-attacked by threatening to have Thalberg, Hum, and the studio's entire technical staff fired. While this might seem just another grandstand gesture on von Stroheim's part, it was in fact a serious threat he fully intended to carry out. In his four years at Universal, von Stroheim had seen production chiefs come and go. Laemmle would either assign an incompetent relative, or undercut the authority of any serious manager by sending conflicting orders from the New York office. Just prior to Thalberg's arrival, for example, the performance of one studio manager was so scandalous that legal action was later taken against him by Universal. The appointment of Thalberg was seen by von Stroheim as another Laemmle caprice, possibly only a stopgap measure until a more experienced hand could be found. When Thalberg began to assert authority over von Stroheim—and through an intermediary, at that—von Stroheim exploded. He had no intention of being dictated to by an upstart and was fully prepared to take his case directly to Laemmle. But when *Merry-Go-Round* went into production on August 25, 1922, Carl Laemmle was in Europe. His four-month stay was due to end by September 28, and he could be expected back at the studio around October 4. Word from Laemmle would settle any argument, but until he returned von Stroheim was prepared to show no quarter in the battle with Thalberg.

Hum left a diary account of the *Merry-Go-Round* shooting which recorded these outbursts in some detail, and which is our only first-hand account of the production. From these notes it is clear that while von Stroheim was the studio's main headache, his behavior was certainly not the only problem, and was in any case often well justified. "Kerry sober" is one recurring comment which implies problems well outside von Stroheim's control, for example. The scenic department is shown as being consistently late in completing the elaborate settings called for, and the accuracy of their work never seemed to please von Stroheim's trained eye. When he saw that the grass on a bridle path was not the proper shade of green (this was a black-and-white film, of course) he stormed around the set, cursing technical director Archie Hall as a "son of a bitch" and threatening to send for Thalberg to bawl him out. "Do you honestly think I am going to shoot it?" he demanded of Hum when he saw the stables, newly constructed but not dressed to von Stroheim's satisfaction. The entry for September 8 is typical:

> Took von and Germonprez aside at 2:30 A.M.—told them they were stalling on café set and that stable had to be shot that night, also to ask Thalberg if they wanted to know who was boss and if they wanted a showdown they would get it. (Von had mentioned lawsuits and showdown several times prior to this) Told him I had been standing around for a week or so and that probably he imagined I was a G.D. fool, but from now on I was going to crack the whip. Von raved, said that neither Thalberg nor me could bluff him—told him I was not bluffing—just telling him—he said to tell Thalberg to kiss his prat (sic) and why in hell didn't Thalberg come down and tell him things. Ran around like a crazy man. Told him I was going home and did. His gang are with him heart and soul—so many chances to put things over—they are all working for Von. Sowders especially sneers at everyone. Sullivan trying to do what is right. King wont do anything until he sees Von.[26] Cameramen nice fellows but do not know about them. Electricians only efficient gang here. He finished the stables—guess he dont want to have a showdown or get fired, the last night he said he didnt give a shit about getting fired or anybody. When this boy gets going he is good![27]

That morning's 2:30 a.m. conference was not unusual. Von Stroheim loved to shoot at night and would do so whenever he could get away with it. But lighting his lavish sets was a tremendous drain on the studio's electrical plant,[28] and infuriating blackouts were common. The worst of these happened on October 3, when two other companies were also shooting and one of the studio's generators burned out.

In addition to delays with the sets, the costume problem was also critical. Western Costuming Co. was creating these to von Stroheim's specifications, under the direct supervision of Albert Conti, an ex-Austrian army captain. Kevin Brownlow relates how Western's Ned Lambert collected hundreds of richly detailed imperial uniforms in the dark days right after the war, picking them up for pennies from impoverished officers and aristocrats.[29] But time after time uniforms would be incorrectly detailed or simply not available when needed. Von Stroheim blamed Hum—he was building up a catalogue of grievances to buttress his case with Laemmle—but Hum had suspicions of a conspiracy between von Stroheim and Lambert. According to this theory, whenever von Stroheim did not feel in the proper mood to film a scene called for in the shooting schedule, it was discovered that Western Costuming had delayed the required uniforms. Hum believed that these delays were artificially created for von Stroheim's benefit. Whether this was simple paranoia or not is debatable, for von Stroheim, Lambert and Conti were close friends who shared an "us-vs.-them" mentality regarding Universal.

Hum's worries were compounded by the general air of disrespect for studio authorities engendered by von Stroheim and his group through their constant roasting of the studio hierarchy. At lunchtime von Stroheim would offer a toast "To Mr. Hum, who is to blame for everything." Only Laemmle seemed safe from the continual scorn of the von Stroheim unit, something Hum recorded with mixed feelings. The presentation of each new set would be met by a stream of threats and curses. When Hum dragged himself off the set at 1:00 a.m. for a few hours' sleep, von Stroheim would announce in a loud voice, "Now that the stool pigeons have gone home we will go to work." Normally Valerie would have been on the set each day to calm von Stroheim's rages, but she was pregnant with their son Josef Erich (born September 18) and missed all the excitement. Had she been on the set the outcome might have been different.

The air of confusion, accusation, and delay was constantly punctuated by threats of lawsuits and firings. Von Stroheim kept promising wholesale retribution on Laemmle's return. Under the circumstances, it is amazing how much progress was actually made. Shooting began in sequence, with the opening scenes of the Count's morning ritual and Gisella's scenes with her groom. Palace and street exteriors for these scenes were done on the Goldwyn lot where suitable standing sets were available (Hum was puzzled to learn that von Stroheim had been secretly conferring with Goldwyn executives there on September 14). Back at Universal City the next two weeks were spent on scenes at Elvira's, including the Count's attempted seduction of Agnes and an orgy scene which cameraman William Daniels remembered for years to come. "He had all the extras playing Austrian officers *really* drunk; he served real champagne by the bucketful and whiskey as well; all the extras got loaded. A girl stepped naked out of a punch bowl . . . stuff like that. I think it was during a shot where I irised in on her that von Stroheim passed out cold!"[30]

It was October before they could finally begin lining up long-shots for the Prater sequences. Laemmle was now back in New York, with no immediate plans to visit the coast, but he had already made his decision on *Merry-Go-Round*. On October 3 von Stroheim was finally ready to shoot in the Prater when the roof began to cave in. He insisted that the long shot be held up until the same orangutan to be used in

Philbin and Kerry on the ornate Prater set at Universal City. Posters advertise Oscar Strauss's *A Waltz Dream*.

later sequences was in place on the set. The studio hadn't counted on this, so there was no shooting that morning while Hum tried to find an animal satisfactory to von Stroheim.[31] After lunch von Stroheim decided that the orangutan really wasn't necessary and prepared to go ahead with the shot when a streetcar ran off its track in the middle of the Prater. "Mr. Hum, you will please note that the streetcar is off the track and now I have to wait till the sons a bitches put it back." As work prepared to go on into the night the entire studio electrical system broke down. Novelist Georges Lewys was visiting the set that night: "There was nothing to see most of the time," she remembered. "A lot of foul actions on the part of the employees of Universal, a lot of double-dealing, a lot of crookedness, a lot of back-biting among the personnel, a lot of fighting around and scrapping, a lot of extras running around the lot without anything to do because the lights were out, a lot of inefficiency and incompetence, and I was thoroughly disgusted."[32]

It was 7:30 p.m. the next night before the set was again properly dressed and the cast assembled. Von Stroheim cursed the electricians as

SOBs for the previous night's blackout, so the power went off again, though only briefly. On October 5 von Stroheim returned to Elvira's apartment for retakes before the set was struck. Kerry arrived drunk and spoiled the shooting. "Von is not fighting me as much now but is lying to me about next day's work I know," Hum wrote. There was more night work scheduled for October 6, but Thalberg cancelled the call. At 5:00 p.m. he informed Hum of his final decision to fire von Stroheim and replace him with another director, Rupert Julian. Von Stroheim arrived on the set at eight and together with Louis Germon-prez was called directly to Thalberg's office. Studio counsel Edwin Loeb had composed a two-page letter over Thalberg's signature, informing von Stroheim of the reasons for his dismissal. The administration had prepared its own ammunition.

Von Stroheim's contract, as we have seen, called for the production of two features per year, but only one film, *Foolish Wives,* had actually been completed in the previous 29 months.

> The fact that more productions have not been completed [the letter claimed] is due largely to your totally inexcusable and repeated acts of insubordination, your extravagant ideas which you have been unwilling to sacrifice in the slightest particular, repeated and unnecessary delays occasioned by your attitude in arguing against practically every instruction that has been given to you in good faith, and by your apparent idea that you are greater and more powerful than the organization that employs you. . . . In spite of the fact that you have occupied a position of trust, dignity and confidence on the lot, you have time and time again demonstrated your disloyalty to our company, encouraged and fostered discontent, distrust and disrespect for us in the minds of your fellow employees, and have attempted to create an organization loyal to yourself, rather than the company you were employed to serve. Among other difficulties with which we have had to contend, has been your flagrant disregard of the principles of censorship and your repeated and insistent attempts to include in the scenes photographed by you, situations and incidents so reprehensible that they could not by any reasonable possibility be expected to meet with the approval of the Board of Censorship. . . .[33]

Although unstated, their main weapon here involved scenes in the Count's dressing room where Kerry disrobes and steps into his bath. Von Stroheim had filmed this action in one uninterrupted take, intending to cut away from any footage actually showing Kerry in the nude. But Universal wasn't interested in explanations and decided to make a point of the scene.[34] Hollywood legend pictures a twenty-year-old Thalberg bravely standing up to his uncontrollable employee, an image which may be true to the spirit of the event. But Hum reports simply, "Loeb fired him."

There were no hysterics. Von Strohcim walked quickly back to the set and informed his people, then left the studio. Thalberg, Loeb, Hum, and Julius Bernheim (practically the entire top echelon of the studio) made their own announcement to the company after von Stroheim had left. Thalberg explained his decision, introduced Rupert Julian, and set a new call for the next evening. News of this firing shot through the studios like wildfire. Von Stroheim disappeared from Hollywood and raced to New York. He confronted Laemmle with his arguments but the old magic was gone. Now it was Thalberg who was irreplaceable.

Von Stroheim had been shooting for six weeks, but how much of the picture had he actually completed? In sworn depositions taken in 1927, Germonprez, Hum, and von Stroheim all agreed that one-third of the script had been shot.[35] Thalberg estimated only 25 percent. In a letter to the *New York Times,* Julian claimed that von Stroheim had shot 271 scenes, which would be closer to Thalberg's figure.[36]

Not only was the studio upset about von Stroheim's costly "stalling," but they felt that the script needed further cutting to bring it in at a reasonable cost and within the censor guidelines. Rupert Julian was brought in to execute these orders. How Thalberg came up with Julian is uncertain. Perhaps he remembered that during the war Julian had been von Stroheim's chief rival as an impersonator of the Hun, directing and starring in Universal's highly successful *The Kaiser—Beast of Berlin* (1918). But the only thing he had directed lately was a cheap little western called *The Girl Who Ran Wild.* It is likely that none of the better known directors on the lot wanted anything to do with von Stroheim's dismissal. Thalberg was establishing a dangerous precedent in asserting the primacy of the studio over any director. Prior to this, men like Griffith and Ingram were considered a class apart, directors whose judgment and experience far exceeded that of any studio executive. No mere businessman would dare tell one of them how to direct pictures. But Thalberg was no simple bureaucrat. He had a fully developed grasp of all the elements of production, and a belief in principles of business management which necessarily reduced all directors to employees. In dismissing von Stroheim he was not acting out of desperation, but implementing a plan which would centralize power in the hands of a studio's production chief. In fact he was expanding on the system long established at the Thomas Ince studios, where drone directors labored on assigned productions like so much piecework. But the

top directors never worked for Ince, recognizing his system for the as-
sembly line it was. Instead they aligned themselves with organizations
which promised a relatively free hand in exchange for the (hopefully)
lucrative fruits of their labors. Thalberg was moving to eliminate that
part of the system once and for all. Director Lewis Milestone remembered the day he heard of von Stroheim's firing as a turning point in
Hollywood history:

> . . . the end of the reign of the director, the mighty oak. The storm
> grew fiercer . . . and when the storm subsided there was no D. W.
> Griffith, no [James] Cruze, no [Rex] Ingram, no [Marshall] Neilan.
> These men knew only one way of working—the way of the director;
> select the story, have a hand in the writing of the story, cast it, cut it,
> etc. Deprived of that method they couldn't function. They were forced
> to go and they went.[37]

Such considerations, if they arose at all, were academic to Rupert
Julian, who needed a chance to re-establish his directorial credentials
and was glad of the opportunity. A stock actor who had toured the
British empire in the days before the war, Julian was a native of New
Zealand and onetime husband of director Elsie Jane Wilson. He had
Merry-Go-Round back into production the day after von Stroheim left,
continuing as best he could with the assembled cast, crew, and settings.
Von Stroheim had wanted Wallace Beery for the part of Huber, and he
was in fact announced for the role when the film first went into production. Legend has it that Beery "walked off the set when von Stroheim was fired,"[38] but there is no evidence that von Stroheim ever shot
any scenes with this actor. On the contrary, a cryptic note in Hum's
diary for 26 September reads "Berry [*sic*] is out as he wont work with
him." *Moving Picture Weekly* reported on 11 November that George
Siegmann would play the Huber role, with Beery moving on to the lead
in *Bavu,* one of the studio's plum dramatic assignments.[39] It is unlikely
that Universal would have so rewarded Beery if he had sided with
von Stroheim in the *Merry-Go-Round* affair. Although Julian admitted
to facing "varying degrees of antagonism"[40] from the company, it is remarkable how few of von Stroheim's people went with him. Eddie
Sowders and Louis Germonprez were under personal contract to von
Stroheim and did not stay on, but the entire acting company remained,
including such old cronies as Albert Conti.

After playing by ear for a few weeks Julian called in Harvey Gates,
an old-time scenario writer, to work out plans for a rewrite of the
von Stroheim script. Just how much of the final film was von Stroheim's (in concept if not execution) has long been debated, and Julian

realized quite early on that it was in his interest to claim as much as possible for himself. In an unusually defensive letter to the *New York Times* following the opening of the film, Julian outlined the extent of his contribution to the project:

> Following several weeks work on the production, I called in Harvey Gates to collaborate with me on the story I had in mind. And the love story of *Merry-Go-Round* as it was presented is absolutely original. In the production, as it stands, the entire footage, with the exception of approximately 600 feet, was directed by me. The introduction of Norman Kerry, Dorothy Wallace and Sidney Bracey, the groom, was not part of my work. One scene of Kerry in a carriage and also that of the banquet sequence and that of the elopement of the Countess and the groom are not mine.[41]
>
> All the scenes carrying the theme of the story were directed by me, and also all the scenes in which crowds were employed. The retreat of the Austrian army sequence was "shot" in forty-five minutes through the use of eight cameras.
>
> I finished the production on January 8. The cost sheet stood at $220,000 when I took the picture over. I spent $170,000 in making all the rest of the production as it was shown on the screen . . . I had no part in any quarrel or controversy between Universal and Mr. von Stroheim. I have had no thought of raising any question concerning the situation in which I was placed, except that I have discovered that through a misunderstanding some of the New York newspapers have credited von Stroheim with making important sequences in this production, when these sequences actually were originated and directed by myself.[42]

Anyone who compares the finished film with von Stroheim's script can see instantly that Julian is lying when he claims to have originated the love story plot. In fact, the Julian film—for so it was advertised, a Julian production with a Harvey Gates script—was a simple revision of von Stroheim's script. All of von Stroheim's characters were retained, and few significant plot changes were introduced. In Julian's version the Emperor orders the Count and Countess to marry against their will. Sylvester does not die in the hospital (from a flower pot wielded by Huber) but recognizes the Count and his new bride when they visit, calling him a liar and a cheat. These changes are not out of keeping with von Stroheim's style, and actually prefigure similar episodes in *The Merry Widow* and *The Wedding March*. The Count and Sylvester do have a confrontation during the war, but the old man dies before anything comes of it. After the war the Count returns with a little gray hair, but with all his limbs intact. There is no dwelling on the horrors of the war or the wreck of Vienna and the postwar world. The Count announces he is free to marry as his wife has conveniently died. Agnes says she has promised to marry Bartholomew, but the hunchback self-lessly gives her up to the Count.

What is really lacking is the sense of loss von Stroheim had built into his script, and the authority of performance one comes to expect from his films. In his letter to the *Times* Julian seems to have honestly indicated the few von Stroheim-directed scenes remaining in the picture, as a study of Hum's diary makes clear. In addition, we know that von Stroheim had directed most, perhaps all of the scene at Elvira's between Agnes and the Count, but Julian claims this as his own. If so, he reshot this material for his own purposes, and on screen it does appear softer, less threatening than the episode in von Stroheim's script. There is no question that the staging of such scenes as the attempted rape at the carousel was Julian's doing, but a look at the script shows him to be following von Stroheim's continuity like a blueprint. When the original script calls for a camera movement, Julian moves the camera. He laundered the script, going a bit heavy on the starch, perhaps, but stayed remarkably close to von Stroheim's original ideas. Julian may have been an opportunist, but he was no fool.

On July 1, 1923, the film opened at New York's Rivoli Theatre to a strongly partisan reception. Everyone was aware of von Stroheim's connection with the project, despite the fact that Universal had removed his name from all credits. Von Stroheim's hard core of supporters, seizing on the fact of his dismissal, tore the picture apart. "It's greatest lack is imagination. All that was put into it seems to have settled in the first reel,"[43] wrote Harriette Underhill. She felt that the film was a good advertisement for von Stroheim insofar as he had *not* directed it. Others weren't so sure. Robert E. Sherwood, who had earlier dismissed von Stroheim as wasteful and even stupid, felt the completed film "lacked the incoherence, the extravagant exaggeration, the total disregard of form, which had marred [von Stroheim's earlier work]."[44] Unlike *Foolish Wives,* the film had few avowed enemies. When *The Film Daily* tabulated critic's "ten best" lists from around the country James Cruze's *The Covered Wagon* emerged as the year's runaway success, with 53 votes. But *Merry-Go-Round* was in second place (26 votes), edging out both *Robin Hood* and *The Hunchback of Notre Dame.*[45] Studio records show the picture returned a profit of $336,181,[46] very substantial for those days, and nearly enough to make up the losses on *Foolish Wives.* Today the film is known mainly from copies of 16mm copies originally distributed by the Show-At-Home Movie Library, although 35mm material does exist in the Cinémathèque Française (and, according to at least one source, in Mary Philbin's private collection). The print department junk file indicates that Universal destroyed the ten reels of negative, along with three cans of "added footage," on December 1, 1949.

There is one baroque footnote to this sorry tale which deserves mention, if only to illustrate von Stroheim's hapless luck in contractual and commercial affairs. While casting the production von Stroheim had been contacted by one Gladys Lewis, who was promoting a candidate for the role of Franz Josef. Under the name Georges Lewys she was the author of several "privately printed and unexpurgated" novels that had come to the attention of federal postal authorities. Von Stroheim had no use for her client, but did invite her to drop in on the set next time she was in Los Angeles. She arrived on the evening of October 3 just as all hell was breaking loose, and left for von Stroheim a copy of her novel, *The Charmed American*. A week or two after being fired by Universal, and realizing that the studio fully intended to complete the picture without him, he ran into Georges and her mother on the corner of Hollywood and Cahuenga. He remembered the "virile style"[47] of *The Charmed American* and suggested they might work together to prepare a novelization of his script. For the next several weeks von Stroheim regaled her with the plot of *Merry-Go-Round,* embroidering the scenario with all the good parts no censor would ever have allowed. He gave her access to all his research notes and even brought along Albert Conti and Count Mario Caracciolo.[48] There was an informal agreement that she should submit three sample chapters and they would proceed from there. When von Stroheim received the three chapters he rejected them as "putrid" and ordered her to stop work on the project. But Ms. Lewis was not so easily discouraged, and on September 25, 1923, copyrighted in her name a novel called *Merry-Go-Round.* Lewis was not without a sense of humor, and the book is subtitled "from the Austrian," and dedicated "to my friend, Erich von Stroheim, who was the inspiration of this work." It is a transparent novelization of von Stroheim's script, and the few incidents which do not appear in any of his treatments are classic von Stroheim stories which he apparently elaborated for her during their weeks together. The book's mild pornography permits the detailing of obsessions forbidden on film, and suggest what all von Stroheim's films might have looked like had they been produced in less censorious times. For example, a long subplot involving the degradation of Gisella through a sadomasochistic relationship with her groom is here lovingly described. The book is also useful for explaining in detail the significance of various Viennese landmarks, ceremonial dates, and court rituals—like the *Fusswashung*—which occur so often in von Stroheim's imperial films.[49]

The book was offered on private subscription, but only 91 copies had been distributed before von Stroheim stopped the sale with an injunction. Dragged into court by a furious von Stroheim, Lewis decided on an especially dirty defense. In a hair-raising letter to Will Hays, president of the Motion Picture Producers and Distributors of America, she threatened to hold the entire industry hostage to a catalogue of scandals:

> Mr. von Stroheim's ideas of life and daily conduct, past and present (at that time) are not such as would benefit the industry of motion pictures if I were called on to testify as to the method of our collaboration. The method actually consisted in Mr. von Stroheim telling me incidents of his life, boastful, nauseating events and incidents in the lives of every motion picture director and many stars of his profession, and in revealing his relations with these stars. He has a warped and immoral viewpoint of life and marital responsibility, and I was forced to listen to these scandalous details, which I merely tolerated in order to conclude my business with him. He revealed himself as utterly filthy-minded, lewd, vulgar, depraved, boastful of his irregular life and his vicious reputation, which he represents so well on the screen. I was amazed and dumbfounded. His "orgies" with certain picture players were simply vile as he recited them, and it shows what utter brazenness and folly is in the man's Teutonic make-up that he is willing to antagonize me by his persecution after he has made me and my family confidants of his illicit amours and debaucheries in the Hollywood film colony . . . I will not take pains to hide any part of this filthy man's life as he recited it, nor will I hesitate to repeat his words, nor can I help divulging certain names which will make "excellent copy," I fear, for the newspapers, and give Mr. von Stroheim all the "publicity" he confesses he is looking for to exploit and promulgate his GREED.[50]

Wild claims like this ran far beyond a pornographer's hypocrisy. Von Stroheim said that Lewis was "unbalanced mentally" and was ready to expose her as a "homosexualist," but was sensibly terrified at the possible impact of her wild tales. Lewis in fact had several well-placed friends and would have no difficulty getting a hearing. Von Stroheim denied ever telling her such stories, but realized that if the papers got hold of them his entire career would be in jeopardy. Morality clauses were already appearing in Hollywood contracts in the wake of the Fatty Arbuckle affair. To keep her quiet he ceded his literary rights to *Merry-Go-Round* to her on April 15, 1925. Immediately Lewis sued Universal for an accounting of the profits of the film, claiming that in firing von Stroheim they had broken their contract with him and therefore had no legal right to the material in his screenplay.[51] At the time

Universal was the defendant in a landmark copyright infringement suit involving Anne Nichols's play *Abie's Irish Rose*. As this case was slowly wending its way to the United States Supreme Court they paid Lewis $750 to discontinue her suit. But in recognizing her claim they fell into another trap. In 1930 the studio planned a remake of *Merry-Go-Round* as a talking film. Von Stroheim had been paid $5000 for his script in 1922, but talkies were considered a new medium and all literary contracts had to be renegotiated. This time the rights would cost $20,000, half to Erich von Stroheim, half to his "collaborator," Georges Lewys. After paying for the privilege, the studio ultimately shelved the whole project.

Greed

Von Stroheim was not unemployed for long. In the three years since *Blind Husbands* there had been many attempts to lure him from Universal, and Carl Laemmle appeared regularly in the trades to denounce the attempted raids. But von Stroheim felt comfortable with Laemmle, and stayed with him until thrown off the lot by Irving Thalberg. In fact, this attitude may have caused him to badly misjudge real conditions at Universal, particularly the true extent of Laemmle's feelings for him, and the growing power and importance of Thalberg.

With conditions growing more difficult each week during the shooting of *Merry-Go-Round,* von Stroheim apparently began to listen more closely to outside offers. His meeting with Goldwyn executives on September 14 was a puzzle to J. Winnard Hum, but in retrospect seems an important clue to his intentions. There was no struggle when Thalberg fired him on October 6, only a perfunctory appeal to Laemmle in New York. On November 20 he was under contract to the Goldwyn Company.

The choice of Goldwyn was characteristic of von Stroheim. A more cautious man might have realized that financial conditions there were so uncertain the very existence of the company was no sure thing. But von Stroheim wanted to believe the promises of creative freedom and artistic responsibility. With a generous share of the profits thrown in, he signed without giving corporate health a second thought.

Founded by Samuel Goldfish and Edgar and Archibald Selwyn in 1916, Goldwyn has always been one of the cinemas's most charming anagrams. So much so, that Goldfish had his name legally changed to Goldwyn two years later, appropriating the corporate title as his own.

Under his guidance the company floundered through an unprofitable series of "eminent authors" and famous Broadway celebrities, few of whom were able to adapt their style to the requirements of the screen. Less pretentious efforts featuring Lon Chaney and Will Rogers kept the studio afloat, while Goldwyn spent thousands on high-priced authors like Maurice Maeterlinck, whose scenario for *The Life of the Bee* proved unfilmable.[1] On March 10, 1922, the Goldwyn Company directors voted Samuel Goldwyn out of the presidency, eventually buying back his stock. Frank Godsol, an investor Goldwyn had brought into the company in 1919 was behind the move, and he installed Abe Lehr, one of Goldwyn's assistants, as production head. But the fortunes of the company continued to decline, and only seven films went before the cameras there in 1922, compared with 28 the year before. Godsol and Lehr had little aptitude for filmmaking, and apparently decided to hire a whole new production staff to manage this side of the business for them. For their part, they busied themselves in a complex negotiation for the screen rights to *Ben-Hur,* eventually agreeing to terms which virtually guaranteed disaster. Marshall Neilan, one of Hollywood's most eccentric talents, was signed to a long-term contract; Victor Seastrom was imported from Sweden; Maurice Tourneur, Tod Browning, and King Vidor were put under contract; June Mathis, the powerful scenario editor who had "discovered" Valentino was lured away from Paramount; and in a "last reckless gamble,"[2] Erich von Stroheim was hired to direct.

His contract was 26 pages long, and despite the assertions of some historians von Stroheim was still far from being given *carte blanche*. In many ways it was even more restrictive than his Universal contract, since budgetary ceilings were spelled out and penalties imposed for excess costs. But von Stroheim knew that there was no Thalberg in the Goldwyn company to breathe down his neck, and therefore no effective way of policing him during shooting. On the other hand, Godsol and Lehr knew they were signing Hollywood's most brilliant—and difficult— director, but they felt that somehow he could be kept in line. Unfortunately, they had little to base this on other than vague hopes and a belief in von Stroheim's promises. Today a studio in such condition would be sold off piecemeal, but Godsol and Lehr knew they were in the movie business and were willing to take risks like this if there was any slight chance of keeping the studio afloat.

Von Stroheim's contract was to be for one year, running from December 15, 1922,[3] and he would direct three films, the third of which he would star in. Each picture was to be between 4500 and 8500 feet

in length, and to cost no more than $175,000, unless Goldwyn agreed
to more. If production costs rose above this figure any excess would be
deducted from his share of the profits, which was to be 25 percent.
During production he would be paid an advance against profits of
$30,000 per picture, in ten weekly installments, with $1000 per week
extra for the film he would act in. Von Stroheim agreed to have a complete work print within 14 weeks of the start of each production, and
that "none of the said pictures shall be of a morbid, gruesome or
offensive character."

On the face of it, this contract was less advantageous than the one
he had signed with Universal in 1920. According to the escalator
clauses in that contract, von Stroheim would have been earning a
$90,000 annual salary in 1923, with an added $1000 per week while
acting. At Goldwyn the numbers would be the same, but only if he
succeeded in completing three features in one year, an unlikely prospect. Goldwyn did offer a share of the profits, but this pie-in-the-sky
has never been very convincing in Hollywood, and it made von Stroheim dependent on the Goldwyn sales force and accounting department.
The contract also put rigid limitations on the length of his films, their
budgets (both unrealistically low in light of previous von Stroheim
productions), and the amount of time he could spend shooting them.
"Excess costs" would come out of his own pocket, and von Stroheim
would suffer financially for any delay, whether he was responsible for
it or not. Godsol and Lehr knew they couldn't police von Stroheim
personally, so they built these negative inducements into his contract,
hoping that his own best interests would help keep him in line. They
had no better luck than Irving Thalberg.

Right from the beginning there were two projects targeted as von
Stroheim productions: the long cherished film of *McTeague,* and an
adaptation of the Leon-Stein-Lehar operetta, *The Merry Widow.* "His
first picture, it is said, will have a continental theme with a large cast,"
reported the *Film Daily* on November 28, but *The Merry Widow* was
soon pushed aside as von Stroheim threw himself into preparations for
McTeague.

Oddly enough, *McTeague* had already been filmed once before, as
Life's Whirlpool, a 1916 release starring Fania Marinoff and Holbrook
Blinn. Barry O'Neil directed the five-reel feature, which was viciously
attacked by critics of the time for its "repellant" realism and over-
abundance of closeups![4] The film was quickly forgotten, and Goldwyn
publicity was careful not to bring it up again; but while the public had a
short memory, industry people did not. When von Stroheim's film ap-

peared some of his supporters glibly dismissed this "primitive" version, but an investigation of surviving still photos and contemporary reviews indicates that he may very well have been influenced by it. The stark visual quality of O'Neil's film is disturbingly reminiscent of von Stroheim's approach, as is his insistence on the "coarseness" of the subject matter. Von Stroheim was already an assistant director when *Life's Whirlpool* appeared, and he would have been familiar with new releases as a matter of course. Later, while filming his own version in San Francisco, he criticized Blinn's performance, implying that *Life's Whirlpool* was still on his mind, but this seems his only recorded comment on the picture.[5] Until more evidence emerges the real connection between the two films remains a mystery.

Von Stroheim had been obsessed with Frank Norris's "story of San Francisco" for years, ever since first picking it up (he claimed) during his down-and-out days in New York. He had been announcing it periodically since 1920[6] but was never able to bring it off at Universal, despite the fact that they did at one time acquire the rights for him. Now he would take advantage of his new position at Goldwyn to put it on the screen with unheard of authenticity and idealism. "It has always been my determination to produce the story exactly as it was written," von Stroheim explained to film critic Edwin Schallert. "They have said I could not make an American story, and I want to prove that I can. Of course, it is foolish to say that *McTeague* is American any more than that *Nana* is French. They are international. You can, in fact, trace the inspiration of *McTeague* to *L'Assommoir* of Zola, and it appealed to me more than any other story written by an American, because it is so universal, and because, perhaps, basically the viewpoint and style are those of the European continental."[7] Schallert characterized von Stroheim's intentions in one line: "He is determined that it shall be a sinister and lasting triumph of sordid, though intense and magnificent, naturalism."[8]

The key word is naturalism. In aligning himself with Zola and Norris von Stroheim bypassed mere realism in pursuit of a more complex notion, a realism informed by psychological and sociological imperatives. The naturalists drew from Darwinian thought the notion of man's development from the beasts and created a literature grounded in "scientific" determinism. Although a descendant of the beasts, man had in his rationality and conscience certain civilizing qualities which enabled him to step away from his origins. He remained, however, a product of these origins, a rational, human beast within whom the higher forces of nature were constantly battling the lower. This interior struggle was matched by a larger struggle taking place in the crucible of society at large, a testing ground in which the weaker fell behind and only the fittest could survive. The class struggle which attended the industrial revolution was thus read in Darwinian terms as an economic law of the jungle. But man's apparent civility was only a mask, a thin veneer concealing the *bête humaine* within. Any strong disturbance in environmental conditions could rupture this shell, allowing the always restive primal elements to dominate. Often this shock would be provided by drink, lust, or sudden social or economic reversal. The novels von Stroheim refers to, Zola's *Nana* and *L'Assommoir,* and Norris's *McTeague,* are among the purest examples of this school. Heredity ordains our course in life. Environmental forces act to freeze the best attempts at upward mobility. The Enlightenment's concept of the will's freedom gradually sinks beneath the attack of biology and sociology, and man is left a pawn of the gods, a rudderless toy at the mercy of irresistible forces.

To chart this deterministic universe in which heredity and environment dictate man's fate, the naturalists resorted to a massive accumulation of "milieu detail." Their novels are filled with lengthy passages describing the things of life, exhaustive reports of objects and activities. To document these environments correctly, research notebooks were stuffed with observations taken from life. Journalism was a background for both Norris and Zola, and the reporter's eye is especially evident in *McTeague.* Norris found his inspiration in an actual crime, visited the scene of the murder, lived for a time at the Big Dipper mine where much of the action takes place, and accurately re-created these locales in his book. The locales in turn defined the characters. Such writing took advantage of the work of local colorists like Bret Harte and George Washington Cable, who detailed with considerable realism the course of life in isolated corners of 19th-century America. But the naturalists went beyond local color, using this detail as the structure on which to hang their grander designs.

While von Stroheim may never have bothered to analyze it in these terms, what attracted him to the naturalists was their preoccupation with fate, the influence of heredity, and the importance of a richly detailed environment. These are concerns evident in all of his own works, and he had been developing a parallel film style since his days with Griffith. Von Stroheim was excellent copy all during his career, and one of the most common angles in any story concerned his obsession with "realism." Often this took the form of veiled mockery and catalogues of bizarre and costly "touches." But it is important to realize that whatever the excesses of this approach, von Stroheim considered it a necessary element of his style. As Eisenstein required discrete shot units to form his montage dialectic, so von Stroheim needed to build up a *mise en scène* from mountains of real—not realistic—details. And what's more, he understood that audiences knew this and had come to expect it of him. "The audience must know that what von Stroheim produces is done with the utmost honesty and is just as reliable as the National Geographic Magazine or the Encyclopaedia Britannica," he said at the close of shooting. "Audiences know this, I believe. They think von Stroheim will stand up and fight for correctness of detail; that he is willing to suffer the consequences; that he is willing to go to damnation for his convictions. And he is. Because everything he puts before the eyes of an audience must be that thing itself—the real thing."[9]

In another director such obsessive fussing might be explained in more simple, Freudian terms. But to von Stroheim it was just one element in a master plan for realist cinema, art direction of "utmost honesty" which required camera style, acting, editing, and later even sound recording to match. Von Stroheim's tenacious efforts to cling to these principles constantly undermined his position in the marketplace, and within a decade pushed him outside that marketplace completely. As he had predicted, he suffered the consequences and went to damnation. The introductory title from Frank Norris tells the whole story. "I never truckled; I never took off the hat to Fashion and held it out for pennies. By God, I told them the truth. They liked it or they didn't like it. What had that to do with me? I told them the truth. I knew it for the truth then, and I know it for the truth now."[10] By this time, Frank Norris could speak for both of them.

Before starting for San Francisco to complete his script and set the production in motion, von Stroheim made some final casting decisions. Gibson Gowland would be McTeague, a decision he seems to have made as far back as 1918 when both were playing in *The Heart of Humanity*. Gowland was the hulking British actor he had used as Sepp in *Blind Husbands,* but that part seems to have done nothing for his career, and Gowland hadn't worked in Hollywood in over a year. Von Stroheim summoned him directly to San Francisco, with orders to let his hair and moustache grow out.[11] Gowland didn't require a screen test, but for the other principals von Stroheim shot reel after reel of elaborate tests, entire scenes from the film played against rudimentary sets constructed at the Goldwyn studio. Paul Ivano, a young French cameraman who had been shooting second camera for director Emmett

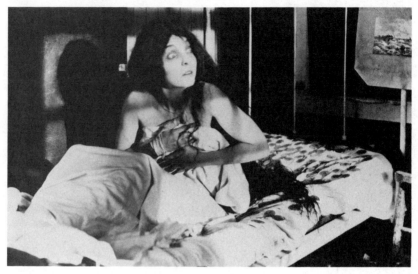

"Having an affair with an invisible person": Zasu Pitts.

Flynn, was called over to film tests of Zasu Pitts in the role of Mc-
Teague's wife, Trina. Von Stroheim had chosen as crucial a scene in
which Trina undresses, fondles a huge pile of gold coins, and climbs
into bed with them. "Stroheim wanted her to have an expression of
great satisfaction by handling the money, and she really didn't know
what he wanted her to express in the tests. And it took us take and
take and take before he got exactly the scene he wanted. And poor
Zasu said 'I don't know what he wants!' He wanted her to look as if
she was having an affair with an invisible person, you know . . ."[12]

How von Stroheim came to choose Zasu Pitts for the pivotal role in
his most important film has never been fully explained.[13] She had
already established herself as a dizzy comedienne, complete with
fluttering hand gestures, in a series of Christie comedy shorts. Her appearances in dramatic films were generally limited to comic relief, but
von Stroheim saw something here that others did not. "The average
person thinks she is funny looking," he once said. "I think she is beautiful, more beautiful than the famous beauties of the screen, for I have
seen in her eyes all the vital forces of the universe and I have seen in
her sensitive mouth all of the suppressions of humankind. I've seen her
lifted to the heights of great acting. Art must weep when Zasu Pitts
plays a comedy role. She should not be in comedy, for she is the
greatest of all tragediennes."[14] This unique assessment of Pitts's talents
was one of von Stroheim's most intense obsessions, and later won her

important roles in *The Wedding March* and *Walking Down Broadway*. But most directors and audiences were unable to see beyond the comic mask and failed to take advantage of what von Stroheim had discovered.[15] Where earlier he had used Dale Fuller to represent the "suppressions" of female sexuality, in the future he would turn to Zasu Pitts, an actress of far greater expressive potential.

For the part of McTeague's friend Marcus Schouler, von Stroheim decided on Jean Hersholt, an experienced supporting actor who had come to America in 1913 from Copenhagen. Despite almost a decade of film work, Hersholt had never found that special role which could establish him as a first-rank performer. He sensed that Marcus Schouler was just such a role and was delighted when von Stroheim signed him. But apparently this decision was reached only through seeing Hersholt on film. As Hersholt remembered later, when von Stroheim first laid eyes on him he was aghast.

> "Are *you* Jean Hersholt? You are not the type I want at all!" he exclaimed. "Your eyes are much too kind." Turning to Eddie Sowders he asked hopefully, "Is Mr. Hersholt actually signed for the part?" When informed that he was, von Stroheim refused to change his mind, and refused to listen to Hersholt's pleadings. "Shouler is a helper in a dog hospital. A greasy, smart-aleck type in a loud suit and derby hat, a cigar always between his lips. Your haircut is wrong, too. His neck is shaved, his hair is smarmed down. I am sorry, but maybe we can find you something else!"[16]

In fact, von Stroheim sounds so taken aback here that perhaps Hersholt's memory was playing tricks on him, for it seems unlikely that von Stroheim would have signed anyone under such circumstances. But Hersholt claims he returned the next day, after shaving off his moustache and submitting to a "Bowery haircut," dressed in a loud suit and smoking a cheap cigar. "I apologize, Mr. Hersholt," said von Stroheim. "You *are* Marcus Schouler."

Whether Hersholt got the details of this story right or not, von Stroheim's behavior is strikingly similar to his first encounter with Fay Wray, when she came to audition for *The Wedding March*. In both cases the director first refused out of hand to consider them for the part, then suddenly relented when the actor returned "in character." Von Stroheim was suspicious of actors who claimed to be able to "put on" a character, another trait inherited from Griffith. An affected "actress" like Mae Murray turned his stomach. But by successfully adopting the details of Marcus Schouler's costume and personality Hersholt earned von Stroheim's highest accolade: "You *are* Marcus Schouler!"

There exists an interesting piece of film showing von Stroheim directing Hersholt in tests for the role, shot not at the San Francisco location, but back on the Goldwyn lot. During the months immediately preceding the shooting of the film, director and author Rupert Hughes was filming a Hollywood-based melodrama called *Souls for Sale.* Part of the action involved the heroine's visit to various studios where famous directors were shown at work. Chaplin, Fred Niblo, King Vidor, and Marshall Neilan made appearances, and von Stroheim was glimpsed directing Hersholt in the role of Marcus Schouler. He demonstrates exactly how he wants the scene to be played, then sits down as the sideline musicians provide a mood-inducing accompaniment. Although we are led to believe that this is an actual behind-the-scenes look at von Stroheim's film, the studio settings, and the known production dates of the two films, reveal it as only a test.

As usual with von Stroheim, the rest of the cast came mainly from screen comedies. Chester Conklin had been a circus clown, and Sylvia Ashton a graduate of Keystone comedies. Frank Hayes was one of the original Keystone Kops. Dale Fuller had played for Mack Sennett, and Cesare Gravina was said to have had a background as "a rollicking clown of Italian classic comedy."[17] Von Stroheim felt such actors would have few dramatic mannerisms to unlearn, and would be more malleable vehicles for his ideas.

The director arrived in San Francisco by the first of the year and moved into the St. Francis Hotel, which would be the company's base of operations until July. He was returning in triumph to a city he had left under a cloud nine years earlier. A group of Norris's friends feted him at a downtown café, giving the production a proper sendoff, and von Stroheim made a spectacular appearance at the annual Quatr'z Arts Ball. One society reporter noted his "monocle, corseted waist line, immaculate evening clothes, swagger stick and clicking heels."[18] Dorothy Wallace, the Gisella of *Merry-Go-Round,* even made the front page of the *San Francisco Chronicle Society Supplement.*

Although he had been working out the details of the film in his head for years, there was still a need for a finished script before the massive production could get under way. When inspired by a story von Stroheim would throw himself into 18-hour sessions, and depend on someone like Louis Germonprez to take it all down. But he had left Germonprez behind and was traveling with Ernest Traxler, whom Goldwyn had supplied as a "business manager" for the picture—in today's terms more a unit production manager.

Thirty years later von Stroheim still had a sense of humor about this part at least.

He was a pretty nice fellow. He only ran away with some of the company's money afterward, but that didn't faze me—it wasn't my money. I told him that I would like to start today in the afternoon on the actual work and he said, "Well . . . where do you get a stenographer?" I said I just passed by the public stenographer's office downstairs and they got a beautiful blonde down there and that's the dame I want. He said all right. Two o'clock—buzz—I opened the door myself (I had an apartment) and there was a girl—Irish, red hair, blue eyes, with an undershot jaw like this—and glasses. Now I don't go for glasses on women—I don't go for women with glasses. I was stunned. I said, "What can I do for you?" She said, "Somebody asked—you want a secretary." I said, yes, come in. I tortured my brain. I said, "what can I do to make this girl so disgusted that she quits and I wouldn't have to say no?" So she sat down in the corner and got a pencil—all laid out next to each other—her pad—and I didn't know how to start. You know when you—a bell rings and says "now start." A big job, you know. Like an adaptation of a great work. Well, I started with this book in my hand . . . and I dictated fast—as fast as I could—but faster than I wanted to. And she kept up with me. And then I dictated about 15 minutes when she suddenly piped up and said, "I don't like that." I came to. I looked in the corner and there was this little dame and she did this (gesture) and she said, "I don't like it." This was something new, and that impressed me so much that I said "Why don't you like it?" and she gave me a very intelligent explanation. Now I said to myself, "Well, I guess I can take the blonde downstairs out some other time and I keep this one." She stayed with me eight years, and one night while I was dictating, oh, until two in the morning, in the same place, she started to cry suddenly. Gazing into space for a moment then the eyes filled and then she laid her head down on her arms and she sobbed. By this time I was more or less intimate with her and I said "what's the matter?" And she said, "Well, I'm homesick for my sweetheart—he's in Boise, Idaho, and he's working in the cigar store, a cigar counter, and I've got the money to let him come here." So I said, "What the hell, I don't want a crying secretary," so I said, "let him come." Then the son of a bitch—when this guy—this pimp was there—one day she was missing from the set. Time had passed and the story was finished and we went into production and one morning we started to work. No script girl. And she was to me by that time really important because she kept track of everything. Now I telephoned the hotel where she lived about her being late . . . and finally at two o'clock in the afternoon she came and cried, of course, and said, "I—excuse me—I got married." I said, "out you go—married—I let your sweetheart come—I paid for it—but to marry on my production—no.!" So, she was discharged at two, she came back at four, and she stayed for eight years.[19]

The woman was Eve Bessette, identifiable in many of the film's production stills by her thick, horn-rimmed glasses. She joined von Stroheim's stock company and was still working with him in 1932 when he wrote the last film he would direct, *Walking Down Broadway*.

In moments off from these extended scripting sessions, von Stroheim roamed the streets of San Francisco and Oakland searching for locations. While Norris had described actual buildings and neighborhoods, many of these had disappeared in the earthquake and fire of 1906, especially the entire area around Polk Street and Sutter. Cedric Gibbons, the head of Goldwyn's art department, had joined von Stroheim in San Francisco, and by late January, Richard Day had come up as well (he appears to have stayed with *Merry-Go-Round* until the completion of shooting).[20] They found a replacement at the corner of Hayes and Laguna and began aging the area to pre-prohibition standards.[21] At 35 Stockton Street, Anna Thorne was "registering faces" for extra parts, screening potential applicants in line with von Stroheim's theories of typage.[22] Harold Henderson, a young miner with considerable knowledge of the Big Dipper Mine area, was hired as technical consultant on the mining sequences, and supervised a second construction unit in Placer County. While von Stroheim completed his script and shot the San Francisco scenes, the crew at Placer reopened the actual Big Dipper Mine and reconstructed a turn-of-the-century mining camp.

Up to now the film had always been referred to in print as *McTeague*, although there was apparently never any intention of actually calling it that. On the Goldwyn Company records the working title was *Greedy Wives*, but no one seems to have taken that very seriously, either, and on February 20 official word came down on the film's new title: it would be called *Greed*.[23]

The budget of *Greed*, theoretically limited to $175,000, was officially doubled to $347,000 after the final estimates on von Stroheim's script were completed,[24] and on March 13 the first scenes went before the cameras in San Francisco. The extraordinary amount of work required to complete the script and get the film into production in only a few months finally began to show on von Stroheim, and within a few days of the start of shooting the director had collapsed, a victim of his own 20-hour work days. Valerie came up from Los Angeles to care for him (he had moved to the Fairmont), but illness and exhaustion would continue to cause delays in the schedule.[25]

It has often been said that the script which von Stroheim had prepared was a literal transcription of the Norris novel, "page by page, never missing a paragraph."[26] This view is part of the obsessive genius legend, and reduces von Stroheim's work on the screenplay to that of a compulsive child. Von Stroheim was quite aware of the difficulties in transferring any text from one medium to another, and was fully prepared to make whatever adaptations were necessary. In addition, he had ideas of his own which he was not about to submerge merely for the sake of Frank Norris. While he did feel an obligation to bring the spirit of the book to the screen, he chose to go about this in a reasonable fashion, and not in the intractable manner so often claimed.

In recent years *Greed* has been the focus of much publications activity. The script has been published, an album of stills has appeared, and at least one monograph on the director devotes most of its space to a prolonged comparison of novel, script, and film.[27] There is no need here to duplicate all of this work, but the manner in which von Stroheim altered Norris's story for the screen is worth attention. At a 1954 news conference von Stroheim admitted that "a little revamping, a little adding, a little taking off" was always needed to produce a successful adaptation.[28] In the case of *Greed* he had gone off by himself to weigh Norris's reaction to each alteration he planned in the text. He hoped to retain the essence of the work, but was not prepared to sacrifice the basic requirements of film style. For example, he felt that the average film audience could not be expected to react as sharply as the average reader, and "[has] to be taught from 'A' on so as to understand."[29] More concrete detail and explanation was necessarily required. "Frank Norris would have put it in if he had been sitting next to me trying to make a film," he replied when questioned on this point. But most importantly, von Stroheim felt that information had to be "planted" early on in order to allow the audience a full understanding of later events in the lives of the characters. This not only mandated a strictly linear development (no flashbacks) but required a full development of episodes only hinted at by Norris which might have a bearing on future behavior. As an example, von Stroheim criticized Norris for showing us McTeague on Polk Street without explaining what events in his life had brought him there. Norris later in the book provides a few lines of background, but this was too little and too late for von Stroheim, who fabricated some thirty pages of script (in the published version) as prologue to the action in Norris's novel. If anything, von Stroheim was a greater believer in the effects of heredity and environment than Norris himself, and planted in these reels (which would have taken nearly an hour of screen time) all the forces that will buffet McTeague throughout a lifetime. These episodes constituted von Stroheim's most significant departure from Norris's text, and covered McTeague's youth in the mining camp, the death of his alcoholic father in delirium tremens, and McTeague's apprenticeship to a traveling dentist. Beyond this von Stroheim felt little need to alter the main outline of Norris's book.

Norris begins with "Doc" McTeague in San Francisco, an amiable giant who enjoys his steam beer and the "six lugubrious airs" he plays on his concertina. His friend Marcus Schouler, another boarder in the same Polk Street apartments, is an obnoxious young tout given to mouthing socialist slogans when not assisting old man Grannis at the dog hospital. McTeague falls passionately in love with Trina (Marcus's cousin and fiancée) when Marcus brings her in for dental work. He loses control of his emotions and kisses her while she lies anesthetized in his chair. Marcus agrees to give her up to his friend, but on the night of the engagement party Trina learns that she has won $5000 in a lottery. This chance winning spells doom for all three. Marcus fights with McTeague over the money, on which he feels he has a claim, and secretly swears vengeance. Not long after the marriage Trina begins to show signs of increasing miserliness, cutting back Mac's visits to Frenna's saloon and swearing that her $5000 "will never be touched." Marcus informs the state dental board that McTeague has been practicing without a license, and McTeague and Trina are on the treadmill to oblivion. During this time Norris has paralleled the main story with several subplots, including the sordid tale of Zerkow, a crazed junkman who marries and murders a cryptic Mexican cleaning woman; two old people who find true spiritual love while everyone around them is falling into corruption; the problems of Trina's German immigrant family; and even the story of two dogs who bark at each other across a backyard fence. After a grim series of events Trina and McTeague hit bottom and are living in Zerkow's old shack in the alley behind Polk Street. McTeague is now a shiftless and brutal alcoholic who grinds Trina's fingers between his teeth when in need of money. Eventually McTeague leaves and Trina takes a job as scrubwoman in a kindergarten. She has withdrawn her winnings and sleeps with the coins, "taking a strange and ecstatic pleasure in the touch of the smooth flat pieces the length of her entire body."[30] McTeague finds her and murders her for the money, planning to escape back to the Big Dipper Mine country where he had grown up. But once there instinct forces him to move on, and he flees across Death Valley, still dragging the gold with him. A member of the pursuing posse is Marcus, who had earlier left San Francisco to go into ranching. Alone he follows McTeague into the very pit of Death Valley. In a brutal struggle McTeague kills him,

The American dream: social criticism or Greek tragedy?

only to find that Marcus has handcuffed them together during the fight. Chained to this corpse, McTeague is left to die in Death Valley.

Never very interested in overt political statements, von Stroheim eliminated Marcus Schouler's attacks on capitalism, and didn't get around to the story of the two dogs. Otherwise, he did a remarkable job of cramming Norris's vast narrative into his screenplay. Of course, the screenplay was the size of a telephone directory, and the published version is larger than the Signet edition of the novel. That Godsol and Lehr approved this script, and doubled the budget for its production, makes them either fools or visionaries. J. J. Cohn was a production manager for Goldwyn at the time, and still cannot explain why the executives approved the script. "They thought they could control him when the time comes," he suggests, but there was no vehicle through which to exericse this control.[31] If von Stroheim simply filmed the script as written the studio would have had no alternative but to cut it to pieces, since a film of this length would have been impossible to distribute. That they let von Stroheim proceed with the project under the circumstances was simply irresponsible, no favor to von Stroheim and a clear waste of scarce studio funding.

In staying so close to Norris's novel, von Stroheim avoided the easy melodramatics of his earlier stories. The simple ironies and coincidences of *The Devil's Pass Key* and *Merry-Go-Round,* the moral lessons neatly learned in *Blind Husbands* and *Foolish Wives,* and the horrible punishments meted out to all earlier villains (while hero and heroine face the sunrise) have here been abolished. Von Stroheim had often fumed about the "tyranny of the happy ending," but he had always been very careful to supply one. Now with Norris's work as a base he abandoned these conventions and was able to concentrate his energies on direction for the first and only time in his career. In future years some of von Stroheim's critics would find his own stories too "novelettish," but the dramatic integrity of the *Greed* script was never attacked on these grounds.[32]

In fact, von Stroheim had little reason to tamper with this text, for in many ways it is a work which he himself might have written had he been an American novelist instead of an émigré Austrian filmmaker. Hanging over it all is the same concern with fate which haunts *Merry-Go-Round* (and will come again with increasing frequency in future von Stroheim films). Characters are locked into their class roles, and atempts to cross over spell disaster; Mother McTeague hopes to improve her son's lot by apprenticing him to the dentist, but he would have done better to remain in the mines. Norris suggests a political reading to class problems through Marcus Schouler's recurrent socialistic outbursts, but von Stroheim, in suppressing them, blunts the film's social and political commentary. When asked directly to comment on the film's picture of "social conditions in America," von Stroheim had no answer—"To me it was like a Greek tragedy, that's all."[33] In a von Stroheim film class barriers are inherited distinctions which limit one's freedom to act. This is the reason he returns over and over to the "old Heidelberg" plot of prince and commoner, where ancient codes are shown to program current behavior. McTeague's tragedy is "like a Greek tragedy" because of something inside himself, and is not the result of external social or economic conditions. Important as they are in *Greed,* they remain catalysts, dramatic devices responsible for triggering primal outbursts.

McTeague was not an original von Stroheim story, but it is clear that he saw much of his own life in its pages. The world of German speaking immigrants in America, working-class struggles in prewar San Francisco, the corrosive effect of financial problems on a young marriage—all these could have been chapters in his own life. Von Stroheim seldom posed for elaborately staged publicity shots in connection with his films, but he did for this one: in one photo he is dressed up in work-man's clothes, swinging a pick and shovel, to illustrate how he had once been a railroad worker in these same parts; another shows him crouched down, shooting craps with a track-laying gang of blacks and chicanos. For this film he put aside his normal contempt for such hokum and took advantage of the opportunity to link his own story to that of McTeague. The script reflects the connection in even more subtle fashion. Norris's novel is set in the 1890s, and von Stroheim's film re-creates this pre-earthquake world in some detail; surviving portions of San Francisco even double for streets destroyed in 1906. But despite the avowed attempt to rebuild Norris's San Francisco, all costumes, street traffic, and calendar dates have been updated to the years 1908-22. The result, if one looks for it, is a bizarre amalgam of Norris's events jammed into the chronology of von Stroheim's life in America.

While many historians give the impression that von Stroheim's filming of *Greed* on location was a revolutionary move away from the Holly-wood studio, in fact such was hardly the case. A *San Francisco Chronicle* article published the week after *Greed* went into production was headlined "San Francisco Taking on Hollywood Air in Film Mak-ing," and listed a whole string of films currently before the cameras, of which "the most important of the operations, locally, is the making of William Dudley Palley's *The Fog* by Graf Productions Inc."[34] By June *Greed* wasn't even the only Goldwyn picture in town, Victor Seastrom's *Name the Man* having come up for a few weeks as well. Silent films were never as locked in to studio production as the talkies would be, although the extremes to which von Stroheim followed the idea of location shooting were in fact rather extraordinary. While San Francisco acted as blasé as possible towards the visitors from Los Angeles, some seventy articles on the production appeared in local newspapers.[35] Most were products of the Goldwyn publicity mill and tell of famous visitors or the use of various locations around town. Accidents and injuries also seemed worthy of space, and we learn that Jean Hersholt was knocked unconscious during a picnic fight sequence with Gibson Gowland ("Picture Actor Hurt in Fall," *San Francisco Chronicle,* June 15, 1923, page 9) while Zasu Pitts "narrowly" escaped death on the Oakland transit lines while filming love scenes there (*"McTeague* Heroine Has Close Escape," *San Francisco Chronicle,* July 15, 1923, page D3). Unlike Griffith, who shrouded the production of films like *Intolerance* in deepest secrecy, von Stroheim agreed to wide local and national publicity during the filming of *Greed*. Judging from the surviving accounts, anyone with half an interest was able to get onto the set during even the most dramatic scenes. Frank Capra was then a gag-writer for a San Francisco-based comedy producer. Asked to deliver a reel of tests from a local lab he stayed to watch from behind the scenes, and was appalled at what he saw. "It was a simple scene, a short, nasty argument between two men in an office. But how Stroheim hammed it up! What posturings, torturings, waits, arguments, retakes, retakes—just to get a simple scene."[36]

Other visitors were more impressed. Edwin Schallert, who had found *Foolish Wives* a disappointment, was sent up from Los Angeles by *Picture Play* magazine. He arrived unannounced and climbed to the second floor of the building at Hayes and Laguna.

They were working on the picture—I could hear. Some one—a man's voice—was shouting frantically about money. Except that I knew that the actors for the bigger companies are promptly paid, he might have been calling for his salary; there was so much noise. It was apparent, though, that this was an altercation between a man and a woman over some hoarded gold, for I could hear him bellowing in a sing-song voice:

"Oh, ain't this fine! Ain't it lovely! We could live like Christians and decent people if you wanted to. You got more'n five thousand dollars, and you're so blamed stingy that you'd rather live in a rat hole and make me live there too before you'd part with a nickel of it. I tell you I'm sick and tired of the whole business."

It was in a little sort of alcove room that the action was taking place. A thick heavy-set lumpish figure of a man, grotesquely haloed by a mass of peroxided yellow hair, towered over a bed on which was a quilt of rags. Cringing beside him was a woman whose face was worn and eyelids bloated from weeping. Her heavy black hair was bound in huge coils about her head, and she wore a faded gray bathrobe stained with cooking and with tears. They were Trina and McTeague. There was no mistaking them—by anyone who read Frank Norris' novel "McTeague."

The room into which they were crowded was miserable beyond belief. There was hardly space for the tangle of electric wires and lamps, and the ceiling was low and the window closed. Stuffy, dead and perspiring was the air, like that of a stoker's hole. On a rude table was a mess of overturned glasses, bottles, cruets and dirty dishes. The stove was a pile of pots and messy kettles. On the wall in correct stupid frames hung a cheap, stiff, wedding picture, a bridal wreath and a bridal bouquet.

Lights looked glaringly down on the players' faces and the sweating atmosphere literally stifled them as they fought their way through rehearsal after rehearsal and scene after scene. And the rehearsals were many and the scenes few, for they were driven, as few players ever have been driven, by the unflagging zeal of the director's militaristic will.

What I saw filming that day was the turning point in the drama—the patent beginning of the decomposition of the various characters in the play. Von Stroheim, that subtly inspired Satanist, who sardonically etched his way to acclaim in *Blind Husbands,* and who disappointed the world and himself—though perhaps not through any fault of his alone—in *Foolish Wives,* was reveling in all the ruddy crude glory of an over-mastering and sovereign realism that he had, with journeying and quest-ing and long painstaking search, come to the heart of the seaport me-tropolis of the Pacific to get, and which was now maturing in tribulation and in pain into a potential shadow epic of disintegration and decay.[37]

Another detailed account was featured in the Sunday drama section of the *San Francisco Chronicle,* and is worth quoting not only for the flavorful description of von Stroheim's methods, but as a record of a scene not in either the novel or the published shooting script:

The scenes that were making when I saw them were taken in Zerkow's junk yard and little shop, a dank, noisome hole that looks a fit place for a murder. Zerkow murders his wife there, the crazy woman he married just to hear her tell the story of the gold table service she had seen somewhere, or imagined she had. He gloated over the telling and he came to believe it as much as (the) woman.

This portion of the story preceded the scenes that were shot while I looked on. The Mexican woman has a pet raven which dies. She buries it in the yard and Zerkow watches her from the iron-barred window of the shack.

He believes it is the gold service she is burying, and when she has gone up to the miserable quarters where the pair live above the shop he digs up the bird. It is after this he kills the woman, and then in terror goes to the water front and jumps into the bay. That gruesome scene was to be taken on the night of the day of my visit.

"Gravina is afraid of the ducking" von Stroheim told Mrs. Warren and me. "That's what is the matter with him. He is thinking of that and not of his work. I have a taxi ready, and a doctor, and the blondest nurse I could find, and a bottle of whisky and another of rubbing alcohol so what more can I do?"

The shack is several steps from the street, and there is a yard about twenty feet long between the gate and the door. This is filled with an indescribable mass of things, old automobile tires, an iron bed or two, broken boxes, piles of bottles—anything and everything that could be thought of—and the shack is filled with much the same heterogenous assemblage of seemingly useless articles, with a pair of big spectacles, such as swing in front of an optician's shop, in a conspicuous place. Cobwebs hang thick from the shingles and the rafters—manufactured cobwebs that seem quite real—and there is dust half an inch thick.

Von Stroheim is very thorough in everything he does; meticulous per-haps, in his attention to detail and in his effort to have everything in his pictures just as it would be in real life.

He wanted a full view of the scene in which Zerkow digs up the raven, so the property boy took the gate off its hinges, after some effort, for it was pretty well nailed, and the two cameras were moved out onto the narrow sidewalk where a group of "peepers" was congregated, every

knot hole in the fence having an eye glued to the aperture and some of
the more venturesome spirits climbing the fence to see, which gave Cor-
poral Maurice Reardon, who is detailed to help the players while they
are here, much work clearing them off.

Finally after a wait of half an hour or so the cameras were in place,
Ben Reynolds, chief cameraman in charge of the big $3500 Mitchell
machine, and William Daniels, his assistant, looking after the smaller
Bell & Howell. They were jammed together, the machines, and von
Stroheim took his place behind them, standing on an empty packing box
to watch the scene.

"Ready!" Von Stroheim called out, and then a cloud covered the sun.
Daniels took a silver framed bit of blue glass from out of his pocket and
looked up in the sky.

"In a minute," he called out.

The sun came out; von Stroheim shouted "Ready" again, then
"Camera" and the machines began to click while Gravina came cau-
tiously out of the door and started for a spade to dig up the raven, which
had already been buried before we reached the place.

"Stop!" Von called out, stepping from the box and going into the
yard where he showed Gravina just how the scene should be played.
Meantime the two helpers of the camera men stepped in front of the
cameras and held up little folding slates bearing the number of the picture, the number of the scene, and the number of the exposure for that
particular scene.

Von came back and the machines moved again, and again there was a
failure. This was repeated nine times altogether, with von Stroheim
finally losing his temper and shouting out, "You'll get the best ducking
of your life tonight, Gravina, I promise you that!"

Mrs. Von Stroheim, a pretty woman, who used to be Valerie Germonprez and met her husband seven years ago when he was making a picture
called *Foolish Husbands* [sic] put her hand on his arm, and smiled at
him.

"I can't help it," he said, but the tension relaxed and he smiled."[38]

Von Stroheim felt that Gravina was the perfect physical type for
Zerkow, had used him before, and would use him again. But com-
municating exactly what he wanted was still a problem. Idwal Jones,
San Francisco Daily News drama critic, observed a similar scene:

> The acting seemed good, but von Stroheim beat his chest like a hollow
> sounding bittern and moaned loudly it was not good. He rose from his
> stool and took Gravina's place. And von Stroheim became Zerkow. The
> effect upon the spectators was hypnotic. He was transmogrified into a
> monster, mouth open, eye fixed, every muscle in his turning face tongu-
> ing suspicion. Gravina took the cue. He acted with what old stagers call
> "that little more," and the trick went over to handclapping from every-
> body in the den. Von Stroheim walked over, patted Gravina's back. The

old actor seized the director's hand, pressing it to his lips, and his eyes watered like a spaniel's.[39]

What Capra found outrageous, Schallert and Jones accepted as necessary in creating that peculiar authority of performance unique to von Stroheim's films. As critic Jonathan Rosenbaum wrote a half-century later,

> Look at any frame enlargement from *Greed* . . . and you'll see not a familiar actor "playing a part," but a fully rounded character *existing*—existing, as it were, between sequences as well as within them (or such is the illusion). How many films in the history of acted cinema would pass this elementary litmus test? Certainly not *Citizen Kane;* perhaps *The Magnificent Ambersons* . . .[40]

Acting wasn't von Stroheim's only concern, of course. Following in the footsteps of Norris and Zola he put demands on the film's entire *mise en scène,* not simply performance and setting. Ben Reynolds and William Daniels were driven to unheard of lengths to achieve photographic effects which could transfer the density of detail required by von Stroheim's treatment of the story. The director demanded tremendous depth of field in his photography, allowing foreground and background action to appear with equal clarity. "We had a big scene they still talk about," Daniels remembered, "the wedding of McTeague and the girl, and during the wedding procession you see a funeral cortege going by, through the window. In other scenes you see the streetcar passing. It was done without process. There was a problem of getting a correct balance of light between interior and exterior so that it looked as though all the scenes were lit by daylight only, and getting enough light on the people to balance the exposure was hell."[41] All this with nothing but a blue glass to check lighting conditions.

One practical interior showed McTeague and Trina living in a 10½′ by 11′ room, with an 8′ ceiling. "Practical" is an art director's term, not a cinematographer's. To photograph this actual room Reynolds's camera was suspended from the roof on a small scaffold, where he shot through a tiny window. Daniels shot another angle through a transom.[42] In the studio such cramped sets could be constructed with break-away walls, but von Stroheim hated this kind of shortcut and insisted on the atmosphere only a practical interior could provide. "I can't cheat. I don't know how. My mind doesn't work that way."[43]

Von Stroheim's demands constantly pressed his cameramen into achievements they would otherwise have shied away from. The smoking of the arc lights in certain shots required that incandescant lamps be substituted, an innovation not generally accepted until years later.[44] More significantly, a substitute had to be found for the fine studio photography developed by Henrik Sartov, Karl Struss, and other pictorialist cinematographers. Von Stroheim was seeking a texture which in future years would be called "documentary."

> The screen must be life's mirror, part of the time, anyway. It is possible to tell a great story in motion pictures in such a way that the spectator forgets he is looking at beauteous little Gertie Gefelta, the producer's pet, and discovers himself intensely interested, just as if he were looking out of a window at life itself. He will come to believe that what he is gazing at is real—a cameraman was present in the household and nobody knew it. They went on in their daily life with their joys, fun and tragedies, and the camera stole it all, holding it up afterward for all to see.[45]

He found few examples of this style among recent films. "There are *Miss Lulu Bett,* some of Will Rogers's pictures, *Grandma's Boy* and *The Kid* in comedies. Certain moments in Marshall Neilan's pictures have possessed the spark, as did the two-reel production of O. Henry's *The Cop and the Anthem* and other O. Henry stories. There was realism in Rex Ingram's *The Conquering Power.* And that, to my mind, is about all."[46] This list is not the hodge-podge it might appear to be. Ingram's film, an adaptation of Balzac's *Eugénie Grandet,* probably had a direct influence on *Greed* in its picture of obsessive miserliness.[47] The rest are all linked by a concern with working-class life, an attitude that had generally been replaced in 20s films by middle-class or upper-class subjects. William de Mille's *Miss Lulu Bett* (1921), the story of a small-town spinster, is still hailed today for the dramatic integrity of Lois Wilson's performance. Many of O. Henry's stories focused on minor incidents in the life of a few working-class characters, although what specifically attracted von Stroheim to *The Cop and the Anthem,* a now forgotten 1917 short, directed by Thomas R. Mills, is impossible to say. Will Rogers's early features were quite remarkable in their creation of believable rural characters and situations, and perhaps von Stroheim was thinking of *Jubilo* (1919), directed with great sensitivity by Clarence Badger. Chaplin's *The Kid* and Harold Lloyd's *Grandma's Boy* are among the first great feature-length comedies, and especially notable for their attention to the affairs of everyday life, with lovingly detailed city and country environments supplying much of their dramatic impact. Since his opinion of the typical silent screen drama was so low, it is not surprising that von Stroheim saw comedy as the main repository of screen realism. His examples are carefully chosen. The brilliant slapstick of Fatty Arbuckle or the technical virtuosity of Buster Keaton do not seem to interest him.

In addition to the apartments at Hayes and Laguna, von Stroheim filmed all around San Francisco and Oakland, including a location on lower Market Street where McTeague was seen practicing in the company of his mentor, Dr. Painless Potter. In this scene McTeague appears flustered when a young girl—a "young lady bum" in the script—mounts his chair for some dental work. Fumbling, embarrassed, McTeague exchanges patients with Potter to general hilarity. The scene was one of von Stroheim's "plants," intended to establish McTeague's sexual naïveté, as well as to introduce an erotic aspect of dental work important in understanding the later scenes of Trina in McTeague's chair. To bring this out more clearly von Stroheim had Zasu Pitts play the girl. When the studio saw this footage they demanded retakes, insisting that Pitts was completely recognizable and that audiences would be confused.[48] Von Stroheim wanted them to see a resemblance. Finally he gave in and shot retakes, although whether he used a more heavily disguised Pitts or another actress is unknown.

At the end of May, Abe Lehr and his wife visited von Stroheim at the location. Everything seemed to be going fine. The two discussed the recent merger of Goldwyn with Hearst's Cosmopolitan, a move intended to strengthen the company's production schedule (as well as its press relations). Lehr had seen some of the early footage back in Culver City and praised the quality of von Stroheim's work to the press. "It has atmosphere, color, and realism that could not possibly have been reproduced in the studio," he beamed.[49] Von Stroheim received the final installment of his $30,000 payment that month, and although he worked on the film another year and a half, it was the last money he would see from this production.

Shooting in San Francisco wrapped by the end of July, and von Stroheim prepared to move on to more rugged locations. On July 26 he addressed the Daylight Post of the American Legion on the topic "Motion Pictures and San Francisco."[50] In 1914 he had left the area by cattle car; now he was a respectable booster, an after-dinner speaker entertaining the city fathers with dreams of a new filmmaking center far from Hollywood. Fate had turned the tables for him, but he would not enjoy his good fortune for long.

"At the end of that time we all returned home, and then began the most terrible experience any of us has ever gone through, shooting the scenes in Death Valley."[51] Jean Hersholt was not the only one stunned by von Stroheim's choice of a desert location. The Goldwyn Company

had hoped he would settle for the dunes near Oxnard, a desert area not
far from Los Angeles where Valentino had charged across the sands in
The Sheik.

> But having read the marvelous description of the real Death Valley as
> Frank Norris had depicted it, I knew that "Death Valley" did not look
> like Oxnard and as I had gone as far as I had for the sake of realism,
> I was not going to conform to the company's desires this time. I insisted
> on Death Valley, and Death Valley it was. This was in '23 when there
> were no roads and no hotels as there are today. We were the only white
> men (41 men—one woman) who had penetrated into this lowest point on
> earth (below sea level) since the days of the pioneers. We worked in
> 142 degrees fahrenheit in the shade and *no* shade. The results I achieved
> through the heat and the physical stress were worth the trouble I had
> gone to. It would have been absolutely impossible to get anything near it
> in Oxnard.[52]

While the film's shooting schedule sprawled over nine long months,
von Stroheim had carefully chosen the worst time of year for the
Death Valley episodes, midsummer. Few of the company would easily
forget. Said William Daniels:

> Of course, being a realist, he really *had* to have it hot! Luckily it was
> dry heat, and we were all young, and could stand it. The only water was
> at Furnace Creek Ranch, which the English Borax Company kept sup-
> posedly for agricultural purposes. There was a lake with palm trees and
> we lived on little army cots in the open air. It was too hot for tents. I
> remember the beautiful stars through the palm trees at night. The food
> was horrible . . . The cast stood up well except for Jean Hersholt who
> became hysterical at one stage with the bad sunburn.[53]

Jean Hersholt:

> Seven car-loads went on the trip . . . During the two weeks that we
> were in the worst part of the Valley the highest temperature was 161
> degrees and the lowest 91. The scorching air seared our blistered bodies,
> making sleep impossible. After a few days and nights not one of us
> spoke to the others unless we had to. It was so hot that an egg only had
> to be broken on a pan to be fried at once! Two of the seven cars were
> kept in use all the time, going back and forth across the valley to Baker,
> the nearest railroad point, to take sick men to the town and bring us
> back water, water, water . . . Out of 41 men, 14 fell ill and had to be
> sent back. When the picture was finished I had lost 27 pounds and was
> ill in hospital, delirious with fever.[54]

Paul Ivano was recruited to shoot inserts of landscapes and sunrises,
but soon became one of the casualties.

> I was roped in to handle an extra camera in Death Valley and like a fool
> I said, "Yes, I'll go." Stroheim used to walk around in shorts, and gloves,

"And Stroheim seemed to like it." Surviving cast and crew in Death Valley.

and a colonial helmet, and I think he had a gun strapped on in case a rattlesnake came out. One of the cooks on the company died—I think he had high blood pressure and the heat didn't help. The paint on the cars curled up and fell off. You couldn't touch a piece of metal. And Stroheim seemed to like it. I could only stand it for about three and a half days.[55]

Ivano had been gassed on the western front and was still recovering; he begged J. J. Cohn to send him back to Hollywood. It would be four years before he was ready for another von Stroheim picture.

Von Stroheim had sought out the worst part of Death Valley at the hottest time of year. It became more than just a "realistic" location, but took on expressive, nightmare qualities of its own. It would provide a suitably hellish background for the work of two actors now hopelessly lost in their roles.

Every day Gibson Gowland and myself would crawl across those miles of sunbaked salt, the hunted murderer pursued by the man who had sworn vengeance on him. I swear that murder must have been in both our hearts as we crawled and gasped, bare to the waist, unshaven, blackened and blistering and bleeding, while Stroheim dragged every bit of realism out of us. The day that we staged our death fight I barely recollect at all. Stroheim had made our hot, tired brains grasp that this scene was to be the finish. The blisters on my body, instead of breaking outwards, had burst inward. The pain was intense. Gowland and I crawled over the crusted earth. I reached him, dragged him to his feet. With real blood-lust in our hearts we fought and rolled and slugged each other. Stroheim yelled at us, "Fight, fight! Try to hate each other as you both hate me!"[56]

There was still a month's shooting to go after the conclusion of the Death Valley episodes, and von Stroheim was in no mood to waste time. On September 13 three Cadillacs up from Hollywood roared through the town of Colfax in Placer County, the heart of the northern California gold country.[57] They were headed for the backwater mining community of Iowa Hill, and its only notable landmark, the legendary Big Dipper Mine. Jean Hersholt had finished his scenes in the film, fortunate since he was still suffering the after-effects of his weeks in Death Valley. Gibson Gowland had emerged in better shape, and von Stroheim prepared to shoot the scenes of McTeague as a young miner, as well as a few episodes taking place years later after McTeague has fled San Francisco. As with his other locations, not just any mine would do, and von Stroheim had the Goldwyn Company lease the actual mine described in Norris's book. It had been closed for more than ten years and required considerable work to restore the shaft areas as well as the old mining camp. "Work is being carried on under the direction of Harold Henderson and Mr. Freeman," reported the *Colfax Record*. "A camp has been established at the Big Dipper mine and all Iowa Hill men desiring work have been employed."[58] Harold Henderson was a young miner who also happened to be a Frank Norris buff. When he heard that a film company had arrived in San Francisco to begin work on *McTeague* he went to the St. Francis Hotel and offered his services. Not only did he know which roads would be impassable and which bridges needed upgrading, but he had a personal knowledge of the mine, as well—his older brother had worked there in the '90s, when Frank Norris had visited as a guest of the management.

To von Stroheim Henderson must have seemed a direct link to the novel, and he was put in charge of all preparations at Iowa Hill—scouting locations, advising on lore and technique, even rounding up special props. When von Stroheim first came up to Iowa Hill Henderson took him to the old cemetery, one of the prime locations called for in the script.

The old church was standing, part of it. Headstones were broken down, amanzanita had grown up, and it was in pretty bad condition. He had two men with him, "Baby Ben" Reynolds, his head cameraman, and another gentleman [Ernest Traxler?], who represented the Goldwyn Company with regard to expenditures. He had control over the purse strings. Von Stroheim explained to him how he would show the last scene first, McTeague coming back after twenty years, trying to find his mother's grave, and finally stumbling on it. Then when he had that wrapped up he was going to clean up the cemetary, rebuild the facade of the church, and show the funeral. He explained it all in detail. His manager alongside him shook his head. "No, Von," he said, "this is going to cost altogether too much money. Forget it."[59]

This story is interesting not only because it shows von Stroheim's tendency to embellish his scripts at a moment's notice (no scene of the funeral appears in the published screenplay), but because it is one of the few recorded instances of the Goldwyn Company putting its foot down over expenses. Von Stroheim went back to San Francisco, and Henderson went to work under Richard Day's direction, scouring the country for antique bucksaws and false teeth. Over the next months new track was laid between the tunnel entrance and the mill, the old cook house, mine office, bar, and commissary were restored, one large building was turned into a bunkhouse for the crew, and an old vin-yardist's residence became von Stroheim's quarters. The giant brothel-saloon was built from the ground up with new lumber, and aged by the Goldwyn art department, astonishing the locals. This establishment was a fantasy of von Stroheim's, not found in Frank Norris, and more at home in old Vienna than staid Iowa Hill. "Miners there sought safer, distant playgrounds when excited by lust," remembers Henderson. "The Big Dipper camp consisted mostly of family groups, where at least a semblance of Puritan morality was maintained."[60]

By mid-September the main production unit, generally recuperated and very well tanned, moved to the Iowa Hill location. Lights, gen-erators, and other apparatus were eased over the pitted roads and open ditches with considerable care. "Nearly every truck in the vicinity" was called into action.[61] During gold rush days this part of California had been completely torn up by hydraulic mining—high pressure water hoses had sliced away entire mountains, leaving deep cuts only slightly camouflaged by scrub and pine. Even the "hill" on which the town stood had been sliced away, so that "the town now clings to a mere back bone, and the rear windows of the houses on both sides of the street look down over sheer precipices into vast pits hundreds of feet deep."[62] Today the area is still four-wheel-drive country, leaving the town's sixty residents among the most isolated in the state.[63]

Although Henderson had been told to round up turn-of-the-century props, he soon realized that von Stroheim and his crew were prepared to update at will, continuing the strange blending of periods evident in the San Francisco shooting. Von Stroheim's miners wore carbide lamps instead of candles, swung anachronistic long-pointed picks, and dressed in white rubber boots instead of the black rubber of Norris's day. Still, there were everyday touches of mining life that von Stroheim did insist on. In one scene forty miners were leaving the tunnel mouth at the end of a shift. Von Stroheim rehearsed again and again, but remained unsatisfied. Finally he stopped the action, smeared his hands with dirt, and wiped them across the flies of the miners' overalls. Henderson and the others immediately recognized "the universal mark of the miner."[64]

Except for those exteriors requiring sunlight, von Stroheim generally worked at night, between 9:00 p.m. and 6:00 a.m. It was at these hours that he filmed deep in the mine shaft, not one hundred feet down, as William Daniels had hoped, but 3000 feet. Many nights were spent on scenes in the brothel-saloon, where McTeague's father wrestles with an old whore and dies in a fit of delirium tremens.

> That scene was rehearsed over thirty times, most of them with the cameras grinding. It seemed that von Stroheim couldn't get exactly what he wanted. He did everything but horsewhip his actors, for it seemed that he would never be satisfied with their performance, but finally he waved his arms, dropped into a chair, and announced, "O.K. Wrap it up!" In many conversations with technicians and actors I came to realize how devoted these men were to von Stroheim. It amounted almost to idolatry. His demands for perfection of detail amounted to a sort of fanaticism. He drove his principal actors with unrelenting fierceness, and yet he was as kind as a benevolent father to those of seemingly lesser importance.[65]

On October 6, 1923, von Stroheim wrapped the production, closing a 198-day shooting schedule. He had shot 446,103 feet of negative, far more than the 326,000 or so used on *Foolish Wives*.[66] His task now was to bring this down to around a dozen reels (apparently Goldwyn had agreed to a greater length than specified in the contract), and he hoped to do so in a few months' time. As the crew left Iowa Hill one of his assistants told the local newspaper that the film would be out in eight months.[67] While Griffith could edit swiftly and decisively, cutting a masterwork like *Intolerance* in a matter of weeks, von Stroheim stalled and fussed over his films. To begin with, he felt restricted by the arbitrary length demanded of a picture by the exhibitors. Then his conception of the work seemed to change from day to day, just as it did during shooting when he would constantly make up new scenes. He had difficulty deciding among the numerous takes he had printed for each scene. Weeks turned into months. Early in 1924 he had a rough cut assembled, a simple ordering of all the footage with outs and duplications eliminated. He began showing it to friends and selected members of the press, hoping to build up a groundswell of public opinion which would prevent a repetition of the *Foolish Wives* fiasco.[68] That spring accounts of an amazing new film began appearing in the press. Harry Carr, perhaps von Stroheim's warmest supporter (and later co-author of *The Wedding March*) was swept away by the fateful romanticism:

> I saw a wonderful picture the other day—that no one else will ever see. It was the unslaughtered version of Eric von Stroheim's *Greed*. It was a magnificent piece of work, but it was 45 reels long. We went into the projecting room at 10:30 in the morning; we staggered out at 8:00 that night. I can't imagine what they are going to do with it. It is like *Les Miserables*. Episodes come along that you think have no bearing on the story, then 12 or 14 reels later it hits you with a crash. For stark, terrible realism and marvelous artistry, it is the greatest picture I have ever seen. But I don't know what it will be like when it shrinks from 45 to 8 reels. Von Stroheim is imploring the Goldwyn people to make two installments of it and run it on two different nights.[69]

Carr gives a 9½ hour running time for this 45-reel version. Another reporter, Idwal Jones of the San Francisco *Daily News,* tells of a 42-reel version which took nine hours to screen on January 12, 1924.[70] Jones compared the "psychological hypothesis" of the film to *The Cabinet of Dr. Caligari,* with overtones of *Dr. Mabuse!* Over the next few months von Stroheim continued struggling with the film. He told his friend Don Ryan, "I could take out sequences and thus get the job over in a day. That would be child's play. But I can't do it. It would leave gaps that could only be bridged through titles. When you do such a thing you have illustrated subtitles, instead of a motion picture."[71] He claimed that he was resisting pressure to have McTeague wake up in the dentist's chair and find it was all a dream. "All this unpleasant but truthful realism a dream—all this exact psychoanalysis taking place in the mind of a boob who was asleep, dreaming it. Impossible!"[72]

Since von Stroheim labored so diligently over the editing of his films we should never lose sight of the most obvious fact: that the editing process was extremely important to him, and that in their final state the impact of his films was largely to be dependent on editing. This emphasis on editing, especially the building up of a sequence through a series of close-ups, was well noted at the time. Many reviewers criticized him severely for it, most notably Welford Beaton in *The Film Spectator,* a journal which otherwise supported von Stroheim. In a typical 1932

text, Andrew Buchanan characterized von Stroheim as a montage director: "Each observation would be captured in a 'close-up,' and at
leisure, he would assemble his 'shots' in just the order which would
most forcibly illustrate the fact . . ."[73] But in later years, when von
Stroheim's films were difficult to see and no longer fresh in the memory,
this general opinion began to change. The power of his images (which
as stills were readily available while the films were not) began to seem
more and more the real key to his work. André Bazin, who was looking
for silent forerunners of the 1940s' long-take style, remembered the
intensity of von Stroheim's style in terms of individual images. "He
has one simple rule for directing. Take a close look at the world, keep
on doing so, and in the end it will lay bare for you all its cruelty and
ugliness."[74] Without providing examples, Bazin claimed that the intensity of von Stroheim's films was largely the result of the long take.
"One could easily imagine . . . a film by Stroheim composed of a
single shot as long-lasting and close-up as you like."[75] Unfortunately
for this argument, von Stroheim's style was never especially tied to the
long take. Instead, as a disciple of Griffith, he depends on an ability to
isolate significant details, building up individual scenes from such units,
or juxtaposing them for dramatic effect. In either case, editing is crucial
to his intentions, not only in the presentation of individual sequences,
but in the development of each work's underlying dramatic structure.
Note the comparison of Hughes and Karamzin throughout *Foolish
Wives,* the opera house sequence in *The Merry Widow,* or the first
meeting of Nikki and Mitzi in *The Wedding March,* all products of
montage. One never gets in von Stroheim that insistent "fourth wall"
feeling apparent in so many of those silent films which did rely (for
better or worse) on the long take. He always prefers to analyze the
mise en scène through the use of close-ups, reverse angles, and inter-
cutting. Still, the pitiful condition of all von Stroheim's surviving work,
cut in every case by alien hands, effectively dampens any detailed analysis of his editing style, and *Greed* suffers more than most. But it is
certainly a mistake to deny the central position of editing in von
Stroheim's work merely because the montage units he deals in are
already so dense.

We know that by March 18, 1924, he had reduced the film to 22
reels, trimming it by half since the rough-cut showings in January.[76]
But he was unable to take it any further, regardless of his agreement
with Goldwyn. Then on April 10, the remains of the Goldwyn Company merged with Marcus Loew's Metro Pictures Corporation. Goldwyn
had a fine new studio in Culver City and contracts with several top

stars and directors. But their distribution was moribund and production was in a hopeless mire. Not only was *Greed* far behind schedule, but the vastly more expensive *Ben Hur* had all but collapsed after months of location shooting in Italy. Most of the Goldwyn executive cadre was purged, and Metro's general manager, Louis B. Mayer, assumed control of the merged operations. His assistant, Irving Thalberg, became head of production.

Coming under the thumb of Irving Thalberg once more must have been a nightmarish shock for von Stroheim. But at least *Greed* was already in the can and edited down to a reasonable work-print length of 22 reels. Von Stroheim had not forgotten that Thalberg had taken *Foolish Wives* away from him at 21 reels, turning it over to a battery of cutters for quick surgery and releasing only "the bones." To try to prevent another such disaster, von Stroheim shipped an edited print to his friend Rex Ingram, who was in New York involved in protracted negotiations with one of Loew's lieutenants, Nicholas Schenck. Ingram had been one of the top Metro directors, and now he and von Stroheim were working for the same boss. When the film arrived, Ingram turned it over to his editor, Grant Whytock, who had worked with von Stroheim on *The Devil's Pass Key*. Whytock remembers receiving about 26 or 28 reels. He studied the film carefully and conferred often with Schenck at his office in Palisades Park, New Jersey. He proposed cutting the film into two sections, an eight reel picture ending with the wedding, and a seven reel picture carrying through to the conclusion in Death Valley. Whytock remembers removing some 1200 feet of very brief cuts, shots that had been trimmed to a flash by von Stroheim and would hardly have registered on an audience.[77] Trimming individual shots was a standard method of saving a few minutes in the editing of a silent film, and von Stroheim had apparently taken this route in preference to eliminating entire sequences.

Whytock spent most of the summer on the project, and made good use of his earlier experience working with von Stroheim, for as far back as 1920 the director had regaled him with plans for a proposed film of *McTeague*. Besides breaking the film in half and cleaning up the ragged ends, he completely eliminated the Zerkow subplot, which he found "very distasteful." But his 15-reel version retained most of the other subplots, including the story of the old people, as well as much of the humor von Stroheim had introduced to lighten the mood of the picture at crucial intervals. For example, Whytock retained a "hilarious" scene in which McTeague bets Marcus that he can't put a cueball in his mouth. Schouler wins the bet, but then finds that he can't open his jaws wide enough to get the ball out again—apparently a well-known practical joke. This, too, is one of the scenes von Stroheim added on the spur of the moment, and does not appear in the script.

"We ran it on the old 'New York Roof' and had all the executives from Paramount and Metro. It was well liked by everybody, including Schenck and Rex [but] somebody from Paramount brought up the objection later [that] 'Well, the second half's a tragedy, and if they ever see the tragedy first, they'll never come back again and see the front end.' "[78] This thinking apparently carried the day, and the film was sent back to the coast without the hoped-for approval of the New York office.

In a 1948 letter to his biographer, Peter Noble, von Stroheim remembered sending 24 reels, and receiving back 18 from Ingram in New York (slightly different from the figures Whytock remembers).

> He [Ingram] sent me a telegram, "If you cut one more foot I'll never speak to you again." I showed the telegram to Mr. Mayer but he told me that he did not give a damn about Rex Ingram or me and that the picture would be a total loss to the company anyway and that the picture must be cut to ten reels. It was given to a cutter at thirty dollars a week who never had read the book nor the script, and on whose mind was nothing but a hat. That man ruined my work of two years. During these two years I had hocked my house my car my life insurance to be able to continue to work . . . At the time when that same company made slapstick and farce comedies of fourteen reels length, my picture was arbitrarily cut down to nine or ten. The rest of the negative was burned to get the forty three cents worth of silver out.[79]

The name of June Mathis has often been linked with the film, but her connection with the finished product is marginal at best. As editorial director at Goldwyn, it was Mathis who gave the actual go-ahead on the project, as a surviving "vault copy" of the original script attests. In January of 1924, when von Stroheim was screening his 42 reel cut for the press, Mathis attempted to edit a version herself. According to material in the M-G-M collection at the University of Southern California, she had prepared a 13-reel version by January 21, and eight days later ordered an additional series of brief cuts. But in February she left for Rome to oversee production of *Ben Hur,* and had nothing further to do with the film.

When the studio lost all faith in von Stroheim's ability to cut the picture himself they turned it over to Joseph Farnham, one of their top title writers, who prepared the 10-reel version eventually released. As von Stroheim had feared, he lopped out huge chunks of action and tried to plug the gaps with title cards. If June Mathis or Marion

Ainslee had been given the job the results might have been better. Anyone attending a screening of the film today knows from experience the audience reaction to such titles as "Such was McTeague," or "Let's go over and sit on the sewer." These are not von Stroheim's titles (as the published script demonstrates) but were added later, probably by Farnham. While the cutting damaged the dramatic flow of the picture, these inept titles had an even worse effect, derailing audience reaction and casting a ridiculous light on an already difficult film. Farnham received screen credit for editing, and June Mathis shared writing credit with von Stroheim, a contractual billing.

Rubbing salt in the wound, various local censorship boards also demanded cuts. The New York State Motion Picture Commission, one of the most powerful in the country, insisted on the following "eliminations" only one week before the scheduled premiere:

Reel 2: Elim. view of administering ether.

Reel 3: Elim. underlined words from title: "I've got her. *By God,* I've got her."

Reel 4: Eliminate title: "Damn his soul."

Reel 7: Elim. all scenes of McTeague biting Trina's fingers.

Reel 10: Elim. last view of horse kicking in agony on ground after it had been shot.

The reasons for the above eliminations are that they are "inhuman" and "sacrilegious."[80]

These cuts would have been made in each release print licensed for exhibition in New York and any neighboring states which (largely for financial reasons) echoed the cuts demanded by the New York Commission. They were not made in the original negative, and so the scenes survive in today's prints, although New York's first night critics may never have seen them.

The film was ready for release by the end of 1924, and scheduled for a December 4 opening at William Randolph Hearst's Cosmopolitan Theatre on Columbus Circle, one of New York's more intimate first-run houses. Hearst's production company was now releasing through M-G-M, and his newspaper chain gave the film strong support. The decision to open it at the Cosmopolitan, instead of one of Loew's downtown picture palaces, is indicative of the delicate marketing the film received. M-G-M knew they had a problem sell, and were hoping to keep it in this smaller theatre for a long run on the strength of expected good reviews and the public's curiosity. If the reviews had been better this scheme might have worked, but the film was attacked

Reviewers found von Stroheim's irony and symbolism lacking in entertainment value.

even more violently than *Foolish Wives*. Most exasperated was the trade press, and the eccentric *Harrison's Reports* was nearly apoplectic with rage.

> If a contest were to be held to determine which has been the filthiest, vilest, most putrid picture in the history of the motion picture business, I am sure that *Greed* would walk away with the honors; I have racked my brains to recollect one like it, but have made a dismal failure of it. In my seven-year career as a reviewer and in my five-year one as an exhibitor, I do not remember ever having seen a picture in which an attempt was made to pass as entertainment dead rats, sewers, filth, rotten meat, persons with frightful looking teeth, characters picking their noses, people holding bones in their hands and eating like street dogs or gorging on other food like pigs, a hero murdering his wife and then shown with hands dripping with blood; I have never in all my life seen a picture in which all the principal characters were people of the gutter and remained such to the end. All these things and more are found in *Greed;* they will turn inside-out the stomach of even a street cleaner.[81]

Variety was somewhat more coherent. To their critic the film was a senseless commercial venture since it was not good family entertainment, the goal of the motion picture business. Worse, the female audience would be alienated. "Imagine any girl keeping company with a young fellow urging him to take her to see *Greed* when she knows the night that she sits through it he is going to sour on every thought that has to do with marriage?"[82]

While the exhibitors might be expected to avoid anything difficult or unusual, it is surprising how unfavorable the rest of the press reaction was. The *New York Times* praised Irving Thalberg and his associate Harry Rapf for cutting the film to ten reels.[83] Robert E. Sherwood in *Life* criticized von Stroheim for having made the film in an unreasonable length, calling him "a genius . . . badly in need of a stop watch."[84] Acknowledgments of the film's unparalleled dramatic force were tempered with complaints of vulgarity or gruesomeness. Von Stroheim had employed the Handschlegl process, a stencil-coloring operation, to color all the golden objects a bright yellow. This was universally seized upon as betraying the otherwise pure "realism" of the picture. The future curator of the Museum of Modern Art Film Library, Iris Barry, complained that "a not very pleasing yellow tinge is smudged in."[85] Perhaps the film's most positive reception came from Richard Watts, Jr., who had replaced Harriette Underhill on the New York *Herald Tribune*. Although he, too, congratulated Thalberg on the editing, he was able to get beyond the film's assault on middle-class sensibilities. "The most important picture yet produced in America," he called it. "It is the one picture of the season that can hold its own as a work of dramatic art worthy of comparison with such stage plays as "What Price Glory?" and "Desire Under the Elms." When the 'movies' can produce a *Greed* they can no longer be sneered at."[86]

But Watts was a voice in the wilderness. Considering the film's atrocious critical reception it is amazing that the studio netted a quarter million dollars in domestic receipts (see chart on page 173). Von Stroheim and his supporters often claimed that the film was simply written off by M-G-M, but statistics show that it was in the foreign market that it really suffered. In fact, the extent of the rejection of the film by supposedly more sophisticated European audiences is hard to explain. German receipts suffered due to a notorious Nazi-inspired riot at the film's Berlin premiere in May 1926 but this could not account for the minuscule grosses world-wide.[87]

Today the situation is different. *Greed* has for decades been a museum classic, at or near the top of most surveys of international cinema. But its current standing has always been tied to critical or political fashions having little to do with von Stroheim and his work. In the 1952 Brussels critics poll, *Greed* tied for seventh place on a list of "the best

films in cinema history," behind Chaplin, Eisenstein, Griffith, even
Flaherty. But ten years later, when *Sight and Sound* renewed the poll,
Greed was tied for fourth place, and had emerged as the top silent
film on the list—*Potemkin* its only rival.[88] In those years *Greed* had
come to be seen as a symbol, a film of worth destroyed by Hollywood
philistines. It was a club with which the Hollywood haters could attack
the studio system, and discussion of the film generally centered on
what the film could have been had not Mayer and Thalberg run amok.[89]
In fact, in 1962 the "greatest silent film of all time" was really the
uncut Greed, a film none of those voting had ever seen. Contempt for
the Hollywood system was so strong in those days that all the weak-
nesses of the Farnham version were indulgently excused: what was
important was to show solidarity with the independent film artist, and
who could represent him better than Erich von Stroheim?

By 1972 the situation had changed again. This time *Greed* was not
even among the 23 finalists. Such studio creations as *Vertigo, The
Searchers,* and *2001: A Space Odyssey* had shot past.[90] While von
Stroheim's intentions were still held honorable, it was no longer felt
worthwhile to ignore the wounds inflicted on the film. *Greed* was moving into a special, meta-critical category of its own. The 1978 Belgian
Film Archive poll seems to have certified this. Asked to list the "most
important and misappreciated American films," more than two hundred
international critics placed *Greed* third, behind only *Citizen Kane* and
Sunrise, and once again ahead of Chaplin, Griffith, and Flaherty.[91]
Greed was one of the most important, but in its current condition you
couldn't say it was one of the best.

Perhaps if the "complete *Greed*" ever turns up the situation will
change once again. Ultimately, the most curious thing about the whole
Greed mystery is how the image of a rough-cut seen by only a few invited guests early in 1924 has come to overshadow so completely the
amazing, though imperfect, film which actually exists. The reputation
of this "uncut" film was established early on by critics like Carr and
Jones, whose reviews hinted at wonders no one else could dare imagine.
As early as 1926 Jim Tully reported that "A British Foundation of
Arts and Sciences wrote and asked von Stroheim if it would be possible
to buy the film in its original length for future generations."[92] Unfortunately, it was not. Over the years many other attempts have been
made to find this grail, and archivists and historians still follow any
feeble lead. The fact that it was never released and existed only as a
work print seems to deter no one. It is known that editors and laboratory personnel occasionally held on to copies of interesting material for

their personal collections. Why could the complete *Greed* not be among them? Hopes of finding the work print of a silent movie are dim, but stories persist, nonetheless. To close this chapter I need only add one of my own, similar to dozens of others, and told me by von Stroheim's son Josef in 1978. During World War II he was stationed at the Army Pictorial Center in Astoria, New York. There were many Hollywood types at the Center, and films of all sorts were often screened. Once *Greed* was on the schedule. Josef didn't recall exactly how long the print was, but he did remember it took two nights to run it.[93]

The Merry Widow

Von Stroheim's production of *The Merry Widow* was his greatest critical and popular success. In mastering the leap from Frank Norris to Franz Lehar he demonstrated a command of style beyond the range of any of his contemporaries. A director who had previously avoided the use of stars, he extracted the only Mae Murray performance of value, and cemented John Gilbert's reputation as a romantic hero. Most impressive of all, he took the silent movie operetta genre—perhaps the most hapless form of adaptation—and incorporated it into his oeuvre without alienating either his own supporters, or those of *Die Lustige Witwe*.

Despite all this, von Stroheim never recalled the film with any affection, and took every opportunity to demean the picture, its star, the production company, and his own role in the proceedings. Despite the fact that the project was his own idea, he later gave the impression that it had been forced on him. Although the glorious "happy ending" originates in his own shooting script, he later disowned it, implying it was the work of somebody else. At a 1955 screening of the film at the Palais des Beaux Arts in Brussels, he went so far as to order the house lights turned up just after the duel scene. "That's where my story ended, but they insisted on the ending you will see now," he told them.[1]

In an interview with the German *Film Kurrier* von Stroheim put his feelings bluntly.

> When I saw how the censor mutilated my picture *Greed,* which I did really with my whole heart, I abandoned all my ideals to create real art pictures and made pictures to order from now on. My film *The Merry Widow* proved that this kind of picture is liked by the public, but I am far from being proud of it and I do not want to be identified at all with

so-called box-office attractions. So I have quit realism entirely . . .
When you ask me why I do such pictures I am not ashamed to tell you
the true reason: only because I do not want my family to starve.[2]

Despite all later claims, it was assumed from the start that *The
Merry Widow* would be an Erich von Stroheim production. As soon as
he signed his Goldwyn contract the publicity department began promoting *The Merry Widow* and *McTeague* as the first two von Stroheim
films, and rights for *The Merry Widow* were actually cleared first. On
January 6, 1923, impresario Henry Savage signed over the motion picture rights to the Victor Leon–Leo Stein–Franz Lehar stage success for
$65,000.[3] Rights to *McTeague,* on the other hand, were not cleared
until January 29. But von Stroheim went into production on *McTeague*
first, spending all of 1923 on pre-production, filming, and assembling
a nine-hour rough cut. Godsol and Lehr had hoped von Stroheim might
be one of the company's saviors, but by the end of the year he had
become one of their chief headaches instead. There was serious discussion about assigning a more tractable director, someone who would
keep administrative problems (and budget overruns) to a minimum.
After wrestling with the decision Abe Lehr finally concluded that
another director "would not give this story the effervescence which it
requires,"[4] and decided to go ahead with von Stroheim. But by the time
of the M-G-M merger in April, he was still cutting *Greed,* and only
when confronted by Mayer and Thalberg did he send the print to Rex
Ingram and begin to think again about Lehar.

Under the terms of the merger, the relatively new Goldwyn studio in
Culver City would become the site of the new M-G-M, and Goldwyn's
stable of highly regarded directors, von Stroheim among them, were an
attractive part of the deal. But Metro Pictures had some cards of its
own to play, notably its connection with the Loew's theater chain, the
aggressiveness of its studio management, and a few noteworthy stars, of
whom the most important was Mae Murray. Known to her fans as "the
girl with the bee-stung lips," Mae Murray was the epitome of early
jazz-age Hollywood. Born Marie Adrienne Koenig in Portsmouth, Virginia, in 1889, by 1908 she was dancing in the Follies for Flo Ziegfeld.
Her first film roles in 1917 were often dance-oriented, and while she
had moved on to standard romantic melodramas in later years, Follies-
style specialty numbers continued to crop up in her pictures with dis-
tressing regularity. She was married to director Robert Z. Leonard, who
had successfully managed her career throughout the early 20s, but by
the time of the merger problems had begun to grow up between them.
Their independent production company, Tiffany, had been releasing

From the start there were problems with Mae Murray over interpretation.

through Metro, but now she would work for M-G-M directly. *The Merry Widow* was the best part of the Goldwyn booty, as far as she was concerned, for she had long seen herself in the title role. She demanded it, and Mayer quickly agreed. Not only was it a sure way of keeping her happy, but it was the sort of ideal casting that might counterbalance any non-commercial notions of von Stroheim's.

According to von Stroheim's own account, he had not wanted Mae Murray or anyone like her, preferring to groom an unknown for the role. How Mayer forced him to capitulate is not hard to figure out. He knew von Stroheim had not been paid in over a year, and took advantage of the director's weak negotiating position in placing Mae Murray in the role. Von Stroheim may have been stubborn, but he was no fool, and knew that Valerie and Josef had to be fed somehow. Had he realized what a nuisance Mae Murray would actually become, he might have thought twice about it. But von Stroheim had never directed a really big star, and was completely ignorant of the tantrums a neurotic silent queen like Mae Murray was capable of. On his pictures, the most outrageous personality had always been von Stroheim. Whatever his reasons, on May 27, 1924, he amended his contract to accept Mae Murray's billing on his picture.

The following day he agreed to another clause, an incentive devised by Mayer and Thalberg to speed along the shooting schedule. The pair had no intention of tying up a big star like Mae Murray for the long months of a typical von Stroheim production. Consequently, they offered him a bonus of $10,000 if the film was shot in less than six weeks, $7500 if completed in seven weeks, and $5000 if finished in eight weeks. This was in addition to the $30,000 advance against profits he was paid while shooting. Von Stroheim's last check from the Goldwyn Company had been cashed many months previous, and the bonus was badly needed. In addition, he was probably glad to see Thalberg wielding a carrot instead of the stick he had used at Universal.

To help him prepare the adaptation Thalberg assigned Benjamin Glazer, a relative newcomer to screenwriting. Glazer had been born in Belfast, and later worked as a lawyer and newspaper editor in Philadelphia. Since von Stroheim was partial to both Irishmen and journalists the pair got along quite well. Glazer immediately realized that the only way to collaborate with von Stroheim was to stay out of his way. "I frankly acknowledge that von Stroheim did the work," he wrote. "If he received any inspiration or ambition from me at all, it must have been from my indolence."[5] Von Stroheim had never worked with a collaborator on one of his film scripts, and felt no need of starting now. But Glazer at least kept his eyes open and left the following account of his weeks of preparatory work with von Stroheim in the summer of 1924.

Modest little ideas grew into sturdy episodes and expanded into sequences of epochal length. A slender, seemingly artificial musical-comedy plot took root in reality and blossomed into a sturdy drama. Heaps upon heaps of manuscript accumulated. Scenes multiplied into thousands. Secretaries almost fainted from exhaustion. And art directors' eyes gave out. But von Stroheim worked on, energetic as an ant, tireless as a horse . . . When you see *The Merry Widow* on the screen you will notice episode after episode done swiftly, briefly, impressionistically. But don't be deceived. Beneath what is there accomplished in a few significant vignettes and a few phantom-like dissolves, lies a solid and elaborate scaffolding. When von Stroheim has chosen to show you merely a muffled drum you may be sure that first he planned and painstakingly worked out the entire funeral procession which it symbolizes. He refuses every short cut. He leaves nothing to chance. Though open-minded as a child in a discussion of general ideas of plot structure and character development, he is pedantic as a professor when it comes to detail. This is his own particular responsibility, and he regards it with all solemnity. He literally directs his pictures as he writes them.[6]

The tone of this account matches exactly the testimony of von Stroheim's later collaborators, Harry Carr and Leonard Spigelgass.[7] Like them, Glazer was impressed and enlightened. After his work on *The Merry Widow* he went on to write many important late silents, notably *Flesh and the Devil* and *Seventh Heaven,* before turning to a career as a producer. He would cross von Stroheim's path again during the filming of *Queen Kelly.*

Already considered a classic, a "lilting musical show of yesterday," according to M-G-M's publicity campaign, *Die Lustige Witwe* was only twenty years old when von Stroheim produced this first full-length screen version. In fact, he claimed to have seen the original 1905 production at Vienna's Theatre an der Wien himself, which seems possible given what little we know of his early years. But the show which most of his audience had seen was based on a substantially different libretto, a text which jumbled names, characters, and subplots to produce a version designed for the tastes and requirements of the London stage. This libretto told the story of Sonia, "the daughter of a poor Marsovian farmer (who) married an animated money bag who left her a smiling widow a week later." The curtain rises on the Marsovian embassy in Paris. Embassy personnel are trying to get Sonia to marry a Marsovian to keep "the Sadoja fortune" from leaving the country. Prince Danilo has been chosen for the task, but this playboy is off somewhere at Maxim's. Danilo, it turns out, had earlier jilted Sonia when his "old uncle" forbade his marriage to a commoner. Now refusing to make a direct play for her hand, he hopes simply to cut out the most likely suitors, an obviously mercenary group. The action involves his attempts to do so, and Sonia's efforts to discover whether he, too, is only after her for her money. A trick ending helps Sonia learn that Danilo loves her for herself alone.

In transferring this text from the restricted confines of the theater to the more open form of the silent cinema, von Stroheim used the bare bones of the libretto to serve as the climax of his plot. In *Greed* he had created reel after reel of introductory material to spell out the background and motivation of his characters, something even Frank Norris had not bothered with. He would do the same in his script for *The Merry Widow,* where out of 477 scenes, 308 take place before the curtain even lifts on the action described in the stage play.[8] The copy of von Stroheim's shooting script preserved by M-G-M is dated October 7, 1924, and is conspicuously labeled "Founded on the Operetta by _____, Music by Franz Lehar." Whether this neglect of Leon and Stein was intended humorously is not known, but it is a fair indication of the connection between film script and libretto. Glazer was right when he said that von Stroheim directed his films as he wrote them, and the *Merry Widow* script bears close analysis for just that reason. This was no forced assignment, but a project that von Stroheim made sure would be regarded as no one's work but his own.

His most significant change was to split the character of Prince Danilo in two, creating a fantastic alter ego, the sneering and lecherous Crown Prince Mirko. Both possess all the stereotypical characteristics of young Ruritanian nobility: an eye for the ladies, aristocratic self-assurance, and the unmistakable air of being born in uniform. But behind these uniforms von Stroheim has created a pair of Jekyll and Hyde characters: a warm, fully developed human being, and his sinister shadow, whose warped behavior mocks the actions of his more social-ized cousin. In the introductory scenes Mirko and Danilo arrive in their separate cars at a mountain inn, having been off on maneuvers with the troops. The locale recalls the area where von Stroheim claimed to have served as an officer in the years before the first World War, and all that follows takes on the character of personal anecdote. Danilo jokes with his adjutant, allows a big police dog to slobber over him in the car, and laughs at the mud puddles and pig sties which crowd the road. By contrast, Mirko brutally whips a friendly dog which rushes to greet him, sneers sarcastically at the accommodations, and threatens unspecified horrors to those responsible.

Sonia is introduced not as a farmer's daughter, but as Sally O'Hara, premiere danseuse of the Manhattan Follies, an obviously second-rate vaudeville company stopping at the same inn. In making a silent film of *The Merry Widow* von Stroheim clearly had to change the musical emphasis from singing to dancing, a course which also took advantage of Mae Murray's experience as a vaudeville dancer—something mocked only slightly by the situation here.

During a wild night at the inn, both Danilo and Mirko make clear their interest in Sally, who never learns that the handsome officer she is attracted to (Danilo, of course) is a true prince of the blood. At the Monteblanco Opera House the next night Sally presents an absurd dance recital attended by Danilo, Mirko, and a third figure, the degen-erate Baron Sadoja. The Baron is specifically characterized as a foot fetishist in the firm grip of *locomotor ataxia,* that degenerative syphilitic paralysis which seems to have fascinated von Stroheim. Like the Count de Trouvere in *The Devil's Pass Key,* he represents these dashing young officers robbed of their few redeeming virtues of youth, charm, and vital-ity. A life in pursuit of women and wine has left him a physical as well as spiritual cripple, whose idea of a good sex life is to slobber over a closet full of high-heeled pumps. If they continue along their current path, both Mirko and Danilo can expect to become second-generation Sadojas.

Von Stroheim typically demonstrates contrasts and parallels through montage, and in this sequence cuts back and forth between close-ups of the three spectators and their view on stage. He uses point-of-view shots with opera-glass masking in each case, emphasizing the level of voyeurism involved, as well as implicating the film audience in the process of observation. As Danilo watches, there is "Nothing visible but Sally's head as she dances." For Mirko, "Nothing visible but Sally's body without head." And for the Baron, "Nothing visible but Sally's feet dancing."[9]

Backstage Sally manages to avoid the attentions of Mirko and Sadoja, and winds up with Danilo at "François," a house of assignation. Music for their tête-à-tête is provided by two hooded, under-age musicians, "apparently blind" and dressed in an arrangement of strategically placed lilies. In contrast to this refinement is a riotous party just down the hall:

> IRIS IN on woman's head and hands holding champagne bottle pouring champagne on her head while two other hands are shampooing hair. Camera on perambulator moves back revealing another private suite of the same architecture as Danilo's apartment . . . About ten officers and eight women on. The officers are in uniform and some of them we know from the Inn. The host of the party is the Romanian military attaché. They are sitting, eating and drinking, and all are in a hilarious mood. As soon as door is in, door opens and Crown Prince enters. All officers rise as well as they can. Crown Prince in very congenial mood waves to them to be seated. The host greets him effusively while some women crowd around him taking his cap and coat off. Camera on perambulator moves forward until Crown Prince and group are in M C U. One woman hangs around his neck and lifts her legs off the floor. He kisses her very intimately but apparently bites her lip as she lets go of him and shrieking feels her bitten lip. They all laugh and start to lead Crown Prince out toward table as camera moves back on perambulator until full scene is in again. In the same scene are sitting somewhere where they can be seen easily—three boys and three girls of about fourteen years of age—all whitened including hair. Their only dress is breast band and trunks for girls and trunks for boys. They are playing white Russian balalaikas and white Russian tom-toms. They are artistically posed in group, sitting on black bear skins against black silk wall.[10]

A third party is being held by the Baron, more intimate, and in which the attending sixteen-year-olds are entirely gilded in gold.[11] Danilo succeeds in getting Sally to remove her dress by spilling soup on it, a device which occurs more than once in von Stroheim's cinema.[12] The Baron hears of Sally's presence and sends a note begging for a rendez-vous which he signs "At your feet." Sally and Danilo find this very amusing and send back a reply telling Sadoja to wait for her at the cemetery. Later, as Sally's resistance to Danilo seems about to collapse, Mirko and his drunken crowd burst in and surprise them. Amid general derision, embarrassment, and confusion, Mirko gleefully exposes Danilo as a philandering prince. Danilo's instant response is to defend Sally's honor by declaring her "the future Princess Petrovich."

But of course the king and queen will not allow any such match, and after a terrible scene at the palace convince Danilo to back out of the wedding. Waiting in her wedding gown, Sally is visited by Mirko, who is delighted to arrive with the bad news. Baron Sadoja now sees his chance, taking advantage of Sally's rage and confusion. Marriage to him would bring wealth and power, especially over Danilo. She accepts, and enjoys her first thrill of power as Sadoja, whose millions support the state, demands Danilo's presence as best man.

Sally and the Baron prepare to consummate their marriage. An "old wrinkled hunchback" maid dresses Sally in a black negligee, and the Baron fortifies himself with a variety of pills and potions. Sally, "shrink-ing with nausea" as the Baron slobbers over her feet, sees him suddenly collapse in an apoplectic spasm. For months Sadoja lies paralyzed in bed, then one day crawls over to his closet and collapses dead in a pile of Sally's shoes. Sally leaves for Paris, and the script catches up with Leon and Stein.

Danilo is sent to Paris, unaware of his mission. He encounters Sally at the Embassy ball, and they dance the Siren Waltz, but she sees his renewed interest as simple fortune hunting. Later when Danilo learns the true reason for his mission he goes into a rage and begins drinking heavily at Maxim's. Eventually Mirko arrives to take over, and soon appears to be making progress. One morning he takes Sally riding through the Bois and they see Danilo, lying in a drunken heap near the roadway. He makes a pathetic impression, but Sally later invites him to a garden fête at her estate in honor of Mirko. The ball is a fiasco—Sally infuriates Mirko by turning down his proposal, and stupidly teases Danilo by claiming to love Mirko. Mirko finds them alone in her bed-room and challenges Danilo to a duel. Danilo spends the night morosely carousing at Maxim's while Sally pleads with Mirko, who is a crack shot. The duel takes place the next morning. Danilo fires into the air, since he believes Sally loves Mirko. She arrives just in time to see Mirko shoot him down.

Audiences saw little of the Baron's wedding night.

Back in Marsovia the king has died and Crown Prince Mirko, the heir to the throne, is marching in the funeral procession. Suddenly a fanatic appears and shoots him from ambush. We see Danilo in bed in his apartments in the palace, still very weak. He tells Sally he cannot marry her because she is so rich and he has nothing. At that moment the minister of war arrives to tell Danilo he is the new king. The finale, in Technicolor, shows Danilo and Sally marching in their coronation procession. Detachments of troops from different countries are in attendance, and as U.S. Marines lower the stars and stripes in salute, Sally picks up a corner of the flag and kisses it. She kisses the flag of Monteblanco, too, as the crowd goes wild with emotion.

What Thalberg and Mayer made of this script is impossible to say. Clearly, they had expected charm, glamour, and romance, with perhaps a hint of nostalgia. Von Stroheim offered something else entirely, a cynical illustration of the more corrupt connections between sex and money. The liaisons in the operetta had all taken place discreetly offstage; here they were multiplied and expanded into full-scale orgies. The operetta Danilo was an enjoyable foil for the Widow; von Stroheim presented a troubled character driven to alcoholism and suicide, shadowed by a grotesquely evil doppelganger. The character of Sally was not quite what Mae Murray had in mind, either; and in Sadoja, von Stroheim offered the screen's first monstrous sexual deviant. Thalberg either didn't realize or didn't care. Unlike *Greed,* the basic box-office elements were all here—stars, property, spectacle, romance, happy ending—and everything else could be controlled.

A few structural changes were made in the script by the time of shooting, possibly suggestions of Thalberg since they simplify rather than embellish the narrative. Instead of finding Danilo drunk in the Bois, then inviting him to the reception, which leads to the duel, all that action was compressed into the Bois episode. This eliminated the need for a costly "Sonia's residence" set, which would have recalled the locale of the play's second act. Cuts were to be made in many of the Baron's scenes, but other evidence indicates that these were actually filmed by von Stroheim and only eliminated later. Audiences saw nothing of the Baron at "François," the lengthy wedding night ritual was reduced to a flash, and his actual death in the shoe closet went unreported. And the very ending, that part which von Stroheim later so stringently disowned, was considerably toned down: no flags were kissed.

Most von Stroheim scripts bear actor indications for many of the parts, and the roles have clearly been written with a particular performer in mind. But this is not the case with *The Merry Widow* where the only actor specified is Lon Poff, the knobby lottery agent in *Greed* who was to play Sadoja's lackey. Mae Murray, of course, would be the Widow, casting to which von Stroheim had already agreed long before the script was completed. Names of other cast members were then leaked to the press, first Tully Marshall as the Baron, then Josephine Crowell as the Queen. Both were old Triangle-Fine Arts players who had appeared with von Stroheim in *Intolerance*. Tully Marshall had played the evil High Priest of Bel, who betrays the Babylonian civilization to the hordes of Cyrus. During the teens he had earned the nickname "king of the dope fiends" due to his performances as an addict in a briefly popular cycle of drug melodramas,[13] and judging from mannerisms he displays in the still extant *The Devil's Needle* (1916) this is exactly what von Stroheim wanted from him. His role in *The Merry Widow* was actually a return to type, since the mid-20s found him playing likeable if crusty old codgers like Jim Bridger in *The Covered Wagon*. He would become a fixed star in von Stroheim's universe, with the mere reference "Tully Marshall" in a script indicating the most sinister depravity.

Josephine Crowell's performance as Catherine de Medici in *Intolerance* set a standard for female villainy, but she had a comic side as well, and as he demonstrated in *Greed,* von Stroheim was interested in casting comedians in dramatic roles. Certainly her "mother-in-law" in Harold Lloyd's *Hot Water* (1925) is definitive, and she enlivened more than a few Hal Roach comedies later in the 20s. Griffith had also found a warm side to her personality as a long-suffering mother in *The Birth of a Nation* and *Hearts of the World,* but von Stroheim had little use for characters like that and cast her as a gargoyle.

As shooting approached all roles had been cast except those of Danilo and Mirko. As usually, von Stroheim had written a "von Stroheim character" into his script, but now his self-image was maturing. He no longer felt obliged to picture himself on screen as Count Karamzin or Lt. von Steuben, villains whose only saving grace is a veneer of surface charm. As his later films demonstrate, his persona was becoming more complex, more introspective. He would achieve this most perfectly as Prince Nikki in *The Wedding March*. Here he emerges as Danilo, a womanizer and a heartbreaker, but one whose own heart breaks when touched by love. This is the new "von Stroheim character," but he is haunted by a double. Throughout the film a leering, grimacing martinet shadows his every action, swaggering behind a monocle in the best "man you love to hate" tradition. This throwback mocks his love affair and eventually shoots him down like a dog. In this transitional work von Stroheim actually wrote himself into both characters, the flesh and blood man he really saw himself as, and the caricatured "Hun" the movies had exploited. In *The Merry Widow* he tried to say goodbye to "the man you love to hate," but fate had another future in store.

Von Stroheim criticism has typically seen Mirko as the "von Stroheim figure" here, and Danilo only as a remnant of the operetta. This interpretation is difficult to support, especially since von Stroheim himself was on record as identifying with Danilo. ". . . not I, but an American actor, the later John Gilbert, played the part of the seducer," he wrote in a 1941 article.[14] More poetic is a bit of internal evidence intended for no one's eyes but his own: backstage at the theater, Danilo leaves roses for Sally with his calling card, on which he writes, "To my sweet Irish Rose. Danilo." Mirko finds the flowers, tears up the card, and leaves his own, identical message, signing his own name. Danilo's message is in von Stroheim's handwriting; Mirko's is that of a stranger.

Perhaps von Stroheim did have hopes of playing Danilo himself, since his contract called for him to appear in one of the three films. But he does not seem to have campaigned for it, and instead urged Thalberg to use Norman Kerry as Danilo. As in *Merry-Go-Round,* Kerry was an acceptable von Stroheim surrogate in the director's eyes, but the studio refused and insisted on John Gilbert. Gilbert had been around for years, but was only recently developing into real star material.[15] He was under contract to M-G-M and the studio wanted to continue building him up—such a role opposite the established Mae Murray was just the vehicle for this. They had absolutely no interest in promoting the career of Norman Kerry, who was under contract to Universal anyway. Gilbert had played a Russian count in his latest film, King Vidor's *His Hour,* and the success he scored in this vaguely similar role made him the inevitable choice in Thalberg's mind. Von Stroheim now found himself stuck with two "stars," one an egomaniacal Follies dancer with no demonstrated acting ability, the other an up-and-coming matinee idol whose real ambition was to write and direct. The recipe for disaster was complete.

The only control von Stroheim was able to exercise over a major role came, ironically, with Mirko. One night at the theater attending Peggy Wood's road company production of *The Clinging Vine,* he and Valerie saw an actor named Roy Giusti. To Valerie, Giusti seemed an obvious Mirko, and von Stroheim agreed.[16] Though born in San Francisco, Giusti claimed to have been educated in Berlin, Leipzig, Vienna, and Paris.[17] And he could wear a monocle. Giusti passed his screen test and was rechristened Roy D'Arcy. As D'Arcy he continued to impersonate von Stroheim throughout the silent period, carrying on a tradition of villainy that the model himself had long since abandoned.

While the actual production of *Greed* was a relatively tranquil affair, *The Merry Widow* was another matter entirely, one long nightmare pitting an immovable von Stroheim against the irresistible team of Mayer and Murray. Shortly after amending his contract to accept Mae Murray as star, von Stroheim began to hear rumors circulating around Hollywood that Robert Z. Leonard was being set up to direct the picture. As Mae Murray's husband, Leonard had been directing her films for years, but now both their personal and professional relationships had deteriorated. Even if Leonard could have convinced the studio that he had the needed "effervescence" it is not clear that Mae Murray would have wanted him.[18] One night in July, von Stroheim came to Mayer's office demanding that he put an official stop to the rumors. The fate of *Greed,* which was now being cut to pieces somewhere in the studio, was another likely topic of conversation. One thing led to another and soon both men were shouting and waving their fists. Mayer either threw von Stroheim out of the office, or had him put out. Von Stroheim "contemplated swearing out a warrant for the arrest of Mayer on a charge of assault and battery,"[19] but thought better of it and went back to his script. The tone had been set for the next year's work.

The tale of Mayer "throwing von Stroheim out of his office" is one that appears often in Hollywood histories. Most frequently it is transposed to the time of shooting, and the meeting is instigated by Mae Murray's complaints. Samuel Marx, who knew both men quite well when he was head of the M-G-M story department in the 1930s, tells it this way:

> Mayer had a lethal muscle. He had worked for his father who was in the junk business in Canada and he handled an awful lot of iron and steel, and very few people realized what a good right fist he could swing. One of those who found out the hard way was von Stroheim, who went to see him when Mayer called him up about Mae Murray's complaints about the part he was getting her to play. And when Mayer confronted him with that, and said, "this is not the original *Merry Widow,*" Von is alleged to have said to him, "She is playing Sonia, and Sonia is a whore." And that particular word was all that Mayer needed to hear, and he swung at von Stroheim and knocked him down and then literally threw him out of the studio.[20]

Of course, it's entirely possible that Mayer continued to knock down von Stroheim and throw him out of his office throughout the production, but more likely this original incident has simply migrated to a more convenient moment.

Production #298 finally went before the cameras on December 1, 1924. M-G-M had five other films shooting that day (as well as the perennial *Ben Hur*), and von Stroheim found himself in good company. Marshall Neilan, Frank Borzage, Victor Seastrom, Monta Bell, and Robert Z. Leonard (sans Mae Murray) all had films in production,[21] and some of these directors had reputations for difficulty almost as notable as von Stroheim's. Victor Seastrom, for example, was second to none in his demands on actors, and Neilan's problems included alcoholism as well as acute egomania. He was the director who had walked out on Louis B. Mayer's address at the grand festivities celebrating the corporate merger, taking all his followers with him.[22] Mayer didn't forget things like that, but neither did he allow them to interfere with the steady flow of product. He allowed Neilan to continue at M-G-M until he had no further use for him. According to studio production records, those five films took an average of just over four weeks to shoot. By contrast, Thalberg and Mayer were prepared to offer von Stroheim a sizable bonus for anything under eight weeks. But von Stroheim had a problem which did not affect Seastrom or Neilan. In those days important films were seen as either the productions of big stars (Swanson, Valentino), or big directors (Griffith, Ingram). One or the other was in command, and lines of authority were clear. But on *The Merry Widow* a superstar director was matched with an equally prominent, and obstinate, performer. While it seems clear that Thalberg was prepared to back his director, von Stroheim's authority was never accepted by Mae Murray, who insisted on seeing the film as a Mae Murray production. To assert this she arrived on the set with her personal crew, hairdresser, costumer, and cameraman who had worked for her on her Tiffany productions. This especially meant her private cinematographer, Oliver Marsh. Marsh had perfected the use of a "baby spot," a small arc light always focused just below her chin which burned out any bags and wrinkles on the 35-year-old dancer's face. The high intensity glow from this special lamp required a make-up which was more than usually mask-like, even for the 20s. In fact, Mae Murray's face is one of the most fanciful icons of the silent screen. Not only did von Stroheim despise this sort of glamourization, he had his own camera crew to offer as well, Ben Reynolds and William Daniels. So there were two separate crews on the set, each with its own electricians and its own chain of command.[23] It is difficult today to tell who actually photographed what. Most production stills show only Reynolds

and Daniels, and William Daniels in interviews implied that the film was
his. But screen credit went to Marsh, and in the elaborate souvenir
book prepared for the film Reynolds and Daniels are not mentioned at
all. Certainly the photographic style is very different from von Stroheim's earlier films, high key glamour work which seems the complete
antithesis of what had been achieved in *Greed*. Instead of the crisp depth
of field and natural lighting employed in San Francisco, *The Merry
Widow* is a textbook example of diffusion, shallow field of focus, and
studio sparkle.

Von Stroheim tried to shoot as much of the picture in continuity as
possible, and the first scenes taken were the arrival of the troops at
the mountain inn. Although he had scrupulously avoided any sort of
"cheat shots" in *Greed,* insisting on the value of real locations, he was
completely open to Hollywood fabrication when creating a European
locale on the backlot. Don Ryan, a journalist with a bit part in the film,
was puzzled by the incomplete sets constructed for this scene, and
amazed when he had the chance to look through the camera finder. Von
Stroheim had incorporated a "hanging miniature," a newly developed
trick shot in which the tops of buildings and mountains were built in
miniature, and suspended between the camera lens and the incomplete
full-size settings.[24] Von Stroheim's script calls for "miniature paris plaster
work" here, so the effect was not the suggestion of the production department, but an idea of his own. In addition to trick shots like this,
von Stroheim was also comfortable with the adaptation of an existing
locale, such as the use of the Examiner building in *Merry-Go-Round*.
Here the San Diego Exposition Park doubles as the cathedral square
for the grand procession which introduces the King and Queen, and
allows the Baron to hobble down an impressively scaled flight of stairs.
Such elaborate tricks never seemed to bother von Stroheim, but on
small bits of detail he remained as manic as ever. Ryan observed him
to stop production in the middle of a shot, curse everyone within earshot, and demand to know why the blanket of Danilo's dog was tied
with string instead of leather straps.[25]

Ray Rennahan found von Stroheim so caught up in these details that
he occasionally lost contact with reality. Rennahan and von Stroheim
were on a six-foot parallel (an elevated camera stand) filming the
coronation and wedding scene. Von Stroheim noticed one of the guard,
a man about four rows back, whose tie was crooked. Without calling
for a ladder he walked straight off the parallel to correct it himself,
breaking his leg in the fall.[26] Rennahan was yet another cameraman on
the picture, an employee of the Technicolor Corporation assigned to

Von Stroheim directs from a wheelchair after falling off a high parallel. At his side is Valerie, who was usually on the set each day.

photograph the film's Technicolor sequence. This covered the last 143 feet of the picture, less than two minutes on screen, and featured several glowing close-ups of Mae Murray.[27] For years Rennahan would find Hollywood technicians who had kept small clips from this scene as souvenirs, for it quickly earned a reputation as one of the finest examples of early Technicolor.

Why would von Stroheim go to such lengths to glamourize Mae Murray? Rennahan, who shot nearly all the Technicolor footage in those days, felt that directors incorporated these brief episodes as extra selling points, and it is certainly true that von Stroheim was looking forward to 25 percent of the profits of this picture. But von Stroheim had a special fondness for color, something evident in the sophisticated color-tinting of *The Devil's Pass Key,* the laborious hand-coloring of *Foolish Wives,* and the insistent use of gold in the original prints of *Greed.* When the Technicolor process was commercially practical in the mid-20s, von Stroheim immediately demanded it, and his script calls for the use of "natural colors" in this scene. As we have seen, his use of artificial color processes tended to be highly subjective, if not overtly symbolic, but with Technicolor he seemed to be reaching for a new layer of realism, and differentiated the "natural" color of this process from the earlier techniques. *The Merry Widow* also contained numerous tinted sequences, and at least one scene in the stencil-colored Hand-schlegl process he had used in *Greed,* a view of the American Beauty roses Danilo leaves for Sally.

Unfortunately, Mae Murray never appreciated von Stroheim's attempts to immortalize her. "I was told by L.B. that she would kneel down and eat out of my hand," he wrote to Peter Noble. "She transposed the kneeling down into stamping her foot most vigorously, hissing that she was 'damned tired of having me know everything,' and the kissing of the hand became the biting."[28] If Mae Murray's behavior recalls that of an animal being broken to harness, von Stroheim's directorial technique was largely responsible. There are documented instances of von Stroheim's physically beating an actress to achieve a desired effect, but this was hardly possible with a big star like Mae Murray. So a less physical form of brow beating was employed.

> They call me hateful, and say I talk to my people as if they were dogs, that I am in truth a typical pre-war German. But I know what I am doing. It is my method. I must undermine this surface of acquired false technique and bring out the real feeling that is like a kernel beneath a girl's superficial charm. I glower at them. Never in their lives have they been spoken to as roughly as by me. I crush them, beat them down with satire, with harsh words, with scorn. They are ready to quit. Then I get at the real soul and guide its natural unfoldment. With Mary Philbin in *Merry-Go-Round* it was simply a process of development, for she had no previous training to be ripped from her childlike naturalness. Mae Murray's artificiality in most of her films, her self-consciousness and cuteyisms had to be torn away, gossamer garments that concealed her real capacity for feeling and her capability for expressing it.[29]

Von Stroheim's contempt for standard silent-film dramatic styles had led him to cast comedy performers like Zasu Pitts and Dale Fuller in so many of his films. When forced to use the most affected of silent stars, his reaction was predictably violent.

While von Stroheim seems to have barely tolerated Mae Murray, there were some aspects of the film he did enjoy. As in *Merry-Go-Round,* he spent considerable time on the "wild party" episodes, which were elaborated here with unprecedented intensity. Wrote one participant:

> The wild party on *The Merry Widow* set has already been given a place of its own in Hollywood history . . . This wild party differed from similar affairs I have seen produced by Cecil De Mille and other specialists inasmuch as the wild party in *The Merry Widow* was the life. The early morning sun revealed a scene of wreckage that beggars description: a piano swimming in cider and broken glass; a lieutenant of the

guards stretched at length beneath it, while from a rent in the bottom of the instrument a stream of liquid descended upon his unconscious face; a bedraggled group of revelers, sticky with cider and covered with feathers. One of the little whimsies of the evening had been a descent upon the sofa pillows of the apartment with drawn swords. An electric fan had added to the confusion. Over in the wardrobe section ten maddened employees toiled all next day picking feathers off of uniforms.[30]

It was von Stroheim's habit to stage such events, then shoot them in documentary fashion, making use of only what the censors would allow; see Hal Mohr's comments on the even more spectacular wild party thrown for *The Wedding March*. While in retrospect this party seems only a sketch for what was to come, it did create quite a fuss at the time, and seems to have completely stopped Mae Murray in her tracks. After sneaking a look at the rushes one day Mae ran screaming to the front office. "This is filth," she told Thalberg. "Kissing people's bottoms and kissing feet, the old man behaving obscenely with a closet full of shoes!" "Von Stroheim has to purge himself," Thalberg said. "The man's a genius. He's giving the picture dimension." "Degeneracy's what he's giving it. And you're letting him."[31] This exchange is related in that curious Mae Murray biography *The Self Enhanced,* in which the production of *The Merry Widow* is seen as a contest between Mae's desire to retain the sparkle of Lehar's masterpiece, and von Stroheim's attempt to make the whole thing as "heavy and hopeless as *Greed.*" While tremendously colorful, Mae's statements are generally so dizzy that their main value lies in showing just what von Stroheim was up against. She felt that Thalberg was secretly collaborating with von Stroheim in an effort to promote Norma Shearer, and spends many pages on an otherwise unreported romance with John Gilbert. Still, she was right about the shoe closet. As his friend Don Ryan knew, von Stroheim was purposely loading the picture with outrageous references to esoteric perversions, in-jokes which he could toss over the head of Louis B. Mayer. The state censor boards would never know what hit them.

> His penchant is Freud, with trimmings by Havelock Ellis and sauce by Krafft-Ebing. Some of the characters he has composed . . . will be recognizable only by those who have pursued a similar bent. . . . In the sequence at the inn there is a bit performed by an angular young lady—a member of the follies troupe—that is typically von Stroheim. The reader may not understand what I mean after seeing it. If not, the reader may enjoy the more usual love scene between Danilo and the innkeeper's daughter, which follows.[32]

Or as von Stroheim would say, "The boobs won't know where the guts of this picture lie."[33]

Of course, one of the most famous of all von Stroheim stories stems directly from these secret references. Irving Thalberg asks why there is so much film showing the collection of women's shoes in Sadoja's closet. "The man has a fetish for feet," von Stroheim explains. "And you have a fetish for footage," retorts Thalberg. Unfortunately, there seems to be no way to verify this probably apocryphal exchange, which nonetheless has come to symbolize the whole range of von Stroheim's troubles with Hollywood.

For *The Merry Widow* von Stroheim created his own officer's cadre, bringing back such old cronies as Albert Conti, and enlisting many of the other ex-officers then haunting the studios. Don Ryan was one of these, and others included Wilhelm von Brincken (a supposed W.W.I German spy) and a British officer named Owen Martin. Von Stroheim devoted an inordinate amount of time to this group, fussing with their medals, and drilling them in the ritual of obscure central European armies. He employed military discipline and they loved him for it, just as they loved the attention he gave to their status and experience as officers in the great war—a war which he had sat out in Hollywood. This group became a part of the cadre of technicians and assistants which he carried with him from film to film, and like that group directed their loyalties not to the studio, but to von Stroheim.

The situation was different with the run-of-the-mill extras, however. This group often bore the brunt of von Stroheim's attacks and insults, and could have cared less about his attention to detail. They were day workers, and even before Hollywood unionization expected to work a humane schedule for their modest pay checks. This group began to grumble during production, and while they did not have Mae Murray's access to Irving Thalberg, they did take their problems to the production manager, J. J. Cohn. Von Stroheim would shoot until 5:00 a.m., then set a call for later that morning. While the studio technicians received overtime pay, extras only earned a flat rate. Cohn answered their complaints by ordering the head of the electrical department to shut off power to the stages at midnight. Von Stroheim was furious, and no doubt marked down Cohn's action to studio sabotage.[34]

As filming progressed into 1925 Mae Murray grew more difficult, Mayer and Thalberg more nervous, and Erich von Stroheim more bitter. *Greed* had opened in New York on December 4 to some of the worst reviews ever published. Von Stroheim was already in agony over the butchery of his masterpiece, but the degree of rage expressed in these notices added insult to injury. It also looked as if a lot of money would be lost on the picture, and von Stroheim had not had a box-office success since *The Devil's Pass Key* almost five years earlier. In this atmosphere tempers were drawn, and the slightest differences of opinion threatened to close down the picture. Valerie was on the set each day and observed many of these tantrums. One morning they were filming in Griffith Park the scene in which Sally and Mirko ride through the Bois. Von Stroheim gave Mae Murray a simple order and she refused to comply. This seems to have involved a controversy over whether Sally would toss the horse's reins over its head on dismounting. Von Stroheim, who knew a thing or two about horses, cracked "Who do you think you *are!*" According to Mae Murray's own account her response was simply, "The queen of M-G-M." It was clear that nothing could be done with the queen that day, so the entire company returned to the studio.[35]

The worst of these incidents occurred during the filming of the "Merry Widow Waltz" scene. Some accounts claim that von Stroheim did not even want to film this sequence, but this is hard to credit. Remember the crucial episode in the *Merry-Go-Round* script where the Count and Gisella decide their future while dancing "The Merry Widow Waltz" at Gisella's birthday ball. But von Stroheim had never gotten to the point of filming that scene, and whenever he was prevented from using some good material in one picture, it was sure to crop up again somewhere else. A glance at the *Merry Widow* script reveals an expansive array of close-ups and "perambulator" shots here, strong evidence that the scene was of real interest to him.

It was Mae Murray's big moment, too, because for her this dance was the centerpiece of a film which had otherwise strayed far from its origins. Here is where she could demonstrate once and for all that this would be remembered as a Mae Murray picture, despite everything. With 350 extras finally in position, filming on the dance was about to begin when von Stroheim went up to Mae Murray and "showed her how to do the step."[36] This was the last straw. "You dirty Hun," she screamed. "You think you know everything!" She threw her peacock headdress to the ground and began stamping her feet. Erich and Valerie turned quickly, left the stage, and went home. Thalberg was ill, and J. J. Cohn was off in Palm Springs. These two were nominally supportive of von Stroheim, and in their absence Louis B. Mayer dealt with the situation personally. He considered von Stroheim to have walked out on his contract and assigned Monta Bell to take over the picture. After the lunch break Bell climbed up on the high camera parallel, but something was wrong. The extras began chanting, "Von Stroheim! We want von Stroheim!" This was no doubt instigated by the

Ultimately, von Stroheim filmed the waltz the way *he* wanted.

"elite guard," but was quickly taken up throughout the stage. Production was impossible.[37] Mayer had made a point of publicly replacing von Stroheim, and Mae Murray was still demanding an apology, so it would be no easy task to patch things up. Von Stroheim stayed home, and Bell tried to continue with the picture. Trouble grew when the stagehands—studio workers and not especially beholden to von Stroheim—also refused to work. Mayer went down to the set with Eddie Mannix, comptroller of the studio and an ex-bouncer at Palisades Park. Similar troubles with Neilan and some of the other directors made it imperative that Mayer assert his authority over the crews. He began to harangue them in the gutter language he would drift into when aroused, and tempers flared. One grip seemed to make a move for Mayer and was flattened by a punch from Eddie Mannix. The mutiny was quelled.[38]

Von Stroheim, meanwhile, had gone back to Madame Ora, his fortune teller, to report what had happened. She had earlier told him to go ahead with the picture despite his misgivings, it would be "a feather in (your) hat." Now he told her that he was in the street, having been escorted to the studio gates by Louis B. Mayer personally. Her reply was that he would continue directing the picture in the morning, and further, that a group of men in uniform were waiting for him in his home that very moment. Von Stroheim found this a bit hard to swallow, but his faith in Madame Ora was justified.[39] Owen Martin and Wilhelm von Brincken were waiting for him when he returned, acting as self-appointed emissaries between studio and director.[40] After shuttling back and forth that night between Mayer and von Stroheim they finally arranged a meeting of all aggrieved parties. Reported a page-one article in the *Los Angeles Record* the next day:

> The city is quiet today after a wild night of fear and rumor. Peace was signed by Erich von Stroheim and Mae Murray at midnight in the office of Louis B. Mayer, head of the M-G-M studios. The terms of the treaty have been withheld, but it was learned that von Stroheim won his demand for absolute authority in the direction of *The Merry Widow*. The treaty also provides, it is understood, that von Stroheim's armed forces, led by officers who served in the world war, will be demobilized. They will retain their uniforms and sidearms . . .[41]

The film finally wrapped on March 9, 1925. It had been in production fourteen weeks, and the studio kept its bonus money. Worse, von Stroheim was personally billed $78,000 in excess charges, thanks to a clause in his contract which made him responsible for cost overruns. Von Stroheim claimed that this figure represented the cost of retakes

ordered by Thalberg, filmed by an assistant, and never even incorporated into the final print.[42] On the studio's books the negative cost
would be $608,016.31, almost the same as for *Greed* (see chart). Von
Stroheim insisted that the real cost of the picture was only $275,000,
and that all the rest was inflated overhead and accumulated star salaries
(i.e., payment to Mae Murray for all the idle weeks since her last picture). But there was no arguing with the M-G-M accounting department.

Von Stroheim had managed to complete the film himself, and in what
for him was a relatively short period of time.[43] But it was impossible to
continue at M-G-M, and on April 14, five weeks after the close of
shooting, his contract was cancelled by mutual consent. In the agreement
signed that day official costs were fixed for both *Greed* and *The Merry
Widow* to serve as a basis for calculating von Stroheim's percentage of
profits. *Greed* was pegged at $585,250, and *The Merry Widow* (offi-
cially still in production) was given as $500,000. Thalberg edited the
film himself while recovering from his first heart attack. He cut surprisingly little, although at ten reels the film was still considered un-
necessarily lengthy by exhibitors. It is unknown whether von Stroheim
was able to assemble a cut himself before leaving the studio, but the
editing (credited to von Stroheim's cutter, Frank Hull) closely parallels
the shot breakdowns given in the shooting script. As noted, audiences
lost a good part of Tully Marshall's role, but even according to von
Stroheim only about one reel was eliminated by the studio.[44] On August
25 the film opened in New York at Gloria Gould's Embassy Theatre,
a 600-seat jewelbox which was one of the smallest first-run houses in
any major city. The critics were ecstatic, and especially surprised at the
miraculous performance extracted from Mae Murray. The *New York
Times* did feel that von Stroheim was mixing Emile Zola with Elinor
Glyn,[45] but all such criticisms were minor and the film ran for months.

As can be seen in the chart, von Stroheim never received a penny
of his 25 percent of the profits of *The Merry Widow,* which became
his most successful box-office picture. The studio held "losses" from
Greed against the *Merry Widow* profits, as had been specified in his
contract. But the incredibly low foreign receipts on *Greed* indicate that
the picture was dumped overseas, despite reasonable domestic grosses
for so depressing a film. Had M-G-M promoted the film properly in
Europe the situation would have been far different. Sadly, the question
of these *Merry Widow* profits haunted von Stroheim for years. When
he was unable to find work following the *Queen Kelly* fiasco in 1929
von Stroheim and his lawyers kept pressing the studio for an accounting,
insisting that the film had earned a $4.5 million profit.[46] But the figures

Erich Von Stroheim Productions—Statement of Costs and Receipts
June 5, 1930

	Greed	The Merry Widow	
Negative Cost	585,250.00	608,016.31	
Less, Advance to Director	(30,000)	(30,000)	
	555,250.00	578,016.31	
Excess Cost Charged Against Director's Share	—	(78,016.31)	
	555,250.00	500,000.00	
Positive Cost	54,971.82	62,544.80	
Advertising & Exploitation	53,654.28	47,300.55	
Motion Picture Dues	1,726.92	5,116.55	
Total Cost	665,603.02	614,961.90	1,280,564.92
Net Receipts:			
United States	224,500.39	665,269.20	
Canada	3,063.11	22,292.20	
Foreign	47,264.05	308,664.84	
Total	274,827.55	996,226.24	1,271,053.79
Balance to Clear			9,511.13
Advance Against Director's Profits: Greed		30,000.00	
Merry Widow		30,000.00	
Excess Cost, Merry Widow		78,016.31	
		138,016.31	

N.B. Although the two films were within $10,000 of breaking even by 1930, the excess costs and advances which had been separately broken out would have been subtracted from von Stroheim's 25% of the profits. It should be noted that the receipts reported for *The Merry Widow* are substantially lower than the figures given in Samuel Marx's *Mayer and Thalberg,* which were drawn from Eddie Mannix's notebooks.

always evaporated. About the only thing von Stroheim wasn't charged for was a lawsuit brought against the studio by the real Prince Danilo of Montenegro, who was awarded 100,000 francs ($4000) by a French court in March, 1930.[47] (Prior to this he had successfully agitated to have the film banned in Yugoslavia.) In 1933 von Stroheim learned that the studio planned a remake of *The Merry Widow,* and he tried to use this as a lever to increase his chances of seeing some of the profits from his version. But by this time he and his family were in such reduced circumstances that after lengthy negotiations he accepted Thalberg's offer of $5000 for all his interests. In a stroke of poetic justice, the remake, directed by Ernst Lubitsch, proved a disaster at the box office.[48]

But *The Merry Widow* did serve to re-establish von Stroheim as one of the industry's top directors, and actually won him a new reputation as a director of stars. Whether he liked it or not, von Stroheim was now

sought after to direct second-string Mae Murrays, a chilling twist of
fate, but one he was soon able to turn to his advantage. When *The
Film Daily* polled the nation's film critics that year, *The Merry Widow*
tied for third place with Fairbanks's *Don Q, Son of Zorro,* behind *The
Gold Rush* and *The Unholy Three,* but ahead of *The Last Laugh, The
Freshman, The Phantom of the Opera, The Lost World, The Big
Parade,* and *Kiss Me Again.*[49]

Von Stroheim's later disavowal of the picture, its image as a "typical
M-G-M star vehicle," and its extreme stylistic contrast with the revered
Greed (as well as its unseemly box-office success) have all conspired
against the film for modern writers. A standard approach is to dismiss
it as an interesting "transitional" work.[50] More recently, revisionist
criticism has turned inside-out the opinions of those 1925 critics and
declared the film subversive of all the values which acted to make it a
success.[51] The problem with such commentary is that the writers are
unable to separate the film from a pre-existing image of von Stroheim.
Foolish Wives, Greed, and *The Wedding March* are held out as yard-
sticks, and the idiosyncratic *Merry Widow* fails somehow to measure
up. For a variety of reasons, von Stroheim was here exploring avenues
he avoided in other films, an exploration reviewers of the period were
quite willing to allow. To appreciate fully his accomplishments here,
The Merry Widow must not be seen simply as a sketch for *The Wedding March,* but as a complete work with themes and values of its
own. That these are necessarily more modest than those present in his
grander works seems obvious given the circumstances of production
outlined here. But few could deny that had *The Merry Widow* been
the only film von Stroheim ever created, he would still seem a match
for all the other directors on the lot the day he put this film before
the cameras.

Shortly before breaking with M-G-M von Stroheim tried to interest
the studio in a script called *The Crucible,* in fact a retread of his unproduced 1918 screenplay *The Furnace.* Von Stroheim submitted a
22-page treatment to Harry Rapf, but the idea never got past the story
department.

In this complex World War I melodrama, Dr. Mortimer, an American physician, has married a Belgian wife after completing a course of
X-Ray training at Heidelberg. He takes up practice in Belgium, where
the couple have three children—identical twins Lucienne and Angela,
and a son named Raoul. The wife dies and Mortimer takes to drink.

Angela develops a talent for music, and Raoul for art, "but a cubist
taint in his thoughts prevented achievement." Lucienne goes to Heidelberg and earns her M.D., returning home on the very day of the

Sarajevo assassination. She had become engaged to one of her professors, Dr. Kraft, who when the Germans occupy Belgium is assigned to the local military hospital. Tensions arise between the sisters over their younger brother, Raoul, who is living with a girl named Mimi. Lucienne does not approve, but Angela supports them with money. Angela's own lover, Bartholome, a violinist attempting to compose an opera on the Oedipus legend, is killed in the war. Raoul is shot and badly wounded.

The women all work at the hospital, which is housed in a former convent. Mimi revenges herself on Lucienne by substituting water for tetanus anti-toxin, knowing Lucienne will be blamed. When several deaths result the Germans investigate and sentence Lucienne to be executed. Dr. Kraft tries to discover a way out and approaches the military commander, Count von Below. He blackmails von Below over a murder he knows the Count committed years before, and von Below agrees to replace the real bullets of the firing squad with blanks. Lucienne will pretend to fall, and be spirited away by the nuns.

But von Below never gets to fulfill his part of the bargain. After catastrophic gambling losses that night he decides to rape the daughter of the Belgian family he is quartered with. Her screams bring help and von Below is shot.

In the morning the execution goes off as scheduled. Kraft is distraught, and meets Angela at the graveside. She accuses him of being no different from all Germans and throws away his flowers. Von Below recovers and again takes over the military command. As the fortunes of war change, American marines are about to overwhelm the town. Von Below orders Kraft to stay behind and surrender the hospital. Mimi confesses to the doctor that Lucienne is not dead: Angela had drugged her, exchanged places with her, and sacrificed her own life so that Lucienne might live. Von Below is the last German to evacuate the town, and kidnaps "Angela" (really Lucienne) as he leaves.

Among the marines is Captain Rogers, who had also been a student of Kraft's and secretly loved Lucienne. Informed of the kidnapping a group races to the rescue, and just as von Below is about to accomplish his rape of Lucienne he is shot by Kraft. Lucienne still claims to be Angela, but Mimi reveals the truth, and when she learns of the doctor's failed attempt to save her sister Lucienne is reconciled to him.

Raoul returns from a German prison camp with a painting that will make him famous, and is reunited with Mimi. Rogers and Kraft sail to America to found a children's hospital, and Lucienne goes with them—although the exact nature of her affections is left unanswered in the surviving material.

The outline certainly does have the flavor of something von Stroheim might have written in 1918, especially in its strong echoes of Griffith's *Hearts of the World.* But while the melodrama is uncharacteristically wild there are strong elements of plot structure and characterization quite typical of von Stroheim's later work. Although nearly lost in the clumsy handling of eight major characters, the stories of Angela/ Lucienne and Kraft/von Below are worth noting. Once again we see the notion of a single character split into two halves, here in terms of male *and* female personalities. Angela and Lucienne are twin graces, blessing humanity through science and music (their Cubist brother has a hand in here somewhere). Kraft, the good German, is shadowed by von Below, who represents those lower instincts of humanity implicit in naturalist philosophy. As in *The Merry Widow* we also have a clear split of the "von Stroheim character" into twin halves, the dedicated physician and the caricatured Hun. The resolution of this story involves eliminating one of these doubles, a tactic von Stroheim would apply in similar fashion to his next film, *The Wedding March,* where one female sacrifices herself for another, while the good Prince Nikki vanquishes his dark alter ego in mortal combat.

The reader's report sent down from the story department felt that the script was perhaps a bit too complicated for its own good, and that the "theme and symbolism" discussed in a foreword to the treatment were not clearly in evidence in the work itself.[52] The foreword is gone now, and the theme and symbolism look fairly straightforward to modern eyes. But von Stroheim and M-G-M had little to say to each other by this point, and the story went back into von Stroheim's trunk, ready to be recycled for later projects.

Out at M-G-M, von Stroheim found himself without a studio, and without an income. During the summer of 1925 he looked for work around Hollywood, but his reputation preceded him. The pain of his asociation with Mayer and Thalberg could not have made him any easier to deal with, and the idea of working under contract again could not have been pleasant. His life with Valerie became more and more difficult. In November it was announced that he would star in and direct an adaptation of George Barr McCutcheon's *East of the Setting Sun,* an old fashioned "tale of Graustark" which Joseph Schenck would handle for United Artists.[53] Nothing came of this, either, although von Stroheim would return to the project a few years later. For the first time since he had blustered through Carl Laemmle's doorway, von Stroheim was looking for work.

The Wedding March

One evening at dinner Erich and Valerie were seated next to independent producer Pat Powers and his current protégé, Peggy Hopkins Joyce.[1] Powers was one of the real film industry pioneers, having been Carl Laemmle's partner in Universal when it was founded in 1912, and only selling out his interests in 1920, just as von Stroheim was establishing himself there. Since then he had done very well as a producer of low-budget action pictures on Hollywood's poverty row. Those theaters unable to afford Laemmle's Hoot Gibson westerns might easily turn to Powers for an inexpensive substitute. At the moment he was very involved in trying to establish Peggy Joyce as a film star, and was looking for a director to take charge of the project. Von Stroheim's success with Mae Murray made him a likely candidate, but when Powers tried to talk him into the project von Stroheim neatly turned the tables. Few people were ever able to talk von Stroheim into anything. Instead, before the evening was out, Powers had committed himself to financing one of von Stroheim's own projects, a great, nostalgic homage to prewar Vienna to be called *The Wedding March*.

Von Stroheim became so involved in outlining this production that he completely disregarded the growing attentions of Peggy Joyce, much to Valerie's relief. Joyce was a notorious celebrity groupie whose most auspicious Hollywood fling had been with Charlie Chaplin, and at another moment von Stroheim might well have become interested. But tonight it was the free-spirited, hard-drinking Powers who appealed to von Stroheim. Fed up with the executive-ridden bureaucracy of M-G-M, he found the chance to tie himself in with Powers's independent operation too good to pass up. Von Stroheim always had his best relationships with Irishmen anyway, people like John Farrow, Don Ryan, and

Father John O'Donnell, pastor of St. Augustine's Roman Catholic Church in Culver City. Except for Joseph Schildkraut, there were few Germans or Austrians in von Stroheim's inner circle.

With another friend, Harry Carr, von Stroheim secluded himself in a mountain cabin early in 1926 and began to flesh out the script. *The Wedding March* at its core was a new version of the story he had failed to put on screen as *Merry-Go-Round*. But the years at M-G-M had made von Stroheim a different person—more reflective, less sure of himself and the world around him—and his story would be different, too. After one false start, where "ghosts" drove the two collaborators back to Hollywood,[2] they settled in a cabin at La Jolla, overlooking the sea about 90 miles south of Los Angeles. Unlike his work with Glazer, the collaboration with Carr on *The Wedding March* was a true partnership, Carr adding shape and direction to the ideas generated by von Stroheim. A night person, von Stroheim did all his best writing —and most of his best directing—after sundown. At La Jolla he would rise at noon and discuss his ideas with Carr for two or three hours, then dictate the new scenes to a secretary as they sat near the beach. According to Carr, von Stroheim was always formally dressed, even wearing a cavalry sabre as he wrote to help induce the proper mood. After dinner the two would talk more about von Stroheim's ideas, and after his collaborator had gone to bed von Stroheim would stay up until 3:00 a.m. writing them down.

In a feature article for *Photoplay* Carr left an unusually revealing account of von Stroheim's working methods:

> In the story there was to be a motherless girl. Von said he couldn't write about a motherless girl—unless he knew what her mother was like. So we had to sit down and spend days on end manufacturing the life story of a woman who was never intended to appear in the story. We told how she fell in love with her husband; their early struggles together; the coming of wealth; his temptations; and her sorrow. Finally her illness and death.
>
> Actually, Von made me invent a placard to be placed outside her house when she was dying: "Please walk your horses quietly through this street: serious illness within." And he translated it into German. And—mind you—this woman was never to appear in the story.
>
> "Now," said Von, when we properly killed off the lady, "I know what the girl is like."[3]

The assemblage of such milieu detail would put Norris or even Zola to shame. But of course it was the work of just these men which inspired his own philosophy of heredity as destiny, and his insistent belief that the world of our parents limits and defines our own. Remem-

A nostalgic return to old Vienna, with von Stroheim now the handsome Prince.

ber that von Stroheim had added to "McTeague" huge sections intended to inform our understanding of the dentist by detailing the life histories of his father and mother, episodes which Norris himself had neglected to draw, but which to von Stroheim were the real heart of the matter. As much as *Greed, The Wedding March* would show how the dead hand of the past shapes the destinies of the present. But now the story would be von Stroheim's own, and the past, his past.

The script was finished in a matter of weeks, a blueprint of the Vienna that existed in von Stroheim's mind's eye. "I got the idea of *The Wedding March* one day when I was so homesick I felt physically ill. It is not because I do not love my adopted land—it is the natural feeling of one far from home, who remembers those carefree, happy days when life flowed at full tide, without responsibility, flashing past one like the drama in a fascinating story of adventure and romance."[4] How carefree von Stroheim's own life was in those days is open to question. The film he was writing is certainly nostalgic, but instead of the Vienna of Strauss and Lehar we find a melancholy town seen through the eyes of Schnitzler and Freud. Von Stroheim's *Wedding*

March would be a *valse triste,* a melancholy air tinged with the pain of great personal loss.

Although never really a part of the Imperial circle, von Stroheim had felt the fall of the Hapsburgs severely, reacting as if he himself had actually lost power or status. In a curious article published after his brief return to Vienna in 1930 he mourned the absence of "the military sound of the feet of officers' horses on cobblestones," and the "soldiers strutting and pulling their moustaches for the admiration of red-cheeked nursemaids." In their place he found a Vienna filled with war profiteers and latter-day socialists, now grown fat and complacent with the end of the Empire. From his youth he remembered a May Day demonstration, unexpectedly energized by the appearance of the Emperor's Life Guard, breaking out into spontaneous cheers of "Hoch der Emperor!" at the first sight of Franz Josef's carriage.[5] For *The Wedding March* von Stroheim tried to recapture this magic: Vienna was gone, but through the power of his imagination it would live again.

The Academy of Motion Picture Arts and Sciences has preserved various treatments of the *Wedding March* script, from an early, single-page synopsis hardly more than a rewrite of *Merry-Go-Round,* to the full and final shooting script. Although the *Greed* script is so far the only von Stroheim screen play to achieve publication, it is really *The Wedding March* which captures his characteristic sense of poetry and epic drama at its best. The story opens at the palace of the Wildeliebe-Rauffenbergs. It is Corpus Christi morning and they are preparing for the day's great "military and religious celebration." Prince Nikki will ride sentinel with the Emperor's Life Guard Mounted, but he has to get out of bed first.[6] Before leaving he tries to raise some cash from his parents, but their only response is "Blow out your brains—or marry money." The procession takes place in front of St. Stephen's Cathedral, and while lining up for duty Prince Nikki spots in the crowd a charming young *susse madel,* Mitzi, accompanied by her parents and an oaf-ish, brute butcher named Schani. Schani is filled with anti-aristocratic invective, but Mitzi is charmed by the Prince, and leaves a bouquet of violets in the lip of his boot. In an astonishing sequence of some two hundred shots von Stroheim relies entirely on editing to establish the rapport between them. There is not one image where Nikki and Mitzi appear in the same frame.[7] Just before the procession leaves the Cathedral Nikki's horse rears up out of control and crushes Mitzi's foot. She is carried away in an ambulance and the protesting Schani is taken off by the police. They miss the glorious procession which unites the ritualistic pomp of the Empire's religious and military establishments—for the last time, as it will turn out. It is the first of the script's three great "marches," and for added emphasis von Stroheim filmed it in Technicolor.

Nikki visits Mitzi in the hospital, but neglects to tell her of his Imperial rank. "Let's make it just plain—Nikki," he says. Later he visits her at the wine garden run by her parents, "Zum Alten Apfelbaum," another Eden decorated with naïve statues of Adam and Eve. She plays "Paradise" on the harp, and later they go down to the Danube, where Mitzi tells him of the Danube maids and the Iron Man, contrasting symbols of good and evil whose appearance portends future destinies. The evening ends in the apple bower, as delicate white blossoms begin to fall on the lovers.

When Schani returns from prison he hears of Nikki's visit and is furious. "I'll kick his glass-eyed mug to goulash!—an' make you wear a necklace o' his teeth!" he screams. Nikki spends much of his time at Madame Rosa's, an elaborate brothel at no. 69 Kelnerhofgasse, but he leaves early one night to see Mitzi again. Their scenes together are intercut with the continuing brothel party, at which Nikki's father arranges his marriage to Cecelia, the lame daughter of a corn-plaster magnate. The old aristocracy hopes to refill its depleted coffers through intermarriage with the most grotesque elements of the status-seeking *nouveaux-riches*. The party reaches its climax in a drunken parody of a wedding procession. Just at the same time Mitzi sees a vision of the Iron Man, and with it a premonition of disaster and death. The specter arouses her dog as well, and its barking wakes Schani, who sees Nikki and goes down to confront his rival. They fight and Schani is thrown into the pig sty.

Mitzi goes to the Cathedral to confess her seduction by Nikki, and in a lovely visual metaphor we see how this ancient ritual cleanses her soul of all stain of sin. Later it is the night before the wedding, and Nikki returns in the rain for a last visit. "Isn't it funeral weather?" he asks. "Yes! And the storm tore off so *many* blossoms," Mitzi answers. "Spring—is *all over*." He tells her of the wedding. The next morning Schani taunts Mitzi with news of the wedding reported in the paper. He tries to rape her but is stopped by his father. In a fury he threatens· to kill Nikki when he leaves the church that afternoon. Nikki and Cecelia are married in the Cathedral. As the bride limps down the aisle, hands playing "Die Hochzeit March" on the organ dissolve into skeletal hands, the march of new life turning into a march of death. Outside it is raining buckets. Schani and Mitzi have arrived, and Mitzi promises to marry him if he will not shoot the Prince. The royal couple pass them by and enter their carriage. Who were those two strange people, Cecelia asks? "Professional class-hater!" says Nikki. "She—one—that—takes in Weddings—and Funerals!—Loves to weep! I suppose!"

The honeymoon trip to their mountain estate gets off on the wrong foot with a variety of ill omens, including Cecelia's falling over the bridal threshold. She naïvely tries to play the suitable bride for Nikki, but her bouquet of apple blossoms brings up painful memories and he abandons her. The next day Nikki climbs to the hunting lodge high on a mountain peak, leaving Cecelia behind. Schani and Mitzi go to be married, but at the last moment Mitzi collapses in a faint, driving Schani to further cries of revenge. Eventually all four find their way to the cabin at the pinnacle, Mitzi bursting in to warn Nikki, and Cecelia stepping in front of the bullet Schani had intended for her husband. Schani is driven away by the hunters, and Cecelia is told by her doctors that she must stay absolutely still or die. But she realizes the true love of Nikki for Mitzi and fatally drags herself to the foot of a giant crucifix.

Back in Vienna, Nikki is free to marry Mitzi, but finds the wine garden closed and the family gone. He spends his time at Madame Rosa's, where he hears one night of the declaration of war. Nikki's assignment is to patrol the Serbian border, where bands of renegades and ruffians are terrorizing the countryside. Mitzi has entered the convent of the Sisters of the Order of the Bleeding Heart, and the convent comes under attack by one of these bands. Leading the group is a bespectacled hunchback, and Schani is one of his lieutenants. Both wear "comic opera" parodies of Imperial Austrian uniforms. They are running riot in the convent when Nikki's troups arrive, and in a terrific battle he personally saves Mitzi from Schani's lust. Nikki marries Mitzi at the convent altar, promising, "If I come back from this campaign—we will follow spring around the world!" He must ride off as the battle reaches the outskirts of the convent. With as much pomp as they can muster the troops gather and ride out, the film's last "wedding march." Says Nikki, "Nobody can say—we didn't have a lot—of music—such as it is!"

This plot served as a perfect vehicle for von Stroheim's various concerns and obsessions, but it is not for his plots that he remains a great filmmaker. Wrote one critic, "Basically, *The Wedding March* is just *The Student Prince* with an odorous background, plus touches of *The Fatal Wedding*."[8] Von Stroheim's debt to *Old Heidelberg* is clear, but the force of his dramatization is entirely the mark of his own imagination. *The Wedding March* is a film of contrasts and parallels. Upper and lower classes, sacred and profane love, ritual and chaos, each are juxtaposed throughout. Just as von Stroheim's characters are typically caught on the horns of a dilemma, so the filmmaker himself is faced with the choice of two conflicting modes of life, dramatic manifestations of the internal conflicts of the Empire. Nikki's world is splendid and glamourous, but burned out and crumbling from within. Marriage is a mockery and true love a joke. Opposed to this is the proletarian world of Schani and the other "professional class-haters," hypocrites who envy the very pageantry they seek to smash. Mitzi is at the center of this struggle and only her love can resolve it. But fate is against it, along with those twin evils of lust, sex and money. The need for money forces a not so unwilling Nikki into the mockery of a marriage to Cecelia, abandoning his true love. Even the boundaries of class fall before the need to prop up the sagging fortunes of the Wildeliebe-Rauffenbergs, and the daughter of the corn-plaster magnate seems a splendid catch. This emphasis on money is, of course, typical of von Stroheim, and goes beyond the simple class-consciousness of the "Old Heidelberg" plot. So is the recurring contrast of sacred and profane love: Nikki goes directly from Madame Rosa's to a late night assignation with Mitzi. Although their lovemaking drives Mitzi to the confessional the next day, this love is truly a sacred love, since it is motivated by underlying spiritual factors. For von Stroheim, this fact overwhelms any problems caused by weakness of the flesh. In an introductory title card he dedicates the film to "the true lovers of the world." This is no mere sentimental gesture, but refers to a special state of grace which the film seeks to celebrate.

Again von Stroheim uses a variant of the romantic triangle on which to structure his personal relationships, and in this film of carefully balanced contrasts it emerges with more than usual symmetry.

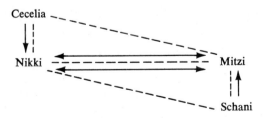

We are given two opposing and overlapping triangles, one with Nikki at the center, the other with Mitzi. Both figures are given romantic choices, and forced by circumstances to make the wrong decision. But the wedding bonds between Nikki and Cecelia are never consummated, and those between Schani and Mitzi collapse at the altar. Only that between Nikki and Mitzi is sanctified by true love, consummated, and ritualistically celebrated (in that order). Cecelia and Schani are the two destabilizing elements in this equation, and have been eliminated by the film's conclusion. Schani, in fact, actually kills Cecelia while aiming at Nikki, and at the end is disposed of by the Prince himself. In those last scenes at the Bleeding Heart Convent the script takes flight, blazing with operatic intensity, as elements of D. W. Griffith melodrama merge with the climax of a fairy-tale romance. In this climactic duel over Mitzi, Nikki battles a symbolic extension of himself. Schani wears a parody of the Austrian Life Guard Mounted uniform, "apparently bought in Masquerade store." He is a personification of the dark underside of Nikki's character, of all the ugly "man you love to hate" qualities. Nikki vanquishes this dragon, and in so doing purges himself of its venom. Redeemed by his love for Mitzi, he is at last worthy of it.

Von Stroheim learned from Griffith the technique of combining an intimate personal story and a larger narrative of epic scale. He saw this device at work in *The Birth of a Nation* and *Hearts of the World,* and adopted it for his own ends. The larger story here is the fall of Empire and the coming of the Great War. As noted, von Stroheim identified completely with the *ancien régime,* no matter what his true origins.[9] He detested the anti-monarchist notions of the socialists in particular, and in Schani we see an image of the mindless violence he finds at the core of revolutionary thought. Here is a cure that is worse than the disease, a new level of hypocrisy to make one nostalgic for the straightforward decadence of the Hapsburg court.[10]

A reporter for the *New York Times* found him wandering about the minutely detailed settings he had ordered built at Pat Powers's studio. " 'It is Vienna,' exclaimed von Stroheim as he walked about through the various sets and scenes, and those with him observed a sad note in his voice—'Vienna, before the great war of 1914—Vienna the melodious, the romantic, the dramatic—my Vienna'!"[11]

Richard Day again was the art director, and designed three dozen elaborate sets, including a detailed replica of St. Stephen's Cathedral. Most of the sets were built at the Associated Studio, still generally referred to as the Selig Zoo Studio from the time when Col. William Selig had shot animal pictures there in the early days of Hollywood. But Mt. Alice in the High Sierras was used for mountain locations, with lodges built there to von Stroheim's specifications. Later parts of these locations would be rebuilt at the Lasky Ranch to facilitate night photography. The man who had luxuriated in the natural surroundings of *Greed* had an entirely different idea in mind for *The Wedding March*. To von Stroheim, *Greed* was a piece of reportage, a page torn from the daily paper. But *The Wedding March* was a secret dream, and no location on earth could contain enough "realism" for that.

> I distrust any method of design other than the direct, not because I do not believe in expressionism or cubism or any other mode, but because the public won't accept them as entertainment . . . The film has won the reputation of defeating the stage in spectacle. Well, we must continue to defeat the stage by outdoing its realistic scenery. There's one of the reasons for solid stuff. Personally, I do not believe in trying to use actual locations. I might go to Schonbrunn for this story about the Emperor Francis Joseph. But fancy dragging a company over there, securing permission to use the castle for a couple of days, and then find it raining. As to the devices for saving money on scenery by double photography, mirror projections, and so on, they are good as long as your technicians don't spend too much *time* perfecting them. Time is more valuable than money, and if you are hung up because the mathematicians go wrong fitting your final picture together, you might as well have spent money building the whole setting solid.[12]

When von Stroheim and Harry Carr had written the script they crafted it to fit the personalities of von Stroheim's stock company. With no one to tell him otherwise, von Stroheim would play Prince Nikki himself. Zasu Pitts would be Cecelia, and George Fawcett and Maude George would be Nikki's parents. Von Stroheim needed to be able to see physical types as he created the characters on paper, and so the script will describe a character as looking, "with squinting eyes and lynx-like expression so typical of Maude George." A new face was Matthew Betz, picked from the ranks of stock villains to play Schani, and the crucial role of Mitzi was also open. Von Stroheim had created an ideal, and would now have to find an actress to live up to it. Mary Philbin was now one of the biggest stars at Universal, and unavailable—and besides, the role called for a new face, a discovery. Casting the female lead in the new von Stroheim picture was big news in Hollywood throughout the spring of 1926, and there was no shortage of applicants. But von Stroheim and Carr had terrible problems in finding a girl with the right mixture of innocence and sensuality. "They are all hard-boiled, or dumb and gooey sweet," wrote Carr. "Nine-tenths of the girls available are more common than gum stuck under the edge of the chair."[13] One of the hopefuls was a young actress whose film experience had been limited to Hal Roach comedies and Universal westerns, a 5' 3" brunette named Fay Wray. An agent convinced her that she was the perfect Mitzi, and together they showed up at von Stroheim's office. At first they couldn't get past the lobby. Von Stroheim was looking for a blonde, a short blonde, since he himself was only 5′ 5″. They went away but returned another day, Fay still a brunette, but this time trying to look as short as possible, hair down and heels flat. This time they made it into von Stroheim's office. "It was a really tremendous experience for me to meet him and sense his electric, dynamic quality. I sat in a chair while he *told* the story, and he paced up and down telling the story, and I simply listened. And finally he said to me, 'Do you think you could play that role?' And I said, 'I know I can!' He took my hand and he said, 'Well, good bye, Mitzi'."[14] At this she burst into tears, not a calculated reaction but an utterly spontaneous outburst. Von Stroheim got terrifically excited and knew, somehow, that he had found his co-star. He signed her without a test.

"When I heard that von Stroheim had reached down and picked up an unknown girl from the cow operas to play the lead in the most important picture he had ever made," wrote Harry Carr, "I was inclined to suggest to his family that they select a pleasant padded cell, and put him under restraint."[15] But von Stroheim's instincts were good. Fay Wray, even as a brunette, really was the ideal Mitzi. And just as important, she was able to stand the rigors of production as well as anyone in the stock company who had been through it all before.

Shooting began on June 2, 1926, as close as possible to the feast of Corpus Christi.[16] For the first time von Stroheim was unable to use either Ben Reynolds or William Daniels behind the camera. Daniels, the real genius of the pair, had stayed behind at M-G-M. He would soon make a reputation photographing Garbo, Shearer, and Crawford. To replace him, von Stroheim's first move was to hire the team of Harry Thorpe and Bill McGann. He had known them since his days with Fairbanks, and they can be *seen* at work in the credits of *When the Clouds Roll By*. Buster Sorenson was working with them as camera assistant, and in an article in *Motion Picture Magazine* he recalled the first day of shooting: "Previous experience had spoiled me. I thought that over eight hours a day was criminal, and to work nights was beyond my comprehension. The first day we started at nine in the morning, at ten-thirty that night we were still going strong with no prospect of quitting, so absorbed had this man become with his work that time meant nothing. Next morning seven of us tried to quit . . ."[17] Sorenson stayed on, but McGann and Thorpe made a hasty exit. Hal Mohr,

a young cameraman with few major credits, was quickly brought in to
take over.

The first big hurdle was the apple orchard scene, which would be
Fay Wray's first work in the picture. Von Stroheim had the trees decorated with hand-made blossoms which were to drift down on cue. Estimates on the number of these blossoms range from 50,000 to 500,000.[18]
After a month of waiting for her scenes to begin, Fay Wray was finally
called to the set. Reporters were all over the lot, as von Stroheim films
were always good copy and sets were only closed for certain sequences.
Dorothy Bay was one who recorded the scene:

> He stood behind the camera and directed the lighting, had someone
> take his place on the seat while he looked through the lens to get the
> right angle for shooting—then stepped in front to play it—he uses no sub-
> stitute directors. This night Fay . . . was noticeably nervous. It was her
> first scene with him, and overwhelmed by the importance of it all—and
> knowing how rarely anyone ever did anything to suit him—she was afraid
> of herself and her work. But von Stroheim, sensing it, drew her down
> on the seat beside him, took her hand *reassuringly,* and with an under-
> standing patience talked to her like a child for over an hour—about
> everything else but the subject at hand—until she forgot herself. And
> when he gave a silent signal for the camera to start grinding, she played
> her part with him almost perfectly—as he had known she could.[19]

Having chosen his actors for specific physical and emotional attributes,
his preferred method of directing was to elicit from them their most natural responses. Only when pitted against a rigid "performer" like Mae
Murray would hysteria be a daily occurrence. "He had a marvelous talent to find something, some mannerism, some attitude you might have
naturally that he liked, and he would say, 'Use that,' " remembers Fay
Wray. "And so he made you feel that you were in fact creating as you
went along. And he was not an imposer of ideas. I think he rather
freed you, because there was a strength about him that made you feel
that whatever you did was all right, and that he would just guide you.
Then when you did something that he liked he would praise you very,
very much. On the other hand, if things didn't go just like he wanted,
then he could be rather severe, and there were highs and lows."[20] Of
course, only the lows made news.

Von Stroheim felt the confession scene one of the most critical in
the film, and shot the sequence as an extended series of dissolves. This
had to be done in the camera, with the cinematographer winding the
film back manually. The procedure had to be timed perfectly, for one
mistake would ruin the whole sequence. Fay Wray had been on her

knees, crying, for a long time, and von Stroheim was giving her instructions for one of the final shots. "He wanted me to blow my nose. And I was almost stiff, and I just felt that I wanted to press the handkerchief against my nose, and that's what I did. Afterward he said, 'Why couldn't you *blow* your nose! Why couldn't you really *blow* it hard?' And he really stormed, but it was too late . . . he was furious with me."[21] Harry Carr was there, too. "He threw his megaphone clear across the stage and stalked in a white fury from the scene . . . He used to shriek at her to go back to the cow operas whence she came . . . In *The Wedding March,* if every scene hadn't ended with Fay Wray in hysterics, we would have thought something wasn't running true to form."[22] Buster Sorenson reported similar outbursts:

> During the shooting and rehearsing of a scene . . . a visitor made the remark, "That man is impossible. If I were in Miss _____'s place I would walk right off the set and tell him to go to Hell." The truth is we had been on that particular close-up since two that morning, and it was daylight then. And every minute of that time was spent in abuse to Miss _____ to break a haughty, stubborn, know-it-all spirit and opinion of herself. To get this result took just such abusive treatment. To print what he said and how he said it would be embarrassing; as a matter of fact, you could say, "I don't believe a man would talk to a lady like that." Had we not known him, we would all have harbored the same thoughts. But after each severe lashing he would look at us and wink. Even Miss _____ knew why he talked the way he did . . . There has not been a day during the picture that some individual has not wanted to thrash him, but thirty seconds later Von apologizes wholeheartedly for his hasty remarks.[23]

Von Stroheim would feel driven to these excesses when he felt a performer was not able to summon up a sufficiently convincing reaction. He would then manipulate that person, using verbal abuse, psychological tricks, sometimes even physical threats. In one scene Matthew Betz was in his butcher shop, having just heard about Nikki's visits from Mitzi's mother. Betz was supposed to appear mean, animalistic, and von Stroheim was not satisfied. Hal Mohr remembered the scene clearly:

> We were dying of the heat. So this butcher shop had several sides of beef and mutton and pork and so on hanging on the hooks. And this set had been standing there for god knows how long, and the stuff was never refrigerated. It was just hanging there and you could smell the set a mile away. And the stuff was—Christ, it was full of maggots and everything else, just rotting away. Well, they did have a fresh hunk of beef for Betz to work on this cutting block for this particular scene . . . Betz was supposed to turn at the end of the scene, cut this chunk of beef off of this thing and stuff it in his mouth and start chewing. He'd stand there

just viciously chewing this thing which was supposed to be the end of the sequence. And Von would never say cut. He'd just keep going and going and going, and this poor bastard, you could see him getting sicker and sicker. And he'd finally run off the set and throw up. And Von would say, "All right, let's try it again. See if you can get it this time!" I have no idea how many takes we made of that scene. Just, he was a sadistic guy. He liked to make people suffer. And poor Matt, he had a bad time with that. He threw up until there was nothing left to throw.[24]

Von Stroheim never had any illusions about his own acting, and always had Harry Carr take his place behind the camera and offer his approval of the performance. "As an actor, Mr. Von thinks himself of the worst," wrote Sorenson. Often he would refuse to play a scene if visiting actors were on the set, feeling painfully self-conscious about his abilities. "He always came up, shaking his head mournfully and despairingly," wrote Harry Carr. " 'No good, huh'? he would say. Once I was so swept away by his genius as an actor that I told him it was good the very first time. He gave me a look of hurt reproach . . . The next time, I made him repeat the scene seven times over. At the end he walked over to the leading lady, bowed with a click of his heels, shook her hand and said, 'The two rottenest actors in Hollywood.' "[25] Hal Mohr remembered that von Stroheim gave him the authority to stop a take at any moment if he discovered a large cyst on the back of his neck was visible. Great pains were taken to hide this from the camera, but von Stroheim refused to have it surgically removed.[26] Eventually he was operated on for this lump in 1932.

Harry Carr was always on the set, not only as von Stroheim's collaborator, but as a soothing force the production office could rely on (Valerie no longer spent every day on the set). The day's work could be abandoned for all sorts of reasons, and it was up to Carr to keep the picture on the tracks.

> One night we had a terrible time over it. He was taking a big scene with an overhead expense like the French national debt. I beckoned him to a studio doorway to see the moon crescent. But he was stopped by a sudden panic. It seems that it is no good unless you jingle silver in your right pocket. And Von had no silver. I offered him two dimes. No good. Had to be his own money. I suggested he do something for which I would pay him twenty cents. Great idea. I suggested that he walk across the set and back. No; no good. In the end we had to go over to his bungalow where he painstakingly worked out a suitable scene. I paid him the two dimes. The night was saved.[27]

Despite such outrage, aggravation, and general nonsense, morale on the set was surprisingly high. The atmosphere was that of a fraternity initiation. Mohr remembered, "It was a kind of family effort insofar as the crew was concerned. I mean everybody liked everybody else. We worked like dogs. Stroheim was a fiend for work. Many nights I never even got away from the studio. I'd just sleep for two or three hours on the set and go to work—the next day's work."[28] Fay Wray would drive herself home each night with her head cradled in her left hand, fighting sleep. And be there again at six every morning.[29] "Were it not for the personal feeling his crew wouldn't stay a day," wrote Sorenson. It would be the great shared experience of their lives.

The film had been highly budgeted from the start, but once again costs began to get out of hand, often because of seeming indecisiveness on von Stroheim's part. He would do scenes thirty or forty times with no hint of added direction. "He wanted a certain thing, but he didn't know exactly how he wanted it and apparently he kept hoping that each new take of the scene might get closer to it. And sometimes he'd just get up and say, 'Oh, to hell with it. Just print them all.' "[30] Other times his compulsion for "realism" would force absurd and expensive delays. He was psychologically unable to use "cheat shots," simple re-arrangements of actors and props that are necessary when the camera angle changes. In coming in for a close-up, for example, the changing perspective reorders the alignment of objects, often destroying the compositional balance. Von Stroheim would prohibit any "fixing" of such problems, and the work had to be done surreptitiously if the shots were later to be cut together without distracting the audience.[31]

"His punctilious insistence on detail has in it a good deal of child—the little boy who wants everything just so—or he won't play," wrote Harry Carr.[32] But what even Carr failed to realize was the significance of these details in the over-all scheme: not merely in terms of plot, but as a way of transcending the limitations of a mass medium which needed first of all to appeal to the lowest common denominator in any audience. "For the benefit of those who bother to use their brains we provide one or two pointers which suggest an additional, more subtle aspect," said von Stroheim. "For people who want to read more into a scene than meets the eye of the mass audience we indicate that the additional attraction is there."[33]

Of course the orgy scenes were the source of the wildest stories, and were here carried out with an exactitude bordering on madness. The set was boxed in with flats, and the stage was closed off to visitors. (Fay Wray was not allowed on the stages for ten days.[34])

The actors were all on the set and they began drinking. It was during prohibition. We had gallons of bootleg gin on the set and all that sort of

Schani, Nikki's rival, a transparent figure of the beast within.

thing, and Von drank along with the rest of them, and everybody got pretty pissed. . . . And then actually it became a Viennese whorehouse in almost every sense of the word. And then we started lining up shots and figuring out what the hell to do and we shot it almost off the cuff . . . They had call girls on the set and a lot of booze, and they had the rugs—there was screwing going on under the rugs on the set. I mean I say it was. It certainly looked like it. If it wasn't screwing it looked like it. And they had a couple of burros on the set and the gals were teasing the burros and giving them erections and all that sort of nonsense. And we photographed all that shit. I don't know what the hell ever became of it, but Von was able to get a few moments of realism out of the thing that told what he wanted to tell . . . The result was, only about a fiftieth of what we shot was usable, but that was the way he would get his realism.[35]

Tales of this spree, and rumors as to the location of the footage, were prime Hollywood stories for many years. When *The Wedding March* was finally released *Variety* coyly reported ". . . one tip being that there's enough out to make a couple of stag dinner reels."[36] Needless to say, von Stroheim's reputation was hardly helped by such stories, which undoubtedly grew even more bizarre as they passed through Hollywood.

By this time Pat Powers realized that the film was outstripping his ability to finance it, and turned over the production to Paramount. Von Stroheim could no longer depend on his personal rapport with Powers to see him through, since Zukor and Lasky were now exerting direct pressure themselves. Things began to cloud over. Hal Mohr quit when von Stroheim's rages began to turn in his direction. His replacement was Roy Klaffki, an old-time cameraman who was a charter member of the A.S.C. The company moved to the Sierras to shoot the location scenes for the mountain episodes. The work was grueling, with much climbing over hard rock required of Zasu Pitts and especially Fay Wray. By the time they returned to the studio only the convent episodes remained to be shot. But Powers had run out of patience and Paramount had run out of cash. On January 30, 1927, production was stopped. After eight months of shooting costs stood at $1,125,000 (although von Stroheim only felt he had spent $900,000).[37]

Again the problem of cutting the film to a reasonable length was countered by von Stroheim's suggestion of a two-part work. The first part, to be called simply *The Wedding March,* would end with the marriage of Nikki and Cecelia.[38] Part two, *The Honeymoon,* would include all the material from the hunting lodge sequences onward. The original shooting script contains no indication of such a break—the idea arose only during the editing process.[39] Von Stroheim urged Powers for funds to shoot the final convent episodes, but apparently was resigned to bring the film to a conclusion as it was—if only he could be allowed to do the cutting himself. For seven more months he worked on the picture, along with Frank Hull, his chief cutter.

> On October 8, however, I was suddenly taken off the film. B. P. Schulberg announced that he was suddenly turning the editing of the picture over to Josef von Sternberg, whom, he stated, would edit the picture in two weeks time.[40] Instead von Sternberg spent several weeks on the editing, and then his version proved so unsatisfactory to Paramount that they took the picture away from him and turned it over to Julian Johnston for a new editing.[41]

Powers went to New York to show von Stroheim's two-part version to Jesse Lasky, but Lasky refused to look at it. Powers refused to accept the Johnston version. Finally, Lasky gave Powers permission to cut down the two-part film into one twelve-reel feature. When Powers showed this new version to Paramount they supposedly approved it, but began previewing the Johnston version in a screening at Anaheim which was reviewed by the trade papers.[42]

Josef von Sternberg's influence on the picture is difficult to trace. According to his own testimony he discussed his suggested changes in advance with von Stroheim, and received his approval for the cut he produced.[43] But von Stroheim's own thoughts, in letters to his biographer, Peter Noble, fail to indicate this.[44] Historian Lotte Eisner, who was close to von Stroheim in his later years, writes that von Sternberg was a "declared enemy" who purposely cut the film to pieces.[45]

There were two previews of two different cuts in the winter of 1927-28, first the Johnston at Anaheim, and another at Long Beach. The Anaheim version was criticized for white-washing the character of Nikki to the point of absurdity. Wrote one critic, "when the seduction scene was reached, it gave the impression that Mitzi, his victim, had been the aggressor."[46] This was remedied in the Long Beach cut, although whose version this was is impossible to state. Again, as with *Foolish Wives,* von Stroheim's long months of polishing and tuning were supplanted by abrupt changes that turned the film on its ear almost overnight. The *New York Times* announced that *The Wedding March* was ready for a January, 1928 release,[47] but instead it went back up on the shelf again. Talking pictures were on the horizon and the industry was in turmoil. Paramount had delayed its release of *Abie's Irish Rose* and refilmed it with talking sequences. *The Wedding March* was an expensive question. Finally it was decided that the film would be issued with a synchronized music and effects score, to be recorded on discs. J. S. Zamecnik and Louis de Francesco composed this music, one of the most sensitive surviving examples of silent film scoring.[48] Although von Stroheim had been off the film for months, Valerie insists that he had carefully planned out all of the musical cues to be used with the film, and it is possible that Zamecnik and de Francesco had access to this material.

Finally, on October 14, 1928, the film made its appearance at New York's Rivoli Theatre. Von Stroheim had wanted its great length to take up all of the space usually occupied by newsreels, shorts, and staged prologues. He failed in this, too. On its first run *The Wedding March* shared the bill with a Max Fleischer "Out of the Inkwell" cartoon. Initial eight-day grosses were a very respectable $51,500, but two weeks later the film drew only $19,900 and was pulled after six days.[49] It drew well at other metropolitan theaters, generally playing the standard single week booking, but was not an exceptional hit even in the big cities (*Wings* ran everywhere for many weeks that season) and died elsewhere.

The film had been so long in the making that at least two members of the cast had since died. The more sarcastic critics prominently referred to them as "the late" George Nichols and Hughie Mack, but they

were not the only aspects of the film that time had passed by. Talking
pictures were all over Broadway the day *The Wedding March* opened,
and audiences could see and hear *Lights of New York, The Terror,
The Singing Fool,* and quite a few others. While their technology was
crude and their aesthetic value mediocre, it was clear that here was the
wave of the future. By contrast, the languorous *Wedding March* seemed
instantly dated and old-fashioned. The lingering lap-dissolves, combined
with von Stroheim's penchant for building up his *mise-en-scène* with innumerable close-ups, caused wide-spread complaint. The *Times* felt the
picture, however truncated, was still "much too long," and suggested it
might "benefit by cutting."[50] It was a "ponderous slow moving production" to one critic,[51] and for another the plot development was "absolutely snail-like."[52] At 10,400 feet the film ran 115 minutes, not an
extraordinary length for the time (*Wings* was 12,267 feet), but the intensity of von Stroheim's *mise-en-scène* proved overwhelming. Welford
Beaton, one of the few reviewers of the period to display a strong and
consistent critical posture, felt the close-ups were clearly at fault. He
accused von Stroheim of creating fabulous love scenes, then chopping
them to pieces with close-ups, "proving that Von treated Griffith's discovery as wildly as he did Pat's bankroll."[53]

Many seized on the first meeting of Nikki and Mitzi just preceding
the Corpus Christi procession, truly one of the most lavish uses of
close-up montage this side of *Passion de Jeanne d'Arc.* "Root of the
evil is the time given the Corpus Christi event, from which the succeed-
ing action never recovers being none too swift in itself."[54] Blissfully
self-indulgent, this "slowness" might today be better described as "intensity," a factor general audiences of 1928 were unable to accept.

While business in the big cities was fairly good, the "general patron-
age" reaction from the outlands was terrible. Among comments from
small-town theater managers quoted in the *Motion Picture Almanac*
are the following: "Well, THE AGONY IS OVER. I am a glutton for punishment but this picture sure made me run up the white flag as the people came out" (Perkins Theatre, Holton, Kansas). Another: "It's a
14-reel messed-up picture. We booked it for three nights, but we didn't
have the nerve to show it the second night. In London or in some foreign country . . . it might be understood and called a big picture"
(Dixie Theatre, Durant, Mississippi). "Fourteen reels of wasted film.
Too bad exhibitors are compelled to show these high-priced flops"
(Harvard Theatre, Harvard, Nebraska).[55] After the respite of *The
Merry Widow,* the exhibitors were back to grinding their teeth.

Late in life von Stroheim did have the opportunity of recutting the film, and was able to make some minor changes and readjustments. Working at the Cinémathèque Française with a release print of the film and the fourteen-disc soundtrack, he produced a 16mm sound-on-film copy, which is the version generally shown today. A detailed comparison of this print with a continuity of the original release version shows only minor changes: an occasional shot shortened or reordered, the introductory stock footage of Vienna replaced with footage clipped from a print of *Merry-Go-Round*. He was limited by the lack of new footage, and the inflexibility of the pre-recorded score. But he did make some substantial cuts in the confession scene, eliminating titles and tightening up the editing. The sequence plays much better here than in a copy of the original release version preserved by the American Film Institute. Unfortunately, poor laboratory work caused the needless cropping of the left-hand part of the frame to make room for the soundtrack, something which drives unprepared audiences to distraction.

The film he cut at the Cinémathèque, however, was only part one. Part two, *The Honeymoon,* had been so poorly put together he could scarcely stand to look at it. The film had never been released in America, and circulated overseas in a 7273 foot version, of which 2685 feet consisted of a ludicrous condensation of the whole of part one. This left about 51 minutes of unique material here, what remained of the hunting lodge episodes. The sole surviving print had also found its way to the Cinémathèque. Von Stroheim felt that this aborted copy was nothing but an embarrassment, and tried to keep Langlois from screening it, but it occasionally turned up, unannounced, at the tag end of screenings of part one. Shortly after von Stroheim's death in 1957 a mysterious fire broke out in the Cinémathèque, and the only print of *The Honeymoon* was destroyed. Henri Langlois insisted it was the work of von Stroheim's restless spirit.[56]

Queen Kelly

Von Stroheim now faced another contractual dilemma. Legally bound to Pat Powers for another picture, he was unable to accept any outside job offers, although Powers had no further personal use for his services. Early during the shooting of *The Wedding March* it had been reported that von Stroheim would film Ziegfeld's *Glorifying the American Girl* with Gilda Gray,[1] but this came to nothing, as did a projected version of *Hotel Imperial* with Pola Negri[2] (although Paramount later filmed both projects using other directors). For a time he planned a return to Universal, and on May 10, 1927, Louella Parsons reported he would be returning there following a split with Paramount[3] although in fact he stayed on at Paramount until August). The rumor reappeared in November in connection with a remake of *Blind Husbands.*[4]

His only substantial work at this time was some anonymous rewriting on a film called *Tempest,* which he did at Catalina with Lewis Milestone. In 1927 V. I. Nemirovich-Dantchenko, co-founder of the Moscow Art Theatre, had arrived in America to study Western film techniques. He succeeded in selling the outline of a story called *Tempest* to Joseph Schenck and John Barrymore, and Russian émigré director Viachetslav Tourjansky was hired to direct. But production bogged down and von Stroheim was brought in by his friend John Considine (the film's producer) to work with Lewis Milestone on an adaptation of Dantchenko's material. The pair worked together for several weeks but when Sam Taylor was brought in to replace Tourjansky both von Stroheim and Milestone left the project; eventually C. Gardner Sullivan received sole screenplay credit. Although there are touches in the completed *Tempest* that might be traced to von Stroheim, it is useless to speculate on them in detail in the absence of any surviving von Stroheim script.[5]

But von Stroheim had other irons in the fire. In March of 1928, readers of the California *Staats-Zeitung* were told of preparations for an Alsatian film with German cavalry, and any veterans of such a cavalry were requested to contact Wilhelm von Brincken at the Goldwyn studios with full particulars.[6] This announcement was far from routine: normally, cowboy extras would suffice in such roles, but this was to be no normal production. Wilhelm von Brincken, who claimed to have been a spy for the fatherland in the late war,[7] was now an assistant to Erich von Stroheim, and the film in question was to become *Queen Kelly*.

But the origins of *Queen Kelly* (and its ultimate fate as well) lay not so much with von Stroheim as with Gloria Swanson, a powerful star/producer eager to repeat a newly won success. In 1926 Swanson had quit Paramount to become an independent producer associated with United Artists. This loosely knit group had been formed in 1919 by Chaplin, Pickford, Fairbanks, and Griffith in order to place control of production in the hands of the filmmakers themselves, removing it from the supervision of big studio executives. By joining U.A., Swanson made a conscious decision to remove her destiny from the hands of Zukor and Lasky, and to take full charge of it herself. The first Swanson production, *The Love of Sunya* (1927), was very much in the tradition of her Paramount releases, wrapped up in sentiment, rags-to-riches opulence, and the romantic dilemma of the film's heroine. Although the opening attraction at New York's vast Roxy Theatre, it did not have the success anticipated. As if in reaction, she next turned to material of a radically different sort, and transformed Somerset Maugham's *Rain* into the absolute antithesis of all she had done before. The story of a San Francisco streetwalker on the run in the South Pacific, *Sadie Thompson* was directed in a consciously deglamourized fashion by Raoul Walsh. Walsh's forceful and assured style must have seemed a revelation after years of working with Allan Dwan, Frank Tuttle, and Richard Rosson, and it should be no surprise that she sought more of the same.

But producing as an independent proved a nightmare of organization and paperwork, and even before *Sadie Thompson* went into release, Swanson was in the process of acquiring a partner to take this managerial load off her shoulders: Joseph P. Kennedy. Hollywood legend has it that Kennedy's motives were a tangled mix of big business and romance, an opinion certified by Swanson's recent autobiography.[8] The book attempts to push full credit for the *Queen Kelly* debacle onto

Swanson's losses on this picture would be considerable.

Kennedy, with Miss Swanson emerging as an unlikely innocent, a character out of an Allan Dwan melodrama. It is probably true that with Kennedy eyeing Swanson, and Swanson eyeing Kennedy, nobody was keeping an eye on von Stroheim. But while the general picture of events in this account is correct, there is a lot more to know about the truth of *Queen Kelly*.

In reorganizing Swanson's production unit Joseph P. Kennedy took it upon himself to reorganize the rest of her life as well, dismissing her old retainers and substituting his own people, a crowd of Boston Irish who knew all about high finance and little about high filmmaking. Kennedy was no neophyte in the picture business, but his association with

Swanson on this film was a decided attempt at something different, a move up from the inexpensive FBO quickies he had previously been associated with. In 1920 the British Robertson-Cole Company built a studio for itself at 780 Gower Street, in the heart of what would later be referred to as "Gower Gulch," a concentration of low budget production firms specializing in westerns. The following year they reorganized as FBO (Film Booking Offices of America) and were soon firmly established as producers of inexpensive program pictures. Hayden, Stone and Company, the American banking firm, bought out FBO in 1926 and named Joseph P. Kennedy as president.[9] Under his regime the studio turned almost completely to westerns, many featuring Ranger, the Wonder Dog. A skillful application of eastern efficiency caused profits to soar for FBO—and Kennedy—but the challenge of producing such fare soon paled. Like many another businessman trying his luck in Hollywood, Kennedy was not satisfied with financial returns alone; he wanted to demonstrate his ability to create a prestige success, and Gloria Swanson would be his vehicle.

Late in 1927 he brought her together with Erich von Stroheim, and allowed the director to spellbind them with a tale he had personally designed for her, then called *The Swamp*. According to Swanson, Kennedy was delighted, Swanson not so sure. But for reasons of her own she had turned the management of her career over to Kennedy, and the decision to go ahead was his. Kennedy saw the new film as an artistic creation of his own, and (from Swanson's point of view) worked to suppress any connection in the public's mind between it and *Sadie Thompson,* Gloria's own production. Instead he wanted to link it to von Stroheim's *The Wedding March,* which Paramount was announcing for release early in 1928. What he thought of the powerful similarities of tone and style that link *Sadie Thompson* and *Queen Kelly* is unknown.[10]

Von Stroheim, however, was not so readily available. Although he had been relieved of all contact with *The Wedding March* in August of 1927, he was still obliged to Pat Powers for one more film. Powers had no wish to produce another von Stroheim picture, but planned to hold on to the contract until someone made it worth his while to do otherwise.

While this three-way negotiation was under way, von Stroheim began to proceed tentatively with his end of the deal. To avoid arousing Pat Powers, he used Wilhelm von Brincken as both surrogate and advance man. It was von Brincken who alerted the readers of the *Staats-Zeitung* while Kennedy, Powers, and von Stroheim were still hammering out the details of their settlement. Von Brincken was almost a miniature von

Stroheim, with a similarly mysterious European background and a close-cropped hair style which gave him a slight resemblance to the director. He had been an actor and assistant director on *The Prince of Pilsen* (1926), and appeared as one of von Stroheim's company of aristocrats in *The Merry Widow* and *The Wedding March.* He would play a part in *Queen Kelly,* although perhaps his best known of many later appearances would come as Von Richter in Howard Hughes's *Hell's Angels.* Von Brincken was placed in charge of research on *Queen Kelly,* and besides producing a thick sheaf of documentation on costumes and decorations, he also managed to locate a considerable number of those authentic German cavalrymen von Stroheim was looking for.

The first public announcement of a deal between Swanson and von Stroheim came on April 30. "Here's one to make your eyes bulge," wrote one columnist, speculating on the possibility of von Stroheim's completing the film within a rumored ten-week shooting schedule. "He's spent longer than that on a couple of scenes."[11] At this point there were two projects under consideration, "the life of a woman evangelist,"[12] as well as von Stroheim's original *The Swamp.* Aimee Semple MacPherson was at the height of her notoriety in 1928, and von Stroheim and Swanson might have made an interesting film by "sticking to her story,"[13] but the material would have been impossibly delicate.

Finally on May 19 it was reported that Powers had capitulated. "A good story would be that Gloria vamped P.A. (Powers) and succeeded in getting the director for whom she has been angling all these months," joked one paper,[14] but its version of the "real" story was equally suspect. Von Stroheim had supposedly agreed to direct some closing scenes for *The Wedding March,* hardly a likely event at this point. Instead, von Stroheim immediately set out for New York, trying, among other things, to locate a leading man for the picture. He returned empty-handed on May 29, and on meeting reporters at the railroad station promised he had turned over a new leaf in production economy. "There will be no delays, squabblings, run-outs or other embarrassing moments," it was reported.[15] This would be a recurrent theme of pre-production publicity, and would come back to haunt all concerned.

Fortunately for posterity, Gloria Swanson preserved a substantial amount of material detailing the production of *Queen Kelly* and, through the courtesy of James Card, I was able to examine these papers at the George Eastman House in 1971. Included were scripts and treatments in various stages of completion, shooting schedules, costume plots, original research materials, and laboratory records. In addition, complete sets of daily reports from the cameraman, script girl, and assistant director broke down the sequence of production in exact detail. A table correlating the main material in these daily reports is included in the Appendix. Now that we can read for ourselves the original von Stroheim treatments of *The Swamp* and *Queen Kelly* (as it came to be known during production) we are forced to consider many of the public statements of Swanson and von Stroheim in a new light. For example, in recent years Swanson has stated that von Stroheim originally specified the African location, the "Poto-Poto Saloon," as a dance hall— then somehow turned it into a brothel by the time of the shooting, much to her surprise.[16] This is not supported by the surviving script material, and while von Stroheim quite probably exaggerated the character of this locale during shooting, the original scripts leave little question as to the exact nature of the place. This is important, because if Swanson (and the Hays Office) were aware of this fact before production began, then the censorship scare which eventually helped close down the picture must have been the result of truly flagrant abuses on von Stroheim's part.

The Eastman House collection contains one incomplete script of *The Swamp,* the first folder of a two-folder treatment. It is not known if the second half has been lost or simply never written down, but what exists differs in several respects from the later *Queen Kelly* script. The story is set in a fictitious Middle European principality. Prince Wolfram arrives home and is dragged out to the balcony to greet the populace on his birthday. His servants actually have to manipulate his arms to get him to wave at the crowds, and he is wearing only a coat, no pants (which cannot be seen from the crowd). The Queen, his intended consort, comes to see him in the morning. "But the dynasty had come to the end of the direct line." There is an ugly scene. She complains about his "girlies," and asks him why he and she are not yet married. She uses her wiles to get him to agree to the marriage, and even cries.

That morning there is a grand review, during which the Prince loses control of his horse and falls off. A convent school crowd is near and he is comforted by one of the girls (Gloria Swanson). They both drink from her canteen and flirt. He keeps her handkerchief and goes back to the procession. Later at the convent the girl, Kelly, is punished by being deprived of dinner and being made to pray before the Virgin until midnight. At a banquet in the palace the prime minister announces the royal betrothal. Back at the convent, Kelly finishes her vigil and goes to bed. The Prince and his adjutant drive up and search for a way to break in; he is anxious about the day's events. They climb over a garden wall, then up a ladder and through a bathroom window; to rouse the girls

the prince sets fire to a tar barrel. An elaborate sequence shows the arrival of fire engines. The pair grab Kelly and escape out the window just
as the firemen break in. The Prince takes her back to his rooms, where
a table is spread with "all the delicacies, especially aphrodisiacs," oysters, caviar, lobsters, etc. He feeds her some oysters and several glasses
of champagne. He compares her to an orchid, kisses her, and she runs
out onto the balcony "while above all illuminating the whole scene,
looms the pale face of that ancient procuress, Luna." While the two sit
under the moon we see shots of fountains, swans, and a nightingale. He
carries her back inside.

Meanwhile the nuns and the firemen realize that Kelly is gone. A little later the Queen leaves her wing of the palace, surprises the pair, and
starts after them with a whip. The Prince is arrested and taken away.
The Queen has promised to send Kelly home properly, but instead
whips her out of the palace. Kelly is about to jump off a bridge when
she is stopped by a policeman, who takes her back to the convent. Just
as Kelly is returning a telegram arrives from Dars es Salaam asking her
to come. The Prince is in jail but he still has Kelly's handkerchief.

Titles introduce Africa. Kelly arrives in the port and is met by Kali
Sam, a black woman "resplendently attired in a large white Merry
Widow hat with numerous white plumes." They are taken through town
in a rickshaw and arrive at "Poto-Poto Gasse 69," a seedy brothel.
Poto-Poto, we are told, means "The Swamp." At the bar there is much
establishing footage of the various races mixing. Men dancing with each
other, fighting, etc. Kelly is terrified. They enter a back room, meet a
frowsy blonde "of the horizontal profession," whose name is Coughdrops, and who takes care of Kelly's aunt when Kali is not around. For
the first time Kelly meets her sick aunt who has been supporting her in
convent school. A nasty old degenerate (Tully Marshall) enters the bar,
buys a round of drinks, inquires about the aunt, and is interested when
he hears about Kelly. Upstairs the aunt confesses that she had to take
Kelly out of the school because her money had run out. Jan Petrovich
(Marshall) enters, overhears the conversation, and offers to take care of
Kelly and marry her. Says he has $100 million, 5000 blacks, and 80,000
square miles of land. He sends for a priest while the aunt, admitting that
he owns everything, agrees to the marriage. They are married and the
priest sends them out of the room as he administers the last rites to
Kelly's aunt. The saloon prepares for a wedding feast.

There is an obscene parody of the "Wedding March" procession as
the brothel orchestra plays "Here Comes the Bride." Jan removes her
mosquito-net veil and kisses her. The orgy that follows is demonstrated

through various optical devices (spinning champagne bottles, etc.). Kelly is led to bed by Kali, and Jan follows. Suddenly she runs into the next room and cowers beside her aunt's bier. She begs Jan to wait, says she will be a good wife, but later. Jan says he can wait for that and presents her to the crowd as the new madam. The crowd (which had followed them upstairs) goes wild. Suddenly Kelly grabs one of Jan's crutches and starts swinging it. "Out of here, you scum." She sits down, weary. Kali and Coughdrops offer her whisky and a cigarette, but she just looks at them. Jan says, "I can wait." The treatment ends with a note that, "There will be an intermission of ten minutes."

Of particular interest here is the first meeting of the Prince and Kelly, an inverted quotation from *The Wedding March*. In that film the prince's horse rears up and causes an injury to Fay Wray, the image of the horseman against the sky clearly indicating the physical and sexual potency of the aggressor male. In *The Swamp* the prince simply loses control of his mount, falls on his face at Kelly's feet, and is comforted by her; the woman has been placed in the dominant role. However, von Stroheim ultimately changed this scene again, as we will see later.

Considerable work was done on the script over the summer of 1928, for in October a "revised" shooting schedule was produced, cued to a 510-scene shooting script. The reason for the revision and delay is not clear, but at one point the *Motion Picture News* referred to "reports that Gloria Swanson and Erich von Stroheim have split . . . following many postponed production dates,"[17] a comment which implies rumors of serious internal strife even before the start of production. This shooting schedule was in two parts, dated October 8 and 15, 1928, and projected October 29 through January 23 as the film's production dates.

But while all this preparation was going on, Joseph P. Kennedy had faded from sight. Instead of supervising the project himself he assigned William Le Baron and Benjamin Glazer to oversee it for him. Le Baron had been a production executive back east for Hearst's Cosmospolitan and Paramount's Long Island studio, and currently was a vice-president of FBO. Glazer was von Stroheim's old "collaborator" on *The Merry Widow*. As producers, they were the least intrusive pair von Stroheim ever had to deal with. In fact, their participation in the project was completely unsuspected until Swanson revealed it in 1980.[18] That spring and summer Kennedy was busy engineering a complex deal which began when the Keith-Albee-Orpheum theater chain, of which he was a major shareholder, had absorbed the FBO studio in February of 1928.[19] Kennedy knew that talking pictures were coming in, and while he had little interest in making talkies, he knew who did. David Sarnoff and

RCA had been looking for an opportunity to promote their own sound process, RCA Photophone, which had been suffering in competition with the Western Electric system.[20] In October, Kennedy sold out his interests to RCA at a huge profit and was out of the studio business.[21] Sarnoff renamed the chain Radio-Keith-Orpheum and established a new production company, RKO Pictures, on the old FBO lot. *Queen Kelly* was in the process of shooting as the new company moved in its personnel.

The cast and crew for the production were not the usual FBO regulars. Nicholas Musaraca, an FBO contract cinematographer, did shoot one day's worth of panchromatic test footage on October 22, but he was not employed during production. Instead von Stroheim hired Gordon Pollock, a special effects cameraman whose "Pollock Process" he intended to use to fake such shots as a German cruiser in the harbor of Dar es Salaam. Von Stroheim had no compunctions about the use of such process shots, and the script contains several references to them (perhaps to indicate how reasonable he intends to be on matters of "realism"). However, while Pollock knew all about special effects, he knew little about the requirements of set lighting. He contacted his friend Paul Ivano, asking him to "come and help him," and offering a position as second cameraman.[22] Ivano was a French cameraman who had come to America after the war with Max Linder. As a contract cameraman at Goldwyn he had shot the test footage of Zasu Pitts for *Greed,* and accompanied the unit to Death Valley, where for three days (before falling victim to the heat) he shot landscapes and other secondary material. Among Hollywood cognoscenti he had won a reputation for his photography of von Sternberg's *The Sea Gull,* a film that had never been officially released. More recently he had been working with Ernest Palmer at Fox on *Street Angel.* Ivano was a willful personality not easily bent to the requirements of studio politics, and his career would suffer for it in later years.

Ivano worked with Pollock on pre-production tests, which Swanson approved. Pollock was in charge the first three days of shooting (November 1-3, 1928) then on Sunday, November 4, Ivano by himself shot more costume tests of Swanson in a style quite different from that of Pollock.

> Next day in the projection room, together with E.v. Stroheim, Joe Kennedy and others, Miss Swanson looked at the tests and she said: How come that these tests look the same as the original tests you and Gordon shot. I could not say it was my lighting and style, did not want

to hurt Gordon, but Gloria understood and from that day on I was in charge.[23]

Production records indicate that the first three days' work were in fact reshot at the end of the following week. William Margulies was first assistant cameraman on *Queen Kelly,* and it was his duty to load the film, follow focus, keep the daily reports, and so on. He assisted Ivano on the Sunday test and also remembers the effect it had on Swanson. "Gordon was really the boss up to a certain point and then, later on, Paul became the head man . . . I think that Pollock left after that."[24] Again according to Ivano, "Gordon got sick (nervous) and did not show up for days, and when he came back, I was still in charge . . . Ask anybody, I photographed *Queen Kelly.* Gordon got the $ [and] I the pleasure."[25]

A personality clash between Ivano and von Stroheim was inevitable. There are some cameramen who seem constitutionally incapable of subordinating themselves to strong-willed directors. Hal Mohr was one of these, and he had walked off *The Wedding March* not long before. Ivano was an idiosyncratic talent who only felt a responsibility to "please myself," and took no guff from directors like Murnau or von Sternberg whom he felt had exaggerated notions of their own abilities. On *Queen Kelly* he often quarreled with von Stroheim, but Swanson always had final say and refused to let him go. Ivano's recollections of von Stroheim are clear:

> He was a great actor, but as a director he was impossible. He used to fire me four times a day and I used to go and thank Swanson, "It was a nice engagement . . ." And she used to say, "Well, if you leave, you'll never work for anybody else. I'll have you blackballed." I said, "But tell von Stroheim I'm still on." So she would call him and bawl the hell out of him and we would make up . . .[26]

William Margulies recalls a time when Ivano was setting up a sunstreak beaming through a window:

> Von Stroheim said to Paul, "Paul, let's shoot it," and Paul says, "I'm not ready." And Von says, "I don't give a goddamn whether you're ready or not, shoot it!" And Paul said, "I will not shoot it until I'm ready." He says, "You're fired." So Paul walks off the set. Gloria comes on the set and says, "Where's Paul?" I says, "Von Stroheim fired him." "So, you sonofabitch, I wait ten years to find a cameraman to photograph me and you fire him." She says, *"You're* fired." And he walked off the set. About a half hour later they all come back with love and kisses.[27]

Margulies would serve as intermediary in these squabbles, which often descended to obscene ethnic epithets. Yet somehow Ivano stayed with the picture, and it achieved a visual style easily identifiable as that of a late von Stroheim film. Ivano himself admits that only a few of his other films were photographically the equals of *Queen Kelly,* implying that von Stroheim should receive a share of the credit for the photographic quality of the film. How did he accomplish this? Although not himself a cinematographer, von Stroheim knew what he wanted to see on screen, and was prepared to accept the contributions of his collaborators—or of fate itself—if he could get that ideal image up on the screen. While he knew that he wanted a lot of diffusion in certain scenes, for example, he never articulated this to the camera crew, merely condoned or condemned their efforts later on in the screening room. A typical anecdote relates to the heavy use of lap-dissolves in the film. These effects were accomplished in the camera, and the assistant was responsible for them. William Margulies remembers an error on his part which von Stroheim was flexible enough to praise. In moving the camera from a long shot to a close-up somehow focus was lost:

> Well, the fellow from the lab comes. "Oh my God, it was out of focus," he says. "Don't tell von Stroheim, it'll spoil his whole day." I says, "the hell with 'im." I didn't care. I was getting what? thirty-five, forty bucks a week? I didn't care who got fired . . . (In the projection room) the second scene comes on and he says, "What's the matter with that?" Nobody says anything. And he says, "What's the matter with that?" I said, "It's out of focus." He says, "Great! Just the effect I wanted!" He wanted that certain softness.[28]

Costumes for *Queen Kelly* were designed by Max Rée who also worked on *The Wedding March;*[29] he stayed on the lot to become head of the costume department when RKO took over. The art director was Harold Miles, who had done *Don Q, Son of Zorro* for Fairbanks, and whose later films included *The Iron Mask* and *The Big Trail.* Some sources credit Richard Day as at least a collaborating art director,[30] but there is no evidence for this in the *Queen Kelly* papers (admittedly sketchy on this point). In fact, he was still completing his M-G-M contract in 1928, although it is of course possible that this long-time collaborator of von Stroheim's contributed some anonymous assistance (only Miles received screen credit in the print released by Swanson). Von Stroheim himself would have had his usual say about the details of costume and decor, especially in regard to military regalia, but he was no designer either, and really does not deserve the credit here that some historians feel compelled to give him. Louis Germonprez signed the as-

Lavish settings and outrageous behavior.

sistant director's reports each day, although most sources say that Eddie Sowders was also an assistant on the picture. The script girl was Viola Lawrence, also a long-time von Stroheim collaborator; after Swanson gave up the idea of completely reforming the picture, it was Lawrence who restored it, as much as possible, to von Stroheim's original plan— as we shall see later.

To play opposite her, Swanson borrowed Walter Byron from Gold-wyn, a British actor whose total lack of charisma agreed well with von Stroheim's growing shift of interest from heroes to heroines. Swanson had a bad habit of casting the most insipid actors opposite her, regard-less of the damage to the film, and Byron followed in the tradition of Lawrence Gray, Eugene O'Brien, and John Boles (*Sadie Thompson* is again the exception).[31] As Queen Regina, von Stroheim cast Seena Owen, whom he had worked with on *Intolerance;* she had since ap-peared in Maurice Tourneur's *Victory* and a few William S. Hart films, but her career had not especially prospered. Tully Marshall again ap-peared as an old degenerate, a role he played for von Stroheim in *The Merry Widow*. He too, was an *Intolerance* alumnus.

Von Brincken was given a role as the prince's adjutant, and Sidney Bracey played the inevitable valet. The black prostitute in the African sequences was played by Madame Sul-Te-Wan (did von Stroheim re-member her from *The Birth of a Nation* and *Intolerance*?), and the white prostitute by Ray Daggett. The part of Kelly's aunt, brief but of some importance (mothers and mother-surrogates are always important in von Stroheim films) was played by Florence Gibson, who played the old saloon hag in the cut opening reels of *Greed*. Her appearance was reported in the *New York Times,*[32] but went unnoticed by von Stroheim scholars. The role was never attributed to anyone until 1967, when Joel Finler stated that the actress was Sylvia Ashton, Trina's mother in *Greed*. This was picked up almost simultaneously by Michel Ciment, and later adopted by Herman Weinberg.[33] In the original French edition of his biography, Thomas Quinn Curtiss credits the role to Josephine Crowell, although in the American edition published the following year this in-formation is "corrected" to Sylvia Ashton.[34] In fact, Josephine Crowell, another veteran of Griffith and of *The Merry Widow,* was indicated by von Stroheim in the script as playing the part. Curtiss must have seen this script and assumed that she had eventually played the role in the film. However, the assistant director's daily reports make it plain that Florence Gibson played Kelly's aunt in *Queen Kelly*.

The surviving shooting script of *Queen Kelly* is a working copy, al-tered during production to conform to changes that had been decided on since shooting began. Some scenes have been removed and others substituted, and there is no pristine copy to indicate what the script looked like before this occurred.

We open on the "miniature kingdom of Cobourg-Nassau" and its capitol, Reginenburg. Prince Wolfram Ehrhart Max Otto Johann Freidrich Albrecht Von Hohenberg Felsenburg arrives home after a night out and falls off his horse. When he is brought up to his rooms the Queen enters, screams and wrestles with him. They are to be married, although it has not been officially announced yet. She orders him to drill with his troops on the road all day, where he and his men encounter a group of forty convent girls. As one curtsies her panties fall down, and in frustration and embarrassment she throws them at the Prince. The nuns take the girls back to the convent, but not before the Prince has returned the panties; he and the girl make a wish on the hay from a passing hay wagon. Back at the convent the girl, Kelly, is punished with no dinner and being made to kneel before the cross until midnight. She reads a letter from her aunt, Molly O'Donovan, which says that she is ill, and that Jan has seen her picture and wants to marry her if she comes to Africa. Kelly prays to see the Prince again.

At the palace the prime minister announces the engagement of the Prince and the Queen. Later the prince and his adjutant, reminded by the hay, decide to go and look for the girl. They arrive at the convent but cannot find her, so they set fire to the building. Under cover of the confusion they seize Kelly and take her to the palace as the first engines arrive. In his apartment he serves her a meal replete with aphrodisiacs. Kelly is puzzled and admits, "You've got to show me! You see, they never give us oysters at the convent!" He compares her to an orchid, and says he will "never see orchids again without thinking of you." As they begin to make love in the moonlight we see a lap dissolved montage of swans, a nightingale, lilac blossoms, jasmine blossoms, azaleas, and orange blossoms.

Back at the convent they wonder where Kelly has disappeared to, and on the other side of the palace the Queen gets restless and decides to go see the prince, apparently with lascivious intent. As she sees Kelly and the prince she attacks them with a whip, shouting, "I thought you would stop dragging harlots into my house—at least—on the night of our betrothal." Kelly starts to go and the Prince is placed under arrest. Although the Queen promises him that she will see that Kelly gets home safely, as soon as he is out of the way she whips the girl out of the palace in a frenzy. Kelly leaps into the river but is saved by a policeman, who brings her back to the convent. A telegram arrives from Jan

Vryheid instructing Kelly to return to Africa at once, as her aunt has
had another stroke. The Prince meanwhile is in prison, beginning a six-
month sentence; his adjutant gives him Kelly's dress, left behind the
night before, and he hangs it up and serenades it on the violin. Kelly
leaves for Africa.

Part two.

Kelly arrives at the port of Dar es Salaam and is met by a black woman,
Kali, who takes her to a sloppy brothel on Poto-Poto street. Here we
see the lowest elements of all the races fighting, dancing, and drinking.
They meet Coughdrops, who offers them a box reading "One Cough-
drop a day keeps TB away." Kelly's aunt is bedridden upstairs; she cannot hear or speak and writes a note saying there is no money and Kelly
should marry Jan. Kelly dazedly agrees. Meanwhile Jan arrives (Tully
Marshall), a degenerate old wreck on crutches, and they all quickly
agree to the wedding. Priests arrive and begin the last rites with great
ritualistic detail. Kali and Coughdrops give Kelly a mosquito-net for a
veil, and tell her that Jan is "the richest guy in Africa." The aunt receives the last sacrament, and as the wedding begins someone gives
Kelly an artificial orchid. This reminds her of the prince, and she has
hallucinations in which she sees many priests (Pollock process) and
people's faces changing—priest to Prince, Kali to mother superior, a long
and complicated montage. Just as the wedding (in Latin) concludes the
aunt dies. While the rest kneel, Jan gives orders for Kelly to get ready
for bed, and goes downstairs to celebrate. Soon he invites the crowd to
come up and view the nuptial festivities. Kelly takes a pair of scissors
and threatens to kill herself, and says she will be a good wife and will
do "anything—but that!" Jan agrees and introduces her to the mob as
"the new madam—she'll deal out the booze, count the towels, take in
the dough—an' everythin'!" The crowd roars and Kelly grabs a crutch
from Jan, chasing them down the stairs with cries of "Out of here—you
scum! Downstairs with you—you dirt!" She stops for a moment to pon-
der a cigarette and a glass of whiskey she has been given.

Ten-minute intermission.

Eight months later the place is the high-class "Poto-Poto." Kelly is a
sexy tart with a police dog, orchids, and whips. She is now their "queen."
As a cruiser arrives in the harbor she is shown running the bar. Jan
comes in and the bartender asks him "Sick o' the swamp—or lonesome

for wifey?" She has never slept with him and the crowd is razzing him about it. She is in a superior position, he reduced to saying, "I can wait." She sees in the paper that it is the Prince who has arrived on the boat, goes to the pier, but changes her mind when she realizes what she has become. She opens a letter he has sent her, but burns it. The Prince on arriving refuses to go to an official ball but goes off instead in a rickshaw. Kelly contemplates suicide—a lap-dissolve of gun, razor, gas jet, and noose. She gets distracted by a poison bottle, but a companion tells her that men are not worth it, and Kelly goes down to the bar to forget her troubles. Here she begins flirting with some sailors from the Prince's ship, the *Aurora*. Later the Prince arrives, finds her drunk, and there is a terrible scene. Kelly sends him away. Jan gets aroused and demands Kelly immediately. She becomes hysterical and offers herself to the mob. "Doesn't anybody want Queen Kelly? Here I am!" The mob rushes Jan, who fires at them with his gun, and a terrific fight breaks out. Jan is killed. The mob is fighting furiously over her. The Prince hears about this and returns just in time to see a huge Oriental run upstairs after her. Kelly locks herself in her room while the Prince fights him, but he is knocked out. She reaches for the poison bottle as the Oriental begins to break the door down. The prince gets up again and defeats him, but just as he enters Kelly swallows poison. He apologizes for his earlier behavior and "she is overcome by the irony of fate." He calls for a doctor and she tells him she has kept herself clean for him. She screams "Have mercy Jesus!" as the doctor arrives with the stomach pump, but it seems too late. The Prince goes to a chapel and prays to the Virgin, and Kelly is saved. A telegram arrives announcing the death of the Queen. Kelly thinks he will leave her now, cries, and it begins to rain. But he says he will take her back and make her a real queen. Back in Europe (indicate use of stock shots and standing sets of *The Wedding March*) we see the marriage and coronation, at which Kelly says, "Majesty—me foot! Just plain Queen Kelly."[35]

There are few changes of note visible here. In the original treatment the Queen had used "feminine wiles," including tears, to coerce the prince into marriage; here she uses her power to order the marriage. And of course at the first meeting of Kelly and the Prince, Wolfram does not suffer humiliation, but Kelly has her pants fall down. These two changes consolidate the "dominant female" in the character of the mad queen, and emphasize the hapless, powerless position of Kelly, even whose underpants are controlled by fate.

A reading of these African episodes inevitably suggests a connection to the jungle-locale melodramas popular in the early decades of this

Kelly in Africa: terminal culture shock.

century. Such Joseph Conrad stories as *Victory* and *Heart of Darkness* mark the highpoint of this genre, which at its lowest ebb descended to simple racist pulp fiction. These stories dealt with action "on the fringes of civilization," where the European is tested in confrontation with primal natural forces. Wild West fiction also dealt with life on such a frontier, but there civilization was typically shown advancing, taming the wilderness, vanquishing the savages, and overcoming all obstacles before it. Jungle fiction was often the reverse of this Social Darwinist exercise. Here the white man had only a tenuous hold, and it was the forces of darkness that were ascendant. Civilization on this frontier was typically tattered and exhausted, its representatives effete rather than industrious. Many examples of the genre bear a surface relationship to *Queen Kelly,* but von Stroheim seems to have been specifically influenced by the popular melodrama *Kongo,* written by Chester de Vonde and Kilbourne Gordon, and produced on Broadway in 1926. Tod Browning filmed this as *West of Zanzibar* early in 1928 (at the same time von Stroheim was writing *The Swamp*) and it was remade by William Cowan in 1932, this time under its original title. An innocent convent girl degraded in the brothels of a steaming African port, and the fiendish revenge of a crippled ivory merchant, are but two of the plot elements of *Kongo* which von Stroheim seems to have appropriated for his own use.

As we indicated earlier, the surviving script incorporates changes devised during the course of production. What were they, and what was the original like? Von Stroheim has left the following comment on the start of shooting of *Queen Kelly:*

> The schedule was okayed and my story also, $25,000 being paid me for it. The first day on the set I was informed that I was $100,000 over budget. When I asked how this could be, they told me it was the accumulation of Gloria Swanson's salary and her personal publicity. So I was told to take $100,000 worth of scenes that were in my script and throw them out.[36]

The shooting schedule of October 15 covers the African episodes, and shows us in broad terms where these changes took place. It indicates that after the wedding sequence the action would shift to the jungle, including five days at Jan's house and seven at a "swamp tree" location. Obviously, Jan was to take Kelly home to his estates, but what about the "swamp tree"? According to one article written during production:

> The high-light of the yarn was to be when Gloria Swanson, clinging desperately to a tree, is rescued just as the huge stick sinks eighty feet into a swamp. This was the scene Von counted on. It was to furnish more excitement, heart interest, *et al.* than the other fourteen or so reels combined. It was his brainchild. It was, so to speak, his baby. But, phooey! Along came a supervisor with his big stick, or knife, and hacked the whole thing out. Too expensive. Out with it.[37]

Von Stroheim's later screenplay and novel, *Poto-Poto,* also contained elements of this African story. But *Queen Kelly* and *Poto-Poto* are not identical, and we cannot merely transpose the ending of *Poto-Poto* to fill out the missing sequences here. There is, however, a swamp tree in the *Poto-Poto* script to which the jealous planter ties his wife and her lover, an American aviator.[38] Orchids grow on it, rising from the slime of the swamp. As the rainy season causes the surrounding waters to rise, the pair will come within range of the swamp's "alligators."[39] In this case Gloria Swanson seems to have been tied to that tree alone, and it is her lover the Prince who comes to save her, not the U.S. Marines. Just why and when this was decided on we will discuss later.

"Following many postponed production dates"[40] the shooting of *Queen Kelly* finally began on Thursday, November 1, 1928. Scenes showing the exterior of the palace and the Prince arriving home drunk had been scheduled for shooting the previous Monday, but the sets were not completed in time. The company stalled for a few days, then decided to shoot the sequence showing the meeting of the Prince's troop and the convent girls. The script indicated this to be shot in Griffith Park (a location von Stroheim had used in *The Merry Widow*) but instead the Lasky Ranch was used, a gently rolling tract in the San Fernando Valley also known as Gopher Flats. Perhaps it was fate which later turned this plot of ground into an opulent cemetery, Forest Lawn Memorial Park. Ironically, this entire sequence was reshot the following week due to the change in cameramen described earlier. Almost before production got under way *Queen Kelly* found itself a week behind schedule.

This was before the union contract, and filming proceeded on a six-day schedule (with some Sundays devoted to tests) each day's work lasting as long as the crew could stay on their feet. Ivano remembers: "Our call was at 8 a.m. Lunch (cold) at 3 p.m. dinner (when?) and at 3 a.m. my chief electrician would pull the switches and we went home."[41] (The appendix lists the time of call, first shot, and end of work for each day of production.) While the first day's work ended at exactly 5:00 p.m., after this von Stroheim began keeping the company until 2:00, 3:00 and even 6:00 a.m., with the morning call soon moved back to 9:00 a.m.

> Property men barely ambled instead of ran. Actors slept standing up. Hollywood at the time was having a struggle with the flu epidemic and members of the Stroheim company, low in energy, swelled the sick list. Everyone was tired—awful tired. Everyone, that is, but Eric von Stroheim. He alone seemed to be enjoying it.[42]

At one point von Stroheim was shooting the sequence in which Seena Owen stalks the palace with her white cat. According to Ivano:

> That was a daylight scene that we shot at night. All I saw is Bill Margulies putting thousand foot magazines—they had just come out at that time—on my camera. We'd run six hundred feet, Stroheim would say, "Cut. No good." Why? "Don't ask me." So we shot until daybreak and he says, "Now we shoot night scenes." I say, "My dear friend, now we go home, because to cover the set in black canvas would take four hours." So. "You refuse to shoot it?" I said, "No, if you want to be here at eleven o'clock in the morning, fine." This was daybreak at four o'clock in the morning.[43]

This appears to have been November 10, 1928. William Margulies remembered the same evening over forty years later, although his recollections differ in detail:

> He was with Seena Owen that night on the balcony, and she gets out of bed and walks down the balcony . . . and all she had to do was look at him (the prince) and say, squint, "I'll get even with that guy." It took him until seven o'clock in the morning to get a close-up of her. He did it over and over and over and over. He didn't like it. Finally, at seven o'clock on a Sunday morning, the sun was up. He says, "I want a long shot of the castle, day," I said, "You go to hell. It's seven o'clock Sunday morning. I'm going home." So he said, "Okay, let's go home."[44]

Actually the company worked until 4:50 a.m. that particular day. They soon became as exhausted, physically and emotionally, as the crew of any von Stroheim picture. At one point even Louis Germonprez began grumbling at the indefinite postponements of the dinner hour. "You go to hell. We want hot soup in our bellies!" he muttered as he walked off the set with the rest of the workers.[45] Swanson lived in the studio and could put up with this; the rest of the crew raced home for a few hours' sleep, or napped on the set. Von Stroheim would spend the night at a brothel, Madame Frances's, whose staff may be seen in the film arriving home with the Prince after his all night binge.[46]

Von Stroheim was noted for his abusive treatment of actors who displeased him. Although he could hardly treat Swanson in this fashion (unlike Mae Murray, she was the producer of the picture), he vented his hostilities on the rest of the cast. "Erich was rough with actors," remembers Ivano, "and played the scenes himself."[47] Von Stroheim did not want to see an actor's interpretation, only a reflection of what he himself would act out in detail before each scene, a proclivity he shared with Chaplin, for example. He would rehearse with the actors before a shot, then "he'd have them do it over again and tell them it stinks and raise hell with them."[48] But Swanson appreciated the results.

> The experience of working with him was unlike any I had had in more than fifty pictures. He was so painstaking and slow that I would lose all sense of time, hypnotized by the man's relentless perfectionism. A scene that Allan Dwan or Raoul Walsh would have wrapped up in an hour might take von Stroheim all day, fondling and dawdling over the tiniest minutiae . . . But his exactitude always paid off in the rushes, and it was a course in the art of filmmaking to hear him defend his choices and explain his reasons . . .[49]

It's doubtful, though, that her appreciation was shared by Seena Owen, usually referred to by Paul Ivano as "poor Seena Owen." The

all-night shooting described earlier by Ivano and Margulies was probably so well remembered because Seena Owen was nude during much
of it. She had to get out of bed and walk to the balcony to watch the
prince as he arrived.

> She got out of bed completely nude . . . Then after about ten takes
> she said, "Sorry, I don't want to be nude." So we got her a pair of flesh-
> colored tights and after a few more takes, "No, I don't want my breasts
> to be exposed," when she walks out on the balcony. So they got her a
> white cat. She got out of bed and she picked it up and she covered her
> breasts with the white cat. But after a couple of hours the cat started
> scratching her. So they went out and got white mittens for the cat. By
> this time it was seven o'clock . . .[50]

If Swanson had once been satisfied that the script could get past the
various censor boards, it must have been von Stroheim's handling of
scenes like this that made her wonder about the film's future. And the
Poto-Poto scenes were still to come. Swanson was nervous about the
situation, particularly for the way it might reflect on Joseph P. Kennedy, whose connections with the Roman Catholic hierarchy were considerable. Early on in the course of shooting Kennedy came to a screening of rushes involving ". . . the scene where she loses her pants in
front of the cavalry, which was very nicely photographed, if you remember. Mr. Kennedy asked me, he said, 'What do you think of the stuff,
Mr. Ivano?' I said, 'Well, photographically it's fine, but I don't know if
you'll get away with it.' Stroheim kicked me, Gloria kicked me (I was
sitting between them). I said, 'What am I supposed to say to the man?
He asked me a question. I have to answer honestly.' Well, so I was in
the dog house for ten minutes."[51]

As Swanson watched reels of sequences like this pile up, she also saw
the costs climb steadily, apparently the result of von Stroheim's excesses. William Margulies remembers the pains taken over shooting the
engagement banquet, a few moments of action on screen:

> It started like nine in the morning, and we got a long shot and two
> close-ups by midnight and that was it. We had . . . a long table and
> everything on that table was authentic: the dishes, the silverware, the
> napkins, the flowers, the food. And all the guests of course were royalty.
> Ambassadors, and the prince and queen, and the ribbons and medals
> had to be perfectly authentic all the way down, you could hardly see
> them they were so far away . . . And then in back of each two people
> was a waiter in livery, and in back of each one of them was a guard with
> the plumes and the sword and the breastplate and the patent leather
> boots . . . It had to be absolutely authentic, you couldn't fake a thing.
> Way down at the end of the table a napkin had to be perfect . . . He

watched everything. He'd say, "I don't like that ribbon." Maybe wait an hour until they got the right ribbon.[52]

Still, von Stroheim's conduct on this picture was regarded as a remarkable improvement over previous films by all observers. Tod Welch described von Stroheim's inspection of a set:

> "At Universal I would kill them if they gave me a set like that." He stomps up and down the stage, gesticulating wildly with his walking stick. Once more he screams: "I ask for silver paint and you give me gold. Must I be a painter, too?"[53]

Yet despite such scenes Welch found plenty of evidence that "It appears Eric has at last got the producers' point of view and is willing to co-operate rather than artisticate." Cedric Belfrage also found von Stroheim less inflexible than before:

> Von Stroheim wanted to make the cat bristle up and look fierce coincidental with the Queen . . . But the cat refused to take any interest in its work. Bored from the first, it gradually fell into a state of lethargy from which it was impossible to arouse it. Even "Ranger" the Wonder Dog, borrowed from the next set, only made the cat yawn with his barking and growling. Stroheim at length gave up and took the scene with the cat asleep. Two years ago he would have got every dog in Hollywood into the studio . . .[54]

Von Stroheim himself told the *New York Times,* "I have changed my attitude. One naturally does as one grows older. I am more philosophical about the making of pictures. I am, so to speak, aged in wood, mellower."[55] But even aged in wood, von Stroheim's directorial style was proving too strong for Swanson and Kennedy.

The collapse of *Queen Kelly* was the final straw in the destruction of von Stroheim's career. Why and how did the film collapse so completely? In an interview with Philip Jenkinson of the BBC, Gloria Swanson reacted to the very mention of *Queen Kelly* with dismay. "Oh dear, do we have to go into poor, dear *Queen Kelly?* She'll never die. That was an experience that was quite something because it was never finished, you know. And there have been many stories about why it wasn't finished. Mr. von Stroheim naturally would have a different story than mine."[56] This is in fact the case. Von Stroheim stated directly in a letter to his biographer, Peter Noble, that it was Joseph Kennedy who stopped production when he realized that talkies would mean "the death knell of silent pictures."[57] Swanson's argument is that "we had censorship then and the picture was going to be in the wastepaper basket."[58] As we have seen, Kennedy unloaded his motion picture holdings to a company interested in exploiting talkies (RCA) even before *Queen Kelly* went into production. He had obviously come to his decision about the future of the medium in the summer of 1928, not in January of 1929. Later we will see how a move was made to turn *Queen Kelly* into at least a part-talkie even while von Stroheim was still directing, so von Stroheim's laying the blame on the arrival of talkies seems weak. We have also seen how the script clearly indicated von Stroheim's intentions, and that Swanson had no cause to claim innocence of, for example, the fact that the Poto-Poto saloon was a brothel. So the basically censorable nature of von Stroheim's script also was no reason to suddenly cease production after a small fortune had been poured into the film. Only the cumulative effect of von Stroheim's directorial extravagance is left as an explanation, and this seems to have been enough.

By the time von Stroheim began filming the African sequences on January 2, 1929, he was already one month behind schedule. On wrapping up the European sequences the company had vacated the FBO lot (now RKO) and had moved to the Pathé studio in Culver City, once the studio of Thomas Ince (and another studio in which Kennedy had an interest). This caused them to lose the entire week between Christmas and New Year's. Production records indicate that the company now began to keep regular hours, and quitting time was always before 8:00 p.m. This put a serious cramp in von Stroheim's style, as he had grown accustomed to his all-night shooting sprees. During 41 days of shooting at FBO, 21 had lasted until well past midnight.[59] That Sunday, January 6, a meeting was held at which von Stroheim agreed to truncate the African sequences. The exact reasons for this have not survived, but it was clearly the intention of all concerned to carry on with the picture, with von Stroheim remaining as director. All of the jungle episodes, including the swamp tree, were torn out of the script, as described earlier.[60] This saved the cost of the entire swamp set as well as Jan's estates, considerably contracting the scope of the film, eliminating the main portion of Tully Marshall's role, and bringing completion of the film reasonably close. This was the "$100,000 worth of scenes" mentioned by von Stroheim to Cedric Belfrage. Belfrage quoted von Stroheim as saying that this happened "the first day on the set," but the director obviously meant the first day on the Pathé set, not the FBO set.[61]

While von Stroheim rewrote the script, the company filmed the scenes of Kelly's meeting with her aunt, the wedding, the aunt's funeral service, and Kelly's threatened suicide. A memo exists of another meeting held on January 17 of Swanson, E. B. Derr (Kennedy's "financial watchdog"), and the writer-director Edmund Goulding. It is not indicated if von Stroheim attended this meeting, but the continuation of work on the African sequences, with von Stroheim in charge, is still clearly assumed. The main thrust of the meeting seems to have been a discussion of how best to inject sound into the picture. Edmund Goulding's part in this may have been crucial. He had spent several months in New York investigating the Movietone process early in 1928, and had published a wide-ranging article on the prospective use of sound in July.[62] He had written the just-completed *Broadway Melody* for M-G-M, and most interestingly, he was a song-writer at a time when theme songs overlaid on otherwise silent pictures were becoming standard.

A script and a note both dated January 19 (but from internal evidence clearly from January 17) reflect the company's attitudes as worked out at the meeting of Swanson, Derr, and Goulding. The script is identical to that discussed earlier in which the Prince rescues Kelly from the riot in the Poto-Poto saloon. It states:

> This script as it now stands shows what is to be shot in the African sequence after January 19. All the scenes cut out at the meeting with Mr. Von Stroheim on Sunday, January 6, have been eliminated from the script in its present form.

Following page 87 is a note reading:

> Scenes 210 to 286 cover Kelly's arrival up to her meeting with her dying Aunt; Kelly's marriage to Jan and the business of Kelly driving the 30 people out of her rooms and down the hall. At this writing practically all of the foregoing scenes have been shot, only enough remaining to keep the company working next Monday and Tuesday (Jan. 21-22). We are breaking off in the shot of the sequence just outlined by shooting the Banquet and Coronation tomorrow and Saturday. All of these sequences are silent except for synthetic sound.

"Synthetic sound" was a method of dubbing dialogue over silent footage that had been shot "wild." A film done largely in this fashion is William Wellman's *Chinatown Nights,* released by Paramount on March 23, 1929. Apparently, it was hoped to do the same for *Queen Kelly.*

The banquet scenes were shot on January 18 at the old Selig Zoo studio on Mission Road (the sequence described by Margulies cited earlier), though the coronation seems to have been postponed. Work at the Selig studio was finished in one day and the company returned to Pathé on Saturday to shoot scenes of Tully Marshall leading the mob upstairs. Sunday, Swanson screened the assembled rushes, and on Monday, January 21, the company continued to shoot more scenes between Jan and Kelly. The script girl's record for January 21 lists the final shots of the film:

> 277. MED. SHOT
>> The curtains part from inside revealing Jan and Kelly who are stepping out. She has scissors in her right hand. She withdraws as she looks at mob.
>> Takes 1 and 2 O.K.
> 277A. MED. SHOT
>> Protection shot to see which set-up would be most impressive. Crowd listening. Curtains open. Jan and Kelly come out. He holds her by wrist.
>> Takes 1 and 2 O.K.
> 277B. MED. SHOT
>> Both in—Kelly loo

This fragmentary account of shot 277B is crossed out in pencil and "Look on Camera Report" hastily scrawled next to it. The cameraman's daily report indicates that for the first time there were "no OK scenes," but only 300 feet of "bad" footage. What had happened? According to Ivano:

> Tully Marshall took her hand and spit fell on Gloria's hand. Tully explained Stroheim asked for this business. I told my first assistant (William Margulies) to strike cameras. Gloria phoned J. Kennedy in Miami and he in turn called Stroheim and fired him.[63]

Swanson's story is identical.

> . . . as soon as I saw the first rushes of the African sequences I knew we were in trouble. First of all, they seemed utterly unrelated to the European scenes or the characters in them. Moreover, they were rank and sordid and ugly, Mr. von Stroheim's apocalyptic vision of hell on earth, and full of material that would never pass the censors . . . On my third day of shooting, Mr. von Stroheim began instructing Mr. Marshall, in his usual painstaking fashion, how to drool tobacco juice onto my hand while he was putting on the wedding ring. It was early morning, I had just eaten breakfast, and my stomach turned. I became nauseated and furious at the same time.[64]

She left the set and made her phone call. "Joseph, you'd better get out here fast. Our director is a madman . . ."[65]

At this instant *Queen Kelly* irreversibly fell apart. It was a moment, richly symbolic in its own right, which capped a growing list of problems that seemed to have no possible solution as long as von Stroheim remained as director. A primary concern was censorship. Swanson may have initially convinced herself that the raw edges of the script would be cleaned up, but eleven weeks of shooting had opened even her eyes.

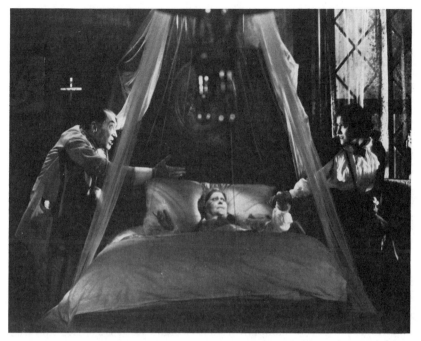

"I knew we were in trouble," Swanson said.

Although she certainly had been examining the rushes all along, the January 20 screening, featuring the riotous behavior of the Poto-Poto habituées, must have seemed the final straw. Cost was a lesser factor. Von Stroheim claimed that $400,000 had already been spent, and another $400,000 budgeted to complete the picture;[66] to Swanson the film represented a flat $800,000 investment.[67] Von Stroheim was still a full month behind the original schedule on January 21, but since the rewriting of the script it would have taken only two or three weeks to complete the film—and that relatively cheaply, on sets which had already been built. By this point, the problem of von Stroheim running up extra expenses was no longer very significant. The talkie situation had little to do with it. As we have seen, it was already decided that some form of sound would be used in the picture. The *New York Times* reported that Swanson was already recording talking and singing sequences for *Queen Kelly* (under von Stroheim's direction!) in an article published shortly after the film shut down.[68] Although this had not happened as yet, it had clearly been on the agenda for the near future. Paul Ivano (whose contact with the film ended when shooting stopped) remembers that "Eddie Goulding wrote a song for *Queen Kelly*,"[69] apparently for use in just this fashion. If all had gone according to plan, *Queen Kelly,* as some sort of prestigious part-talkie, would probably have been released in the summer of 1929. There were a few elaborate all-talkies released before mid-1929, but over a dozen of that year's most important films were released in *completely* non-dialogue versions. These included von Sternberg's *The Case of Lena Smith,* Keaton's *Spite Marriage,* large-scale adventure films such as *The Trail of '98, The Four Feathers,* and *The Viking,* two Lon Chaney features, and three Greta Garbo films. *The Kiss,* released as late as November 16, 1929, with only a music and effects track, proved to be one of Garbo's biggest moneymakers.[70] Contrary to popular belief, *Queen Kelly* would not have seemed a unique anachronism that season—especially with its talking and singing sequences—and there was a chance of its returning at least some profit.

But of course it was never intended to stop *Queen Kelly* dead in its tracks, only to eliminate von Stroheim, alter the censorable portions of his work, and complete the film with sound of some acceptable sort. Records indicate that sounds tests and script work were immediately undertaken, with the company told to "stand by." But after about a month various members of the cast were let go, and on March 2 the company stopped filing daily reports. During this time Edmund Goulding had taken over as script doctor and prospective director,[71] and *Queen Kelly* seemed headed down the same path as Howard Hughes's *Hell's Angels,* another elaborate silent production which retooled as a talking picture over many weary months. Between April 2 and April 9 Paul Stein directed a week of sound tests featuring Swanson, Byron, and as many as thirty convent girl extras, using a convent chapel set which had been erected at Pathé. It became clear that the film would require a great deal more effort before it could be turned into a talkie. In any case, Goulding had little interest in patching up von Stroheim's material, and "suggested it would be cheaper to make a new picture with the money necessary to spend on salvaging *Queen Kelly.*"[72] This picture was an all-talkie, *The Trespasser,* written by Goulding (with Swanson and Laura Hope Crews) in three weeks and directed by him in eighteen days.[73] Swanson and Goulding turned all of their attentions to *The Trespasser,* and it was released on October 5, 1929. Very much a return to the format of Swanson's mid-20s successes, *The Trespasser* was enough of a box office success to enable her to think about *Queen Kelly* again.

That fall a new script was prepared, with "story and dialogue by Lawrence Eyre and Laura Hope Crews, technical interpretation by

Richard Boleslawsky." It appears to have been based on an undated treatment prepared by Sam Wood and Delmer Daves, one a veteran director, the other a young screenwriter who would become a director himself years later. A shooting schedule was submitted on November 6 which gave December 6 to December 31 as the dates of production. The final script is dated November 30, 1929; it is organized around von Stroheim's European footage and suggests a lot of "synthetically synchronized" dialogue for his scenes. In this script Queen Regina takes over the country and forces the royal family to flee. A priest named Father Kelly rescues the young heir to the throne and places her in a convent. Later we see the scene on the road with the Prince, the fire in the convent, the Queen whipping her out of the palace, and so on. But a group of patriots has grown up, and starts a revolt. The patriots storm the palace, Kelly is saved by the mob and revealed by the priest as the rightful heir. The standing Poto-Poto saloon set was to be used as the headquarters of the student rebels.

Boleslawsky began shooting tests on December 2, and over the next few days the cast was decided upon. Swanson, Walter Byron, and Seena Owen repeated their roles from the original version. David Torrence played the priest, and Sarah Padden the Mother Superior. Others in the cast included Richard Cramer, George Hackathorne (of *Merry-Go-Round*), Dennis d'Aborn, Fred Burt, June Stewart, Nat Madison, Sydney Bracey (also a member of the original cast), C. Macy, and B. Stuart. The first actual footage was shot on December 9 (three days late) and featured Swanson and the convent choir singing "Ave Maria." The company worked 16 hours that day, and 15 hours on the second day of shooting—rivaling von Stroheim's pace. The third day of shooting proved to be the last, as Kennedy abruptly pulled the plug once again. Boleslawsky completed a total of 12 minutes, 24 seconds of usable dialogue, and he might have succeeded in finishing the film within his 19-day shooting schedule. But he was at this time primarily a stage director and had little or no experience in motion pictures. He had spent several years as an actor and director with the Moscow Art Theatre, and after coming to America worked with Reinhardt on his production of *The Miracle,* and staged *The Three Musketeers* for Ziegfeld. He had directed musical numbers for the film *Grand Parade* which Edmund Goulding had just written and directed for Pathé, and was apparently working on *Queen Kelly* because of Goulding's lack of interest in the project.

Perhaps Kennedy shut down the film again because of disappointment with Boleslawsky, but it is also possible he was not happy with the new script and had hit on another way of licking *Queen Kelly*—turning it into an operetta. On January 7, 1930, it was reported that Franz Lehar had been signed to write the music for *Queen Kelly*, his first commission for the cinema.[74] Swanson and Kennedy approached Goulding to direct the operetta version but he refused, claiming that he "wouldn't touch" the script prepared by Eyre and Crews.[75] Swanson and Kennedy then attempted to force Goulding to direct the film by threatening to withhold his royalties for "Love Your Magic Spell Is Everywhere," a popular song he had written for *The Trespasser*. During the legal dispute which followed, *Queen Kelly* was once more left in the lurch.[76]

Undaunted, Swanson set other writers to work on the material throughout 1930, while Gloria Productions turned out *What a Widow!*, directed by Allan Dwan. A script entitled "New Story Version 'Queen Kelly,' " written by Harry Poppe (who was on the staff as a production manager) is dated November 4, 1930. This, too, is based on von Stroheim's footage and overlaid with similar European intrigues and court struggles. It never even approached production. Instead, Swanson made *Indiscreet*, a musical comedy directed by Leo McCarey. At this point she abandoned the idea of "synthetic synchronization" and attempted to salvage *Queen Kelly* by rewriting the titles and issuing it as a silent film. Throughout 1931 various treatments of *Queen Kelly* as a silent film were submitted, and slowly the raw material once more began to approach von Stroheim's original. Viola Lawrence, a cutter associated with von Stroheim off and on since *Blind Husbands*, had since *Queen Kelly* become Swanson's editor; with the exception of a new ending she managed to restore the tone of his original script with surprising fidelity—especially in light of the far-out treatments Swanson had been considering since 1929. Swanson now filmed the last of her independent American production, *Tonight or Never*, another film with musical overtones (operatic this time), which was directed by Mervyn Leroy. The final draft of revisions for *Queen Kelly* required the shooting of a new conclusion, and on November 24, 1931, Gregg Toland (cameraman on *The Trespasser, Indiscreet,* and *Tonight or Never*) photographed the final sequence.

Von Stroheim had shot footage of Swanson leaping off the bridge, than being rescued by the policeman and returned to the convent, where she discovered the telegram telling her to come to Africa. He also photographed the Prince's release from prison at the end of his sentence, and his trip to the convent to ask Kelly why his letters have not been answered. The Mother Superior tells him that Kelly is not there.

Swanson perceived that if Kelly never made it out of the river alive, the film could end right there. By changing some titles she made it appear that the Prince returns to the convent the very next day. She used von Stroheim's footage of the Prince's arrival, shot in 1928, and spliced onto it a new sequence which showed him discovering Kelly's drowned body laid out on a bier in the convent chapel (a set in storage since Boleslawsky's version). A musical score was composed by Adolf Tandler and recorded on December 28-30, 1931. Swanson finally had a completed print on her hands, if anyone still wanted to see it.

It is often claimed that von Stroheim's contract prohibited the release of this version in America,[77] but that seems hard to credit. It is more likely that there was no longer any market for a silent Gloria Swanson–Erich von Stroheim picture in 1932 America. When Swanson traveled to Europe for a long stay in 1932 she took the film with her, and in November opened it in Paris at the "Falguiere," an art house. Here it was received well and widely commented on throughout Europe, hailed as "Ein Meisterwerk des Films" even by the German press, which had often been hostile to von Stroheim.[78] But the film received little circulation. Just before the outbreak of World War II it was reported that Walter Futter had purchased the *Queen Kelly* footage for $10,000 and would use it as stock material in a feature dealing with "anti-democratic activities in a mythical Balkan kingdom."[79] Futter was a producer of one-reel "Curiosities" and "Travelaughs" who had recently moved into feature production; he was responsible for Paul Robeson's *Jericho,* although better known as a producer of westerns. Apparently he never made use of the material.

Later Swanson gave prints to various film archives, including one to New York's Museum of Modern Art in 1945 (which she has since repossessed). When she appeared with von Stroheim in *Sunset Boulevard,* a film which includes a clip from *Queen Kelly,* this print was dusted off and given a special "press preview" there on July 20, 1950. *Variety* gave it a lengthy page-one review, albeit as a "museum piece."[80] In 1965 two reels of the footage sold to Walter Futter turned up in the collection of Dudley Murphy, who had acquired the material; the other 200 reels had since been lost in a flooded basement.[81] In 1967 Swanson made personal appearances with a nostalgia double-bill of *Queen Kelly* and *The Trespasser,*[82] but in recent years has grown tired of discussing the film, an albatross which damaged her career almost as much as von Stroheim's. In 1971 she sent a large quantity of her papers

to the Eastman House, including the surviving production records of
Queen Kelly, and in 1980 published her version of the story in *Swanson on Swanson.*

In many ways *Queen Kelly* was a reworking of the basic ideas von
Stroheim developed in *The Wedding March,* not surprising considering
his two-year preoccupation with that film just before writing *The
Swamp.* In his earlier films circular relationships among a group of
characters seemed to intrigue him, and in *Merry-Go-Round* this *reigen*
was the focal point of the action. But in *Queen Kelly,* as in *The Wedding March,* von Stroheim is less interested in the interrelationships of
characters, and more interested in the individual characters themselves.
The film is studded with "types," representatives of various social and
sexual categories, often naturalist in origin. A graph of these relationships in *Queen Kelly* is very similar to one for *The Wedding March:*

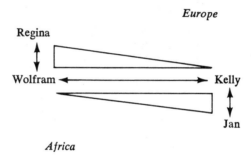

The typical von Stroheim format of one female situated between two
males is balanced by having a hero caught between two women as well.
However, the scripting (and acting!) of this role de-emphasizes this
balance and leaves Kelly as the unchallenged dominant personality.
This echoes the structure of *The Wedding March,* but the Wolfram-
Kelly relationship is more lopsided than the Nikki-Mitzi relationship in
The Wedding March.

Note that there is an "African" triangle and an overlapping "European" triangle. It is not so much the juxtaposition of characters, but the
contrast between these two worlds which interests von Stroheim here,
and he bases the dramatic action on a series of parallels which contrast Europe and Africa in terms more psychic than geographic. Europe
and Africa represent two sides of the same bent coin, a contrast von
Stroheim often displays in such characters as friends or romantic rivals
(Marcus and McTeague, Mirko and Danilo, Nikki and Schani, etc.).
Here, for perhaps the only time, the geographical metaphor allows him

to explore this idea through the creation of a totally Stroheimesque *Weltanschauung*. The effect was so stark, that when Swanson saw the first African rushes she felt that they were "utterly unrelated" to what had gone before.

One of von Stroheim's favorite authors, John O'Hara, once said that America was unique in having leapt from barbarism to decadence without an intervening period of civilization. Von Stroheim in *Queen Kelly* brings into collision the decadence of Europe and the barbarism of Africa; the story of how Kitty Kelly survives this collision is the story he has to tell here. As usual, ritual is at the heart of his portrayal of any society, with sex not far away. The dark priest performing his obscene wedding/funeral prefigures the glorious wedding/coronation of the script's conclusion, with the title "Queen Kelly" at issue in both services. This was to be the central action of *Queen Kelly,* just as the various processions provided the dramatic focal points of *The Wedding March.* One can easily see the brothel and its inmates as the transposition of the convent with its nuns and orphans, a connection von Stroheim encourages us to make through the use of a "Pollock process" shot. The aunt bears a physical resemblance to the mother superior, with similarities of duty and responsibility implied. Likewise, the palace is duplicated in Jan's vast estates, just as the power Regina holds over Wofram echoes the power of Jan over Kelly.

Europe and Africa represent poles of ossified regimen and lawless anarchy, and the script finds even the smallest gestures ripe for contrast. In Europe breaking the rules is punished by drilling with the troops or kneeling in prayer; in Africa an infraction is met with a punch in the nose, and life is perpetually on the borderline of riot. Yet von Stroheim is always busy showing us how these apparently dissimilar worlds are really alike underneath. When "Queen Kelly" assumes control of the brothel she adopts the black gown, whips, and ostrich plumes of Queen Regina. Von Stroheim delights in such business. Not surprisingly, the elimination of the African sequences in the released version does not merely damage the film, but destroys it. The carefully established iconography of the European episodes relates to nothing, leaving it simply a one-dimensional caricature of little interest. Even audiences unaware of the planned African episodes sense this, and find the film troublesome and unsatisfying.

Not visible in the script, but apparent from a study of the stills and the surviving footage, is the visual correlative of this style, the tonal opposition of black and white which runs throughout the film. Europe is white, Africa black, and the art direction of the palace and the

Poto-Poto saloon reflects this in no uncertain terms. Queen Regina's palace is awash in vast expanses of white marble, and a lack of the clutter usually associated with von Stroheim's palaces emphasizes this even more strongly. By contrast the Poto-Poto saloon shows ceilings and dark walls, a claustrophobic, lightless trap. Chairs and tables are arranged in chaotic fashion, the symmetrical lines of the palace staircase completely erased.

Of course the presence of black actors here is also important to von Stroheim. It is clear that he is using the image of the African in the crudest naturalist terms, as the lowest level of mankind on the evolutionary ladder. The decadent aristocrats, their European counterparts, have come full circle (unable to escape their origins) and are likewise shown as typical *bêtes humaines*. As in *Greed* (or *L'Assommoir*) alcohol is the key which unlocks the beast, and both Europeans and Africans are shown at their most depraved in fits of drunkenness. But while he tries for a sort of balance, there is no question that von Stroheim sees Africa as the lowest and most foul "sewer" of humankind. The insistence in the early description of the saloon on the presence of all races makes this clear. This human refuse heap contains the worst elements of black, white, yellow, and brown, some never raised very far above savagery, others inevitably relapsed into it.

We are never allowed to forget the clash of black and white values, and even before the action moves to Africa it is clearly being set up for us. After arriving at the palace drunk the Prince is dressed in his white pajamas and the Queen approaches in her black negligee; their wrestling match is reflected in the squabble between her white cat and his black dogs. In Africa the prostitutes come in black/white pairs, and a black priest will officiate in a white surplice, the chromatic inverse of the dour minister at McTeague's wedding, for example.

We have seen how von Stroheim incorporates these European and African motifs in the structure of his film, but what about the characters that flesh out this landscape? As we mentioned, their main importance comes from their existence as symbols, and it is more useful to examine them individually than to bother sorting out their rather mechanical relationships.

Walter Byron's performance as the prince only serves to emphasize the quality of von Stroheim's own performance in *The Wedding March*. Byron is an actor of no charisma, and barely succeeds in making the prince a character of two dimensions; when Kelly tells him that he is a picture-postcard hero to the girls in the convent, we know exactly what she means. This does not happen because his performance wound up on the editing room floor—indeed, in the released version, he is on screen as much as Swanson. Byron is simply a lifeless actor, in the tradition of many lifeless Swanson heroes. As written his part is no weaker than John Gilbert's in *The Merry Widow,* but his own limitations as an actor destroy the role. As Prince Nikki, von Stroheim was able to demonstrate a wide, though believable, growth of character. Byron shows us nothing. This factor would not have been as apparent if the film had been completed as scheduled, for the Prince has no real part in the African sequences, his place being taken over by Jan. But in the version as released this non-performance leaves a serious gap in the film's dramatic structure: technically, the prince is the center of Swanson's version, torn between Kelly and Regina, and on screen nearly all the time. This was not von Stroheim's intention, nor was it within the capacities of Walter Byron as an actor.

Although even in *The Devil's Pass Key* there is a hint of von Stroheim's interest in the decadent man of power, only in *Queen Kelly* is this role fully sketched. Tully Marshall was the image in von Stroheim's mind when he wrote this part, but with the loss of the "swamp tree" episodes his most important scenes vanished, and we cannot fairly evaluate his role from the surviving script material. It is significant, however, that this time the epitome of decadence is not an aristocrat, but a member of the bourgeoisie, a *nouveau riche* planter. Von Stroheim was growing increasingly critical of this class (as witness his picture of Schani in *The Honeymoon*) and in *Queen Kelly* his strongest contempt is directed there for the first time. But while Tully Marshall as the last representative of a decadent *noble* line makes sense in von Stroheim's universe, his position as a decaying bourgeois is more troublesome. How did this come to pass? The hereditary explanation is unsatisfying here, since we lack the careful presentation of background material which von Stroheim concocts for a character like McTeague. We see little or nothing that could explain his character for us, and Jan is merely a monster, though a *monstre sacre,* after all.

On the other hand, it is flatly stated that Queen Regina is the last of a degenerate line, but that explanation of her character is soon supplemented by more substantial material. Queen Regina has power, and she tries to use this power to make someone love her. If she had seen *The Wedding March* she would have realized the disasters inherent in such a program. Although she is a queen, this role is less about being queen than about being a jealous woman. Her position as a would-be wife is often referred to, and she relates to Wolfram not as a queen does to a prince, but as a wife to a husband. When the prince escapes for a night out on the town, he is escaping from the clutches of a nagging, suspicious wife. This image is exaggerated into monstrosity, a jealous, dominant woman shown as an omnipotent psychopath, a nymphomaniacal junkie frothing at the mouth. Von Stroheim was fascinated enough by this character to increase the vehemence of the role in *Queen Kelly* over his original conception in *The Swamp,* and she is certainly one of his most grotesque creations. What is disappointing is her convenient disappearance from the film in the last reel, though this is in line with the director's fatalistic fondness for the *deus ex machina.*

Earlier we saw that von Stroheim's first female characters were poorly observed, and lacked the richness of characterization supplied for the males. This was especially so in the case of his heroines, particularly those lackluster American wives of his first three films. This problem has largely been overcome by the time of *Queen Kelly,* but Kitty Kelly is still a little too much the heroine for von Stroheim to relax and develop her character in a more complex fashion. Instead she remains little more than a symbol, an indomitable "Irish" spirit posed between African savagery and palatial decadence. She is a cork tossed about both in Europe and in Africa, seemingly powerless in both locales, but somehow achieving a happy destiny thanks to good old fate. Von Stroheim shows her as a truly pure spirit who cannot be sullied even by the ridiculously blasphemous events that befall her in Africa, when she moves in one step from convent inmate to brothel madame. Almost like a Griffith heroine, her purpose is to demonstrate the incorruptibility of true virtue. Although her situation changes, *she* doesn't change, a lesson which is probably the main point of the picture. In this case Kelly is less interesting than Sadie Thompson, who is forced to make a decision between powerful emotional forces which deeply affect and alter her personality. Kelly is never touched in this way; she meets the Prince, keeps herself pure for him, and achieves a happy end after considerable melodramatic suffering.

Queen Kelly was the last major project von Stroheim was ever to direct. When Swanson and Kennedy shut the film down they effectively closed the book on his career as a top director, but the blame cannot be placed on their heads alone. They approved one of von Stroheim's raunchiest scripts, put a great deal of money at von Stroheim's disposal, and were ready to brave the advent of talking pictures by making (with him) whatever changes *Queen Kelly* might require. It was von Stroheim's well-documented excesses, both financial and directorial, which brought the picture down on top of him. These were more than enough to trigger the panicky closing-down of the production, a "temporary" suspension from which the film never recovered. Although riddled with various minor flaws (mainly stemming from his all-too-apparent re-use of *The Wedding March* as source material), *Queen Kelly* could quite possibly have emerged as one of his major works. The truncated version which survives, while apparently "intact" to a remarkable degree, remains one of the most frustrating of von Stroheim fragments—a half-completed jigsaw puzzle somehow trying to stand in for something much, much greater.

The suspension of shooting on *Queen Kelly* was the single most damaging blow to von Stroheim's career. Coming only three months after the disastrous premiere of *The Wedding March,* it convinced producers and public alike that not only was von Stroheim an intractable wastrel but that the type of film he was so strongly identified with was now definitely out of touch with audience fashion. And this double blow fell at the worst possible moment, when all Hollywood was in turmoil over the introduction of sound. There was a concerted effort to sweep out the old and import from the east anyone and anything connected with talk.

While most film histories focus here on the fortunes of stars like John Gilbert and Vilma Banky, many directors and writers were also given the sack. Major figures like Herbert Brenon, Rex Ingram, and Marshall Neilan saw their careers plummet. D. W. Griffith, like von Stroheim already reeling from a run of bad luck, suffered from the coming of sound in precisely the same fashion. These directors were said to be old-fashioned, and ignorant of the requirements of microphones and dialogue. In fact, they were stubborn individualists who had never been comfortable as part of a studio team and the executive hierarchy took advantage of the new order to edge them out once and for all. Those directors who did survive and flourish, like Ford, Lubitsch, Curtiz, Walsh, and Vidor, were certainly no more knowledgeable about sound and dialogue, but they did enjoy reputations as reliable team players, something Griffith and von Stroheim had never bothered to acquire.

Von Stroheim must have seen the handwriting on the wall, for suddenly he agreed to work as an actor in a film directed by James Cruze, *The Great Gabbo.* Cruze was another free spirit about to see his career crash in the talkies, and *Gabbo* would become as much of a millstone for him as it would be for von Stroheim. Cheaply produced for Sono-Art, a poverty-row independent, the film's technical crudities made it appear worse than it actually was. Von Stroheim played a crazed

The Great Gabbo: an artist driven mad.

ventriloquist, a great vaudeville artist driven to madness, who has eliminated the line between his personal life and his professional career. In retrospect this performance is terribly poignant, and much of the dialogue has an eerie autobiographical quality. But audiences of 1929 saw only a standard "crazy artist" melodrama. Von Stroheim did recognize himself in the role, however, and attempted to buy the rights years later, only to find they had already been acquired by Edgar Bergen.[83]

But appearing in *The Great Gabbo* would not have been seen as a simple respite from his directing chores by the rest of the Hollywood community, where the appearance of prosperity and success matter tremendously. To be associated with big-budget disasters like *The Wedding March* and *Queen Kelly* was one thing; to be linked to a poverty-row melodrama like *The Great Gabbo* was something else entirely. Von Stroheim had crossed to the other side of the tracks, and in doing so he had irrevocably branded himself a has-been. There would still be directing projects, of course, but from this point more and more of them would be stillborn. And as von Stroheim's condition grew more desperate, the tone of these works took on an increasingly unrealistic, even bizarre character.

He revived his plans for an adaptation of *East of the Setting Sun,*
this time intended for Norma Shearer, but he kept only the bare bones
of George Barr McCutcheon's 1924 novel. McCutcheon's hero journalist became the representative of a Ford agency, and the invasion of
Graustark by the neighboring communist state of Axphainia (modeled
on the Hungarian Béla Kun regime) was completely omitted. This
seems odd, since von Stroheim was known to be concerned with the
rise of socialist states from the fragments of the Austo-Hungarian Empire, but perhaps he felt the whole question too painful to deal with
here. In place of this climax he substituted the abduction of the
Princess Milena by the dissolute Prince Vladimir and a last-minute
rescue by U.S. Marines. A reader's report on this treatment noted:

> Not unusual in plot, but containing all the amusing satire against royalty
> that is so characteristic of von Stroheim. The temperamental scenes be-
> tween Milena and her father are delightful, and the vulgarity of Queen
> Draga is stressed, also the dissolute, loathsome nature of her son
> Vladimir. It is a sort of fairy tale thing, but don't we like them . . . and
> Miss Shearer is particularly lovely in such a part with a background of
> court life.[84]

Walter Pidgeon, George Fawcett, and Josephine Crowell were to be
in the cast, and von Stroheim would play the loathsome and dissolute
Vladimir himself, a character who horsewhips the hero, and then
breaks a hornet's nest over his open wounds. In trying to escape the
marines Vladimir leaps from the window of an inn called "The Sign of
the Devil," and impales himself on the devil's pitchfork, a character-
istically symbolic end reminiscent of the death of Karamzin. "The film
never went into production as in the last moment Joe Schenck had
misgivings of letting me play a part in a picture which I directed myself because he feared I might run away and make another *Foolish
Wives* . . ."[85]

Von Stroheim did sign a contract with M-G-M on September 4,
1929, to write an original story, his first work as a contract writer. He
was to have been paid $15,000, but on January 20 the studio rejected
the idea he had developed, a project called *Wild Blood,* and the contract was settled for only $5000. Almost nothing is known about this
assignment, but when von Stroheim returned to M-G-M as a writer in
1935-36 he came up with another treatment under this same title.

Finally, von Stroheim accepted another acting role, this time at
Warner Brothers in a remake of the old melodrama *Three Faces East.*
He had studio chief Darryl F. Zanuck's permission to suggest improve-
ments in the script, but director Roy del Ruth and co-star Constance

Bennett displayed nothing but contempt for von Stroheim and his suggestions. After kissing scenes Constance Bennett would loudly order a bottle of mouthwash, while del Ruth, when informed that von Stroheim feared he had swallowed some glass from a cracked thermos, quipped, "Well, we'll shoot your stuff first in case you die later."[86]

A few bits and pieces of this florid early talkie do seem to have benefited from his advice, notably a scene in which he unpacks Constance Bennett's lingerie while two maids peak through a keyhole, but these are few and far between. Once more he was playing the horrible Hun, and while he did his best to infuse some humanity, even pathos into the character, in the final analysis he was still the Hun. It was one more step in the wrong direction.

While working on *Three Faces East* von Stroheim gave a long interview to *Motion Picture Classic* in which he spoke of nothing but the lost world of old Vienna. In this powerfully nostalgic monologue he once again associated himself with the fallen regime and deplored the petit bourgeois society which had replaced it.

> If I speak of Vienna it must be in the past tense, as a man speaks of a woman he has loved and who is dead. As a man speaks of his youth. For my Vienna is as different from what they call Vienna now as the quick is different from the dead . . . I shall never go back to the city where I was born. It would be like going to the morgue to identify the body of a sweetheart one remembers as a lovely living woman with whimsical ways and a thousand dear beauties. Heartbreaking.[87]

But von Stroheim did return to Vienna, and sooner than he might have expected. Carl Laemmle, Jr., the 21-year-old son of the president of Universal, was now in charge of production at that studio and had instituted a program of upgrading the company's releases. He planned to phase out the westerns, serials, and B-movies with which Universal had generally been associated, and replace them with big budget films like *All Quiet on the Western Front* and *King of Jazz*. Paul Kohner, now one of Laemmle's producers, insisted that von Stroheim should be brought back to remake one of his early successes as a talking picture.[88] In June of 1930 it was announced that *Merry-Go-Round* would be the new von Stroheim picture, and Universal paid $10,000 each to von Stroheim and his "collaborator," Georges Lewys, for the talking rights. But for some reason the project was shelved and *Blind Husbands* was announced instead.[89] Another $5000 was paid to von Stroheim for the talking rights to this story, and in July he left for Europe to visit relatives, secure costumes and furnishings, and see Vienna for the first time in over twenty years.

He took Valerie and Joseph along, and a high point of the trip was a private audience with Pope Pius XI, who pinned the order of St. Theresa to young Joseph's uniform.[90] Afterward they journeyed to the Tyrol and began acquiring the peasant costumes, handicrafts, and furnishings which would be needed for the picture. But von Stroheim never took his family to see Vienna. He had found a caricature of himself in a German language newspaper, drawn with a black border and a rope around his neck, indicating what would happen if he ever returned to the city he had so "slandered" in films like *The Wedding March*. Valerie saw him disguise himself in a false beard, and go off alone.[91]

In Vienna he saw his mother, whose illness had been a major impetus for the trip, and his brother Bruno and the rest of the family. But why was the visit such a secret? It seems improbable that von Stroheim really felt his life was in danger. More likely he did not relish a meeting between his American family and his European family. Valerie had no idea at this time that Erich was Jewish, and he apparently wanted to keep it that way. She stayed behind at Innsbruck with Joseph and the order of St. Theresa.

On returning to California von Stroheim began work on the *Blind Husbands* script, and hid away at Lake Arrowhead for eight weeks until the first draft was ready. When he returned to his house in Brentwood, Paul Kohner came over to see the results. "He came out with what looked like two telephone books—*today's* telephone books—*that* thick! I said, 'Von, you must be insane! You don't think Mr. Laemmle will ever read this? I told you, we have to have a script of not more than 90 or 100 pages!'"[92] Von Stroheim went back to work and produced at least nine drafts between December 15, 1930, and April 4, 1931. The longest of these ran 618 scenes, and all were predictably over-written, a common fault of most early talkies.

The final draft followed the text of the original in great detail, although this time the lieutenant—here Lt. Hans Carl Maria Baron von Treuenfels—escapes with his life. There is particular attention to the details of sound—the ringing of bells, the cries of animals, the rattle of carriage wheels over mountain paths. Much German is spoken. Von Stroheim issued detailed preparation sheets listing dozens of items—like pig's bladder tobacco pouches—which needed to be manufactured *en masse* according to samples or sketches he provided. Scores of peasant, military, and civilian costumes were ordered, supplies of pre-war Austrian kronen demanded, and particular issues of 1913 medical journals specified. Every extra was individually characterized. An old woman seen as part of a crowd was not just an old woman, but "one very old woman—1000 wrinkles." All the lieutenant's decorations are described—the Jubilee Cross of 1908, the Annexation Medal, and the Marianer Cross—and these turn out to be decorations von Stroheim himself claimed to have won.

When von Stroheim finally had a script which Kohner could support the two started off to see Laemmle for final approval. "We walked out of the house . . . and when we came to the sidewalk he turned around and walked back! I said, 'Von? What's the matter with you?' 'Didn't you see? A black cat crossed over!' He wouldn't go that day."[93]

Eventually Laemmle saw the script and did grant approval. Norman Kerry, Mady Christians, and Salka Viertel were cast, and von Stroheim would re-create his original role. Bit parts were written in for Albert Conti, Maj. John Farrow,[94] and Erich von Stroheim, Jr., the director's older son. The film would be entirely in two-color Technicolor, with location scenes taken at Arrowhead—where von Stroheim had rowed tourists around the lake in the crucial summer of 1914. Kohner remembers:

We got to the point where production was just three days off. This was a Friday, early afternoon, at Universal studio. We were supposed to go on Sunday up to Lake Arrowhead to shoot exteriors. I sat in my office when an assistant director came running. He said, "Paul, you better come over to the stage where the bells are, because von Stroheim is going berserk!"

"What is it?" I rushed over there. Here was von Stroheim strutting up and down, breaking his cane. The assistant gave him another cane—he broke the other cane! That was his sign of extreme displeasure. I said, "Von, what is it?" He says, "You told me I have to select the bells, because when we are up there the bells are ringing [over the lake]."

"Tell us those, the sounds of which you want."

"What do you mean, 'the sounds'? I want the bells up in Arrowhead hanging over the lake!"

I said, "You must be crazy, Von! Why do you want to have the bells hanging over the . . ."

"Because don't you know that bells sound different, the sound is different when it's over the water?"

I said, "That may be the case, but that's not how you make talking pictures, sound pictures today. We record the sound of the bells and then we lay the sound over the scene."

"The next thing you're going to tell me, there isn't going to be a band playing while the dance is going on!"

I said, "Of course, Von, the band will not be playing. There will be a band, and they will pretend to play, but the music will be recorded separately."

"You must be crazy if you think I'm going to direct a picture like this!"

I said, "Von, the people have dialogue while they are dancing. They

will be talking to each other. You cannot do it and have the music
playing!"

Well . . . he just stormed off the set like a wild man. I knew eventually Von would give in, but it never came to this because ten minutes
later I was called in to the office of Mr. Laemmle.[95]

Both Laemmles were there, surrounded by the entire retinue of
studio managers and assistants. Uncle Carl spoke first. "Kohner, before
you say anything—I don't want to hear anything—I want you to fire
von Stroheim. He is out! The picture is off!"[96]

The incident of the bells was clearly a pretext. Von Stroheim's
"ignorance" of the realities of sound recording seems in retrospect
another example of his "inability to cheat," something which would be
charming if it had not had such tragic consequences. But Universal
saw that this was going to be a very expensive picture. Junior Laemmle's
program of big budget pictures was a failure, *King of Jazz* in particular
running up catastrophic losses, and all budgets were now being severely
cut down. They were not about to go into production with another von
Stroheim picture, especially one in which he acted as well as directed.
They had been through all that before. Said Carl Laemmle, Jr., years
later, "firing von Stroheim was the smartest thing I ever did."[97]

But as usual, von Stroheim had another project up his sleeve, this
time a pastiche of several of his earlier pictures which he called *Her
Highness,* and which he first tried to sell to M-G-M. The story takes
place just before the war in the small village of Rzcezcov on the Austro-
Russian border. It is a sleepy garrison town, so dull that the officers
amuse themselves by meeting the express train from Vienna and fan-
tasizing about fashionable travelers who remind them of life in the
capital. The local barber, Kornikoff, hides his socialist and anti-mili-
tarist beliefs while hypocritically catering to the officers. His daughter
Sonya has ambitions to better herself, and exudes a superior air which
causes her to be sarcastically labelled "Her Highness."

Sonya is in love with the dashing Lt. von Ebenstein, who occupies
rooms over the barber shop. When she realizes that he has no plans to
marry her she hides from him the fact that she is expecting his child.
Instead she accepts the proposal of the decrepit old Baron von
Gutschintzky. Life with the Baron is hell, and when Sonya in a fit of
anger reveals that she still loves Ebenstein, the father of her child, the
old man collapses in a rage and dies.

Now a wealthy widow, Sonya travels to Vienna and is entertained by
Prince Dubrovsky, the middle-aged commandant of the garrison town
who has long admired her. She also meets Ebenstein, who is still
attracted to her but not interested in marriage. Instead she weds Du-

brovsky, with whom she has a rich and rewarding life. But when war breaks out, and she learns that Ebenstein is being sent on a mission which means certain death, she rides after him, tells him the truth about the child, and confesses her love. Then she returns home to Dubrovsky, bids him farewell as he, too, leaves for the front, and prays for his safe return.

His first original script since *Queen Kelly, Her Highness* is a work very much in the tradition of von Stroheim's other projects in this period. The shift of emphasis to the female lead, the relatively light-weight quality of the young lieutenant, and the appearance of the degenerate man of wealth, all link it directly to scripts like *The Merry Widow* and *Queen Kelly*. But while perhaps too close for comfort to *The Merry Widow,* there are interesting variants at work here. The lieutenant steadfastly refuses to marry Sonya and always sees her as a plaything, a frivolous, facile attitude which never does succeed in killing her love. And the presence of Prince Dubrovsky, an attractive, middle-aged representative of the aristocracy, is completely new, for the first time indicating some saving grace in this noble tradition (although only in the most sterile terms). As von Stroheim grew older this character began to put in more frequent appearances in his scripts. Today we might call him the "Lewis Stone character," and in fact von Stroheim later indicated Lewis Stone for this role.

The idea that Sonya can be true to the good Prince Dubrovsky, while reserving her passion for the much less worthy lieutenant, seems to have its roots in von Stroheim's own marital situation. By this point his marriage to Valerie was nearly devoid of passion, but the nature of his obligation as husband and father was such that he never ceased to support her, even in the face of the most grinding adversity.

A reader at M-G-M noted, "Mr. von Stroheim's work is always interesting and finished as to atmosphere. This might offer an idea that could be developed for Garbo, though the ending seems to need a little better working out, for it leaves us rather up in the air."[98] M-G-M's story editor, Samuel Marx, also found the ending weak and asked von Stroheim to rewrite it.[99] While working this out he accepted yet another acting role, this time at RKO in Victor Schertzinger's *Friends and Lovers.* Adolphe Menjou and Laurence Olivier were in this film as well, but it proved another time-marking exercise. Chances were beginning to run out, and von Stroheim could no longer be so particular about his debut as a director of talkies. If he was ever to make the transition he would have to take quick advantage of whatever opportunities developed.

Walking Down Broadway

In 1930 William Fox had been forced from the presidency of the Fox Film Corporation, the result of governmental actions and civil suits involving a series of extraordinary stock manipulations. Control of the profitable production and exhibition empire passed to the Chase Bank, which for the next two years engaged in a vicious court-room wrangle with Fox, his lieutenants, and his would-be-successors.[1] Confusion reigned at the studio while the fate of the corporation was decided in east coast board rooms and judicial chambers; as might be expected, production suffered, and comfortable profits turned into substantial losses. With the studio in disarray, various executives vied for control, and Erich von Stroheim came into the picture at a moment when Winfield Sheehan was in charge of production. In the summer of 1931 he managed to promote a one-picture deal with Sheehan for the direction of a minor program picture, in scope the least ambitious film of his career, *Walking Down Broadway*.

Sheehan had been one of the founders of Fox Film in 1914, and in 1926 had assumed control of the west coast studios. He was responsible for the construction of Movietone City, an enormous complex in Westwood created for the production of talking pictures, and under his guidance the quality of Fox releases had advanced considerably. Once noted mainly for its Tom Mix pictures, the studio in 1926 had imported F. W. Murnau, a move which signaled a new desire for prestige. Murnau's influence quickly spread throughout the lot, affecting the styles (and budgets) of such contract directors as John Ford (*Hangman's House*), Howard Hawks (*A Girl in Every Port*), and Frank Borzage (*Street Angel*). Erich von Stroheim had an undisguised respect for Sheehan, one of the few important studio executives with a college degree. In a world of "pants pressers" turned producers, von Stroheim had come to prize any sort of book learning.

But while sympathetic to the director, Sheehan felt obliged to put more than the usual restrictions on his new employee. In a memo to John H. Tracy, assistant legal counsel to the corporation, Sheehan proposed a contract specially calculated to keep von Stroheim under control:

> Please draw up a contract between the Corporation and ERIC VON STROHEIM, incorporating all the usual provisions for the direction of one picture to be based upon the story "WALKING DOWN BROADWAY" which we agree to purchase for not in excess of $10,000, and if we cannot obtain rights another story is to be substituted by agreement.
>
> Von Stroheim has the right to prepare, advise, change and supervise continuity, etc., but is to so supervise the same that the film will not exceed 8500 linear feet.
>
> We will pay him $30,000 as his entire compensation upon completion of the picture, but he may draw at the rate of $1,000 per week after commencement of production for not in excess of seventeen weeks.
>
> There will be no time limit in the contract and we further wish a special provision that either party may cancel and terminate the contract at any time without cause and in such event any work that he has performed up to that date shall belong to us and any money that he has drawn shall belong to him, but we shall be under no obligation to pay him anything further.
>
> He will have a business manager appointed by the studio, and Von Stroheim is to make no purchases, contracts or arrangements without the written authorization of the business manager. Von Stroheim is not to play a part in said production without our consent in writing. The entire contract is of course contingent on our being able to purchase this story and if we cannot obtain complete rights within a reasonable time after execution of the contract, or if another story cannot be agreed upon, we may terminate our obligations under this contract.[2]

The contract was dated and signed September 2, 1931, and von Stroheim retroactively went on salary as of August 31. The first newspaper accounts of the signing intimated that von Stroheim "will not be paid a penny until the picture is signed, sealed and delivered,"[3] and while this was not the case, such reports reflect fairly clearly his tenuous position in Hollywood after *The Wedding March* and *Queen Kelly*. One notes, for example, the special clauses in the Fox contract designed to keep von Stroheim in check: a business manager to be responsible for every expense; the film to be under a specific length (nearly 95 minutes, a generous limit, but a contractually stipulated limit nonetheless); the legal power to fire von Stroheim at will; and the *de facto* power to fire him as well, by not allowing him to appear on screen. However, the contract makes it clear that the project is no mere assignment, but will be specifically acquired for him to direct.[4]

The author of the original play, Dawn Powell (1897-1965), was a writer of some ability not widely known in her own day and largely forgotten since her death. She wrote for magazines, radio and television, was the author of two produced plays and thirteen novels (the last published in 1962) and received a Peabody Award in 1964. Powell's topic was invariably the American middle-class, and often the country girl come to the city to avoid the provincialism of small-town life. At times accused of satirizing this class with unnecessary cruelty, she replied, "I don't think satire is what I do. I think it's realism. It's not making fun. It's just telling the truth"[5] (a response von Stroheim might have appreciated). Her obituary in the *New York Times* is that of a modest, highly personal writer with more than a trace of von Stroheim's own uncompromising sense of artistic creation:

> Miss Powell brought to her work a merciless scalpel of satire . . . and a probing wit that some call mordant and others called fierce and destructive . . . She never courted fame, nor compromised her decision to please her readers. She avoided publishers' cocktail parties, publicity people, and interviews.[6]

In addition to *Walking Down Broadway,* one other film was based on a Powell original, *Man of Iron,* a 1935 First National production directed by William McGann (coincidentally, one of the original cameramen of *The Wedding March,* who later became a director of low-budget features).

There is no reference to *Walking Down Broadway* in any of the biographical literature on Dawn Powell, but the unpublished manuscript is available at the United States Copyright Office. There are marked similarities to Powell's novels of the period, notably *She Walks in Beauty* (1928), *Bride's House* (1929), and *Dance Night* (1930), novels rich in regional character and working-class ambience. Von Stroheim had only once, with *McTeague,* been attracted to material of this sort, yet here was a work of no reputation which had come across the Fox transom as an unproduced playscript, and once again his interest was aroused. The play was strong meat indeed for 1931, an unsentimental tale of young people in the big city, loaded with streetwise sexuality, fatalism, and acute psychological character analyses.

Two girls from the country share a room in a Manhattan boarding house near Riverside Drive in the West 90s. Marge is somewhat lonely and even embittered at her inability to find a boyfriend in the big city. Elsie is awkward and just a bit flighty. Their only friend is Eve Elman, a tough Broadway blonde who represents that cynical sexuality which in the films of von Stroheim had been so often portrayed by Maude George. The pair have met two boys on Broadway, Lewey and Chick, one a wisecracking New Yorker, the other a nice boy just arrived from the country. Marge and Elsie are very edgy over this pick-up, and Marge finally leaves—to go see a Gloria Swanson movie, she says. Eve Elman gets the boys to come over to her apartment after Lewey recognizes her as the "fallen arches Girl," the model for "Striegel's Strap for Fallen Arches." Chick eventually gets together with Marge and their shared loneliness forms a bond between them. "It's like fate, isn't it—our bumping into each other."

Act two takes place in the boys' apartment three months later. Chick confesses that he has to marry Marge, who is pregnant. Their roommate Mac, who is the evil influence in this play, tries to talk him out of it by implying a female conspiracy to take advantage of unwary men. Marge arrives with Eve Elman, who demands $200 from Chick to pay for an abortion. Chick is convinced Mac is right about Marge's gold-digging intentions.

The third act shifts back to Marge's room, where she announces she will go off by herself to have the baby, and name it Sonny Bascomb (an allusion to the classic stage melodrama, *Blue Jeans*). Eve gives her money for an abortion. In a final scene, a long-planned party brings all the principals together. Marge and Chick are being very sophisticated, returning each other's gifts. Gradually they realize the true love they have for one another. Did she have the abortion? "Eve Elman helped me" is all she says.

This may not on the surface sound like the sort of material which would attract von Stroheim, but in fact the dramatic conflicts and even many of the characters are highly reminiscent of his earlier work. There is no sentimentalizing the sexual nature of the relationship between Marge and Chick. In fact, it is often reduced to the level of pure economics. "A little less love and a lot more business and you wouldn't be in this fine mess," says Eve Elman, echoing the cynical statements of a character out of *Foolish Wives* or *The Wedding March*. The splitting of good and bad attributes into two or three related characters is also typical of von Stroheim's style, as is the general acceptance of fate and the almost grubby attention to the details of daily life. Eve Elman is quite clearly a transplanted von Stroheim type, but it is Elsie that seems to have appealed to him from the start. Elsie is a relatively minor character here, a foil for the play's heroine, and yet von Stroheim saw it at once as a perfect vehicle for Zasu Pitts, a chance to do in talking pictures what he had accomplished with her in *Greed* and *The Wedding March.*

Whether the manuscript was first discovered by the studio or by von Stroheim himself is unknown. Leonard Spigelgass was a reader for Fox in New York and remembers passing it along with a recommendation, although von Stroheim might have been aware of it independently.[7] But if von Stroheim had his own reasons for filming this story, so did the Fox company. Their biggest hit in the summer of 1931 was Frank Borzage's *Bad Girl,* a very similar story which paired James Dunn and Sally Eilers as depression-era lovers in back-lot Manhattan. The film was a surprise hit, established the team's box-office potential, and even won Borzage an undeserved Academy Award for direction. It is clear that the studio hoped *Walking Down Broadway* would be a follow-up success to *Bad Girl,* and set about ensuring this through a similar mix of players, setting, and dramatic situation.

But before much work could be accomplished on the *Walking Down Broadway* film, von Stroheim was offered the part of "De Forest" (later changed to "Von Furst") in Paul Sloane's *The Lost Squadron* at RKO. The role was an obvious self-caricature. Von Stroheim would play an arrogant and explosive film director whose mania for realism leads him to murderous excess. But he was eager for the chance to play it, and on October 7, 1931, his Fox contract was suspended to allow him six weeks on the RKO picture starting October 15. Then the illness of Paul Sloane caused a delay in *The Lost Squadron,* and on November 25 Fox granted up to six additional weeks' leave. George Archainbaud replaced Sloane, completed the film quickly, and on December 31 von Stroheim was back on salary at the Fox studio.[8]

As always he wrote the script of the film, this time in collaboration, Leonard Spigelgass being assigned to help him with the intricacies of the talking film. In an article in *Academy Leader,*[9] Spigelgass tells of working on the film at night over a six-month period, which suggests that von Stroheim was moonlighting from his acting chores at RKO in October, November, and December of 1931. According to Spigelgass, von Stroheim's staff consisted of "a charming red headed secretary and a young priest."[10] Often during their all-night sessions other priests and nuns joined the group. "They'd just sit around and watch us compose (while Mr. Von Stroheim sipped his Scotch, a quart a night), and at some point Mr. Von Stroheim would take them into another room and have a private conversation."[11] Spigelgass's personal opinions of von

Outright self-parody: an insane film director in *The Lost Squadron*.

Stroheim are unflattering (he has referred to the director as "a stupid, foolish, bigoted, narcissistic, bestial individual")[12] and he seems miffed at having been used as an errand boy for midnight hamburger runs.

In addition, he was shocked to hear von Stroheim muttering under his breath in Yiddish, a clear contrast to the stream of Catholic clergy who were constant late-night visitors. "For me, a Jew, thinking he was a Jew, meant that he was 'geshmatt.' I cannot tell you . . . what regret there is in it. We dislike people who are converted."[13] It would be another thirty years before von Stroheim's Jewish origins would become generally known. Nonetheless, Spigelgass had a grudging admiration for the director's dramatic skills.

> It was hard to understand why Mr. von Stroheim, who had been associated with pictures like *Greed, The Wedding March,* and *Blind Husbands,* would find this simple kind of American story so appealing, but as we discussed it, and I began to put it down on paper, it became clear that he was chiefly interested in the neuroses of these people. We turned the simple American characters into far more complicated ones, Vienna-oriented. And Mr. von Stroheim's sense of drama and unity were enormously impressive.[14]

After many weeks of effort the pair had produced a script which stayed relatively close to the spirit of Dawn Powell's original, but took off in predictable directions. "The first scene we had in the picture was in a ladies room," Spigelgass remembers, "and a lady's hand went in and put a dime or a nickle in a slot, and she turned (it) and something came out. And von Stroheim *adored* it. And I didn't know what the hell was going on. I never knew what she got out of the thing. He explained it was Kotex. Well, I thought Kotex was something with which you polished your nails."[15] Another scene in this draft showed raw sewage erupting into the river, a touch out of *Foolish Wives* or *Greed*. The big love scene was played in front of a drugstore window advertising "douche bags, on sale." Spigelgass had to find a proper dramatic shape for all these incidents.

> He was *determined* that I would say and write down and *indicate* to Mr. Sheehan, for whom the whole picture was being done, that this was the most passionate, sexual, violent love affair that there had ever been in the world. That this girl apparently had been a virgin, but that Jimmy Dunn was very good at what he was doing. And so we had to describe it. And I guess I wrote the first pornography—though nobody ever saw it![16]

It seems there were problems brewing behind the scenes at Fox. On January 20, 1932, Winfield Sheehan was sent off on a "three-month vacation,"[17] and Sol Wurtzel and his assistant Al Rockett were temporarily in charge of production. Edward Richmond Tinker, board chairman of the Chase National Bank, had succeeded Harley Clarke as Fox president in November, and he arrived at the studio soon after to institute an economy drive. "Certain contract cancellations on his part caused much bitter comment on the lots,"[18] reported *Time* magazine's business page, and one of the contracts was von Stroheim's. He was told that "the studio did not want to go through with the production,"[19] which really meant that they didn't want to go through with it with von Stroheim. The property was immediately given to staff writer Edwin Burke to rewrite for Alan Crosland's direction. An extant script prepared by him reads "WALKING DOWN BROADWAY, (Based upon the play by Dawn Powell), Story by Erich von Stroheim, Dialogue and Continuity by Erich von Stroheim, Leonard Spigelgass, Harry Ruskin, Maurine Watkins (compiled, edited, revised by Maurine Watkins) (started February 17th) (complete March 11th) Changes by Edwin Burke." Within a week, then, the script was under revision by other hands, and several new names had entered the film's checkered history.

The contributions of this crew of scenarists are questionable. Harry Ruskin was a writer of Broadway sketches for Florenz Ziegfeld and John Murray Anderson. He came to Hollywood to work on Anderson's *King of Jazz,* and would spend most of his career at M-G-M, where he wrote innumerable "Dr. Kildare" scripts. Maurine Watkins was the author of the popular stage comedy *Chicago,* as well as the screenplays of *Up the River* and *Doctor's Wives.* Her later films included *No Man of Her Own* and *Libelled Lady,* and she apparently was considered an expert on slangy dialogue. Edwin Burke had been a contract writer at the studio since at least 1928, and was credited with the dialogue on *Bad Girl.* He would be used as a hatchet man on this film, reworking the material whenever required.

After von Stroheim was dismissed from the project nothing much was done with it for several months. Von Stroheim took advantage of the situation as best he could and entered the hospital for some minor surgery, then was lucky enough to win an acting role at M-G-M in *As You Desire Me.* In an interview with the *Los Angeles Times* on June 5, 1932,[20] he comments that the *Walking Down Broadway* deal with Fox is apparently off, but suddenly the studio reactivated the project. Sheehan had returned from his enforced vacation while Sidney Kent replaced Tinker as president of the company. On June 21, 1932, George Bagnall, comptroller of the west coast studio, entered into a new agreement with von Stroheim reviving the full force of the September 2, 1931, contract. By so doing it would only be necessary to pay von Stroheim an additional $16,500 to make the picture, a bargain which seemed quite irresistible at the moment.[21] Von Stroheim immediately went back to work and submitted two more treatments before the start of shooting in mid-August.

The July 14 draft supplied the actor indications typical of von Stroheim's scripts. James Dunn was the hero, and Zasu Pitts the flighty roommate. George Raft was indicated as Dunn's pal, but no one had been found as yet to play the heroine—the studio was still looking for another Sally Eilers. The copy of this draft preserved by Fox has penciled comments in an unknown hand scrawled across the cover, many concerned with censorable material. "Tone down the slang for Eng(lish) audiences," says one note, below which is provided a list of offending terms: hell, damn, catch on, raspberry, louse, bum. "Too many fights with Mona and Mac," says another, referring to the new names given to Powell's Eve Elman and Lewey. The text is filled with expletives like "fish fur" and "Miste all Crighty."

The final shooting script, dated August 9, 1932, put Terrance Ray in the George Raft role, but there was still no heroine. Boots Mallory, an untried Fox discovery, would be cast in the lead only days before the start of shooting. By this time all the names of the characters had been changed, and the three male characters had been reduced to two by combining Lewey and Mac into one generally sinister figure. The play had been "opened up" by the introduction of a spectacular fire sequence, and by the simple tactic of showing events which could only be discussed in the play. And the Zasu Pitts character had emerged as the most complex and interesting.

From the crowds of people walking down Broadway on a warm summer evening the camera picks out Peggy and Millie, who are being followed by Jimmy and Mac. The boys attempt a pick-up, and while Peggy is a bit annoyed, Millie runs on glibly about her hobby of accident chasing and funeral watching. The fast-talking Mac quickly pairs off with Peggy, and leads the group to a dingy speakeasy where the boys try to loosen up their dates with a couple of drinks. In the powder room Peggy expresses misgivings, but Millie is glad they followed Mona's advice to "walk down Broadway and look *willing!*" The group moves on to a dance hall for some hot jazz and Millie tells about her experiences with a fortune teller. "I'm just a fool about Fate!" she admits. By a strange coincidence the group discovers that they live across the street from one another on the corner of 47th street and Ninth Avenue. On the way Jimmy and Peggy befriend a dog which they find lying injured in the gutter, but before they can get it home Millie falls into an open sewer excavation. While she goes in to clean up, Peggy and Jimmie give first aid to the little pup, which he nicknames "Pick Up." The girls' friend Mona shows up, a tough blonde who invites everyone to her room for a party. Mac recognizes her as the model in the deodorant ad he has tacked up on his wall. "You know—'Your Best Friend Won't Tell You.'" Miffed that Mona has made off with the men, Peggy goes to her room, but Jimmy takes a sandwich up to her while Mona entertains Mac. Peggy is glad to see him, and shows off her skylight view of New York, climbing up on a chair to share it with him. As they kiss, Millie sees them and falls into a deep despair.

Jimmy stays the night, and after he leaves Mac (who has spent the night with Mona) sneaks up to Peggy's room and tries to rape her. Mona hears the struggle and wrestles Mac back out of the room.

Millie confesses to Peggy that she had wanted Jimmy for herself. "I ain't blamin' you! You can't *force* anybody to love you," she says. Later Millie receives a visit from her hunchbacked librarian friend, Miss Platt. Millie elaborates for her a story of her secret love affair with one of the Vanderbilts, and how he once saved her life while rowing at his hunting lodge in the Adirondacks. When Miss Platt leaves Millie turns to her pet turtle, Lady Godiva.

At the seed-packaging factory where the girls work, Peggy is fired for fainting once too often. After visiting a doctor at the local medical center she tells Jimmy they must get married. He is delighted. Jimmy is able to get a raise from Mr. Brewster, the president of the bank where he works selling mechanical savings-banks, but before he can meet Peggy at the marriage-license bureau he runs into Mac. To get back at Peggy for resisting his advances, Mac tells Jimmy that he had gone up to her room after Jimmy had gone home. Jimmy misses Peggy at the license bureau and goes looking for her at her apartment. He finds Millie instead, who compounds the trouble by telling a wild story of all the lovers the girls' had before they knew Jimmy and Mac. When he runs into Peggy on a rain-swept street he explodes with accusations and calls off the wedding.

When the girls hear what has happened first Mona and then Millie come to get Jimmy to change his mind. But Mac has predicted this would happen, and Jimmy refuses. Mac sets them up with "two o' the snazziest bims you ever laid your eyes on," in an effort to cheer Jimmy up, but as they are leaving their building they see the girls' apartment house explode in flames. Jimmy rushes in to save Peggy, but he cannot find her. Millie is carried to Roosevelt Hospital. Peggy reads about the fire in the afternoon paper—she was in Grand Central, about to leave town—and rushes back. Millie blamed herself for breaking up the engagement and tried to gas herself, but the building blew up instead. She confesses her actions in a traumatic death scene as snow falls outside, Christmas music drifts in from the church across the street, and a procession of nurses files down the corridor. Months later Jimmy and Peggy meet Mona pushing a baby carriage down Broadway—she has married Mac. A thin watery stream is trickling from the carriage but there is no baby inside, only a broken bottle of bootleg hootch. The camera pulls back to lose them once again in the Broadway crowds.

At the time there was little publicity devoted to the filming of *Walking Down Broadway,* and apparently no substantial accounts of the shooting were published. The publicity which was issued by the studio was mainly concerned with establishing Boots Mallory as a bright young starlet. After appearing in such New York revues as the George White "Scandals" and Ziegfeld "Follies," Boots Mallory was signed to a Fox contract and made her first appearance in *Walking*

Down Broadway. An article in the film's pressbook describes how she landed the part, and while probably apocryphal, has enough von Stroheim flavor in it to bear quoting here:

> Miss Mallory was there but a few days when, browsing around the big studio, she came upon a pair of large cuirassier boots. She was unable to resist her childhood fetish, and thinking no one was looking, stepped into them. But at that very moment their owner, a director, stepped from behind a large light reflector. He smiled and Miss Mallory flushed crimson with embarrassment. The next day he called her into his office and told her that if she thought herself so capable of filling shoes larger than her own dainty 4½ A's she could have the leading romantic role in the new picture . . .[22]

One gets the feeling that von Stroheim had left the boots out as a trap, to see which young starlet would be unable to resist a "childhood fetish" and climb into them, and so win the part for herself. Publicity stills illustrating this scene were also provided by the studio, showing Boots Mallory with skirt hiked up and riding crop at the ready, smiling coyly next to a director's chair labeled "Eric von Stroheim." Many other stills showed von Stroheim greeting visiting east coast bankers—clear indications that the publicity department was not losing any sleep over this picture.

Von Stroheim was fortunate, however, in obtaining James Wong Howe as his cinematographer, a brilliant young cameraman who had been working under contract to the studio for the past year. His career had been sidetracked around 1929, after he spent a year in China shooting location footage for a projected documentary. On returning to Hollywood he was told that he had missed the talkie revolution and was unable to find work in the "new" medium. Eventually William K. Howard, aware of the quality of his silent films, hired him to photograph *Transatlantic,* and a Fox contract resulted.[23] But Wong Howe was still undervalued at the studio, and the major assignments typically went to Ernest Palmer (*Cavalcade*), George Schneiderman (*Pilgrimage*), or one of the other men with greater seniority. Von Stroheim worked with him for a week or two prior to the start of shooting, plotting the visual style of the film and working out in advance any difficult shots which might be forthcoming. This in itself was rare for anything but a major production, for cameramen typically were assigned to a film with little or no advance notice.

Although Wong Howe found von Stroheim a "hard taskmaster," he realized the director possessed a unique knowledge of the potentialities

James Wong Howe's dancing camera.

of the camera, and admitted to learning a great deal from him. In a 1971 interview he remembered one of the director's "extravagant" demands:

> He says, "Jimmy, I want this camera to dance, dance with the people." I said, "What do you mean, Von, 'dance with the people'?" He said, "You see that light stand over there? That light, three-wheeled lamp stand?" He got hold of it and he started pushing it, waltzing with it. "Now," he said, "just get something like this, and if this was strong enough, you could put a little platform, put the camera on top of it. Or you could have something built." I thought he was out of his mind to do that. I went into the production office, the man in charge at the time was Sol Wurtzel. I told him, I said, "Look, get me off this picture. This guy is crazy. He wants a dancing camera now!" He says, "Jimmy, go ahead, go back there. See what you can work out with him." He says, "Keep him happy."[24]

Wong Howe returned and devised the dancing camera, as well as other extraordinary visual effects. But von Stroheim's constant challenges began to wear him down, perhaps began to make him feel that von Stroheim was trespassing on his authority as cinematographer. He remembered that, "if I weren't under contract, I probably would have given up the job, because he was a very tough fellow to work for."[25] Apparently the lengthy days and nights which plagued the *Queen Kelly* company were being repeated on the Fox lot:

> We were working twenty-six hours; not twelve hours, not twenty-four hours, but twenty-six hours. We worked over Saturday and he wanted to continue working Sunday into Monday. I couldn't—it got so I couldn't look through the camera. My eyes are all puffed up. So I went in and I told Mr. Wurtzel. I says, "I'm going home because I can't work." He said "That's right. Go home, Jimmy. I got to put a stop to this. That Von—he gets going, he doesn't know when to stop."[26]

Von Stroheim's working habits caused considerable worry during the filming of the tenement fire scenes, and the Beverly Hills Fire Department was called out to stand by, "because that fellow's liable to burn our studio down." It was a damp, chilly evening, and von Stroheim was passing drinks out among the crew. Although the Fox regulars were able to restrain their thirsts (this was still during prohibition), the visiting firemen were soon so groggy that they were unable to return their equipment to the firehouse.[27]

The direction of actors we saw in the silent films was continued here. At times von Stroheim would patiently act out each scene for his cast, but on occasion he could coax, cajole, bully, or otherwise attempt to extract the proper emotions in a more physical manner. He continued the silent film technique of using music to put his actors in the proper mood, and played a gramophone during rehearsals to achieve this. Other inducements were not so subtle, particularly in one scene with Boots Mallory:

> He wanted her to be hysterical, crying. He just didn't get it out of her the way he wanted it and he slapped her, oh so hard, that the crew, they were ready to jump and pounce on him. That poor girl, her face almost black and blue, it swole up the next day. I think he was sadistic the way he was.[28]

Von Stroheim had been known to assault actresses before when he failed to note the proper degree of anxiety in their performances. William Daniels remembered that in the rape scene of *Foolish Wives,* Malvine Polo "became hysterical" after a long day and night's work on the brutal scene.[29] On the other hand, in working with Terrance Ray, von Stroheim employed a bio-mechanical system of direction:

> Well, Minna Gombell [playing Mona] had a scene with this fellow and he was supposed to laugh, and he couldn't laugh. And so what von

Stroheim did, he had a guy tie a string around the end of his pecker. He put it down his pants, so whenever von Stroheim wanted him to laugh he would pull this string and that made the guy laugh.[30]

This unique approach was described by Charles van Enger, at the time also a Fox contract cameraman, who was assigned to assist Howe for a day or two on scenes showing the party in Mona's apartment. Howe's own recollection was even more detailed, and ended with von Stroheim jerking the string and shouting, "Reaction! Reaction!"[31]

On the other hand, Leonard Spigelgass, who heard this story from his friend Minna Gombell, remembers James Dunn as the victim. Gombell also told him that in directing the love scenes, von Stroheim instructed the performers to visit the lavatories prior to each take and masturbate "almost to the point of completion."[32] Stories like this were the talk of the lot throughout production.

Despite such occasional indulgences, von Stroheim completed the film in 48 days for approximately $300,000.[33] According to R. L. Hough, the business manager assigned to the film, "I don't think we were much over budget,"[34] and von Stroheim himself claimed to be $150,000 *under* budget—although that seems a bit hard to believe.[35] Admittedly, the $300,000 cost of *Walking Down Broadway* was a far cry from the fortunes spent on *Foolish Wives* or *The Wedding March,* but how significant was it as compared with other films of the 1932-33 season? Keep in mind that a really cheap programmer, even from a studio the size of Universal, could be made that year for well under $100,000. For example, *The Secret of the Blue Room,* with Paul Lukas and Gloria Stuart was completed by that studio for $69,000.[36] The following chart compares the cost of *Walking Down Broadway* to selected 1932-33 releases from Universal and M-G-M (no comparable Fox figures are available). The Universal figures may be taken as the rock bottom cost of a class A picture (one suitable for exhibition in a first-class theater) while the M-G-M figures may include a bit more overhead than a comparable film produced at Fox:[37]

The Mummy (U)	$196,161
Gabriel Over the White House (MGM)	216,000
Once in a Lifetime (U)	246,527
The Kiss Before the Mirror (U)	260,192
WALKING DOWN BROADWAY (Fox)	300,000
Airmail (U)	305,000
Red Dust (MGM)	408,000
Tugboat Annie (MGM)	614,000
Grand Hotel (MGM)	700,000

So while *Walking Down Broadway* was never intended as a blockbuster on the level of *Grand Hotel,* it did receive a very comfortable budget, especially considering the relative unimportance of the cast. *Airmail,* produced for a nearly identical figure, was the most expensive production of the season at cost-conscious Universal, while *Red Dust,* a film loaded with high salaried talent and a substantial studio overhead, was only one-third more expensive.

At the close of production in mid-October, relations between von Stroheim and the studio were quite amicable, and the *New York Sun* reported that Fox had purchased Louis Bromfield's *A Modern Hero* to be directed by either von Stroheim or Frank Borzage (eventually G. W. Pabst directed it for Warner Brothers). Things were so good at this time that von Stroheim even managed to sell the studio an unfilmable story of his called *Her Highness* for $25,000.[38] His *Walking Down Broadway* contract was settled on November 5, 1932, indicating that the project was now officially completed. Publicity began going out. The Theatre Collection of the New York Public Library retains a set of stills it received on November 21, 1932, along with a pressbook carrying full credit to von Stroheim. Most amazingly of all, the fan magazine *Screen Romances* carried a highly detailed novelization of the film in its January 1933 issue[39] (the previous number had carried a large ad for the von Stroheim film).

But when the executives saw the picture everything began to unravel. Sheehan was now beginning to lose influence to Sol Wurtzel, who was appalled at what he saw in the film. At a closed screening at the studio Wurtzel yes-men tore the film to pieces. "I heard someone say it could only be shown to a convention of psychoanalysts," Spigelgass remembers. A preview in Glendale was even more disastrous, as the audiences began to laugh mercilessly.[40] This might have been predicted, since Zasu Pitts was then at the height of her popularity as a dizzy comedienne. Two years earlier Lewis Milestone had cast her as Lew Ayres's mother in *All Quiet on the Western Front,* but had to reshoot all her scenes with another actress when audiences unexpectedly laughed as soon as she appeared on screen. The same thing was happening here, but this was no question of reshooting a couple of scenes. Now forced into a position where he had to justify his actions, Sheehan began to behave differently. According to Spigelgass, "when Mr. Sheehan saw the work print he threw von Stroheim off the lot."[41]

From the start Sol Wurtzel had never had any use for von Stroheim or his films, and the director returned the sentiment, characterizing Wurtzel as "a low brow if ever there was one."[42] In his biographical

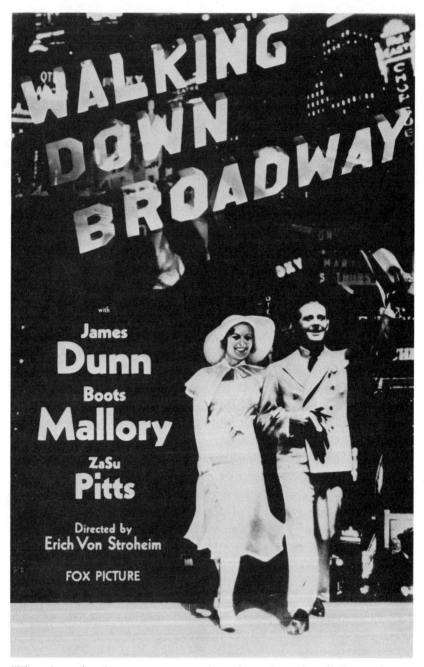

"Fit only to be shown to a convention of psychoanalysts." Poster for an unreleased film.

note in the 1936 *Production Guide and Directors Annual,* it is said of Wurtzel that he "is convinced most people want entertainment, not preachment, in motion pictures."[43] While this might indeed have been the opinion of the large majority of Hollywood producers, it was considered very *déclassé* to issue such statements publicly (biographical entries would be submitted, or at least approved, by their subjects). Indeed, von Stroheim was not the only victim of Wurtzel's operations: a few years later when Fox allowed the quality of their Ritz Brothers films to fall, the Brothers complained that they were going "from bad to Wurtzel."[44] Von Stroheim was about to go beyond even that.

It was always von Stroheim's contention that Wurtzel had used the issue of *Walking Down Broadway* as a convenient excuse for attacking his rival Sheehan's managerial capabilities, implying that nothing would have happened but for Wurtzel's intervention. Yet while Wurtzel was clearly the chief villain it seems that Sheehan supported him without much of a fight. In retrospect it appears that both men were genuinely disturbed by the film, and Sheehan's own uncertainties were only exacerbated by Wurtzel's complaints. On November 30, 1932, Wurtzel sent a memo to George Wasson in the legal department: "Please look up our contract with Eric Von Stroheim and advise me if we are compelled to give him credit on the screen and advertising matter as director. We plan on making a considerable number of retakes on the picture with another director."[45] The answer was no.

How many hands came into the film at this point is uncertain. Apparently the first scenes to be shot for the new version were Coney Island sequences directed by Raoul Walsh (James Wong Howe remembered shooting these scenes with Walsh, his only contact with any of the retake material).[46] Spigelgass mentions Sidney Lanfield as one of the group behind the new version.[47] But the main person responsible was Edwin Burke, who had taken over when von Stroheim was first bounced from the project in February of 1932. Burke came onto the project once again, and by February 6, 1933, had produced a "retake script" carefully divided into "old scenes" (those that could be salvaged from von Stroheim's material) and "new scenes" (material which was either completely his own creation, or altered versions of scenes that had originally been developed by Spigelgass and von Stroheim).

The new scenes generally served to soften the raunchy tone of the piece, although the illegitimacy plot remained central (this was still possible before uniform implementation of the Production Code). Burke added scenes at Coney Island and in a Chinese restaurant, as well as a strange episode in the doctor's office where we learn that there is nothing shameful about illegitimacy. He altered the ending so that neither of the girls is trapped inside the building, which explodes due to the activities of a dynamite-stealing drunk, a comic character who appears throughout the new version.

Later that month the *New York Sun* reported that *"Walking Down Broadway* is being remade now that Erich von Stroheim is no longer directing."[48] Alfred Werker (whose later films included *House of Rothschild, Adventures of Sherlock Holmes,* and *Walk East on Beacon*) was assigned to help Burke put his material on screen. According to Werker:

> The re-take version, which I co-directed with Edwin Burke, took about five weeks to shoot. We used the Stroheim long-shots, street scenes, etc., but the body of the script followed Mr. Burke's scenario. I believe Mr. Walsh did one sequence before Burke and I took over . . . I was under contract to the studio at the time and worked with Mr. Burke as a favor to Mr. Sheehan, but the retakes were really a project of Mr. Burke. The picture was released, but I don't know what happened to it and I certainly did not want credit for it.[49]

Under the title *Hello, Sister!* the film was copyrighted on March 23, 1933 (the film *Walking Down Broadway* was never copyrighted, although its pressbook claims a 1932 copyright). *Variety* on April 3, 1933, announced that Burke and Werker had spent only $62,000 on these retakes, but that neither would get screen credit, "as Von Stroheim's contract called for him having it."[50] (not the case, as we have seen). While there is no director credit on the prints and advertising for *Hello, Sister!,* a short blurb in the pressbook for that film does name Werker as the director. In fact, the only one of the various writers or directors to receive *official* credit was Leonard Spigelgass, who was none too happy about it. Publicity went out again on the film, and the New York Public Library received a new packet of stills on April 4, this time under the title *Hello, Sister!* The *Hello, Sister!* pressbook now carried no mention of von Stroheim whatsoever, although a careful reading of some of the prepared articles indicates a campaign originally planned around von Stroheim's popular image. For example, a blurb entitled "Realism good for art, but bad for Gombell," not only makes obvious use of von Stroheim's reputation, but refers to a scene between Minna Gombell and Terrance Ray which had been eliminated in *Hello, Sister!*

The film opened to poor reviews at the Seventh Avenue Roxy on May 5, 1933, considered a weak choice as the theater's sixth anniversary attraction. It followed a stage show which included Ann Pennington,

Martha Raye, assorted singers, dancers, musicians, and a donkey act. Of the major reviews only *Variety* and the *New York Sun* indicated von Stroheim as the original director. The *New York Times* and the *New York American* both credited Alan Crosland, while the other papers mainly kept their silence.[51] For them the film was "indifferent," "routine," "a stupid little trifle, aimless and dull." It quickly disappeared. Herman Weinberg's notice in the spring 1933 *Cinema Quarterly* settled the question for later historians: someone had "re-shot the whole film,"[52] and that was the end of it.

Under whatever title, the film quickly disappeared from sight and was effectively "lost" until 1970, when historian William K. Everson discovered one surviving print in the Fox vaults. What existed was, unfortunately, the Burke-Werker version, which incorporates only fragments of von Stroheim's material. For the record, we should indicate which scenes of *Hello, Sister!* now circulating are left over from von Stroheim's version. We know this by referring to stills issued at the time of *Walking Down Broadway's* production in 1932 as well as the so-called "retake script" of February 6, 1933, with its convenient division into "old scenes" and "new scenes." According to this evidence the surviving von Stroheim scenes are as follows:

1. The beginning and end of the scenes showing the first encounter of the two couples on Broadway, except for the actual introductions, down to Millie's speech about last week's big funeral.

2. The group arriving at the corner of 47th and Ninth Avenue and finding the dog, up until Millie is pulled out of the sewer.

3. Four shots of Jimmy taking the sandwich up to Peggy's room and knocking at the door.

4. The retake script indicates that the conclusion of the following scene is to be retained, from the time Peggy stacks the chair on top of the table until the end of the balcony love scene. However, in the film as released the dialogue is unlike any of the available treatments, implying that it was rewritten on the set—but whether by von Stroheim or Werker is unknown.

5. Mac entering Peggy's room, his confrontation with her and his fight with Mona. But intercut with this are new scenes of Millie looking on from her doorway, and a man in bed on the floor below having plaster fall on his head.

6. Peggy entering the medical building and consulting the directory (although the scene with the doctor is new).

7. Jimmy's scene with the bank president, Mr. Brewster.

8. All the footage showing Peggy at the marriage bureau.

9. Three shots of Jimmy running up to Peggy's apartment, but not the scene with Millie that follows.

10. All of the scenes in the rainstorm.

11. A shot of Peggy returning to the building, greeted by Mona's line, "How's your trousseau getting along?"

12. The retake script indicates that Mac's conversation with Jimmy, in which he convinces him to go out with the new girls, is also to be retained. In fact it was reshot with completely new dialogue to eliminate specific references to these girls.

13. All the surviving material relating to the explosion and fire, except for those shots showing Jimmy rescuing Peggy, and the fireman joking with the drunk.

While von Stroheim was justifiably famed for the epic quality of his films, *Walking Down Broadway* shows that he could achieve equal success when working in a more intimate mode. More importantly, it demonstrates that he was able to bring to *all* of his films a similar vision of man and society, unified by characteristic stylistic and thematic concerns. Not many directors have been able to accomplish this, and again D. W. Griffith appears as a significant precursor. In films like *A Romance of Happy Valley* and *The White Rose*, Griffith showed how a story which is restricted both in scale and subject matter could comment as significantly on the human condition as a more extravagantly conceived production. While other directors of the period, particularly Vidor, De Mille, and King, worked successfully in both modes, their epic and intimate films hardly ever seem cut from the same cloth. This is where Griffith and the von Stroheim of *Walking Down Broadway* share a unique position. While *Walking Down Broadway* apparently lacks the grand social concerns of von Stroheim's more impressive projects—the fall of empire, class distinction, social Darwinism—on closer examination it is not so far from the center of von Stroheim's universe. The fact that his characteristic concerns are not writ large here only means that the investigation is set in a minor key. *Walking Down Broadway* marks a change of pace, but not a change in mood or expectation.

The grubby details of working class life. James Dunn, Terrance Ray, Minna Gombell, Zasu Pitts, Boots Mallory.

In narrowing the scope of his film von Stroheim eliminated those obvious contrasts and parallels which dominate most of his work. Instead we have characters of the same class located in the same section of town, people whose similarities are more important than their differences. Those who know von Stroheim's other films can compare the courtship rituals of these working-class types with that found in *The Merry Widow* and *The Wedding March,* but von Stroheim is not interested in making that connection within this one film. In *Queen Kelly* he contrasted Europe and Africa in order to show the two-sided face of a universal situation. But here he only shows us life on Broadway, and we can create our own similes. It is no surprise that the obsessive topic of concern here is "love," that hardly a frame is wasted on anything but its contemplation (with relief provided only by some strange discusions of banking practices). All the characters in von Stroheim's universe share a common concern with sex, and while their situations might vary, their ultimate objectives hardly differ at all (although the

routes to that objective may be "pure" or "impure"). Mac tells us that
he acquired his French postcard collection through his barber, echoing
a line of Prince Danilo's in *The Merry Widow,* a line which in that film
was intended to identify sex as the common ground of all classes. But
Walking Down Broadway is not just *The Wedding March* in mufti. In
his imperial films von Stroheim creates a world of splendor, then shows
us the corruption at its heart. Here that idea is made to stand on its
head: the world is a crowded street jammed with tenements and hot
nuts stands, but a pair of true lovers can still be found uncorrupted by
its tawdry attractions.

Near the start of *Walking Down Broadway* the film's central character admits that "I'm just a fool about fate," putting into words one of
the film's most characteristic von Stroheim obsessions. As a naturalist
von Stroheim felt that the lives of men were fully pre-determined by
heredity and environment, helpless pawns in a game of the gods
marked by inexplicable strokes of fate. While fate plays a large part in
such films as *Greed* or *The Wedding March,* it is no less present here.
A severely literal critic might attack von Stroheim for the reliance on
coincidence and accident which runs throughout his body of work, a
holdover from the conventions of stage melodrama, perhaps. Remember that a title card in *The Wedding March* tells us that "There is no
such thing as accident—only fate—misnamed." The simplest coincidence,
the most off-hand accident, must inevitably be read as the hand of fate
toying once more with humanity. In a film like *Greed* this hand makes
a personal appearance, a nightmare come to life in one of that strange
film's fantasy sequences. But while the more restrained *mise en scène*
of *Walking Down Broadway* eschews such effects, fate is no less present
here. In the early script drafts, von Stroheim developed the idea of a
lottery ticket sold by Mac to Jimmy which appears to win $10,000.
Mac is underhanded enough to try to get it back, although ultimately
we learn that the whole lottery was a fake. In *Greed* the winning of a
$5,000 lottery prize marks a change in the characters' fortunes. Fate
has picked out McTeague and Trina, but its attentions are not benefi-
cial; the prize instigates the jealousy of Marcus and ignites the psycho-
pathic behavior of Trina, setting in motion the slide to destruction of
a group of otherwise ordinary individuals. Von Stroheim introduced the
idea of such a winning ticket here, but apparently withdrew it at the last
moment. It served no vital function, but merely cropped up as another
instance of fate's intercession. Perhaps he eliminated it after plotting
the consequences to their conclusion: what if Jimmy and Peggy actually
won the money? Do we run through *Greed* all over again? But if all the

tickets really were "printed in Hoboken," what is the point of the incident? The late films of many directors (Howard Hawks, for example) are awash with the detritus of early successes, filled with stylistic tics and obsessions that all too often are just along for the ride. It is to von Stroheim's credit that he realized that this was happening with his $10,000 lottery ticket, and junked the whole idea. But there are other "accidents" whose value von Stroheim magnifies perhaps beyond their actual importance. The two couples meet on Broadway and discover only afterwards that they live across the street from one another on West 47th Street. This is hardly an unlikely event, and one would think that given the similarities of their situations the meeting is inevitable. Yet von Stroheim sees this as a star-crossed rendezvous and emphasizes that "fate" has brought them together (like Millie, Shakespeare's Romeo is also "fortune's fool"). As an added bonus, Mona is discovered to be the deodorant ad model on Mac's pin-up wall, another Stroheimesque coincidence. There are visual correlatives to this idea as well. Von Stroheim began his film with a crane shot which descended into the crowds of Broadway, fiinally settling on the characters whose story we follow; they are lost in the crowd again at the film's conclusion. Such a random selection implies that the story relates to people of no special significance, just any convenient member of the passing parade. But it is also a selection by chance, as the camera eye chooses *these* people, not the group next to them. Why this happens cannot be explained any more than fate's other choices, but we should recognize that fate frames this story. Von Stroheim makes Dawn Powell's story his own by enclosing it in these brackets which stress the element of chance. Finally we should consider another "fated" action, as Jimmy misses Peggy when he runs to the marriage license bureau. They pass in a revolving door—so close! To another director this is mere irony, but for von Stroheim the wheel of fate is spinning once more. We may remember the multiple levels of meaning in the title *Merry-Go-Round,* a locale, a structuring element for the narrative, a wheel of fate. Something similar is operating here, and von Stroheim hopes for us to see that door as another kind of roulette wheel, spinning the fates of its players.

Fate was one concern von Stroheim shared with Dawn Powell, but what else attracted him to her work? We must look back to another of his smaller films, *The Devil's Pass Key,* and its concerns with innocence, suspicion, and belief. The plot machinations of *Walking Down Broadway* reach their climax in a rainstorm, one of von Stroheim's most extreme uses of the pathetic fallacy. The characters scream to be heard above the din of storm and street noise. "He showed me what a *phoney* you are!" sneers Jimmy. "And you believe *him*—against me?" asks Peggy. The question is the same as that confronting Warren Good-wright, the need for true love to be proven through an act of faith. As it happens, neither Warren nor Jimmy pass this test, but von Stroheim allows each a second chance for a happy ending, however unlikely. Here the emotional storm is capped by an explosion which blasts through the characters' hardened positions—a melodramatic advance over the groundless epiphany of the earlier film. Again, a film like *The Wedding March* will announce that it is "dedicated to the true lovers of the world," but here the insistence is not so direct. Von Stroheim gives us this essay on sacred and profane love without the need of labels. The film's balance of various brands of "love" is one of its most successful attributes, accomplished with considerable skill. The "pure" love of Jimmy and Peggy is no easy icon, but a relationship wracked with doubt and founded on a morality peculiar to the films of Erich von Stroheim (peculiar for Hollywood, that is). It bothers von Stroheim not a bit that his heroine becomes pregnant by his hero on their first date; their *love* is pure because it adheres to the vague roman-tic regulations of von Stroheim's universe. Romantic love is a license for just about anything in a von Stroheim film, but "Love is one thing and marriage another," as Maude George tells us in *The Wedding March*. Being true to the passion of the moment is the most important kind of truth.

The characters which von Stroheim uses to play out this drama are not among his most singular creations, but instead are intended to blend into a recognizably "realistic" streetscape. Thus the straining to include as much street jargon as possible, an attempt which fails him in much the same way that it failed D. W. Griffith in *The Struggle*. The charac-ters become excessive due to an excessive attempt to make them or-dinary. Mona seems the one character who might be more at home in some other von Stroheim picture. Her feather boas and leopard coats remind us of Queen Regina and are intended to clash quite visibly with Peggy's simple white or black outfits, and Millie's busy polka dot prints. As a character she is in direct line of descent from Maude George and Mae Busch, so crassly cynical that she is incapable of thinking about "love" except in terms of financial reward. (It is a genuine surprise that this characterization stems directly from Powell's original.) Yet she is a good friend, defending the innocent Peggy against both Mac and Jimmy, and suffering for it on both occasions. Late in his career von Stroheim began to add this second dimension to his cynical women (just as he had done earlier for his predatory males) and the move reflects his changing attitudes toward all his female characters. Along these same lines Mac should have blended good and evil qualities as well, but the characterization falls flat, hardly more than a bush league Prince Mirko. Perhaps George Raft might have breathed a more ambiguous quality into the role, but the material in the script is thin to begin with and Terrance Ray cannot be held totally to blame. As in all von Stroheim films the two males represent variations on one specific type, and according to Leonard Spigelgass, Mac and Jimmy were intended to represent "lust on one hand and sterility on the other."[53] It would be surprising if von Stroheim characterized Jimmy as disparagingly as this during pre-production, for the script is full of references to him as "just a nice, straight kid from the country." Perhaps the characterization is merely that of the acerbic Spigelgass? In any case, the word "just" seems a distinct limitation on Jimmy's potential, a naturalist trap which pre-ordains his possibilities. Peggy won't see apple blossoms and a nightingale when she kisses him, but he will provide a nice, straight home in Brooklyn or the Bronx. He is one of von Stroheim's most passive heroes, closer to the husband in *Foolish Wives* than to anyone else. Even Warren Goodwright in *The Devil's Pass Key* is allowed a lot of time to be obnoxious and thus to provide some motivation for the other characters, but Jimmy has little to do, as far as the development of the plot is concerned. In that case, *Walking Down Broadway* is clearly a film about its women. We see the love affair through their eyes (Mona's included), and once it has started Jimmy almost seems apart from it all. We have a triangle with only two sides, and our experience of the film's romance comes almost completely through Peggy and Millie. Boots Mallory does surprisingly well with Peggy, and it is a pity that her career never prospered. As written the character all too often resembles one of those tedious American wives, but she brings out an element of warmth and sensuality missing in the performances of Francellia Billington (*Blind Husbands*) or Miss Dupont (*Foolish Wives*). While lacking the animation of Swanson's Kitty Kelly, she is certainly more successful as an exemplar of innocence, pregnant or not. Indeed, the character is much warmer and more appealing than the cranky heroine of Powell's play. But in the long run the romance of Jimmy and Peggy is too lightweight to prevent our attention from drifting to Millie. Their affair is about as crucial as the love interest in a late Marx Brothers movie: useful, but hardly memorable. It is worth comparing the roles of Zasu Pitts in *The Wedding March* and *Walking*

Down Broadway. She plays the tragic lover in both films, but in *The Wedding March* her presence (even in the complete version) is overshadowed by the story of Mitzi. That is Fay Wray's film, but *Walking Down Broadway* clearly belongs to Zasu. A minor character in the original material, her role gradually developed as von Stroheim worked on the screenplay, and in his synopsis of the film published years later it appears that she is all he was ever interested in here.[54] In that synopsis he insistently refers to the character of Millie by the name "Zazu," identifying the character completely with the actress who played her. The importance of Zasu Pitts to von Stroheim cannot be exaggerated.

Tragedy for von Stroheim lies in having one's desires circumscribed by uncontrollable forces: heredity and environment again, here in the form of a beautiful soul trapped within a not-so-beautiful body. In *The Wedding March,* Zasu Pitts as Cecelia tries desperately to smoke and drink just like Prince Nikki's "girlies," but the attempt is disastrous. The same scene is played out by Millie at the start of *Walking Down Broadway,* pathetically flirting and drinking in an effort to make some sort of romantic impression. But since man cannot affect his destiny by will alone, Millie's efforts fail as do Cecelia's. This may seem more like pathos than tragedy, but for von Stroheim it is the most personal expression of tragedy imaginable. It is no coincidence that Millie fantasizes a romance straight out of *The Wedding March,* a hunting lodge in the mountains and an affair frustrated by problems of great wealth. Prince Nikki can "love" Cecelia because "you have six millions!" or so her father tells her, but Millie has nothing. Add a few unfortunate twists of fate (a fall into the sewer, for one) and *Walking Down Broadway* slips comfortably into von Stroheim's naturalist universe, with Zasu Pitts as its star-crossed protagonist.

The eventual fate of *Walking Down Broadway* was also decided by events beyond the control of its director—one last von Stroheim tragedy, it seems. Just as he was beginning to acquire a toehold at the studios, von Stroheim found himself back on the street again, his film maligned and cut to ribbons. He had survived an even more elaborate ousting a decade earlier when Universal removed him from *Merry-Go-Round.* But it had happened too many times since then, and it was no use explaining that this time it was not von Stroheim who was at fault. The supposed shock of the studio when they viewed the rough cut seems a red herring at best. There was nothing in *Walking Down Broadway* to equal that studio's *Hoopla* or *Call Her Savage,* to mention just two of their spicier releases. And the unmarried pregnancy of the heroine, perhaps the most sensitive issue as far as the Hays Office was concerned, was retained in the remade version. This time von Stroheim's explanation seems as good as any: he was the victim of a fight between giants.

I was in the middle, and because my story went over the head of Wurtzel, and my realistic characters were not to his liking, and because he believes that all other people are morons as he is one, he . . . practically remade the film. When the people were supposed to laugh they cried, and when they should have cried—they laughed.[55]

Last Years in Hollywood

The Sun is slowly (by progression) pulling in to parallel to the birth position of Neptune, and will become manifest in about two years, and lasting about eight years.

This is a fortunate influence of its kind. It tends to stimulate your intuitive faculties, bringing periods of unusual inspiration and happiness, and a possible unfoldment of your spiritual faculties, investigation of the occult sciences, and philosophies of life, as theosophy, astrology, etc.

This vibration will be of tremendous help to you, in your present line of work, in that it awakens the perceptive faculties.

Further, in approximately 1934, the progressed sun will have come to the sextile aspect to the birth position of Jupiter, marking 1934-35 and 1936 as the most prosperous years that you will have ever experienced in your entire life time.

The above planetary conditions are all major progressions which bring out the outstanding events of our lives.

In my thirty years of study and practice with this science, I do not recall having ever seen so many fortunate influences, all operating at one time in a horoscope . . ."[1]

As it happened, the horoscope which Paul Brachard cast for von Stroheim on January 14, 1933, was optimistic. Perhaps not knowing the true details of his birth had muddied the results. In any case, the years 1933-36 were probably the *worst* in a long and troubled career, years in which von Stroheim and his family faced poverty, illness, rejection, and ultimately, suicide.

Most astrologers are sensitive to clues offered by current events, but Brachard ignored the collapse of *Walking Down Broadway,* which was at that very moment in the hands of Sol Wurtzel. And when *Walking Down Broadway* fell apart the resurrected *Her Highness* went with it,

266

a unique loss since von Stroheim had sold it to Winnie Sheehan not as a straight melodrama but as an operetta.

With his attorney I. B. Kornblum composing the score, and L. Wolfe Gilbert providing the lyrics, von Stroheim recycled the treatment which M-G-M had rejected in 1931.[2] To augment his usual performance in presenting the story of his new film to a prospective backer, von Stroheim dragged along a pair of opera singers and 25 musicians. As he paced up and down, painting a vivid word picture of the new film and improvising as the mood struck him, the orchestra and chorus provided a running accompaniment, spiked with set-piece arias and duets in the best "Viennese" tradition.[3] The old magic was still working, and Sheehan had quickly snapped up the material for $25,000. The brief season of popularity enjoyed by filmed operettas like *The Vagabond King* in 1930-31 had not completely faded, and it helped that Mrs. Sheehan, Metropolitan Opera soprano Maria Jeritza, was also favorably impressed. Fox announced that Lillian Harvey and Henry Garat, stars of the English-language version of *The Congress Dances,* would play the leads, supported by El Brendel and June Vlasek (von Stroheim's script called for Jean Hersholt, Lewis Stone, and Tully Marshall although not necessarily in these same roles).[4]

We can see what Sheehan had in mind if we look at William Dieterle's 1931 musical *Adorable,* in which Fox starred Garat and Janet Gaynor, or even Erik Charrel's 1934 *Caravan.* But after von Stroheim was thrown off the lot the studio tried its best to get rid of the property, which represented a considerable investment during a lean period in the Fox fortunes.[5]

On his own again, von Stroheim reactivated the unfilmed African episodes of *Queen Kelly,* devised a new prologue for them, and began peddling the result under the title *Poto-Poto.* In this story Roulette Masha travels up and down the east African coast supporting herself by gambling; she toys with fate by staking her body against her opponent's gold. One day she loses to Poto Jan, a degenerate multimillionaire planter who takes her up country to his vast estates. The day they arrive he is bitten by a tse-tse fly and begins a long and slow decline. A downed aviator provides romantic complications, and eventually the pair are rescued from the fiendish planter by the United States Marines. An M-G-M reader summarized it all under the heading "Melodrama: a betrayed husband's fiendish revenge." He criticized the believability of the characters but praised the atmosphere of the piece.[6] A French novelization of this was published in Paris in 1956.[7]

Brachard had specially predicted September 1933 as "a most fortunate and happy month, but it began in disaster when Valerie was severely burned in a beauty parlor explosion on September 2. Preparing for a party that evening she had gone to a fashionable Hollywood beauty salon for a dry shampoo. As a beautician applied this solution it burst into flames, ignited by a small stove used to heat marcelle irons which had been left on from the previous customer. Instantly Valerie became a human torch, flames shooting from her face and hair. An attempt to smother the flames with a nearby fur was met with a cry of "Not my coat!" from one of the stars present, but somehow the blaze was extinguished and Valerie was rushed to Our Lady of Angels Hospital.[8]

She lay there for many weeks, and Erich moved into the hospital to be near her. He was already drinking a quart a day of Black and White Scotch, and when I. B. Kornblum visited him he was visibly shaken.[9] Von Stroheim had recently invested his savings in a modest but elegant home on Bristol Court in Brentwood, a step upward from the little frame house on North Oxford Street where they had lived since 1920. Months of legal and medical expenses lay ahead, with no serious hope of income or employment. Then in a stroke of fate right out of a von Stroheim script, M-G-M decided to remake *The Merry Widow* with Ernst Lubitsch directing. Because his work in establishing a screen treatment for the operetta gave him a claim to any talkie version, the studio needed to negotiate again with von Stroheim. Thalberg located him at the hospital.

Although Kornblum tried to arrange for von Stroheim to direct the remake himself, M-G-M had no interest in that, and in October, von Stroheim and Thalberg came to a verbal agreement on a $5000 payment for his rights. But then von Stroheim broke off the negotiation, hoping to use the issue as a lever to obtain his 25 percent of the silent *Merry Widow* profits. It was the kind of bluff that could only succeed under the best of circumstances, and von Stroheim had nothing in his hand. After an embarrassing delay he took the $5000 and signed away his entire interests on December 29.[10]

Still another blow fell when his son Josef was stricken with what appeared to be infantile paralysis. Although the diagnosis later proved inaccurate, the immediate picture was hopelessly grim. Such a string of personal and professional calamities, if encountered in one of his films, would have been dismissed as purest coincidence, a grotesque obsession with fate approaching the irrational. How it felt to be inside such a scenario can only be imagined.

"Under that terrific mental strain and stress," von Stroheim wrote to Peter Noble, "I stooped as low as one can possibly stoop, and acted in a picture for 'Mascot Company.' "[11] The film was *Crimson Romance,* which David Howard directed, and it was soon followed by Invincible's *Fugitive Road,* directed by Frank Strayer. Unlike *The Great Gabbo* these low-grade quickies lacked all pretense of quality or imagination. Appearing in these films was much worse than spoofing "the man you love to hate" for James Cruze or RKO. Von Stroheim was certifying the whole image as little more than an outdated joke. His work in *The Great Gabbo* was well received, but there was no coming back when the Mascot Company was involved.

In March of 1934 the von Stroheims went to court seeking $275,000 in damages from the beauty parlor operator. While they eventually received what Kornblum says was a record judgment of $125,000 the defendant was unable to pay. A deal was struck in which Mrs. von Stroheim became a partner in the shop, to receive one-third of the profits for the next ten years. But as in most such Hollywood deals the expected profits somehow never materialized, and continuing litigation dragged on for many years.

During his wife's convalescence von Stroheim wrote his first novel, *Paprika.*[12] This seems to have grown from a project first proposed to Sam Goldwyn in November 1933, which Goldwyn had rejected as more suitable to the silent screen.[13] Undaunted, von Stroheim dictated the manuscript to Valerie, who diligently wrote it out on a large legal pad. *Paprika* is a wonderfully feverish work which once more brings together all of von Stroheim's favorite characters and situations. The locale for the first time is changed to the Hungarian part of the Austro-Hungarian Empire, with Budapest replacing Vienna. "Paprika" is the fair-skinned daughter of a gypsy princess, child of an ill-starred love affair with a Hungarian nobleman. Sought after by both the brutal Gabor Zoltan and the sensitive gypsy violinist Rogi Jancsi, she spurns both, even though she secretly loves Jancsi. After a series of adventures Jancsi becomes a famous violinist in Budapest, and lover of the degenerate Princess Ilonka. Paprika hears of his success and comes to the city, but learning of his relationship with Ilonka she takes up with the princess's brother, the lecherous Prince Estervary. The Emperor Franz Josef himself hears about the affair and demands Estervary marry the girl; on the wedding night Jancsi kills his rival, and both he and Paprika are hunted down and killed as they try to escape. *Paprika* is a novel of strongly naturalist tendencies, with much emphasis placed on fate, heredity, and the accumulation of milieu detail (indeed, von Stroheim's descriptive passages are rich and extraordinary). As in the

Lewys novelization of *Merry-Go-Round,* only more so, the sexual undercurrents which were never able to surface in von Stroheim's films here reign unchecked. These are primarily sado-masochistic, and focus on Paprika's continual taunting of Jancsi, and the lack of vigor in his courtship. As the original publisher's blurb puts it: *"Paprika* as a story uncovers with the blunt scalpel of realism the sadism inherent in the sexual plexus of a woman's being."[14] On the book's appearance von Stroheim tried to sell it as a film, but readers found it "a trashy story, written for sensationalism only. Long and dull."[15] In 1937 there was talk of his directing a film version in France, and again in 1943 in Mexico, this time with Pola Negri,[16] but these were doomed projects.

The time had come to look for work elsewhere. In 1931 the Soviet director S. M. Eisenstein and his associates Tisse and Alexandrov had visited von Stroheim to express their admiration for his work.[17] Now grasping at straws, von Stroheim cabled him in Moscow late in 1934:

> Remembering your appreciation for my work, I beg you to try secure work for me, private or government. Consider me also as actor and writer. You know my ability and experience. Am going through crisis of my life. Please answer soon. Merry Christmas and Happy New Year.[18]

Now Eisenstein was hardly in a more favorable position than von Stroheim himself, and while there were in fact negotiations with Soviet film industry officials, this too came to nothing. Supposedly, they wanted to pay von Stroheim in furs and would not allow him to take hard currency out of the country.[19]

The low point finally arrived on December 19 when his second wife, Mae Jones, took von Stroheim to court on charges of non-support. The case made international headlines. "Erich von Stroheim, famous 'Prussian Guardsman' of the screen, who once earned £1000 a week, has been forced to pawn his personal belongings to make ends meet," wrote the London *Daily Express.* "This is the plea which he is making in a Los Angeles court, where he is defending a complaint by his former wife that he has failed to provide for his eighteen-year-old son [Erich Jr.]. Von Stroheim claimed . . . that he received only £800 as salary this year, and was forced to pawn his personal belongings to pay expenses . . ."[20]

While von Stroheim had alienated all the big studios and many of the top executives, there were still those in Hollywood who recognized his contributions and respected his principles. Just before Christmas a self-appointed delegation from M-G-M came to the door of his Brentwood home. It was easy to locate: the von Stroheim's house was the only one on the street without a shred of holiday decoration. A group led by John Considine and Robert Z. Leonard had taken up a collection on the lot and delivered a leather wallet containing $850, along with a souvenir scroll signed by "all your old friends at M-G-M." Valerie was amazed to see the names, not only of old friends like John Farrow and William K. Howard but of men like Louis B. Mayer, who von Stroheim was certain had blacklisted him in the industry.[21]

Ultimately the von Stroheims were able to repay all the donors, sending checks with little Christmas ribbons tied around them.[22] This was not always so easy though, since many people refused to accept the money. Clark Gable, who von Stroheim had used as an extra on *The Merry Widow* kept sending the check back over and over again.[23]

But for the moment the effect was one of crushing humiliation. On Christmas Eve, 1934, von Stroheim telephoned I. B. Kornblum, a toll call to Beverly Hills which immediately surprised the lawyer as an extravagance. Von Stroheim said he was calling to say goodbye, that he was going to commit suicide. "I don't want any charity," he said. "You don't have to feel sorry for me."[24]

Kornblum made him promise to wait until he could come over to kiss him goodbye. In the meantime he called Father O'Donnell, who also rushed to the house, and between them the pair were able to talk von Stroheim out of it. "Would you leave Valerie as disfigured as this? With Josef? And take the easy way out?"[25] They convinced him he could retain his self-respect by paying back the money. They appealed to his sense of responsibility. They assured him that his luck must change.

We are told that all such "final goodbyes" are cries for help, that prospective suicides hope desperately to be stopped by those who love them. In a sense this makes all such attempts grand theatrical gestures, attention-getting devices of last resort. Von Stroheim was nothing if not theatrical, and spent a lifetime attracting attention wih various tricks and ploys. Perhaps this was the last of them.

Suicide plays a significant part in von Stroheim's work, and we think of Bartholomew's sacrifice in *Merry-Go-Round,* Kitty Kelly's two failed attempts, or Millie's extirpation of her guilt in *Walking Down Broadway.* But the most revealing episode is that in his first serious work, *In the Morning.* In a part von Stroheim wrote for himself, Nicki decides on suicide as the only solution to the hopeless squeeze between the responsibilities of his position and the lack of funds to carry out these responsibilities. His goal in life, so he tells us, is "to live as our class lives— not merely to exist. And when that would one day be impossible—better disappear—quietly—in beauty."[26] Nicki is saved by a *doppelganger,* and a helpful inheritance which arrives just in time for the final curtain. But after twenty years in Hollywood, von Stroheim knew better than to wait for miracles.

On January 13, 1935, a newspaper account of a murder in Vienna jogged him back into action. Immediately he fleshed out the brief item with primary and secondary characters, a highly melodramatic plot structure, elaborate milieu detail, and a host of Stroheimesque incidents. He called his friend Joseph Schildkraut and suggested the new story as the basis of the vaudeville sketch he knew the actor was looking for. Schildkraut felt it wasn't suitable for him but suggested it might do for von Stroheim himself, and recommended he contact the writer Wallace Smith to work on an adaptation. Smith was an ex-newspaperman who since 1927 had done a good deal of writing for films. In fact, his name appears on the credits of *The Lost Squadron.* On January 16 von Stroheim outlined his idea to Smith, who was to work up the story and place it through his agents. Shortly thereafter von Stroheim spoke with Al Rogell at Columbia, who seemed interested in the work as a screenplay; accordingly, von Stroheim directed Smith to cast the work as a screen treatment instead.

Unfortunately, the verbal agreement between von Stroheim and Smith was never clear. Von Stroheim felt that Smith could have short story rights, but that credit and payments for any other version would be split 50/50. Smith claimed that von Stroheim was to share in the proceeds of any screen treatment, but that Smith would retain full credit and payment elsewhere. The disagreement emerged a month later when Smith produced two nearly identical manuscripts, one a short story which he submitted for publication under his own copyright, the other a "screen treatment" in which von Stroheim's name appeared after his own. Von Stroheim contended that once the short story appeared under Smith's name, no studio would buy the "treatment," an identical document signed by both of them. Instead the story would be purchased directly, leaving von Stroheim exactly nothing for his contribution. When von Stroheim complained, Smith's agents offered him $200 for all his interests; he refused and the matter wound up in arbitration court.[27]

The story in question, "The Alienist," is one of von Stroheim's most provocative, a cross between Robert E. Sherwood's *Reunion in Vienna* and James Whale's *The Kiss Before the Mirror.* Professor Ernst Volk is one of Vienna's most prominent psychoanalysts, a colleague of Freud and Krafft-Ebing. He specializes in the study of sado-masochism, for which he will receive the Nobel Prize. But his understanding of the human mind is based on clinical study alone; his devotion to his work has cut him off from everyday contact with the rest of humanity, especially women. He is blind to the devotion of his Russian assistant, Dr. Vera Petrovanoff, and confides instead to a waxen female mannequin named Lilith which he keeps locked in his private study.

The doctor falls victim to two adventurers, Kuno, Graf Adelhorst, and his mistress Marie, Baroness von Schweinitz, decayed members of the Austrian nobility now living by their wits. A "spring madness" seizes the doctor, who becomes hopelessly enamoured of the Baroness (he replaces Lilith with a figure of Marie). He marries her without knowing the truth of her relationship with the Count, much less the pair's none-too-subtle plans to recoup their fortunes at the wealthy doctor's expense. They honeymoon as a threesome in the Tyrol.

When even the newspapers begin to whisper about the strange relationship the doctor finally begins to suspect what has happened, but is too repressed to confront his feelings directly. Instead he adds two new figures to his collection, one of Kuno, and another of Vera, whose true love is only now dimly apparent to him.

Driven to madness by the sight of Marie in the Count's arms, the doctor draws a pistol and murders all the wax figures. He confesses his crime to the police, who arrive at the scene to take him away to a lunatic asylum.

The Count and Marie are classic von Stroheim characters, charming rogues most impressively drawn in *Foolish Wives*. But here they are not vaguely grounded "Russians," but the true Austrian noble line, their natural role as parasites made even more clear than in the days of the empire. This is underlined by having the Russian Vera mouth occasional anti-aristocratic imprecations. When von Stroheim was feeling particularly down on the Hapsburgs he would create a socialist to hurl the strongest of class epithets, but he seldom was able to make these radicals as interesting or fully developed as the parasites themselves.

The fascination with dummies recalls his own affection for *The Great Gabbo*,[28] although at the arbitration hearing von Stroheim claimed that Valerie had been the one to come up with the idea. But the way the doctor manipulates these figures is quite special, suggesting the activity of a mad director who works out with mannequins what he cannot accomplish in the world of men.

In fact, while the Count seems the classic von Stroheim figure, the doctor offers more possibilities as a character. In playing this role von Stroheim could once more have traced the fall of a creative mind into madness, something that he had enjoyed doing with *Gabbo*. And the figure of the doctor as a world famous authority on life who is at heart a simple soul, hopelessly prey to his emotions, offered new possibilities. As he grew older von Stroheim stopped creating in his films a comfortable persona through which he could project his own personality. Instead he began examining this figure and the cracks that were beginning to appear, growing less fascinated with the mask than with the man behind it. The original "man you love to hate" was a callous beast, the revised version a suave and calculating seducer. Von Stroheim had been able to put on both characters like a glove, and enjoyed having his public guess where the man ended and the myth began. Now he had created this new figure, one not all that different from those early, foolish husbands, a small man trapped behind an overgrown public image. Not a man firmly in control of all situations, but one capable in an instant of madness or suicide.

Von Stroheim was right in pressing his connection with "The Alienist," because Smith was soon able to turn it into a Broadway property. He interested Frank Mandel and Laurence Schwab in the work, which he called "The Happy Alienist," and under the title *May Wine* it opened at the St. James Theatre on December 5, 1935. Mandel and Schwab had turned it into a musical, with a score by Oscar Hammerstein II and Sigmund Romberg. The show was notable for its lack of a chorus and the way in which its songs furthered the dramatic action, after the fashion of *Music in the Air* and *The Cat and the Fiddle*. Walter Slezak was well received as the doctor (von Stroheim's version has no actor suggestions, but Frank Morgan inevitably comes to mind) but some critics felt the connection to Robert Sherwood's play was a bit too strong. "Another reunion was held in Vienna last night," wrote one,[29] but audiences approved and the show ran 213 performances. Despite the fact that Mandel and Schwab had sold a 60 percent interest to Paramount the show was never filmed.[30] Von Stroheim never spoke of the project and none of his biographers seems aware of its existence, despite the fact that von Stroheim's name was used and his contributions widely noted at the time. In 1978 neither Valerie nor I. B. Kornblum remembered anything about the whole affair.

There was one last film, an incredibly cheap Republic production called *The Crime of Dr. Crespi,* filmed on a few cramped sets in the old Bronx Biograph studio (where Griffith had ended his career in 1931 with *The Struggle*). It offered von Stroheim yet another mad genius role, and the rare chance for eight days' work. With undisguised sarcasm he referred to it as the "pièce de resistance" of his string of low-budget melodramas, and for good reason. The awfulness of this film is still astonishing.

Eventually those at M-G-M who had earlier offered charity were able to provide some opportunity for work as well. In March 1935, von Stroheim was hired as "technical adviser" on *Anna Karenina,* a three-week job for which he was paid $500.[31] Then on March 21 he went on regular salary as a staff writer in the M-G-M writers' building. He held this job, week in and week out, until he left for Paris twenty months later.

Von Stroheim recalled that M-G-M paid him $150 per week during this stint,[32] the low end of a scale which we might compare with William Faulkner's $250 in 1932 or F. Scott Fitzgerald's $1250 in 1938.[33] In fact, von Stroheim was not hired to deliver finished manuscripts, but to collaborate at story conferences where he would be called upon to add "touches" to a work in progress, very much the same way that studio would use Buster Keaton as a gag man for Red Skelton a few years later. Von Stroheim's specialty became adult bits of business. As writers department head Sam Marx remembers, "his mind ran to sex."[34] For this he would be specifically requested by directors like Tod Browning, Clarence Brown, and George Fitzmaurice, all of whom knew him from better days. As far as the studio was concerned there were no problems; von Stroheim was a model employee, well liked by his co-workers and diligent in his efforts. For that year-and-a-half all that had gone before, the storms and the rages, all of that seemed quite forgotten.

The chart indicates those projects with which von Stroheim was associated, although the extent of his contribution in each case is difficult to judge. This information came from releases filed in the legal department, but according to von Stroheim himself there were three unproduced originals done at this time for M-G-M, *Blind Love, The Purple Death,* and *Wild Blood.*[35] There is no available information on *The Purple Death,* which may be a working title for one of the other projects, but outlines and reader's reports exist for the other two titles. *Blind Love* is the story of the hunchbacked son of a Jewish junkman and the blind daughter of an Irish embalmer, who live next door to each other in Mintville, Ill. Bennie has loved Erin from childhood, and she loves him for his many kindnesses, not being able to see his twisted body. A third friend, Chris, is the tall and fair son of the local banker, and he also grows to love Erin. Chris grows up to become an aviator while Erin and Bennie go to Rome to study music, she as a singer and he as a composer of operas. Bennie supports their lessons by working as a junkman until his opera is accepted for production, with Erin as

Von Stroheim's M-G-M Writing Assignments, March 1935–November, 1936

(original title)	(assignment date)	(release title and director)
BLIND LOVE	May 18, 1935	not made
HELL HOLE	June 18, 1935	? possibly HELL AFLOAT, unfilmed Lang project
DOLLY	June 18, 1935	? possibly SUZY, George Fitzmaurice
THE WITCH OF TIMBUKTU	October 10, 1935	THE DEVIL DOLL, Tod Browning
GENERAL HOSPITAL	February 7, 1936	BETWEEN TWO WOMEN, George B. Seitz
ARSENE LUPIN	July 21, 1936	ARSENE LUPIN RETURNS, George Fitzmaurice
THE EMPEROR'S CANDLESTICKS	September 10, 1936	THE EMPEROR'S CANDLESTICKS, George Fitzmaurice
BENEFITS FORGOT	September 25, 1936	not made
GRACE MOORE ORIGINAL	September 25, 1936	OF HUMAN HEARTS, Clarence Brown
ONE CAME HOME	September 25, 1936	SPORTING BLOOD, S. Sylvan Simon
MAN IN POSSESSION	*	PERSONAL PROPERTY, W. S. Van Dyke

* Von Stroheim did not hand in any material or sign an assignment release before leaving M-G-M on November 27, 1936.
Information compiled from M-G-M legal department records.

the star. The opera deals with a blind girl who seeks to be miraculously cured by Jesus Christ, and her grotesque lover who is afraid of the consequences. On the day of the gala premiere Chris coincidentally flies the Atlantic and is feted by Mussolini, who takes him to the performance. A miracle occurs on stage and Erin is cured, runs immediately to Chris, and Bennie returns to his junkpile. Von Stroheim here reused some elements of his earlier works (as well as a few ideas from Victor Hugo's *L'Homme Qui Rit*) adding what he thought were topical genre strains (opera film, aviation pictures). A reader's synopsis dated May 18, 1935, is without comment, but a revision was prepared by Vicki Baum on June 8, indicating some studio interest in the property. The frivolously fickle nature of woman, the triumph of the storybook hero, and the inevitable tragedy of the crippled protagonist are ideas that stem from *Merry-Go-Round* and *Paprika*. Although it is difficult to judge from the extant synopsis, *Blind Love* would seem to contain the most blatant examples of von Stroheim's incorporation of religious symbolism. What M-G-M might have done to the project is uncertain, but it was briefly dusted off again in 1943, again without result.

Although von Stroheim claims to have written *Wild Blood* at this time, he may have been referring to the work he submitted to M-G-M in 1929. A 262-page manuscript does exist, but it is dated July 15, 1941, and was reported on by the readers department on September 12 of that year. It is possible that he tried to float *Wild Blood* again during 1935-36, but the evidence seems to indicate that it actually dates from his return to Hollywood during World War II. In any case, *Wild Blood* seems a bizarre joke of von Stroheim's at M-G-M's expense, a twisted parody of a Mickey Rooney picture. Set in and around New York, it deals with the lives of five young people of different backgrounds and their experiences together through grammar school and high school. Tainted by degenerate parents whose "wild blood" they have inherited, their lives are spent in drinking and whoring at the local hangout, a decadent club known as "The Devil's Garden." Only one of the girls resists the moral slide of her friends, and she eventually redeems the man she loves. Prostitution, *locomotor ataxia,* and a botched abortion are only a few of the elements that seem calculated to raise Louis B. Mayer's blood pressure. Again an extremely naturalist work, *Wild Blood* bears some relationship to William K. Howard's *Back Door to Heaven* (1939)—more evidence of a 1941 composition. The existence of one "pure" spirit in a corrupt environment, and the overwhelming importance of hereditary factors are typical of classic von Stroheim, but his interest in following the characters' lives from childhood is a later development, first seen in his 1930s' scripts.

Von Stroheim readily admitted working on the scripts of *The Devil Doll* and *The Emperor's Candlesticks,* although his touch is hard to discern in either film. William K. Everson has pointed out the most likely von Stroheim contribution to Tod Browning's *The Devil Doll,* a wisecrack about the Christmas season always bringing out religious fanatics. As for George Fitzmaurice's *The Emperor's Candlesticks,* one scene comes to mind in which Luise Rainer and William Powell, competing spies, have retired to adjoining bedrooms in a second-rate hotel. Each wishes the other to think he/she has gone to sleep in order to facilitate some late night spying. First one, then the other, hits upon the idea of bouncing up and down on the creaky bedsprings in a pattern meant to mimic the tossing and turning of a restless sleeper. The scene intercuts shots of Powell and Rainer bouncing up and down on the bedsprings with mischievous intent. This may have been an idea of von Stroheim's, but it is really impossible to trace his influence on any of these films with any degree of certainty.

Von Stroheim's most important M-G-M project was an original screenplay entitled *General Hospital,* devised for Clark Gable, Virginia Bruce, and Bruce Cabot. Also a genre picture (in line with the current vogue for hospital pictures) the film has its deepest roots in the tragic disfigurement of his wife Valerie and the weeks von Stroheim spent with her in Our Lady of Angels Hospital. The hero, a poor but committed young intern, is swept into a loveless marriage with a flighty society girl. The nurse who really loves him is married to a brutal drunkard, a typical human-beast character. Another intern, wealthy but dissolute, is a sadist with a mania for amputations, who while drunk on duty botches an unnecessary amputation on the nurse's husband, brought in from an automobile accident. He is thrown out of the medical profession and begins an affair with the wife of the hero, now growing bored of her husband's dedication to his work. While trying to escape to Paris together their train is wrecked, both his legs crushed and her beautiful face horribly burned. The hero manages to save the man's legs so that he can walk on crutches, but the wife remains disfigured. Unwilling to abandon his disfigured wife the doctor sits brooding at her bedside on a Christmas vigil, as a bill collector arrives for the last payment on her wedding ring.

Von Stroheim was very excited by the project and had hopes of directing it himself, but the studio delayed its production until after he had left Hollywood.[36] Two doctors, good and bad, are involved with

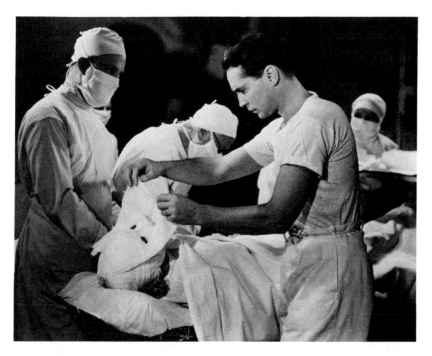

Dr. Franchot Tone discovers his wife's face has been horribly burned.

two women, also good and bad. The way von Stroheim manipulates these relationships echoes the complex structure of his best silent work, and is far more deft than the usually rambling development of his sound film scripts. He gives various people a choice of two lovers and then watches as they make the wrong choice. His new fascination with a dissolute layer of American high society finds its best expression here, but the story also serves as a sturdy vehicle for some of his older obsessions, e.g., the wave of amputations which sweeps through the film. Finally, the pathetic conclusion reflects only too strongly on a clearly autobiographical subtext.

George B. Seitz eventually directed the film under the title *Between Two Women* (for a time the working title was *Scarred Woman*). The final shooting script is signed by Carey Wilson (although he received no credit on the film) and follows von Stroheim's original very closely, except for the substitution of a new ending. Now the disfigured wife is cured, the doctor can separate from her in good conscience, and true happiness with the nurse seems to lie in the hero's future. M-G-M also altered von Stroheim's casting, having Virginia Bruce play the wife instead of the nurse, and putting Franchot Tone into the lead instead of

Gable. The film received mediocre notices, and reviewers stumbled over von Stroheim's fatalism as well as his fetishism. Said the *New York Times:* "Dr. Tone and his colleagues amputate everything in sight except the long arm of coincidence."[37]

Despite Paul Brachard's miserable success as a seer, von Stroheim had not lost his faith in the mystical. During his stay in the M-G-M writer's building an offer came from France to act in a film, *Koenigsmark,* a substantial production to be directed by Maurice Tourneur. He took this offer to Madame Ora, who had done so well during the *Merry Widow* struggles with Murray and Mayer. Much to von Stroheim's chagrin, Madame Ora told him no, that this was not the time to leave, and that another opportunity for great success in Europe was still to come.[38] Von Stroheim was dubious, but continued punching the clock at Culver City.

Then another offer did arrive, this time to appear in a Raymond Bernard film called *Marthe Richard.* The answer was yes. On November 27, 1936, von Stroheim quit his M-G-M job and began his journey to France. He had a round-trip ticket and planned to return to Hollywood immediately, hopefully to direct. In fact, he was putting an end to that career, which had begun 22 years earlier when he arrived in Los Angeles by cattle car. He would be back in Hollywood again, and even do some of his most effective work there—as an actor. But as a *creative* force, as a presence on the Hollywood scene, this part of his life was finished.

Epilogue

In 1936 von Stroheim began a long European exile, broken only by circumstances over which he had no control. But for five years he had already been an exile *within* Hollywood. He had become one of the gallery of ghosts haunting the Hollywood stages. D. W. Griffith made his last film in 1931, Rex Ingram in 1933, James Cruze in 1935. Marshall Neilan was still hanging on with B-movies, but he would have no more work after 1937. Von Stroheim was a leading member of the forcibly retired, that entire generation of industry pioneers put out to pasture in the early sound years for reasons which often had nothing to do with recording technology.

But unlike Griffith or Ingram, von Stroheim was unable to lie back, enjoy his annuities, and grumble about the misplaced priorities of Hollywood's latest generation of moguls. He had never been able to save very much during his peak earning years, largely the fault of bad business judgment and a careless exercise of personal generosity. Certainly his own living standards were never excessive; while directing such lavish spectacles as *Foolish Wives, The Merry Widow,* and *The Wedding March* he was content to live with his family in a modest frame house on North Oxford Street. When financial crisis really hit he was forced to take whatever employment offered itself, first in acting roles which traded crudely on his personal and professional reputation, then as an ill-paid cog in the machinery of the M-G-M writers building.

The move to Europe was a way of shutting the door on such demeaning employment, of working honestly again in his profession, even if only in acting roles. For the Europeans did not consider von Stroheim a freak or a dinosaur. While the cheap Hollywood films in which he acted often forced him into the threadbare "man you love to hate"

mould, the (often just as cheap) European films tried to tap those dynamic qualities which brought him to the public's attention in the first
place, and exploited the man, not simply his image. This may seem a
fine distinction, but it made a real difference to von Stroheim. When
D. W. Griffith died von Stroheim was asked by the BBC to record a
eulogy. As usual, it did not take long for von Stroheim himself to become the real topic of the piece, and this is part of what he said:

> If you live in France, for instance, and you have written one good book,
> or painted one good picture, or directed one outstanding film, fifty years
> ago, and nothing ever since, you are still recognized as an artist and
> honored accordingly. People take off their hats and call you *maître*.
> They do not forget. In Hollywood—in Hollywood you're as good as your
> last picture. If you didn't have one in production within the last three
> months you're forgotten, no matter what you have achieved ere this.[1]

Europe provided a sort of ego gratification that to von Stroheim was
more important than cash, as well as a creative atmosphere which carried the *potential* of further calls to greatness. Yet even in France these
were rare enough, and Jean Renoir's *La Grande Illusion* was the first
and most rewarding.

Von Stroheim was again a World War I German officer, but Renoir
was not interested in the automatic reactions of his audience to this
autocrat with a monocle. The audience may draw on its collective experience of von Stroheim, but what they see is a *modern* film which
uses the von Stroheim figure in a positive and imaginative fashion. By
contrast, von Stroheim in Mascot's *Crimson Romance* is also a World
War I German air ace, appearing in a film similarly touched with fashionable pacifism. But *Crimson Romance* offers this character on the
same note as *Heart of Humanity:* a caricature straight off the recruiting
posters. There has been no real development over fifteen years, merely
the repetition of a type with no understanding of what caused this type
to root itself so powerfully in the public's imagination in the first place.
Renoir was able to take what the von Stroheim persona had to offer
and process it for his own ends. In fact, he wove this role into the fabric of his film so successfully that *La Grande Illusion* is unthinkable
without it.

The attitude with which Renoir approached von Stroheim the actor
was mirrored in the way he handled the director von Stroheim as well.
Renoir encouraged him to use his own creative skills to fill out the
role, and unlike Roy Del Ruth he was smart enough to follow up on
the suggestions. When first called in for the film von Stroheim was offered one of two parts: the German flying ace who downs Gabin and

Fresnay at the start of the picture, or the commandant of the prison camp later on. Von Stroheim's first thought was that the two parts could be combined, which any actor eager to extend his role might have realized. But von Stroheim the director was able to construct a link between the roles which in the context of von Stroheim's cinema had tremendous resonance. The original character, the warrior/prince, has gone down in flames. Burned and broken, he directs comic opera troops in a sterile containment of captured officers. This is the only way remaining to serve his country, to fulfill the role he was trained for and which until recently he was carrying out in such spectacular fashion. As in the early "horrible Hun" films, von Stroheim invites the viewer to read his off-camera personality into the character up there on the screen. Von Stroheim was not interested in an audience's suspension of disbelief, in its appreciation and approval of fine acting. He wanted us to sense something *real* on screen. In the old days he was delighted when the public, seeing him in the street, cursed and vilified him, reacting to him as an actual Hun. They knew that Miss Gish was a great actress, not a war-stricken Belgian waif. But von Stroheim they saw as something out of a newsreel, and he encouraged this.

When he established a career as a director he fostered the link even more self-consciously, implying that he was exposing the foibles of an aristocracy of which he had been an intimate part. Audiences were again encouraged to think that *his* orgies and military rituals were not elaborate jobs of stage managing, à la De Mille, but gossipy re-creations of the world of von Stroheim's past. For Renoir the background screen had shifted again. We are expected to know all about the great director broken by Hollywood, living out a useless existence as an itinerant player in other people's films. This is what informs our understanding of this latest von, von Rauffenstein.

Examine the scene which introduces the commandant. We open on a giant crucifix, an unlikely bit of military decoration, but understandable here since von Rauffenstein has chosen the chapel for his living quarters. Before we see anyone we see the things of this room: its occupant's riding crops laid out, his potted geranium, his copy of *Casanova's Memoirs,* his champagne bucket. Renoir gives us all this in a single, unbroken moving shot; von Stroheim would have linked all these images with lap-dissolves. The moving shot is Renoir, all else is von Stroheim.[2]

The most touching of these details is the geranium, "the only flower in the fortress," an image which traces back to the beginning of von Stroheim's career. It is the "hopeful geranium" of Mae Marsh and *In-*

Slave bracelet, black arm band, and hopeful geranium. Memories of "the good old times."

tolerance, a token which has moved from Griffith to von Stroheim, and now to Renoir. Its significant reappearance later on in the famous scene where von Stroheim and Fresnay discuss the passing of the old order indicates just how far Renoir was prepared to let von Stroheim's ideas influence his script.[3]

Renoir allowed von Stroheim to extend his personal vision into this film not merely for nostalgic reasons. Von Stroheim's ideas added an emotional level to the script which was simply not present earlier, where the two separate Germans were considerably less rich as dramatic figures. Try to imagine this film with all von Stroheim's contributions subtracted and his role taken by someone like Harry Bauer.

Von Stroheim was never again to find an opportunity of this sort, but he kept treating his film appearances as episodes in an ongoing au-

tobiography nonetheless. In *Les Disparus de St. Agil,* for example, he
is a kindly and sensitive schoolmaster in a boys' boarding school. But
for obscure reasons not entirely connected with his nationality he is
shunned by the boys and avoided by the rest of the faculty. He is a
lonely sort and spends much of his time in his room, writing. On his
desk is a picture, totally unexplained in the script. It is Valerie and Josef, the family he has left behind while traveling overseas to find work.

He appeared in seventeen European features before the start of the
war, and when hostilities began—and squelched his most recent plans
for a directorial comeback—he tried to sign on with the French army.
Von Stroheim, who had served in Hollywood during the first war, was
not looking for a Signal Corps or other government service job; he
wanted combat duty. Fortunately, Jean Renoir was able to convince
him to leave for America and accept a role being offered him there by
Fox. With Denise Vernac, an actress whom he had met in Paris, and
who would be his companion for the rest of his life, he flew out of Lis-
bon on November 29, 1939. They had round-trip tickets.[4]

The film he was to make at Fox, *I Was an Adventuress,* was directed
by another émigré actor turned director, Gregory Ratoff. Ratoff's script
was full of holes and he allowed von Stroheim to rewrite large portions
of it.[5] The result was surprisingly successful, a caper film centered on
the actions of three crooks played by von Stroheim, Peter Lorre, and
Vera Zorina. The scene in which von Stroheim, sitting in a boulevard
café, analyzes the personal lives of pedestrians by studying their feet,
could only have been written by the director of *The Merry Widow.* But
von Stroheim still wanted nothing to do with Hollywood. Immediately
after the close of shooting he traveled with Denise to Washington in an
effort to sell an invention of his, a combination helmet and gas mask.
But this didn't work out, and an effort to arrange their return passage
to France was also fruitless. When the Germans marched into Paris on
June 17 von Stroheim was again faced with sitting out the war in
America.

He found a few days work in John Cromwell's *So Ends Our Night,*
as a Nazi officer, and then came a long dry period in New York. He
tried for work in the theater and was considered for the part of Kurt
Muller in Lillian Hellman's *Watch on the Rhine.* But it was felt that
the public would never accept him as a sympathetic type, that he was
still any audience's favorite villain. Paul Lukas was cast instead.

There was no money. No one was interested in his new story ideas,
and the old scripts he tried to float seemed stale. He was living with
Denise in a boarding house in Chelsea. The landlady kept her loose

pennies in an old milk bottle; they dipped into it one day in order to eat.[6]

Finally he landed a part. He replaced Boris Karloff in the long-running *Arsenic and Old Lace,* taking it on a lengthy road trip and returning to complete the run in New York. It was a solid year's work, tough and exacting, especially for a 56-year-old filmmaker with minimal experience of the theater. While he was in Philadelphia with the show D. W. Griffith came backstage and kissed him on both cheeks. They had first met in 1914 during the filming of *The Birth of a Nation.* If von Stroheim respected anyone in Hollywood it was Griffith. He saw Griffith not only as the father of cinema, but as a personal mentor, the progenitor of his own style. They were never close socially, but von Stroheim felt a deep professional bond between them, a shared love for the potential of cinema and a shared hatred for the big studio bosses. It was their last meeting.[7]

While working in *Arsenic and Old Lace* von Stroheim published two of his most revealing articles, both written for the anti-fascist quarterly *Decision: A Review of Free Culture.* The first was a study of sexuality in cinema which inevitably focused on his own films, but even more curious was his ambiguous review of *Citizen Kane.* Here he sought common ground with Welles as actor-writer-director, but was unable to accept Welles's fragmentation of time or, in fact, any violation of the strictly linear temporality so crucial to his own films. He praised the technical work and was especially aware of the problems and possibilities of deep focus staging, but claimed to find the theme of the picture unacceptably small.[8]

When Billy Wilder called him for the part of General Rommel in *Five Graves to Cairo* von Stroheim was glad to give up the grueling life of a traveling player. He gave the role a certain dignity and a strong touch of sympathy as well—highly unusual for a wartime release. It may be true that Rommel was an officer admired by his enemies, but the portrait here is remarkably positive, a reflection of von Stroheim's long standing tendency to see his villains as thoughtful and even noble fellows.

Wilder really did greet von Stroheim by telling him he had been ten years ahead of his time, and von Stroheim really did reply, "Twenty!" Von Stroheim busied himself with the details of his uniforms, still using costume and decor to define the personality within. He created his own "desert" make-up, deep tan up to the cap line and pure white above, since the General never removed his hat outdoors. He ordered a special protective metal grid for the crystal of his wrist-watch, something he claimed was always used by the German military. It was hand-made for him. He ordered special German binoculars and Zeiss cameras. They were obtained. He ordered film to be put in the cameras, and Billy Wilder was incredulous. "Who will know whether the cameras have film in them?" was Wilder's question. "I will know!," von Stroheim replied.[9]

Other roles were not so good, although his "mad artist" performances in *The Great Flammarion* and *The Mask of Dijon* through sheer force of personality manage to carry the films. As the war wound down he came east, determined to get back into the French film industry on the ground floor. With Denise he shipped on the first freighter returning after the liberation.

Unfortunately, the chaotic state of the postwar French film industry made it nearly impossible to tell the good offers from the bad. The films never seemed to turn out as advertised, and he had to content himself with checks which came at irregular intervals. The greatest disappointment was *La Danse de Mort,* a Franco-Italian co-production in which he appeared with Denise. Von Stroheim had written a screenplay, very appropriate since his own work shared a great deal of Strindberg's imagery. But it couldn't be used, or wouldn't be used, the whole production was a nightmare, and the film became another of von Stroheim's might-have-beens.

There was an offer to come to Vienna and he went eagerly, his first visit since 1930. But as he walked Denise around the city all of the landmarks, the neighborhoods that he remembered from his youth, were blasted and decayed. Passes were required to travel from one sector of the city to another. "God knows that I've seen him unhappy, but never as unhappy as he was that day," Denise remembers.[10] Did he realize that he was replaying the Prince's homecoming in *Merry-Go-Round,* the return to the burned out shell of Vienna in the film's last reels?

By now his health had begun to decline noticeably, and the chemotherapy which kept him alive those last years came to affect his personality, making him even more difficult than usual. In this atmosphere Billy Wilder's next call met a definitely mixed response. He had a project called *Sunset Boulevard.* Von Stroheim would play Max von Mayerling, once one of the three great directors of the early cinema, now reduced to working as butler for his former star—and former wife—Norma Desmond. Gloria Swanson would be Norma. The script had possibilities, but carried with it the pain of opening old wounds. Just being in Hollywood was painful enough, but to return to play this part seemed asking too much. Still, *Sunset Boulevard* clearly was going to

Opening an old wound. The cameras turn on themselves.

be an important film, the kind he always liked to be associated with. But that role was something else again, a crudely "autobiographical" appearance which seemed to use him only for his pathetic iconographic value. In *La Grande Illusion* and even *Five Graves to Cairo* von Stroheim could slip on his familiar persona and play off the rest of the film, using his already established image to add a new layer of meaning to the proceedings. But he didn't like the part of Max von Mayerling, "that goddamned butler role," he called it. In some ways the character was too much like von Stroheim himself, and in other ways not enough like him. To play an officer or prince, even in decline, was part of the grand charade of von Stroheim's life and a role which he accepted easily on screen and off. But Wilder was asking for the mad director again, with sentimental and pathetic flourishes this time, and von Stroheim was not happy about it. He resisted the idea that his life and career might even obliquely have suggested the story of this artist turned lackey. He only came to terms with the part when he accepted the fact that his own life contained events even more pathetic.[11]

He returned for a last trip to Hollywood, and as usual when he was involved in a role began to find ways of shaping and redefining it. It was von Stroheim who came up with the idea that the fan letters received by Norma Desmond should all come from Max. It was von Stroheim who realized that the one film of Norma's we see must be *Queen Kelly.* But Wilder was hardly able or willing to accept all von Stroheim's suggestions. Von Stroheim thought it would be a great idea to have Max washing and ironing Norma's underwear, but Wilder drew the line at this.[12]

On the surface the atmosphere on the set was full of smiles and good will, Swanson and von Stroheim praising each other to anyone within earshot. What von Stroheim really felt behind this façade we can never know, but when the film was finished he returned to Paris as fast as he could.

Erich von Stroheim was nominated for the Academy Award for his work in *Sunset Boulevard,* the only such recognition Hollywood ever gave him. But when the votes were counted he had lost to George Sanders; *All About Eve* won most of the Oscars that eluded *Sunset Boulevard* that year. Hollywood found it easier to accept an exposé of the theater than an investigation of its own dark secrets. In fact, the Hollywood establishment absolutely hated *Sunset Boulevard* and refused to support it in the voting. At the first major screening on the Paramount lot, Louis B. Mayer, still the most fearsome character in Hollywood, broke into a blind rage. "You bastard," he screamed at Wilder, "you have disgraced the industry that made you and fed you. You should be tarred and feathered and run out of Hollywood."[13] Von Stroheim's reaction, if he ever heard this story, is unreported but predictable.

He was always active in his last years, working on screenplays (all unproduced), novels (two published), and acting in one or two films each year. He made sure to stay in touch with the film and theater scene in Paris, attending opening nights and dining with a circle of old friends and new acquaintances.[14] When his finances could afford it he indulged his tastes in champagne and horses. He couldn't afford a stable of his own, but enjoyed the dogs he and Denise kept at Maurepas, their comfortable home outside of Paris. As he grew older the cancer which would eventually kill him made it more and more difficult to work or even travel, but he was unable to stop these activities. Unlike his friend D. W. Griffith, he would not allow himself to be shunted into complete inactivity; his mind continued to produce characters and situations, and he worked long hours each day writing them down. He was not going to disappear.

At the end he lay paralyzed, forcibly immobilized, a fate that to his friend Tom Curtiss recalled that of von Rauffenstein. In this state he received the Legion of Honor shortly before he died on May 12, 1957. He had worn many decorations in Hollywood, all from the prop department and all awarded by himself. The medals were fake, but von Stroheim convinced us they were real. That was his magician's secret. Now that the final act was finished his audience awarded him a decoration of his own, a real one. He must have enjoyed the irony.

Notes

Prologue

1. United States Department of Justice, Immigration and Naturalization Service, manifest of the *S.S. Prince Friedrich Wilhelm.*
2. "A European Red," *The New York Times,* June 27, 1920, VI, 2:1.
3. Sylvia Cushman, "The Man No One Likes," manuscript of planted newspaper release, author's collection.
4. Kevin Brownlow, *The War, the West and the Wilderness* (New York: Knopf, 1979), p. 143.
5. Denis Marion, *Stroheim* (Paris: Etudes Cinematographiques #48-50, 1966), pp. 10-12.
6. Thomas Quinn Curtiss, *Von Stroheim* (Paris: Editions France-Empire, 1970) and (New York: Farrar, Straus & Giroux, 1971). Subsequent references will be to the American edition.
7. Ibid., pp. 22-23.
8. Interview with Valerie von Stroheim, Los Angeles, June 1978.
9. Von Stroheim remembered the name as Captain McLean. Curtiss, p. 22.
10. My thanks to John Hagen for providing this information on von Stroheim's enlistment record.
11. Von Stroheim did make good use of his experience in the fashion industry for *The Devil's Pass Key.*
12. Irene A. Coffin, "West Point Inn: A Hiker's Haven on Mt. Tamalpais for Half a Century," unpublished manuscript [San Francisco, 1953]. Thanks to Dale Henderson for bringing this valuable article to my attention.
13. Curtiss, *Von Stroheim,* p. 25.
14. Ibid., p. 26.
15. A further irony is that the actor Holbrook Blinn was the screen's first McTeague in the film *Life's Whirlpool,* seven years before von Stroheim filmed *Greed.*
16. Curtiss (p. 30) refers to a playlet called "Brothers" which was probably an alternate title for this work. The cast of three males and one female is identical, and the "Brothers" title would be suitable here as well. Von

Stroheim may have registered the work as "In the Morning" since several plays named "Brothers" were already on record with the copyright office. See also Peter Noble, *Hollywood Scapegoat* (London: The Fortune Press, 1950), pp. 7-9, 133.

17. Curtiss, *Von Stroheim*, p. 27.
18. Complaint, Margaret von Stroheim vs. Erich O. H. von Stroheim, Superior Court of the County of Alameda, 28 May 1914. This quotation, and other information regarding the decay of von Stroheim's first marriage, is taken from the legal records of the von Stroheim divorce proceedings. I am grateful to Dale Henderson for locating these records for me.
19. Jim Tully, "Erich von Stroheim," *Vanity Fair,* March 1926, pp. 50, 128.
20. Curtiss, *Von Stroheim*, pp. 31-32.
21. Brownlow, *The War* . . . , pp. 142-43; Curtiss, *Von Stroheim*, p. 31.
22. *Film Culture,* Griffith I: *The Birth of a Nation* (1965, no. 36), p. 52.
23. In an unpublished memoir Joseph Henabery, who was one of Griffith's closest aides and plays Abraham Lincoln in *The Birth of a Nation,* flatly stated that von Stroheim never set foot on the Griffith lot until the filming of *Hearts of the World* three years later. It seems to me that not only is Henabery's negative attitude toward von Stroheim (in this manuscript) highly suspect, but there is ample printed and photographic evidence connecting von Stroheim to a wide range of Reliance-Majestic and Fine Arts productions under the Griffith banner at least as far back as early 1915.
24. "Corrected Index of the Work of Erich von Stroheim as Actor, Writer and Director," a series of three letters written to Peter Noble by von Stroheim in 1947-48, bearing corrections in von Stroheim's own hand; in the library of the Museum of Modern Art, 81.5/St. 87/N668, letter I, page i (hereafter referred to simply as "Letters"). A valuable source for von Stroheim's own point of view, which was later filtered by Noble and other biographers.
25. The relationship of all these trade names and corporations is often confusing. Eileen Bowser clarifies it: "In October 1913 Griffith joined Reliance-Majestic, which distributed through the Mutual Film Corporation . . . [and] remained titular production head until the formation of Triangle in July 1915" (Iris Barry and Eileen Bowser, *D. W. Griffith, American Film Master,* New York: Museum of Modern Art, 1965, p. 44). When Griffith joined Ince and Sennett in the Triangle he produced under the Fine Arts banner, but throughout this period he occupied the same studio at the corner of Hollywood and Sunset.
26. Curtiss, *Von Stroheim*, pp. 45-47.
27. Anita Loos, who was married to John Emerson not long after, was very surprised when I suggested to her that Emerson had anything to do with a film version of *Ghosts.* As a child actress Loos had played in the first American company of *A Doll's House,* and was always very much interested in Ibsen. Interview with Anita Loos, New York City, Feb. 2, 1972.

28. *Reel Life,* May 22, 1915, p. 32. See also description on page 17 of May 15 issue.
29. The only modern reference to von Stroheim's appearance in *The Failure* is the Italian *Filmlexicon degli Autori e delle Opere,* an often unreliable miscellany which somehow called this one right. But the *Filmlexicon* errs in saying that von Stroheim appeared in *A Bold Impersonation.* It was Erich von Ritzau who appeared in that film, an actor often confused with von Stroheim, and one with whom he would later share billing in *Intolerance.*
30. When he became a director von Stroheim drew on his years with the Griffith company when it came to assembling actors for his own films. Sam De Grasse, Francellia Billington, Spottiswoode Aitken, Gunther (Erich) von Ritzau, Dale Fuller, Tully Marshall, Josephine Crowell, George Fawcett, George Nichols, Seena Owen (Signe Auen), and Madame Sul Te Wan were only some of the actors on the lot in those days who later would appear in von Stroheim pictures.
31. *Reel Life,* August 21, 1915, p. 15.
32. The only modern reference comes in an undated photo and caption appearing in *Classics of the Silent Screen* (New York: Citadel, 1959), p. 223.
33. Curtiss, *Von Stroheim,* p. 49.
34. Anita Loos, *A Girl Like I* (New York: Viking, 1966), p. 123.
35. Letters, I, v.
36. Loos, *A Girl . . . ,* p. 124.
37. Herman G. Weinberg, "Coffee, Brandy and Cigars," *Film Culture,* April 1958, p. 22.
38. Curtiss, *Von Stroheim,* p. 89.
39. Margaret von Stroheim vs. Erich O. H. von Stroheim, op. cit. Birth date of Erich von Stroheim, Jr., from pension records of the Directors Guild of America—he later worked as an assistant director for Nicholas Ray, Vincente Minnelli, and others, occasionally appearing in small parts in films like *Two Weeks in Another Town.* He died in 1968.
40. "Macbeth," *The New York Times,* June 5, 1916.
41. Loos, *A Girl . . . ,* p. 124. Cost given in Frederick A. Talbot, *Moving Pictures: How They Are Made and Worked* (Philadelphia: J. B. Lippincott, 1923), p. 376.
42. Robert Hamilton Ball, *Shakespeare on Silent Film* (London: George Allen and Unwin, 1968), pp. 229-35.
43. Von Stroheim's position on the Fine Arts lot may be judged from a column in the *Motion Picture News* for March 25, 1916 (page 1745), which reports on a farewell dinner for Tree given at the Alexandria Hotel. Douglas Fairbanks presided as toastmaster, and the *News* reported toasts offered by "D. W. Griffith, Dustin Farnum, Erick von Stroheim, John Emerson, Mary Alden, Constance Collier, De Wolf Hopper," and a descending order of others. Heady company for a young assistant.
44. Loos, *A Girl . . . ,* p. 124.

45. Curtiss, *Von Stroheim,* p. 68.

46. Russell Merritt in interview with author, 1976.

47. Erich von Stroheim, "Tribute to the Master," in Harry Geduld (ed.), *Focus on D. W. Griffith* (Englewood Cliffs, N.J.: Prentice-Hall, 1971), pp. 155-57.

48. Peter Bogdanovich, *Allan Dwan: The Last Pioneer* (New York: Praeger, 1971), p. 43.

49. *"Wild and Woolly," Wid's,* July 5, 1917. For reference to *Reaching for the Moon* see Peter Noble, *Hollywood Scapegoat,* p. 22.

50. Letters, I, ix.

51. Fred Balshofer and Arthur Miller, *One Reel a Week* (Berkeley: University of California Press, 1967), p. 132.

52. Loos, *A Girl . . . ,* p. 125.

53. Curtiss, *Von Stroheim,* p. 86.

54. Interview with Anita Loos.

55. Iris Barry and Eileen Bowser, *D. W. Griffith: American Film Master* (New York: Museum of Modern Art, 1965), p. 53.

56. Was Mae Jones the costumer? She turns up on the Griffith payroll as a seamstress in 1917-18, and in early 1918 her name appears often on petty cash vouchers for sewing machine rental, sewing of costumes, and other services. But always as Mae Jones, not as Mrs. von Stroheim.

57. Lillian Gish, *The Movies, Mr. Griffith, and Me* (Englewood Cliffs, N.J.: Prentice-Hall, 1969), p. 174.

58. "Cheer Up, Erich von Stroheim—the Worst Is Yet To Come," *Moving Picture Weekly,* July 30, 1921, pp. 20, 39.

59. "Might is right—there is no place in the world for weakness," he says at one point, echoing a familiar Prussianism also quoted by Siegmann.

60. Brownlow, *The War . . . ,* pp. 171-72.

61. Sol Lesser to D. W. Griffith, March 22, 1919, telegram in the Griffith collection of the Museum of Modern Art, New York.

62. Letters, I, x. This is sometimes given as happening on *Hearts of the World,* but von Stroheim himself claims not.

63. Interview with Valerie von Stroheim.

64. Ibid.

65. Ibid.

66. *Moving Picture World,* July 5, 1919.

67. Hollingsworth, "Reader's Report, *The Furnace,*" Jan. 11, 1919.

68. Interview with Valerie von Stroheim.

Blind Husbands

1. Although *The Heart of Humanity* itself did very good business well into 1919.

2. In fact, Universal would have close ties to Germany throughout Laemmle's career, absorbing a higher percentage of émigré Germans than any other studio.

3. This was always the claim, but studio records suggest he was paid $400 per week.

4. Interview with Valerie von Stroheim, Los Angeles, June 1978.

5. Interview with Carl Laemmle, Jr., Beverly Hills, June 1973.

6. Interview with Valerie von Stroheim.

7. Mordaunt Hall, "Persistent von Stroheim Conquered Film Magnate," *New York Times,* Dec. 14, 1924, VIII, 7.

8. *Moving Picture Weekly,* Jan. 24, 1920, pp. 16, 35.

9. Celia Brynn, "An Hour with a Villain," *Picture Play,* Nov. 1919, pp. 60-61, 103.

10. *Memoranda of Important Facts,* Universal Film Manufacturing Company vs. Fox Film Company Inc., Dec. 1920. This is a lawsuit concerning Fox's release of a film called *Blind Wives.*

11. Interview with Grant Whytock, North Hollywood, July 16, 1971.

12. Julian Johnson, *"The Pinnacle," Photoplay,* undated clipping.

13. *Motion Picture News,* Sept. 27, 1919, p. 2504.

14. *Motion Picture News,* Oct. 4, 1919, p. 2678. Most probably this was written by Cochrane, who wrote all the copy which was published above Laemmle's signature.

15. Rob Reel, "Film News and Reviews." *Chicago Evening American,* Nov. 25, 1919.

16. Also on the bill was a comedy, a newsreel, Ned Wayburn's Revue, Pryor's Band, and a short produced by the Stage Women's War Relief called *Tom's Little Star,* in which Henry Miller, Daniel Frohman, Otis Skinner, Florenz Ziegfeld, and other celebrities of the legitimate theater appeared.

17. Agnes Smith, *"Blind Husbands," New York Telegraph,* undated clipping.

18. *"Blind Husbands," Variety,* Dec. 12, 1919.

19. Laurence Reid, *"Blind Husbands," Motion Picture News,* p. 3044, undated clipping.

20. "The Screen," *New York Times,* Dec. 8, 1919, p. 20.

21. Ibid.

22. *Memoranda of Important Facts,* op. cit.

23. For a discussion of this religious imagery, see Arthur Lennig, *Von Stroheim* (Albany: State University of New York 1973), pp. 19-23.

24. Reprinted in *Moving Picture Weekly,* Dec. 27, 1919, p. 11. E. C. Segar was the creator of Popeye and the Thimble Theater.

25. Von Stroheim told his biographers Noble and Curtiss that Margaret was an M.D. herself, but an investigation of period medical directories shows only her mother listed.

26. Cue sheet indicates a projector speed of 14 minutes per 1000 feet.

The Devil's Pass Key

1. In August of 1971 Henri Langlois told me that it was "generally known" that the owner of the Silent Movie Theatre in Los Angeles owned a print

of this film and had publicly screened it. This man, John Hampton, does own a fabulous collection of silents, and screened many rare Universals for me in the summer of 1973, but he denied ever having a print. He claimed to know one collector who did say he had a copy, but who was never willing or able to produce it. In January of 1979 Denise Vernac told me that she and von Stroheim had seen the film in Los Angeles in the early 40s. It was being run by a traveling showman as an "old time movie," and when they inquired about the print he refused to answer. Of many reported sightings, these remain the most convincing.

2. Kevin Brownlow, *The Parade's Gone By . . .* (New York: Knopf, 1968), p. 417.
3. Erich von Stroheim, "Movies and Morals," *Decision,* March 1941, p. 52.
4. "A European Red," *New York Times,* June 27, 1920, VI, 2.
5. Bob Bergut, *Eric von Stroheim* (Paris: Le Terrain Vague, 1960), p. 45.
6. Robert Brandau and Philippe Jullian, *De Meyer* (New York: Knopf, 1976).
7. Letter, Philippe Jullian to author, Dec. 10, 1976.
8. Georges Lewys / Gladys Lewis /, *Merry-Go-Round* (Los Angeles: Citizen's Print Shop, 1923).
9. *Moving Picture World,* Sept. 20, 1919, p. 1790.
10. Maude S. Cheatham, "Erich von Stroheim and the Miracle," *Motion Picture Classic,* Jan. 1920, pp. 34-35, 69, 98.
11. Thomas Quinn Curtiss, *Von Stroheim* (New York: Farrar, Straus & Giroux, 1971), p. 112.
12. Inez and Helen Klumph, *Screen Acting* (New York: Falk Publishing Company, 1922), p. 222.
13. Curtiss, *Von Stroheim,* p. 113.
14. Interview with Grant Whytock, North Hollywood, May 29, 1973.
15. Ibid., July 16, 1971.
16. *New York Times,* Jan. 25, 1920, VIII, 6.
17. For a description of how King Vidor trimmed 800 feet from *The Big Parade* in this manner see King Vidor, *A Tree Is a Tree* (New York: Harcourt Brace and Company, 1953), pp. 123-24.
18. *Moving Picture Weekly,* Sept. 11, 1920, p. 30.
19. Alice Leslie, "She's Just Mrs. Von Stroheim," *Motion Picture Magazine,* April 1926, p. 112.
20. Curtiss, *Von Stroheim,* p. 117.
21. "A European Red," *New York Times.*
22. Gordon Trent, *"Devil's Pass Key* at the Capitol," *New York Morning Telegraph,* Aug. 9, 1920.
23. *Moving Picture Weekly,* Sept. 11, 1920, p. 30.
24. Ibid., p. 30.
25. Ibid.
26. Ibid., Aug. 7, 1920, p. 30.
27. Arthur H. Lewis, *La Belle Otero* (New York: Trident Press, 1967), p. vii.
28. Quoted in Lewis, *La Belle Otero,* p. 33.
29. Ibid., p. 1.

30. *Motion Picture Classic,* Aug. 1920, pp. 88, 96.

31. "On the Screen," *New York Tribune,* Aug. 9, 1920, p. 6.

32. Ibid.

33. Ibid.

34. *"The Devil's Pass Key," Billboard,* Aug. 21, 1920.

35. *Moving Picture Weekly,* April 30, 1921, p. 29.

36. *"The New Film," New York Globe,* Aug. 9, 1920.

37. "Von Stroheim's Realism," *New York Morning Telegraph,* Aug. 10, 1920.

38. *"The Devil's Pass Key," Billboard.*

39. Denis Marion and Bathelemy Amengual, *Stroheim* (Paris: Etudes Cinematographique #48-50, 1966), p. 31. My translation.

40. "The Screen," *New York Times,* Aug. 9, 1920, p. 6.

41. "On the Screen," *New York Tribune.*

42. "The Screen," *New York Times.*

43. *Moving Picture Weekly,* Jan. 24, 1920, p. 16.

44. "Noticed and Noted," *New York Times,* Sept. 5, 1920, VI, 2.

45. André Bazin, *Jean Renoir* (New York: Simon and Schuster, 1973), p. 212.

46. "Noticed and Noted," *New York Times.*

47. Eric Elliott, *Anatomy of Motion Picture Art* (Dijon: Pool, 1928), p. 38.

48. "Color Plays Important Role in *The Devil's Pass Key," Moving Picture Weekly,* Aug. 1, 1920, p. 19.

49. *Tinting and Toning of Eastman Positive Motion Picture Film* (Rochester: Eastman Kodak Company, 1927), p. 36.

50. Erich von Stroheim, *Greed* (New York: Simon and Schuster, 1972), p. 143.

51. Bergut, *Eric von Stroheim,* p. 46.

52. *New York Evening Mail,* Aug. 10, 1920.

Foolish Wives

1. Interview with Valerie von Stroheim, Los Angeles, June 1978.

2. Interview with Samuel Marx, Los Angeles, June 1978.

3. "A European Red," *New York Times,* June 27, 1920, VI, 2.

4. Interview with Valerie von Stroheim. Valerie is very sure of this story, but it should be remembered that von Stroheim was not overly fond of the *Blind Husbands* title, and that *Foolish Wives* was one of the titles which had been entered in the sales office's *Pinnacle* sweepstakes.

5. *The Art of Hollywood* (London: Thames Television Limited, 1979), pp. 67-68.

6. Cedric Belfrage, *"Classic* Holds Open Court: The Case of the World Against Eric von Stroheim," *Motion Picture Classic,* June 1930, pp. 36-37, 82.

7. *Wid's,* June 13, 1921, p. 1.

8. Interview with Samuel Marx.

9. See picture of this sign in *Moving Picture Weekly,* Aug. 13, 1921, p. 16.

10. Stanchfield and Levy records, Gleb de Vos file.

11. Arthur Lennig, *Von Stroheim* (Albany: State University of New York, 1973), p. 61.
12. Interview with Samuel Marx.
13. *Moving Picture Weekly,* April 16, 1921, p. 15.
14. Helen Bullitt Lowry, "Mortal Actors and Immortal Film Faces," *New York Times,* May 22, 1921, III, 6.
15. The studio also announced lengths of 320 and even 360 reels, but this figure comes from a final cost sheet reproduced in *Moving Picture Weekly,* July 30, 1921, p. 28.
16. For von Stroheim's figure on the original budget see Gordon Gassaway, "Satan on a Leash," *Motion Picture Magazine,* Oct. 1921, p. 84; for his figure on the total cost see Cedric Belfrage, op. cit. Universal's figures come from an inter-office memo dated Sept. 30, 1926.
17. *Moving Picture Weekly,* Jan. 28, 1922, p. 11.
18. *Moving Picture Weekly,* Sept. 10, 1921, p. 11-12.
19. The studio gleefully published a two-page article on this excursion in *Moving Picture Weekly,* "*Foolish Wives* Comes East," Dec. 17, 1921, pp. 10-11.
20. Daniel Mandell, Oral History interview by Barry Steinberg, UCLA-AFI Oral History Project, 1969.
21. "Fourteen Reels of *Foolish Wives* Allows Few Preliminary Flourishes," *Moving Picture World,* Jan. 21, 1922, p. 259.
22. Fritz Tidden, *"Foolish Wives," Moving Picture World,* Jan. 21, 1922, p. 316.
23. "Julius Stern's Dynamic Energy and Efficiency Speeds Editing of Universal's *Foolish Wives," Moving Picture World,* Jan. 14, 1922, p. 175.
24. Harriette Underhill, "Von Stroheim's *Foolish Wives* Not So Foolish," *New York Tribune,* Jan. 22, 1922, IV, 4.
25. Fritz Tidden, op. cit.
26. *Moving Picture Weekly,* January 28, 1922, p. 11.
27. Fritz Tidden, op. cit.
28. Willis Goldbeck, "Von Stroheim, Man and Superman," *Motion Picture Classic,* Sept. 1922, pp. 18-19, 82-83.
29. "Picture Plays and People," *New York Times,* Jan. 22, 1922, VI, 8.
30. Willis Goldbeck, op. cit.
31. *"Foolish Wives* Titles Vivid," *New York Times,* Aug. 28, 1927, VIII, 3.
32. Interview with Ted Kent, Sherman Oaks, Jan. 20, 1972.
33. Bob Bergut, *Eric von Stroheim* (Paris: Le Terrain Vague, 1960), p. 52.
34. Eileen Bowser, *Film Notes* (New York: Museum of Modern Art, 1969), pp. 44-45, for example.
35. Arthur Lennig, *Von Stroheim,* pp. 35+. Lennig's work was further complicated by the fact that foreign versions were not prepared from the same negative as domestic versions. Sometimes the negatives were taken simultaneously, with two cameras side by side. At other times the foreign negative represented an entirely different take. Did all the "best" takes always wind up in the domestic version? And knowing the cutting history of this film, does it make any difference? The version assembled by Lennig is not purely one or the other, but represents *his* assessment of

which take seems best, with the ravages of time a significant factor. At any rate, no one can argue with Lennig's boast that he was the only von Stroheim editor who added footage.

36. The script refers to him as Apraxin, as does all the early publicity material. Only shortly before release was the name Karamzin used.
37. André Bazin, *Jean Renoir* (New York: Simon and Schuster, 1973), p. 15.
38. Fritz Tidden, op. cit.
39. Ibid.
40. *"Foolish Wives,* A Review of a Picture That Is an Insult to Every American," *Photoplay,* March 1922, p. 70.
41. Erich von Stroheim, "Movies and Morals," *Decision, a Review of Free Culture,* March 1941, pp. 49-56.
42. Harriette Underhill, op. cit.
43. "The Screen," *New York Times,* Jan. 12, 1922, p. 15.
44. Frederick James Smith, "The Celluloid Critic," *Motion Picture Classic,* April 1922, p. 48.
45. Universal Inter-Office memo, Sept. 30, 1926. This gives the cost of the film as $1,124,498 and the loss as $255,213. But despite the beating they took on this one picture Universal still made a comfortable profit that year.
46. *Moving Picture World,* Jan. 14, 1922, p. 175.
47. *Moving Picture World,* June 3, 1922, p. 496.
48. *Moving Picture World,* Jan. 21, 1922, p. 267.

Merry-Go-Round

1. Harriette Underhill, "Von Stroheim's *Foolish Wives* Not So Foolish," *New York Tribune,* Jan. 22, 1922, IV, 4.
2. He mentions his desire to film *Anatole* in James Fredericks, "A Crusader Against Provincialism," *Motion Picture Magazine,* Aug. 1920, pp. 73-74, 113. He also makes the claim here that "Schnitzler, the famous playwright, was the physician of my regiment."
3. Frederick Kohner, *The Magician of Sunset Boulevard,* unedited manuscript.
4. Interview with Paul Kohner, Beverly Hills, June 1978.
5. Frederick Kohner, op. cit.
6. *Moving Picture Weekly,* April 22, 1922, p. 16.
7. This account of the scripting of *Merry-Go-Round* is drawn from sworn testimony of von Stroheim, Germonprez, Thalberg, and Lucien Hubbard during a 1927 copyright infringement suit.
8. Hubbard's version was known as the "Bartholomew as Dictator" version.
9. Georges Lewys vs. Universal Pictures Corporation and Carl Laemmle, Supreme Court of the State of New York, testimony of Lucian Hubbard, April 21, 1927.
10. Von Stroheim once said, "Lubitsch shows you first the king on his throne, then as he is in the bedroom. I show you the king first in the bedroom so

you'll know what he is when you see him on his throne." Herman G. Weinberg, "Coffee, Brandy & Cigars XXX," *Film Culture,* April 1958, p. 21.

11. Von Stroheim returned to this ritual in an unproduced 1938 project, *La Dame Blanche.* See script extract in *Erich von Stroheim,* Edizioni di Bianco e Nero, Italy, 1959, pp. 103-27.

12. A nearly identical version of this script preserved in the Museum of Modern Art, New York, lacks this sequence, suggesting that it was eliminated as part of the "abridged continuity."

13. *Lady Chatterly's Lover* was published in 1928.

14. "Closeup Count, quite taken in by her beauty—but not moving picture love-on-first-sight expression."

15. Von Stroheim later uses hunchbacked characters in his novel *Paprika* and unproduced filmscript *Blind Love* for the same ends. Could he have seen Lubitsch's *Sumurun,* released here in October of 1921, in which Lubitsch himself appeared as the hunchbacked protagonist?

16. Dorothy Calhoun, "The Vienna of von Stroheim," *Motion Picture Classic,* April 1930, p. 30, 78, 85.

17. *Universal Weekly,* July 15, 1922, p. 15.

18. Part of the "just plain Danilo Petrovich" syndrome also apparent in *The Merry Widow, The Wedding March, Queen Kelly,* the unproduced *Her Highness,* and other later works.

19. Sam de Grasse was another Fairbanks-era veteran whom von Stroheim used in his own films years later. But Curtiss (page 143) claims that von Stroheim knew Kerry when Kerry was in the theatrical agency business in New York.

20. "Most Hated Villain Here To Pick Contest Beauties," *Chicago Herald and Examiner,* May 22, 1920.

21. Information from *Merry-Go-Round* pressbook.

22. Philbin's career is very much in need of reappraisal. She was for a time engaged to Paul Kohner, who cast her in several of his most ambitious productions, including *The Man Who Laughs* and *Love Me and the World Is Mine* (a version of *The Story of Hannerl and Her Lovers* directed by E. A. Dupont which attempted to serve as a successor to *Merry-Go-Round*). Her performances opposite Mosjoukine in *Surrender* and Conrad Veidt in *The Man Who Laughs* are extraordinary.

23. *Moving Picture Weekly,* Sept. 30, 1922.

24. The lobby of the Herald-Examiner Building was still intact the last time I visited it in 1978, probably the only standing von Stroheim set in downtown Los Angeles.

25. Valerie says that von Stroheim never put everything into his scripts because in that case they could be directed without him. Interview with Valerie von Stroheim, Los Angeles, June 1978. In fact, von Stroheim was unable to accept any work as final, and was constantly changing and improving his material.

26. James Sullivan was one of the technical staff. King might be Charles King, an actor playing one of the Count's cronies.

27. J. Winnard Hum, Typescript of *Merry-Go-Round* diary, author's collection.
28. Universal City had transformers to step down the AC current received from the local Edison lines, as well as its own DC generators.
29. Kevin Brownlow, *The War, the West, and the Wilderness* (New York: Knopf, 1979), pp. 198-203.
30. Charles Higham, *Hollywood Cameraman* (Bloomington: Indiana University Press, 1970), pp. 62-63.
31. Von Stroheim refused to use Joe Martin, an orangutan who was the star of his own series of comedy shorts. Martin was said to be evil tempered and difficult to work with. Later another animal was sent over from the Selig zoo, an early Hollywood studio on Mission Road which now supplied animals for the movies. It is possible that Joe Martin eventually played the role after von Stroheim was fired, but Universal's publicity was strangely silent on this.
32. Georges Lewys vs. Universal Pictures Corporation, examination before trial of Georges Lewys, April 8, 1927, stenographer's minutes.
33. Universal Film Manufacturing Company to Erich Von Stroheim, Oct. 6, 1922.
34. Interview with Denise Vernac, Maurepas, January 1979.
35. Years later von Stroheim wrote to Peter Noble that he had completed shooting three-fourths of the script, impossible since scenes in the Prater had only been started. Letters, II, i. Perhaps he refers to the amount of his original story material remaining in the completed film.
36. "Production Difficulties," *New York Times,* July 22, 1923, VI, 2.
37. Lewis Milestone, "The Reign of the Director," *New Theatre and Film,* March 1937.
38. Herman G. Weinberg, *Stroheim: A Pictorial Record of His Nine Films* (New York: Dover, 1975), p. 74.
39. *Moving Picture Weekly,* Nov. 11, 1922, p. 11.
40. "Production Difficulties," op. cit.
41. The scenes between Sidney Bracey and Dorothy Wallace which he mentions are now missing from circulating prints of the film.
42. "Production Difficulties," op. cit.
43. Harriette Underhill, *"Merry-Go-Round* Starts with a Rush, but 'Fades Out,' " *New York Tribune,* July 2, 1923, p. 8.
44. Robert E. Sherwood, *The Best Moving Pictures of 1922-23* (Boston: Small, Maynard & Co., 1923), p. 87.
45. "The Ten Best Pictures of 1923," *Film Daily Yearbook of Motion Pictures,* 1924, p. 123.
46. Inter-office memo dictated Sept. 30, 1926 which also shows total cost of $416,627.
47. Lewys vs. Universal, op. cit., testimony of Erich von Stroheim, April 22, 1927.
48. Was this Caracciolo related to the Baroness De Meyer? See page 47.
49. Georges Lewys [pseud. Gladys Lewis], *Merry-Go-Round,* Los Angeles, Citizen's Print Shop, 1923.

50. Gladys A. Lewis to Will Hays, March 10, 1924.
51. "Says Novel Was Pirated," *New York Times,* Nov. 5, 1926.

Greed

1. Arthur Marx, *Goldwyn* (New York: Norton, 1976), pp. 102-6.
2. Bosley Crowther, *Hollywood Rajah* (New York: Holt, Rinehart and Winston, 1960), p. 103.
3. This would give him time to complete his sessions with Gladys Lewis, and Goldwyn publicity on this point later caused him considerable embarrassment.
4. See clippings in the Fania Marinoff collection of the New York Public Library, especially Lynde Denig's undated review in the *Moving Picture World,* and the Jan. 8, 1916, review in the *Saturday Evening Mail.*
5. Quoted in Johanna Laird, "Von Stroheim's San Francisco," *San Francisco Sunday Examiner and Chronicle,* Oct. 31, 1976.
6. "Picture Plays and People," *New York Times,* Jan. 25, 1920, VIII, 6.
7. Edwin Schallert, "Stark Realism—At Last!," *Picture Play,* Oct. 1923, pp. 47, 104.
8. Ibid.
9. Don Ryan, "Erich von Stroheim, the Real Thing," *Picture Play,* June 1924, p. 115.
10. This prologue is not from *McTeague,* but has been identified by George Pratt as coming from Norris's "The True Reward of the Novelist," a paper about the historical novel in the collection of writings published posthumously in 1903 as *Essays in Authorship* (George Pratt, "Restoring the Context," *Image,* XV, 2, July 1972).
11. "McTeague Grows Hair To Order," *San Francisco Chronicle,* Feb. 23, 1923, p. D3.
12. Interview with Paul Ivano, Culver City, June 1978.
13. She had appeared with Fairbanks in *A Modern Musketeer,* made late in 1917, but von Stroheim had probably left the Fairbanks company by then, and is certainly not credited on the picture.
14. *"The Greatest Actress," Photoplay,* April 1931.
15. When Lewis Milestone cast her as Lew Ayres's mother in *All Quiet on the Western Front* preview audiences were so convulsed at her appearance that all her scenes had to be reshot with Beryl Mercer.
16. Peter Noble, *Hollywood Scapegoat* (London: The Fortune Press, 1950), pp. 48-49.
17. "Frank Norris's Novel *McTeague* at Last Shown in Pictures," *New York Herald Tribune,* November 30, 1924, VIII, 15.
18. "At the Quatr'z Arts Ball," *San Francisco Chronicle,* Jan. 28, 1923, p. S-1.
19. Erich von Stroheim, transcript of news conference at the National Film Theatre, London, January 5, 1954, courtesy of Liam O'Leary.
20. "Von Stroheim Plans for *McTeague,*" *Goldwyn Pictures,* Jan. 27, 1923, p. 1.
21. It was claimed that getting permission to erect the sign for "Frenna's

Saloon" was one of the company's more difficult problems. Harry Carr, "On the Camera Coast," *Motion Picture Magazine,* Aug. 1923, pp. 69-70.

22. "Work on *McTeague* Picture Progressing," *San Francisco Chronicle,* Jan. 31, 1923, p. 9.

23. Memo from Frank Godsol, Feb. 20, 1923.

24. Memo from Abe Lehr to Erich von Stroheim, March 16, 1923.

25. "Goldwyn Picture Halted by Illness," *San Francisco Chronicle,* March 23, 1923, p. 11.

26. Kenneth Rexroth, "Afterword," *McTeague* (New York: Signet, 1964), p. 342.

27. Erich von Stroheim, *Greed* (New York: Simon and Schuster, 1972); Herman G. Weinberg, *The Complete "Greed" of Erich von Stroheim* (New York: Arno Press, 1972); Joel Finler, *Stroheim* (Berkeley: University of California Press, 1968).

28. Erich von Stroheim, news conference, op. cit.

29. Ibid.

30. Frank Norris, *McTeague* (New York: Signet, 1964), p. 277.

31. Interview with J. J. Cohn, Beverly Hills, Jan. 21, 1972.

32. For example, see Paul Rotha's criticism of von Stroheim's "whimsical fancies," in *The Film Till Now* (London: Spring Books, 1967), pp. 155-62.

33. Erich von Stroheim, news conference, op. cit.

34. *San Francisco Chronicle,* March 30, 1923, p. 11.

35. Johanna Laird, "Von Stroheim's San Francisco," *San Francisco Sunday Examiner and Chronicle,* Oct. 31, 1976.

36. Frank Capra, *The Name Above the Title* (New York: Macmillan, 1971), p. 35.

37. Edwin Schallert, op. cit., pp. 46-47.

38. "Von Stroheim Making Film in Heart of Busy San Francisco," *San Francisco Chronicle,* April 15, 1923, pp. D1+

39. Quoted in Johanna Laird, op. cit.

40. Jonathan Rosenbaum, "Second Thoughts on Stroheim," *Film Comment,* May 1974, p. 10.

41. Charles Higham, *Hollywood Cameramen* (Bloomington: Indiana University Press, 1970), pp. 63-66.

42. "Von Stroheim Works Hard for Realism," *San Francisco Chronicle,* July 15, 1923, p. D-4.

43. Erich von Stroheim, news conference, op cit.

44. Charles Higham, *Hollywood Cameraman,* p. 66.

45. "Screen Needs Realism," *New York Times,* Aug. 5, 1923, VI, 2.

46. Ibid.

47. Although at his 1954 NFT news conference he denied ever having seen the picture.

48. Interview with J. J. Cohn, op. cit.

49. "Goldwyn Chief Lauds San Francisco," *San Francisco Chronicle,* May 29, 1923, p. 11.

50. "Von Stroheim Will Address Legion Post," *San Francisco Chronicle,* July 25, 1923, p. 9.

51. Peter Noble, *Hollywood Scapegoat,* p. 49.

52. Letters, II, v.

53. Charles Higham, *Hollywood Cameramen,* p. 63.

54. Peter Noble, *Hollywood Scapegoat,* p. 49.

55. Paul Ivano interview, op. cit.

56. Noble, *Hollywood Scapegoat,* p. 49.

57. *Colfax Record,* Sept. 14, 1923.

58. *Colfax Record,* March 9, 1923.

59. Filmed interview with Harold Henderson included in *The Man You Loved To Hate,* Film Profiles, 1979.

60. Harold Henderson to William Loeffler, Sept. 27, 1976, in collection of Film Profiles, Inc.

61. *Colfax Record,* Sept. 14, 1923.

62. Frank Norris, *McTeague,* p. 293.

63. Jerry Carroll, "Town Where Prop. 13 Doesn't Matter," *San Francisco Chronicle,* June 26, 1978, p. 6.

64. Harold Henderson to William Loeffler, April 6, 1976, in collection of Film Profiles, Inc.

65. Harold Henderson to William Loeffler, April 22, 1976, in collection of Film Profiles, Inc.

66. Memo from Mott and Vallee, legal department, to Abe Lehr, March 18, 1924.

67. *Colfax Record,* Oct. 5, 1923.

68. In recent years one thinks of Robert Altman screening a workprint of *Nashville* for Pauline Kael, whose pre-release review caused considerable comment.

69. Harry Carr, "On the Camera Coast," *Motion Picture Magazine,* April 1924, p. 76.

70. Thomas Quinn Curtiss, *Von Stroheim* (New York: Farrar, Straus & Giroux, 1971), pp. 339-44.

71. Don Ryan, op cit., p. 27.

72. Ibid.

73. Andrew Buchanan, *Films, the Way of the Cinema* (London: Pitman, 1932), p. 23.

74. André Bazin, *What Is Cinema?* (Berkeley: University of California Press, 1967), p. 27.

75. Ibid.

76. Mott and Vallee, op. cit. This is the only reference in studio files to the actual length of von Stroheim's last cut of the film, which is occasionally given as 24 or 28 reels. In any case, reference to print length given in reels must always be taken casually.

77. Interview with Grant Whytock, North Hollywood, July 16, 1971.

78. Interview with Grant Whytock, Culver City, June 1978. Paramount executives had a voice in the decision because they regularly interchanged product with the Loew's chain and would be expected to play the two-part film if ever released.

79. Letters, II, iv.

80. Motion Picture Commission to Metro-Goldwyn Pictures Corp., Nov. 25, 1924.

81. *"Greed," Harrison's Reports,* Dec. 13, 1924.
82. *Weekly Variety,* Dec. 10, 1924.
83. "Frank Norris's *McTeague," New York Times,* Dec. 5, 1924, p. 28.
84. Robert E. Sherwood, *"Greed," Life,* Jan. 1, 1925.
85. Iris Barry, *"Greed*—A Film of Realism," *The Spectator,* March 14, 1925, p. 402.
86. Richard Watts, Jr., "Landmark in Film Annals," *New York Herald Tribune,* Dec. 14, 1924.
87. *Klassiker des amerikanischer Films* (Berlin: Freunde der Deutsche Kinemathek, 1977), pp. 74-79.
88. "Top/Ten," *Sight and Sound,* Winter 1961-62, pp. 10-14.
89. As recently as 1978, in Hans-Jurgen Syberberg's *Hitler: A Film from Germany,* the cutting of *Greed* is compared to the destruction of the Jews and Louis B. Mayer to Adolf Hitler.
90. "Top Ten 72," *Sight and Sound,* Winter 1971-72, pp. 12-16.
91. *The Most Important and Misappreciated American Films Since the Beginning of the Cinema* (Brussels: Royal Film Archive of Belgium, 1978). Does the Belgian poll point to an incipient *Greed* revival? In the 1982 *Sight and Sound* poll *Greed* had climbed back to a tie for the number fourteen position, with *Potemkin* and *The General* the only silent films listed above it. By contrast, *The Passion of Joan of Arc, The Gold Rush,* and *Sunrise,* all prominent on the 1972 list, have now dropped from sight. "Top Ten 1982," *Sight and Sound,* Autumn 1982, pp. 242-46.
92. Jim Tully, "Erich von Stroheim," *Vanity Fair,* March 1926, pp. 50, 128.
93. Interview with Josef von Stroheim, Los Angeles, June 1978.

The Merry Widow

1. Thomas Quinn Curtiss, "The Last Years," *Film Culture,* April 1958, p. 5.
2. Quoted in Lewis Jacobs, *The Rise of the American Film* (New York: Teachers College Press, 1968), p. 351.
3. The sum eventually reached $70,470.83 due to escalator clauses keyed to the film's delayed production.
4. Cable, Abe Lehr to Frank Godsol, Jan. 11, 1924.
5. Benjamin Glazer, "Collaborator, Scenario, and von Stroheim," *The Merry Widow* souvenir book, p. 18.
6. Ibid.
7. Although it must be admitted that while Spigelgass was equally impressed with von Stroheim's grasp of dramatic form, he didn't think too highly of him as a human being. See his comments on the production of *Walking Down Broadway.*
8. It should be noted that such liberties were hardly unprecedented. At the height of the operetta's popularity in 1909 the G. W. Dillingham Company published a novelization which also spent much of its time creating a Marsovian background for the characters. When von Stroheim's film was released this work was reprinted by the A. L. Burt Company and offered as a "Photoplay Edition" of the film. Despite the inclusion of several stills and a colorful cover featuring Mae Murray, this text had even less connection with von Stroheim's work than the original libretto.

9. *The Merry Widow,* final shooting script, scenes 78-83.
10. Ibid., scene 120.
11. Ibid., scene 137.
12. Remember that von Stroheim claimed to have met his first wife by spilling soup on her while working as a waiter at the West Point Inn.
13. Gertrude Gordon, "King of the Dope Fiends," *Motion Picture Classic,* Feb. 1917, p. 32.
14. Erich von Stroheim, "Movies and Morals," *Decision,* March 1941, p. 55.
15. One can see both Gilbert and Jean Hersholt as extras in such early Thomas Ince productions as *Hell's Hinges* (1916).
16. Interview with Valerie von Stroheim, Los Angeles, June 1978.
17. *The Merry Widow* souvenir book, p. 16.
18. *Circe the Enchantress,* which they made in mid-1924, proved to be their last film together.
19. "Inside Stuff on Pictures," *Variety,* July 23, 1924, p. 25.
20. Interview with Samuel Marx, Los Angeles, June 1978.
21. For the record these were *The Sporting Venus, Daddy's Gone A-Hunting, Confessions of a Queen, Lady of the Night,* and *Cheaper To Marry.*
22. Bosley Crowther, *Hollywood Rajah* (New York: Holt, Rinehart and Winston, 1960), pp. 100-101.
23. Charles Higham, *Hollywood Cameramen* (Bloomington: University of Indiana Press, 1970), p. 67.
24. Don Ryan, "Trouping with von Stroheim," *Picture Play,* April 1925, p. 109. Ryan also published a curious novel called *Angel's Flight* which deals in part with the production of a film called *The Siren,* directed by Karl von Stechmann. Incidents which appear as fact in his series of articles for *Picture Play* return here as part of an autobiographical newspaper novel.
25. Ibid., p. 47.
26. Interview with Ray Rennahan, Encino, Jan. 24, 1972.
27. Specifically, reel 10 scenes 163-97.
28. Letters, II, vi-vii.
29. Quoted in Bob Thomas, *Thalberg* (New York: Bantam, 1970), pp. 65-66.
30. Don Ryan, "Boredom, Bacchanal, and Beauty," *Picture Play,* May 1925, p. 96.
31. Jan Ardmore, *The Self Enchanted* (New York: McGraw-Hill, 1959), p. 147.
32. Don Ryan, "Boredom, Bacchanal, and Beauty," p. 28.
33. Bob Thomas, *Thalberg,* p. 67.
34. Interview with J. J. Cohn, Beverly Hills, Jan. 21, 1972.
35. Jane Ardmore, *The Self Enchanted,* p. 150, and interview with Valerie von Stroheim.
36. Interview with Valerie von Stroheim.
37. Don Ryan, "Getting Under the Greasepaint," *Picture Play,* June 1925, p. 20.
38. Bosley Crowther, op. cit., p. 118. This story seems to have come to Crowther from Eddie Mannix, but it has never seemed completely believable to me. When I asked J. J. Cohn about it, all he could say was, "I

wasn't there, (but) I'll tell you, I would have known about it. I would have known about it because no sonofabitch would have stayed there. . . . It's inconceivable to me that a crew would say, 'We're not going to work!' Because in those days you'd say, 'That's fine! Take your paychecks and go!' There wouldn't have been any difficulty at all . . . because the crews were complaining about the treatment they were subjected to." Interview with J. J. Cohn, Jan. 21, 1972.

39. "Erich von Stroheim Introduces *The Merry Widow*," Film Culture, April 1958, p. 10.
40. Don Ryan, "Getting Under the Greasepaint," p. 20.
41. "Mae—Von Sign Peace," *Los Angeles Record,* Jan. 29, 1925.
42. Letters, II, viii.
43. Although by comparison King Vidor shot *The Big Parade* on a 7½ week schedule in April and May of 1925.
44. Herman G. Weinberg, "Coffee, Brandy and Cigars XXX," *Film Culture,* April 1958, p. 22.
45. Mordaunt Hall, "Miss Gould's New Theatre," *New York Times,* Aug. 27, 1925, p. 14.
46. Letters, II, viii.
47. Information from M-G-M legal files.
48. Samuel Marx, *Mayer and Thalberg* (New York: Random House, 1975), p. 262.
49. *Film Daily Yearbook of Motion Pictures,* 1926, p. 31.
50. Arthur Lennig, *Von Stroheim* (Albany: State University of New York, 1973), pp. 95-101.
51. Jonathan Rosenbaum, "Second Thoughts on Stroheim," *Film Comment,* May-June 1974, pp. 11-12.
52. W. F. Willis, "Reader's Report, *The Crucible,*" M-G-M, May 11, 1925.
53. Unidentified clipping in the Theatre Collection of the New York Public Library, dated Nov. 15, 1925.

The Wedding March

1. Interview with Valerie von Stroheim, Los Angeles, June 1978.
2. Herman G. Weinberg, *The Complete "Wedding March" of Erich von Stroheim,* Boston: Little, Brown, 1974.
3. Harry Carr, "Hollywood's One Real Genius—Von," *Photoplay,* May 1928, pp. 39, 138-39.
4. "Von Stroheim Tells of Making *The Wedding March*," *Hollywood Filmograph,* April 7, 1928, p. 14.
5. Dorothy Calhoun, "The Vienna of von Stroheim," *Motion Picture Classic,* April 1930, pp. 30, 78, 85.
6. Continuing his tradition of showing "the king first in his bedroom so you'll know just what he is when you see him on his throne." See also *Merry-Go-Round, The Merry Widow, Queen Kelly,* and several unproduced works.
7. This sequence was left intact even by later editors, and quickly gained

the reputation of being the only episode left untouched after von Stroheim was removed from the picture.

8. Frederick James Smith, "Passion and Pomp," *Liberty,* undated clipping.
9. During the shooting he was unexpectedly visited by a real Hapsburg, H.I.H. Archduke Leopold. His Imperial Highness did not record his opinion of the proceedings, but he did recall that von Stroheim was "speechless" on his arrival (H.I.H. Leopold, Archduke of Austria, "A Hapsburg Sees Hollywood," *Photoplay,* May, 1928, pp. 30-31, 92). This was probably a good thing, since von Stroheim's accent was that of "a Viennese cab driver" according to Paul Kohner, Josef von Sternberg, and others in a position to know.
10. Dorothy Calhoun, "The Vienna of von Stroheim," p. 85.
11. "Old Pre-War Vienna Reproduced in Film," *The New York Times,* Jan. 2, 1927, VII, 5.
12. L'Estrange Fawcett, *Films: Facts and Forecasts* (London: Geoffrey Bles, 1927), pp. 182-83.
13. Harry Carr, "She's Beautiful and Sweet," *Motion Picture Magazine,* pp. 37+ (undated clipping in the Fay Wray collection, USC).
14. Interview with Fay Wray, Beverly Hills, July 20, 1971.
15. Harry Carr, "She's Beautiful and Sweet."
16. Clifford Howard, "Erich von Stroheim," *Close-Up,* April 1928, p. 18.
17. B. Sorenson, "An Unretouched Close-Up of Von," *Motion Picture Magazine,* July 1927, p. 39.
18. The memories of those present at the time, reports in the trade press, and the claims of later historians who insist they have seen some of the still-existing blossoms disagree as to what proportion of wax, paper, and/or felt blossoms was used.
19. Dorothy Bay, "First the Artist, Then the Human Being, That's Von," *Motion Picture Classic,* Dec. 1927, pp. 23, 72.
20. Interview with Fay Wray.
21. Ibid.
22. Harry Carr, "Hollywood's One Real Genius."
23. B. Sorenson, "An Unretouched Close-Up."
24. Interview with Hal Mohr, Brentwood, Jan. 22, 1972.
25. Harry Carr, "Hollywood's One Real Genius."
26. Hal Mohr interview.
27. Harry Carr, "Hollywood's One Real Genius."
28. Hal Mohr interview.
29. Fay Wray interview.
30. Hal Mohr interview.
31. Ibid.
32. Harry Carr, "Hollywood's One Real Genius."
33. L'Estrange Fawcett, op. cit., p. 135.
34. Fay Wray interview.
35. Hal Mohr interview.
36. "Sid," *"The Wedding March,"* *Variety* (undated clipping in the Fay Wray collection, USC).
37. See Clifford Howard, "Von Stroheim," and Letters, II, x. But the

Exhibitor's Herald-World quoted the studio's figure as $1,800,000 ("Stroheim States Own Version of Tilt Over *Wedding March*," Feb. 11, 1928, p. 22). Von Stroheim's salary for this picture was apparently $100,000, the figure quoted in a confidential memo of Nov. 6, 1926, from Paul Kohner to Carl Laemmle listing all major Hollywood directors and their current salaries. As a confidant of von Stroheim, Kohner was in a position to have accurate information.

38. Remember that editor Grant Whytock felt that the marriage of Trina and McTeague was the obvious place to divide the full-length *Greed.*
39. "Stroheim States Own Version of Tilt Over *Wedding March*," *Exhibitors Herald-World,* Feb. 11, 1928, p. 22.
40. But another source indicates this happened as early as August 25. See "Powers and Stroheim in Final Break," Aug. 25, 1927, unidentified clipping in the library of the Academy of Motion Picture Arts and Sciences.
41. "Stroheim States Own Version of Tilt Over *Wedding March*," op. cit.
42. Ibid.
43. Josef von Sternberg, *Fun in a Chinese Laundry* (New York: Macmillan, 1965), p. 34.
44. Letters, II, x.
45. Lotte Eisner, "Notes on the Style of Stroheim," *Film Culture,* April 1958, p. 14.
46. Welford Beaton, "At Last One Fragment of Von's Opus Reaches Screen," *The Film Spectator,* March 17, 1928, p. 7.
47. "Von Stroheim's New Film," *New York Times,* Jan. 8, 1928, VIII, 7.
48. There was even a vocal, "Paradise," which the Paramount Publix house paper insists was "sung in the score" after the fashion of *Seventh Heaven*'s "Diane." But no vocal survives in existing prints. See "Theme Songs in Pictures," *Publix Opinion,* Dec. 8, 1928.
49. *Film Daily Yearbook of Motion Pictures,* 1929, p. 878.
50. Mordaunt Hall, "Von Stroheim's Latest," *New York Times,* Oct. 21, 1928, IX, 7.
51. "Sid," *"The Wedding March,"* op. cit.
52. John S. Cohen, "The New Photoplay," *New York Sun,* Oct. 13, 1928.
53. Welford Beaton, "Is Eric von Stroheim Really a Good Director?" *The Film Spectator,* March 17, 1928, p. 8.
54. "Sid," *"The Wedding March,"* op. cit.
55. *The Motion Picture Almanac,* 1929, p. 208.
56. Interview with Henri Langlois, Paris, August 1971.

Queen Kelly

1. Unidentified clipping in the library of the Academy of Motion Picture Arts and Sciences, dated Aug. 11, 1926.
2. *Paramount Fifteenth Anniversary Campaign Book, 1912-1927.*
3. Unidentified clipping in the library of the Academy of Motion Picture Arts and Sciences, dated May 10, 1927.
4. *Hollywood Filmograph,* Nov. 26, 1927, clipping in the Laemmle collection of the Hollywood Museum.

5. Interview with Lewis Milestone, Beverly Hills, Jan. 1972.

6. From material in the *Queen Kelly* file, George Eastman House/International Museum of Photography.

7. Peter Noble, *Hollywood Scapegoat* (London: The Fortune Press, 1950), p. 70.

8. Gloria Swanson, *Swanson on Swanson* (New York: Random House, 1980).

9. Tim Onosko, "RKO Radio: An Overview," *Velvet Light Trap,* Fall 1973, p. 2.

10. Gloria Swanson, *Swanson on Swanson,* pp. 345-47, 357-58.

11. Unidentified clipping in the library of the Academy of Motion Picture Arts and Sciences, dated April 30, 1928.

12. Ibid.

13. Frank Capra and Barbara Stanwyck later made a version of their own, *The Miracle Woman* (Columbia, 1931).

14. Unidentified clipping in the library of the Academy of Motion Picture Arts and Sciences, dated May 19, 1928.

15. Unidentified clipping in the library of the Academy of Motion Picture Arts and Sciences, dated May 30, 1928.

16. Gloria Swanson, "About *Queen Kelly*" in *Hommage à Erich von Stroheim,* edited by Charlotte Gobeil (Ottawa: Canadian Film Institute, 1966), p. 27. Her autobiography also makes this claim.

17. *Motion Picture News,* Nov. 3, 1928, p. 1382.

18. Gloria Swanson, *Swanson on Swanson,* p. 358.

19. "Keith-Albee-Orpheum buys into FBO," *The Film Daily,* Feb. 27, 1928, p. 1.

20. Eric Barnouw, *A Tower in Babel* (New York: Oxford University Press, 1966), pp. 232-33.

21. "RCA Buys Control of Keith-Albee-Orpheum and FBO; Kennedy To Retire Under Deal," *The Film Daily,* Oct. 6, 1928, p. 1.

22. Interview with Paul Ivano, Sherman Oaks, May 26, 1973.

23. Letter, Paul Ivano to author, Aug. 12, 1972.

24. Interview with William Margulies, Burbank, Jan. 22, 1972.

25. Paul Ivano letter.

26. Paul Ivano interview.

27. William Margulies interview.

28. Ibid.

29. *Film Daily Yearbook of Motion Pictures* (1929), p. 317.

30. Herman G. Weinberg, *Stroheim, a Pictorial Record of His Nine Films* (New York: Dover, 1975), p. 209.

31. Although her autobiography (pp. 363-64) blames Byron on von Stroheim.

32. "Miss Swanson's New Role," *New York Times,* Jan. 27, 1929, IX, 8.

33. Joel Finler, *Stroheim* (London: Movie Magazine Ltd., 1967); Michael Ciment, "Erich von Stroheim," *Anthologie du Cinema,* vol. III (Paris: L'Avant-Scene, 1968); Weinberg, *Pictorial History.*

34. Thomas Quinn Curtiss, *Erich Von Stroheim* (Paris: Editions France-

Notes

Empire, 1970), p. 301; *Von Stroheim* (New York: Farrar, Straus & Giroux, 1971), p. 350.

35. This line of course recalls a similar title in *The Merry Widow,* in which the Prince asks to be referred to as "just plain Danilo Petrovich." Both films end with a marriage-coronation ceremony which unites a prince with a lively Irish lass he has loved through much adversity, but in the later film it is the woman who speaks the closing title.

36. Cedric Belfrage, "Classic Holds Open Court," *Motion Picture Classic,* June 1930, p. 82.

37. Tod Welch, "Von Schedule!" *Motion Picture Magazine,* May 1929, p. 104.

38. Jessie Burns, "Reader's Synopsis," *Poto-Poto,* M-G-M, May 8, 1933.

39. Von Stroheim's obsession with realistic detail did not extend to areas he was unfamiliar with. There are no alligators in Africa, only crocodiles.

40. *Motion Picture News,* Nov. 3, 1928, p. 1382.

41. Letter, Paul Ivano to author, Oct. 21, 1971.

42. Tod Welch, "Von Schedule!"

43. Paul Ivano interview.

44. William Margulies interview.

45. Ibid.

46. Paul Ivano letter (Oct. 21, 1971) and interview.

47. Paul Ivano letter (Oct. 21, 1971).

48. William Margulies interview.

49. Gloria Swanson, *Swanson on Swanson,* p. 369.

50. William Margulies interview.

51. Paul Ivano interview. In her autobiography, Swanson points to this particular sequence (pp. 370-71) as her first inkling that something was amiss.

52. William Margulies interview.

53. Tod Welch, "Von Schedule!"

54. Cedric Belfrage, *Film Weekly,* Dec. 31, 1928, quoted in Peter Noble, *Holywood Scapegoat,* p. 76.

55. "Miss Swanson's New Role," *New York Times.*

56. Gloria Swanson in filmed interview with Philip Jenkinson, BBC (n.d.).

57. Letters, II, xiii.

58. Gloria Swanson, "I Am Not Going To Write My Memoirs," *Sight and Sound,* Winter 1969-70, p. 60.

59. For exact dates and times see appendix.

60. Tod Welch, "Von Schedule!"

61. Cedric Belfrage, "Classic Holds Open Court."

62. Edmund Goulding, "The Talkers in Close-Up," *National Board of Review Magazine,* July 1928.

63. Paul Ivano letter (Oct. 21, 1971).

64. Gloria Swanson, *Swanson on Swanson,* pp. 372-73.

65. Ibid., p. 373.

66. Letters, II, xiii.

67. Gloria Swanson, "I Am Not Going to Write My Memoirs."

68. "Miss Swanson's New Role," *New York Times.*

69. Paul Ivano letter (Oct. 21, 1971).

70. Returning a profit of $448,000 according to Samuel Marx, *Mayer and Thalberg* (New York: Random House, 1975), p. 256.

71. Unidentified clipping in the library of the Academy of Motion Picture Arts and Sciences, dated Jan. 25, 1929.

72. Dorothy Herzog, "Scouting the Sinema," *Los Angeles Evening Herald,* Jan. 30, 1930.

73. For information on writing see Gloria Swanson interview with Jenkinson; for directing schedule see Herzog, "Scouting the Sinema." Swanson's autobiography gives the number as 21 days (p. 385).

74. "Franz Lehar To Write Swanson Film Music," *New York Times,* Jan. 7, 1930, p. 21.

75. Herzog, "Scouting the Sinema."

76. The properties and standing sets were still there, taking up space. The Poto-Poto saloon, however, did not remain idle. As a Havana dancehall it can be seen in Tay Garnett's *Her Man,* shot at Pathé in the spring of 1930.

77. Curtiss, *Von Stroheim,* p. 251.

78. Rudolf Leonhard, *"Queen Kelly," Die Weltbuhne,* Dec. 23, 1932, p. 879.

79. Herman G. Weinberg, "Celluloid Trumpet Blasts," *Sight and Sound,* Summer 1939, pp. 58-59.

80. Herb Golden, "1929 Swanson Fiasco Is Finally Reviewed as a Museum Piece," *Variety,* July 26, 1950, p. 1.

81. Information provided by Patrick Montgomery.

82. Lee Beaupre, "Nostalgia Eve: Gloria Swanson and Organ Music," *Variety,* May 10, 1967.

83. Letters, II, xv.

84. A. Cunningham, "Reader's Report, *East of the Setting Sun,"* M-G-M, Oct. 7, 1929.

85. Letters, 11, 16.

86. Curtiss, *Von Stroheim,* pp. 265-68.

87. Eric von Stroheim, as told to Dorothy Calhoun, "The Vienna of Von Stroheim," *Motion Picture Classic,* April 1930, p. 30.

88. *Universal Weekly,* June 21, 1930.

89. "Film Chief Lands New Assignment," unidentified clipping in the library of the Academy of Motion Picture Arts and Sciences, July 30, 1930.

90. Curtiss, *Von Stroheim,* pp. 273-74.

91. Interview with Valerie von Stroheim, Los Angeles, June 1978.

92. Interview with Paul Kohner, Beverly Hills, June 1978.

93. Ibid.

94. Farrow was one of von Stroheim's close friends. A graduate of the Royal Naval Academy, he became a screenwriter and then a director of action pictures. An unidentified clipping in the library of the Academy of Motion Picture Arts and Sciences says that Farrow (in 1931) has written for von Stroheim an original called *Mitzi,* although there are no further references to this project.

95. Paul Kohner interview.

96. Ibid.
97. Interview with Carl Laemmle, Jr., Beverly Hills, June 14, 1973.
98. Franclien M. MacConnell, "Reader's Report, *Her Highness*," M-G-M, July 6, 1931.
99. Letter, Samuel Marx to Erich von Stroheim, July 9, 1931.

Walking Down Broadway

1. See Upton Sinclair, *Upton Sinclair Presents William Fox* (Los Angeles, 1933).
2. Memo, Winfield Sheehan to John H. Tracy, Sept. 2, 1931.
3. *Los Angeles Examiner,* Sept. 2, 1931, clipping in the library of the Academy of Motion Picture Arts and Sciences.
4. Eventually the property was acquired for $7500.
5. "Dawn Powell," *Contemporary Authors,* Vols. V-VIII (Detroit: Gale Research Company, 1969), p. 915.
6. "Dawn Powell" (obituary), *New York Times,* Nov. 16, 1965.
7. Interview with Leonard Spigelgass, Culver City, June 1978.
8. Information from Twentieth Century-Fox legal department files.
9. Leonard Spigelgass, "There Once Was a Place Called Hollywood," *Academy Leader,* Nov. 1972.
10. Ibid., p. 6.
11. Ibid., p. 8.
12. Leonard Spigelgass in seminar at the American Film Institute, Center for Advanced Film Studies (n.d.).
13. Leonard Spigelgass interview.
14. Spigelgass, "There Once Was a Place Called Hollywood," p. 8.
15. Leonard Spigelgass interview.
16. Ibid.
17. Glendon Allvine, *The Greatest Fox of Them All* (New York: Lyle Stuart, 1969), p. 142.
18. *Time,* Feb. 15, 1932, p. 47.
19. Memo, Al Rockett to John H. Tracy, Feb. 13, 1932.
20. John Scott, "Von Stroheim Confesses Purpose in 'Eccentricity'," *Los Angeles Times,* June 5, 1932.
21. Telegram, George Bagnall to S. E. Richardson, June 21, 1932.
22. "Boots Mallory Making Career in Big Strides," *Hello, Sister!* Pressbook (1933).
23. Charles Higham, *Hollywood Cameramen* (Bloomington: Indiana University Press, 1970), pp. 83-85.
24. James Wong Howe in interview with author, July 17, 1971. And yet he seems to have forgotten the even more sophisticated "dancing camera" he himself employed over a year before on William K. Howard's *Transatlantic.*
25. Ibid.
26. Ibid.
27. Ibid.

28. Ibid.
29. Charles Higham, *Hollywood Cameramen,* p. 61.
30. Interview with Charles van Enger, Los Angeles, July 29, 1973.
31. James Wong Howe interview.
32. Leonard Spigelgass interview.
33. For budget see "That Makes It $362,000," *Variety,* April 3, 1933; for schedule see *Los Angeles Times,* Oct. 15, 1932, untitled clipping in the library of the Academy of Motion Picture Arts and Sciences.
34. Telephone interview with R. L. Hough, Aug. 10, 1976.
35. Letters, III, v.
36. Information from files of Universal Pictures accounting department.
37. Information on Universal productions from studio accounting department records; information on M-G-M productions from Samuel Marx, *Mayer and Thalberg* (New York: Random House, 1975), pp. 260-61.
38. Letters, III, vi.
39. "Walking Down Broadway," *Screen Romances,* Jan. 1933, pp. 67+.
40. Interview with I. B. Kornblum, Culver City, June 1978.
41. Spigelgass, "There Once Was a Place Called Hollywood," p. 8.
42. Letters, III, v.
43. *Production Guide and Directors Annual* (Los Angeles: The Film Daily, 1936), p. 245.
44. Leonard Maltin, *Movie Comedy Teams* (New York: Signet, 1970), p. 227.
45. Memo, Sol Wurtzel to George Wasson, Nov. 30, 1932.
46. Higham, *Hollywood Cameramen,* p. 86.
47. Spigelgass, "There Once Was a Place Called Hollywood," p. 8.
48. *New York Sun,* Feb. 21, 1933, untitled clipping in the New York Public Library Theatre Collection.
49. Letter, Alfred Werker to author, Oct. 12, 1971.
50. "That Makes It $362,000," *Variety.*
51. Char., *"Hello Sister!" Variety,* May 9, 1933; John S. Cohen, *"Hello, Sister!,* a Weak Romance," *New York Sun,* May 8, 1933; A.D.S., "A City Romance," *New York Times,* May 6, 1933; Regina Crewe, "James Dunn Does Splendidly Trying To Be Soft Hearted," *New York American,* May 8, 1933.
52. Herman Weinberg, "Another Film Carnage," *Cinema Quarterly,* Summer 1933, pp. 230-31.
53. Spigelgass, "There Once Was a Place Called Hollywood." p. 8.
54. "Two Synopses," *Film Culture,* Jan. 1955, pp. 33-34.
55. "The Greatest Actress," *Photoplay,* April 1931.
56. Letters, III, v.

Last Years in Hollywood

1. Paul Brachard, horoscope of Erich von Stroheim, drawn January 14, 1933. Courtesy of Denise Vernac.
2. Von Stroheim (Letters II, v-vi) claims this was thrown together in

"eleven nights and two Sundays," although I. B. Kornblum in a 1978 interview remembered spending "six or seven months writing the score."

3. Interview with I. B. Kornblum, Culver City, June 1978.
4. *Los Angeles Examiner,* Oct. 8, 1932. Clipping in the Library of the Academy of Motion Picture Arts and Sciences.
5. Letter, Samuel Marx to John Zinn (Fox Film Corporation), June 13, 1934.
6. Jessie Burns, "Reader's Report, *Poto-Poto,*" M-G-M, May 9, 1933. Some of this story also appears, not credited to von Stroheim, in Paramount's 1934 *White Woman,* starring Carole Lombard and Charles Laughton.
7. Erich von Stroheim, *Poto-Poto* (Paris: Editions de la Fontaine, 1956).
8. Interview with Valerie von Stroheim, Los Angeles, June 1978.
9. Interview with I. B. Kornblum.
10. Information from M-G-M legal department.
11. Letters, III, vi.
12. Erich von Stroheim, *Paprika* (New York: Macauley, 1935).
13. *Los Angeles Times,* Nov. 10, 1933, clipping in the Theatre collection of the New York Public Library. See also Curtiss, *Von Stroheim,* p. 296.
14. Erich von Stroheim, *Paprika.*
15. Lucille Sullivan, "Reader's Report, *Paprika,*" M-G-M, February 25, 1935.
16. "Von Stroheim Set in Paris Pic World," *Variety,* February 24, 1937; "Mexican Promoters Seek Negri for Pic," *Hollywood Reporter,* May 3, 1943.
17. Interview with Valerie von Stroheim.
18. Quoted in Curtiss, *Von Stroheim,* p. 293.
19. Interview with Valerie von Stroheim.
20. "Von Stroheim Forced To Pawn His Belongings," *London Daily Express,* Dec. 22, 1934.
21. Interview with Valerie von Stroheim.
22. Interview with Anita Loos, New York City, Feb. 2, 1972.
23. Interview with Valerie von Stroheim.
24. Interview with I. B. Kornblum.
25. Interview with Valerie von Stroheim.
26. *In the Morning,* original typescript in United States Copyright Office.
27. From material in the Wallace Smith collection, University of Oregon Library.
28. This business with mannequins also strangely antedates Karl Freund's *Mad Love* produced at M-G-M soon after.
29. Gilbert Gabriel, *"May Wine," New York American,* Dec. 6, 1935.
30. *Variety,* Nov. 27, 1935, clipping in the Theatre Collection of the New York Public Library.
31. Memo, J. J. Cohn to W. J. Craig, March 4, 1935.
32. Letters, III, viii.
33. Tom Dardis, *Some Time in the Sun* (New York, Scribners, 1976), pp. 44, 82.
34. Interview with Samuel Marx, Los Angeles, June, 1978.
35. Letters, III, viii.

36. Ibid.

37. "Between Two Women," *New York Times,* Aug. 6, 1937, p. 21.

38. Interview with Thomas Quinn Curtiss, Paris, July 1978.

Epilogue

1. Quoted in Peter Noble, *Hollywood Scapegoat* (London: Fortune Press, 1950) p. 25.

2. Von Stroheim made these claims in a period interview (Elizabeth Copeland, "Von Stroheim in *Grand Illusion* Plays German General," *Richmond (Va.) News Leader,* March 15, 1939) and Valerie von Stroheim repeated them to me in Los Angeles in 1978.

3. When Prince Wolfram is imprisoned by the Queen in *Queen Kelly* a solitary geranium graces his prison window. Peggy's tenement skylight in *Walking Down Broadway* is decorated with a pair of hopeful geraniums. These are not isolated examples. Geraniums, like crucifixes, are ubiquitous symbols in von Stroheim's universe.

4. Interview with Denise Vernac, Maurepas, Jan. 1979.

5. Interview with I. B. Kornblum, Culver City, June 1978.

6. Interview with Denise Vernac, Jan. 1979.

7. Peter Noble, *Hollywood Scapegoat,* p. 28.

8. Erich von Stroheim, "Movies and Morals," *Decision,* March 1941, pp. 49-56; and *"Citizen Kane,"* June 1941, pp. 91-93.

9. Interview with Billy Wilder, Beverly Hills, June, 1978.

10. Interview with Denise Vernac, Maurepas, July, 1978.

11. Ibid.

12. Interview with Billy Wilder. There is a similar scene, however, in *Three Faces East,* where von Stroheim unpacks Constance Bennett's lingerie as two maids peek through a bedroom keyhole. Roy del Ruth allowed him that one, at least.

13. Maurice Zolotow, *Billy Wilder in Hollywood* (New York: Putnam, 1977) p. 168.

14. Curtiss has the best and most flavorful account of this period.

Bibliographic Note

The literature on von Stroheim is voluminous, and serious study dates back at least to 1927, and the appearance of Atasceva and Korolevich's 14-page monograph *Erich Stroheim* (Moscow: Kinopechat). The major works in English include Peter Noble's *Hollywood Scapegoat* (London: The Fortune Press, 1950) and Thomas Quinn Curtiss's *Von Stroheim* (New York: Farrar, Straus & Giroux, 1971). Von Stroheim originally cooperated with Noble and engaged in a lengthy correspondence which still provides much valuable first person testimony. But he later disclaimed the published work. The Curtiss book is the equivalent of a ghost-written memoir, penned by von Stroheim's old friend to set the record straight as von Stroheim would have told it. Other works in English include Joel Finler's *Stroheim* (Berkeley: University of California Press, 1968), a slim volume focused mainly on *Greed;* Arthur Lennig's *Von Stroheim* (Albany: State University of New York, 1973), a useful compendium of Lennig's own writings with period texts and documents; Herman G. Weinberg, von Stroheim's most energetic supporter, has *Stroheim: A Pictorial Record of His Nine Films* (New York: Dover, 1975); and the luxurious albums *The Complete "Greed" of Erich von Stroheim* (New York: Arno Press, 1972) and *The Complete "Wedding March" of Erich von Stroheim* (Boston: Little, Brown, 1974).

Also worth noting are: *Erich von Stroheim* by Jon Barna (Vienna: Osterreichisches Filmmuseum, 1966), a unique assemblage of texts and references; *Erich von Stroheim* by Bob Bergut (Paris: Le Terrain Vague, 1960); *Erich von Stroheim* by Freddy Buache (Paris: Editions Segheurs, 1972); *Umanita di Stroheim ed Altri Soggi* by Ugo Casiraghi (Milan: Poligono, 1945); Giulio Cesare Castello's *Von Stroheim* (Rome:

Dell'Ateneo, 1959); *Erich von Stroheim* by Castello and Buache (Lyon: Serdoc, 1963); Michel Ciment's entry in volume three of the *Anthologie du Cinema* (Paris: L'Avant Scene, 1968); *Erich von Stroheim* by Guido Fink (Parma: Piccola Biblioteca del Cinema, 1963); *Erich von Stroheim, Sa Vie, Ses Films* by Georges Fronval (Paris: Visages et Contes du Cinema, 1939); Charlotte Gobeil's anthology *Hommage à von Stroheim* (Ottawa: Canadian Film Institute, 1966); and the very valuable *Erich von Stroheim* by Denis Marion and Barthelemy Amengual (Paris: Etudes Cinematographiques, 1966). Marion's *Erich Von Stroheim* (Brussels: Club du Livre de Cinema, 1959) is an earlier example of his work. I was unable to locate Jean Mitry's scarce *Erich von Stroheim* (Paris/Brussels: Classiques du Cinema, 1963) and unable to translate Jørgen Stegelmann's *Erich von Stroheim* (Copenhagen: Det Danske Filmmuseum, 1963).

Special numbers of *Cahiers du Cinéma* (January 1957), *Film Culture* (April 1958), *Bianco e Nero* (February-March 1959), *Cinema* (Zurich) (December 1973), and *Filmkritik* (February 1976) all contain much intriguing material. Books by von Stroheim include the novels *Paprika* (New York: Macauley, 1935), *Les Feux de la Saint-Jean* in two parts, *Veronica* and *Constanzia* (Paris: André Martel, 1951 and 1954), and *Poto-Poto* (Paris: Editions de la Fontaine, 1956). The script of *Greed* was published initially by the Cinémathèque Royale de Belgique in 1958, again by *L'Avant Scène du Cinéma* in their July-September 1968 issue, and most recently by Simon and Schuster (New York, 1972).

A full bibliography can be found in my *The Unknown Cinema of Erich von Stroheim* (Ph.d. dissertation, New York University, 1977).

The present work is based largely on unpublished materials, including studio records and documents in various public and private collections. Von Stroheim's letters to Peter Noble (referred to in the text as "Letters") are in the library of the Museum of Modern Art in New York. The Erich von Stroheim research project at the American Film Institute's Center for Advanced Film Studies in Hollywood consists of interviews I recorded in 1971-72, along with a large collection of von Stroheim treatments and scripts. Interviews on film can be found in the feature-length documentary *The Man You Loved To Hate,* produced from my script by Patrick Montgomery (Film Profiles, 1979), and intended as a visual companion to this volume.

Appendix

Queen Kelly
Daily Record of Shooting

Date; time convened, first shot, time broke; number of scenes taken; description of action.

11/1/28   7am, 10am, 5pm; 5 scenes; Gopher Flats, Lasky Ranch; convent girl's parade.

11/2/28   7am, 9am, 6:15am; 7 scenes; Gopher Flats in AM, Mother Superior chastises Kelly in PM.

11/3/28   3pm, 3:45pm, 9:50pm; 3 scenes; chapel.

11/5/28   7am, 9am, 12:45am; 8 scenes; Prince's dressing room.

11/6/28   7am, 10am, 4:30pm; 4 scenes; Gopher Flats; soldiers on parade.

11/7/28   8am, 9:30am, 12:15am; 4 scenes; Prince's room (plans convent raid).

11/8/28   8am, 9am, 4:30pm; 4 scenes; retakes of 11/1/28.

11/9/28   8am, 9am, 4:30pm; 1 scene; same as yesterday.

11/10/28 8am, 10:30am, 4:50am; 3 scenes; in morning same as yesterday, in evening Queen's bedroom nude scene (set not ready until 11:50pm).

11/12/28 7:30am, 10:45am, 2:30am; 7 scenes; palace ext; Queen's bath.

11/13/28 9:30am, 11:15am, 7:15pm; 8 scenes; convent upper hallway.

11/14/28   8:30am, 8:45am, 8pm; 6 scenes; convent upper hallway (fire).

11/15/28   9am, 11am, 2:55am; 6 scenes; convent upper hallway.

11/16/28   12n, 4pm, 1:40am; 5 scenes; upper hallway and dormitory.

11/17/28   10:30am, 11:15am, 7:15am; 2 scenes; same as yesterday.

11/19/28   8:30am, 2:45am, 6:15pm; 1 scene; ext palace side entrance.

11/20/28   8:30am, 9:55am, 5:10am; 6 scenes; same as yesterday (prince arrives drunk)

11/21/28   8:30am, 9:15am, 2:15am; 7 scenes; same as yesterday, and ext convent garden (n.b. 27 set-ups, 2 or 3 takes each).

11/22/28   11am, 1:30pm, 6pm; 3 scenes; Prince's bedroom.

11/23/28   9am, 10:30am, 6:45am; 6 scenes; same as yesterday (Queen berates Prince).

11/24/28   2pm, 6:15pm, 8pm; 1 scene; convent lower hall.

11/26/28   8:30am, 9:10am, 6:05pm; 6 scenes; Prince visits convent, finds Kelly gone (n.b. 24 set-ups today).

11/27/28   9am, 9:20am, 6:45pm; 2 scenes; mother superior's office (Prince hears about Africa)

11/28/28   9am, 12:20pm, 12:30am; 6 scenes; Prince's salon (Kelly arrives)

11/30/28   9am, 9:30am, 6pm; same as 11/28; 1 scene.

12/1/28   9am, 9:30am, 7pm; apparently no scenes taken; same locale.

12/3/28   9am, 9:30am, 7:15pm; 4 scenes; same; oyster business (n.b. comment on one shot, "Mr. Von lighted this scene.")

12/4/28   9am, 9:50am, 8:15pm; 2 scenes; same.

12/5/28   9am, 9:30am, 7:15pm; 5 scenes; same locale; orchid business.

12/6/28   9am, 11am, 8:10pm; 11 scenes; same locale.

12/7/28   9am, 11am, 7:15pm; 4 scenes; same locale (Queen finds them).

12/8/28   9am, ?, 12:15am; 7 scenes; same as yesterday.

12/10/28   9am, 10:15am, 12:50am; 7 scenes; same.

12/11/28   10am, 12:30pm, 12:50am; 6 scenes; same.

12/12/28   10am, 12:30pm, 12:30am; 5 scenes; palace upper hall-
            way.

12/13/28   9am, 4:20pm, 2:50am; 3 scenes, int and ext side en-
            trance (n.b. delay for story conference is noted).

12/14/28   7pm, 8pm, 6:25am; 4 scenes; ext bridge river bank (Kelly
            jumps).

12/17/28   notation: no work.

12/18/28   9am, 9:45am, 5am; 3 scenes; lower hallway and palace
            exit (whip scenes reshot in stronger vain—earlier, only a
            threat).

12/19/28   2pm, 3:15pm, 5:55am; 8 scenes; convent ext and lower
            hallway (Kelly arrives back at convent).

12/20/28   2:30pm, 3:40pm, 2:20am; 3 scenes; ext convent, int
            Prince's salon (retakes).

12/21/28   1pm, 5:45pm, 5:30am; 5 scenes; int prison (violin bit).

12/22/28   inserts on laps.

12/24/28   retakes.

12/26/28   conference, 8pm until 2:30am.

1/2/29   9am, 5pm, 7pm; 1 scene; upper hallway cafe (first day at
            Pathé studio).

1/3/29   9am, 10:15am, 7:25pm; 2 scenes; same; Kelly arrives at
            bar.

1/4/29   9am, 11:45am, 8pm; 4 scenes; Aunt's bedroom.

1/5/29   9am, 10am, 7:30 pm; 3 scenes; same.

1/7/29   9am, 9:30am, 7:25 pm; 4 scenes; same.

1/8/29   9am, 9:40am, 7:50pm; 6 scenes; same.

1/9/29   9am, 9:35am, 7:25pm; 6 scenes; same; priest arrives.

1/10/29   9am, 10am, 7:35pm; 3 scenes; same.

1/11/29   9am, 10:30am, 7:15pm; 2 scenes; same.

1/12/29   9am, 12:45pm, 7pm; 6 scenes; same and Kelly's bedroom
            (wedding service begins).

1/14/29   9am, 11:20am, 7:20pm; 6 scenes; same; marriage and
            funeral.

1/15/29   9am, 10am, 7:50pm; 8 scenes; aunt's and Kelly's rooms
            (with wedding finished, Jan chases Kelly around room).

1/16/29   10am, 5pm, 7:15pm; 6 scenes; lined up banquet and coronation scenes at Associated, went back to Pathé to shoot more chasing around bed.

1/17/29   9:30am, 10am, 5:40pm; 2 scenes; Aunt's and Kelly's rooms (threatens suicide with scissors).

1/18/29   9am, 11am, 9pm; 6 scenes; banquet, Associated Studios (announcement of engagement).

1/19/29   7am, 1:30pm, 7:40pm; 3 scenes; upper hallway cafe (mob gathers to watch Jan).

1/21/29   9am, 9:30am, 7pm; 1 scene; upper hallway and Kelly's room (mob scene; she assumes control of brothel).

Figures from daily reports as of 1/21/29, date Stroheim stopped shooting; 10 days idle; 60 days work

stills:	380		
script scenes:	533	added scenes:	513
taken	257	retakes	30
to be taken	276	negative	206,304′

Pollock's camera record for 1/21/29 lists 206,304′ of negative drawn;

129,835′ good,
76,469′ bad.

Films Directed by Erich von Stroheim

Blind Husbands (Universal)

Director: Erich von Stroheim
Story and Screenplay: Erich von Stroheim
Titles: Lillian Ducey
Director of Photography: Ben Reynolds
Second Camera: William Daniels
Editors: Frank Lawrence, Viola Mallory (later Viola Lawrence), Eleanor Fried, Grant Whytock
Working Title: "The Pinnacle"
Dates of Production: April 3, 1919 to June 12, 1919

Copyright Date: October 21, 1919 (LP14317)
First Shown: Washington, D.C., Oct. 19, 1919.
Length: 7,711 feet
Cost: $125,000

Cast:

The Husband	Sam DeGrasse
The Wife	Francellia Billington
The Other Man	Erich Stroheim
The Mountain Guide	T. H. Gibson-Gowland
The "Vamp" Waitress	Fay Holderness
A Village Blossom	Ruby Kendrick
Honeymooners	Valerie Germonprez,
	Jack Perrin
The Village Physician	Richard Cummings
The Village Priest	Louis Fitzroy
Three Men from "Home"	William Duvalle
	Jack Matheis
	Percy Challenger
The Dog, Bob	Himself

The Devil's Pass Key (Universal)

Director: Erich von Stroheim
Original Story: "Clothes and Treachery" by the Baroness De Meyer
Screenplay: Erich von Stroheim
Director of Photography: Ben Reynolds
Additional Photography: Howard Oswald
Second Camera: William Daniels
Assistant Directors: Edward Sowders, Jack Proctor, Jeanne Spencer
Editor: Grant Whytock
Art Titles: J. H. Buffum
Working Titles: Clothes and Treachery; His Great Success; The Charge
    Account; The Woman in the Plot.
Dates of Production: September 8, 1919 to December 4, 1919
Copyright Date: September 3, 1920 (LP15513)
New York Premiere: August 8, 1920
Length: approximately 7,500 feet
Cost: $185,000

Cast:

Warren Goodwright	Sam DeGrasse
Grace, his wife	Una Trevelyn
Capt. Rex Strong	Clyde Fillmore
Renée Malot	Maude George
Amadeus, her husband	Leo White
La Belle Odera	Mae Busch
Count de Trouvere	Jack Matheis
Yvonne, his wife	Ruth King
Director of Theatre Français	Ed Reinach
Alphone Marier, reporter	Al Edmondson

Foolish Wives (Universal)

Director: Erich von Stroheim
Story and Screenplay: Erich von Stroheim
Titles: Marian Ainslee
Directors of Photography: Ben Reynolds and William Daniels
Assistant Directors: Edward Sowders, Louis Germonprez, Jack Proctor
Editors: Arthur Ripley, assisted by Edward Sowders, Bob Roberts and
   Daniel Mandell
Supervising Art Director: E. E. Sheeley
Unit Art Director: Richard Day
Costumes: Western Costuming
Chief Engineer, illumination and lighting effects: Harry J. Brown
Scenic Artist: Van Alstein
Technical Directors: William Meyers, James Sullivan, George Williams
Sculpture: Don Jarvis
Master of Properties: C. J. Rogers
Landscape Gardening: Victor André
Hand Coloring of Film: Gustav Brock
Original Musical Score: Sigmund Romberg
Dates of Production: July 12, 1920 to June 15, 1921
Copyright Date: February 11, 1922
Release Date: January 11, 1922
Length: 14,120 feet
Cost: $1,103,736.38

Cast:

Count Wladislas Sergius Karamzin	Erich von Stroheim
Princess Olga Petschnikoff	Maude George
Princess Vera Petschnikoff	Mae Busch
Andrew J. Hughes	Rudolph Christians and Robert Edeson
Helen, his wife	Miss Dupont
Marushka, a maid	Dale Fuller
Pavel Pavlich, a butler	Al Edmundson
Caesare Ventucci	Cesare Gravina
Marietta, his daughter	Malvine Polo
Dr. Judd	Louis K. Webb
His wife	Mrs. Kent
Albert I, Prince of Monaco	C. J. Allen
Sec. of State of Monaco	Edward Reinach
An Actress	Mme. Kopetzky
A Monk	Nigel de Brulier
Crippled Girl	Mary Philbin

Merry-Go-Round (Universal)

Directors: Rupert Julian and Erich von Stroheim
Original Story and Screenplay: Erich von Stroheim
Revised Treatment: Harvey Gates and Finis Fox
Titles: Mary O'Hara
Directors of Photography: Charles Kaufman and William Daniels
Assistant Directors: Edward Sowders and Louis Germonprez
Editors: Maurice Pivar and James McKay
Supervising Art Director: E. E. Sheeley
Unit Art Director: Richard Day
Technical Director: Archie Hall
Art Titles: Harry B. Johnson
Dates of Production: August 25, 1922 to January 8, 1923
   (Julian replaced von Stroheim on October 7, 1922)
Copyright Date: June 16, 1923 (LP19121)
Release Date: July 1, 1923
Length: 9,178 feet
Cost: $389,831

Cast:

Count Franz Maximilian von Hohenegg	Norman Kerry
Agnes Urban	Mary Philbin
Sylvester Urban	Cesare Gravina
Ursula Urban	Edith Yorke
Batholomew Gruber	George Hackathorne
Schani Huber	George Siegmann
Marianka Huber	Dale Fuller
Aurora Rossreiter	Lillian Sylvester
Minister of War	Spottiswoode Aitken
Komtesse Gisella von Steinbrueck	Dorothy Wallace
Nepomuck Navrital	Al Edmundson
Rudy, Baron von Leichtzinn	Albert Conti
Nicki, Baron von Uebermut	Charles King
Prince Eitel Hochgemut	Fenwick Oliver
Gisella's Groom	Sidney Bracey
Emperor Franz Josef	Anton Wawerka
Madame Elvira	Maude George
Jane	Helen Broneau
Marie	Jane Sherman
also:	Betty Morrissey

Greed (Goldwyn; released by Metro-Goldwyn)

Director: Erich von Stroheim
Original Story: "McTeague" by Frank Norris (New York: Doubleday, 1899)
Screenplay: Erich von Stroheim
Titles: June Mathis, Joseph Farnham
Directors of Photography: Ben Reynolds and William Daniels
Assistant Directors: Edward Sowders and Louis Germonprez
Editors: Frank Hull, Grant Whytock, June Mathis, Joseph Farnham
Supervising Art Director: Cedric Gibbons
Unit Art Director: Richard Day
Production Manager: J. J. Cohn
Coloring of Film: Handschlegl Process
Dates of Production: March 13, 1923 to October 6, 1923

Copyright Date: February 10, 1925 (LP21123)
Release Date: December 4, 1924
Length: 10,607 feet
Cost: $585,250

Cast:

(Prologue)
McTeague	Gibson Gowland
McTeague, Sr.	Jack Curtis
Mrs. McTeague	Tempe Piggott
Old Hag	Florence Gibson
Dr. "Painless" Potter	Gunther von Ritzau
Recalcitrant Patient	Zasu Pitts

(San Francisco)
Marcus Schouler	Jean Hersholt
Trina Sieppe	Zasu Pitts
Mr. Hans Sieppe	Chester Conklin
Mrs. Sieppe	Sylvia Ashton
August	Austin Jewell
Max and Moritz (twins)	Oscar and Otto Gotell
Selina	Joan Standing
Uncle Rudolph Oelbermann	Max Tryon

(Characters in Subplots)
Maria Miranda Macapa	Dale Fuller
Zerkow	Cesare Gravina
Charles W. Grannis	Frank Hayes
Miss Anastasia Baker	Fanny Midgley

(Friends and Neighbors in Polk Street)
Mr. Heise	Hughie Mack
Mrs. Heise	Mrs. E. "Tiny" Jones
Mr. Ryer	J. Aldrich Libbey
Mrs. Ryer	Rita Revla
Joe Frenna	S. S. Simon
The Photographer	Hugh J. McCauley
The Palmist	William Mollenheimer

(Others)
The Minister	William Barlow
Lottery Agent	Lon Poff
Sheriff of Placer County	James Fulton
Deputy Sheriff	James Gibson
Cribbens	Jack MacDonald
Balloon vendor	Erich von Stroheim

The Merry Widow (M-G-M)

Director: Erich von Stroheim
Original Story: "Die Lustige Witwe" by Leo Stein and Victor Leon (Opera libretto, Vienna, 1906)
Screenplay: Erich von Stroheim, assisted by Benjamin Glazer
Titles: Marian Ainslee
Directors of Photography: Oliver Marsh, William Daniels, and Ben Reynolds.
Assistant Directors: Edward Sowders and Louis Germonprez
Editor: Frank Hull
Supervising Art Director: Cedric Gibbons
Unit Art Director: Richard Day
Supervision of costumes and uniforms: Erich von Stroheim and Richard Day
Original Musical Score: David Mendoza and William Axt, after Franz Lehar
Artificially colored sequence: Handschlegl Process
Natural color sequence: Technicolor Process
Technicolor Photography: Ray Rennahan
Dates of Production: December 1, 1924 to March 9, 1925
Copyright Date: September 14, 1925 (LP21826)
Release Date: August 26, 1925
Length: 10,027 feet
Cost: $608,016.31

Cast:

Sally O'Hara	Mae Murray
Prince Danilo	John Gilbert
Prince Mirko	Roy D'Arcy
Baron Sadoja	Tully Marshall
Queen Milena	Josephine Crowell
King Nikita	George Fawcett
Danilo's Adjutant	Albert Conti
Danilo's aide-de-camp	Wilhelm von Brincken
Danilo's Footman	Sidney Bracey
Mirko's Adjutant	Don Ryan
Innkeeper	Hughie Mack
Innkeeper's wife	Ida Moore
Innkeeper's daughter	Lucille van Lent

Flo Epstein	Charles Margelis
Jimmy Watson	Harvey Karels
Dopey Marle	Edna Tichcnor
Hard Boiled Virginia	Gertrude Bennett
Frenchie Christine	Zalla Zarana
Madonna	Jacquelin Gadsdon
French barber	Estelle Clark
Horatio	D'Arcy Corrigan
Hansen Sisters	Clara Wallucks, Frances Primm
George Washington White	Zack Williams
Francois	Eugene Pouget
Ambassador	Edward Connelly
Ambassador's wife	Meriwyn Thayer
Doortender at Francois'	George Nichols
Sally's Maid	Dale Fuller
Sadoja's Lackey	Lon Poff
Blindfolded Musician	Anielka Elter
Black Dancer	Carolynne Snowden
Chorus Girls	Louise Hughes, Anna Maynard, Helen Howard Beaumont, Beatrice O'Brien

The Wedding March (Paramount)

Director: Erich von Stroheim
Story and Screenplay: Erich von Stroheim, assisted by Harry Carr
Producer: Patrick A. Powers
Directors of Photography: Hal Mohr, Bill McGann, Harry Thorpe, Roy Klaffki (see text)
Camera Operator: "Buster" Sorenson
Assistant Directors: Edward Sowders and Louis Germonprez
Second Assistant Directors: Eddie Malone and Art Jell
Editors: Frank Hull, Josef von Sternberg (see text)
Art Director: Richard Day
Costumes: Max Ree
Military Advisers: Albert Conti and D. R. O. Hatswell
Original Musical Score: J. S. Zamecnik and Louis de Francesco
Theme Song: "Paradise" by Harry D. Kerr and J. S. Zamecnik
Music Recording: Nathaniel Finston, Victor Talking Machine Company
Natural Color Sequence: Technicolor Process

Technicolor Photography: Ray Rennahan
Dates of Production: June 2, 1926 to January 30, 1927
Copyright Date: October 8, 1928 (LP25696)
Release Date: October 6, 1928
Length: Part One—10,400 feet; Part Two—7,273 feet
Cost: $1,125,000

Cast:

Prince Nikki	Erich von Stroheim
Mitzi	Fay Wray
Cecelia	Zasu Pitts
Schani	Matthew Betz
Prince von Wildeliebe-Rauffenburg	George Fawcett
Princess von Wildeliebe-Rauffenburg	Maude George
Schweisser	George Nichols
Katerina, Mitzi's Mother	Dale Fuller
Martin Schrammel, Mitzi's Father	Cesare Gravina
Schani's Father	Hughie Mack
Maid to Prince Nikki	Lucille van Lent
Maid to Cecelia	Lurie Weiss
Emperor Franz Joseph	Anton Wawerka
Nikki's valet	Sidney Bracey
Archduke Leopold Salvator	Don Ryan
Black Servant at Brothel	Carolynne Snowden
Mountain Idiot	Danny Hoy
Servant	Lulee Wilson
Officers of the Imperial Guard	Capt. John Peters, Capt. Peter von Hartman, Carey Harrison, Schuman-Heink, Harry Rinehardt, Albert Conti, Wilhelm von Brincken

Queen Kelly
(Gloria Productions/United Artists)

Director: Erich von Stroheim
Story and Screenplay: Erich von Stroheim
Titles: Marian Ainslee

Directors of Photography: Paul Ivano and Gordon Pollock
First Assistant Cameraman: William Margulies
Assistant Directors: Edward Sowders and Louis Germonprez
Editor: Viola Lawrence
Art Director: Gordon Wiles
Costumes: Max Ree
Production Manager: E. B. Derr
Technical Assistant: Wilhelm von Brincken
Original Musical Score: Adolf Tandler
Dates of Production: November 1, 1928 to January 21, 1929
Length: 8 reels
Cost: $800,000

Cast:

Kitty Kelly	Gloria Swanson
Queen Regina	Seena Owen
Prince Wolfram	Walter Byron
Prince's Adjutant	Wilhelm von Brincken
Mother Superior	Madge Hunt
Valet	Wilson Benge
Lackey	Sidney Bracey
Maid to Prince Wolfram	Lucille van Lent
Nun who escorts Kelly to altar	Ann Morgan
Jan Bloehm Vryheid	Tully Marshall
Kelly's Aunt	Florence Gibson
Kali	Mme. Sul Te Wan
Coughdrops	Ray Daggett

See text for production credits of aborted revised version.

Walking Down Broadway (Fox)

Director: Erich von Stroheim
Original Story: "Walking Down Broadway," unproduced play by Dawn
    Powell
Screenplay: Erich von Stroheim and Leonard Spigelgass
Additional Contributions to Screenplay: Geraldine Nomis, Harry Rus-
    kin, Maurine Watkins
Director of Photography: James Wong Howe
Second Camera: Charles van Enger

Assistant Directors: Edward Sowders and Louis Germonprez
Editor: Frank Hull
Sound: Alfred Bruzlin
Art Director: William Darling
Costumes: David Cox and/or Rita Kaufman
Production Manager: R. L. Hough
Dates of Production: August to October, 1932 (48 days)
Copyright Date: (as "Hello, Sister!") March 23, 1933 (LP3778)
Release Date: May 5, 1933
Length: 5,800 feet
Cost: $300,000, plus $62,000 for retakes

See text for full information on retake version.

Cast:

Jimmy	James Dunn
Peggy	Boots Mallory
Mona	Minna Gombell
Millie	Zasu Pitts
Mac	Terrance Ray
Bank President	Henry Kolker
Man Visiting Bank President	Walter Walker
Black Woman in Apartment House	Hattie McDaniel

(In retakes only)

Drunk	Will Stanton
Fireman	Wade Boteler
also:	Claude King, James Flavin, Astrid Allwyn

Index

Italicized numbers refer to illustrations